Josie and the Pussycats®

VOLUME ONE

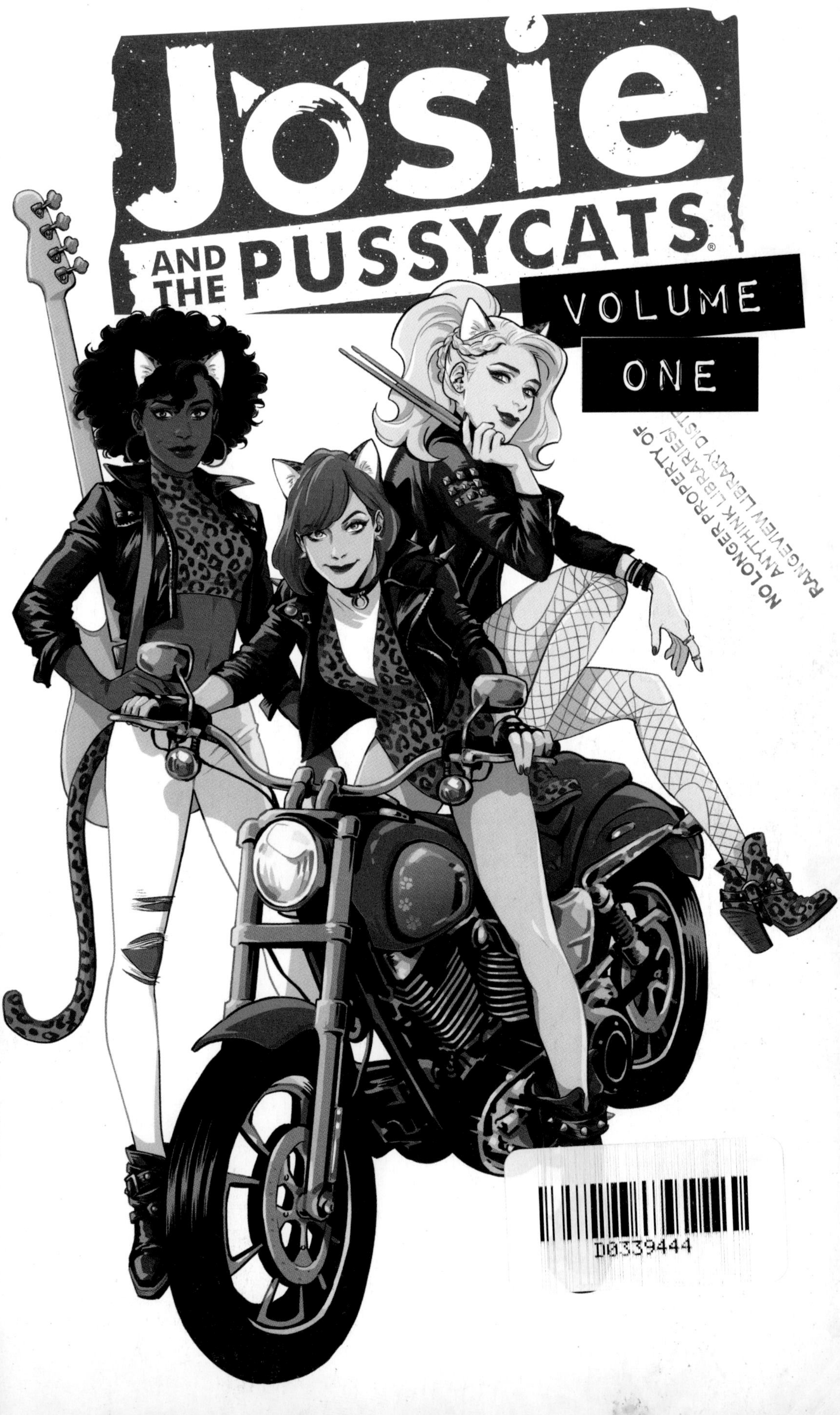

ART BY
AUDREY MOK

STORY BY
MARGUERITE BENNETT
AND CAMERON DEORDIO

COLORING BY
ANDRE SZYMANOWICZ   ISSUE #1
KELLY FITZPATRICK   ISSUES #2-5

LETTERING BY   GRAPHIC DESIGN
JACK MORELLI   KARI McLACHLAN

EDITORS   ASSOCIATE EDITOR
ALEX SEGURA AND   STEPHEN OSWALD
MIKE PELLERITO   ASSISTANT EDITOR
                            JAMIE LEE ROTANTE

EDITOR-IN-CHIEF
VICTOR GORELICK

PUBLISHER
JON GOLDWATER

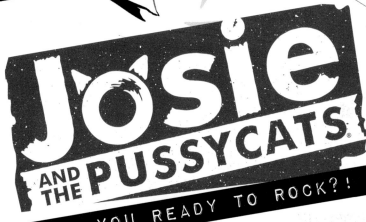

Josie AND THE PUSSYCATS®

ARE YOU READY TO ROCK?!

Discover how the most famous comic book band was formed! What you hold in your hands is a brand new introduction to the three musical mavens, and how the aspirations of a wide-eyed solo artist in her early 20s started something bigger than she'd ever imagine.

There was no question that superstar writer **Marguerite Bennett** (*Bombshells*, *Batwoman*) would be up to the task of re-telling the origins of the Pussycats. Joining her is up-and-coming writer **Cameron DeOrdio**, whose love of music infiltrates every page. Couple them with the fabulous rising star artist **Audrey Mok**, who perfectly grasps every expression and makes sure the ladies are always wearing the coolest fashions, and you've got a recipe for success.

It's not just a matter of introducing new readers to one of the most iconic musical acts of all-time, though. It's about creating the diverse personalities of each of the band members. Josie McCoy is a songstress who wants to break out of performing at college bars and make it big time. Veterinary tech Valerie Brown is the level-headed leader of the pack, who does her best to be the voice of reason. Melody Valentine is a lot more than the ditzy drummer, she's a self-aware bibliophile whose love of puns and breaking the fourth wall runs abundant. Throw in some rad tunes and a bit of action-adventure and each issue of *Josie and the Pussycats* proves to be one wild ride after another.

Above all else, *Josie and the Pussycats* is about friendship. It's about three women who want nothing more than to make awesome music, be best friends and celebrate grrrl power.

ISSUE ONE

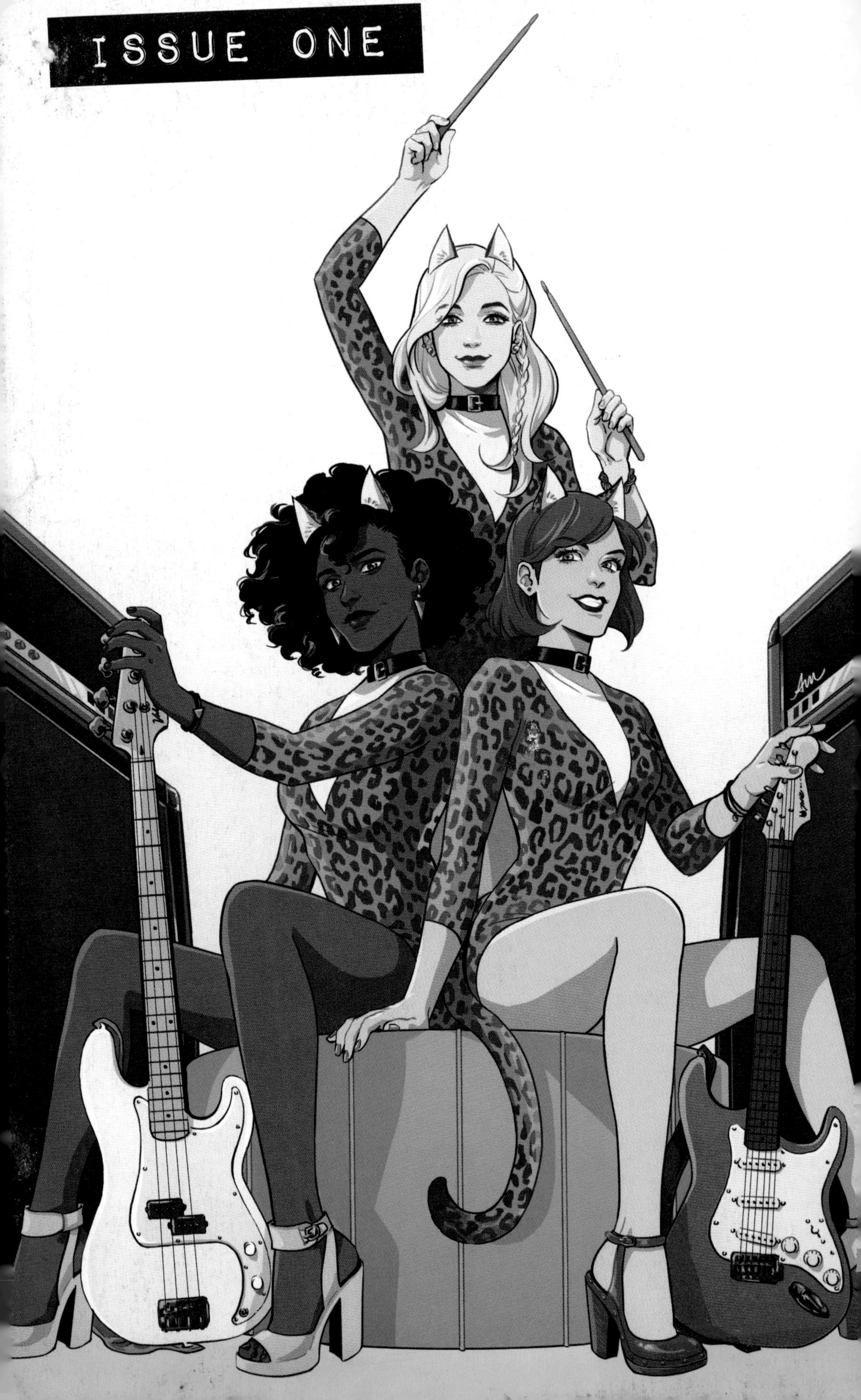

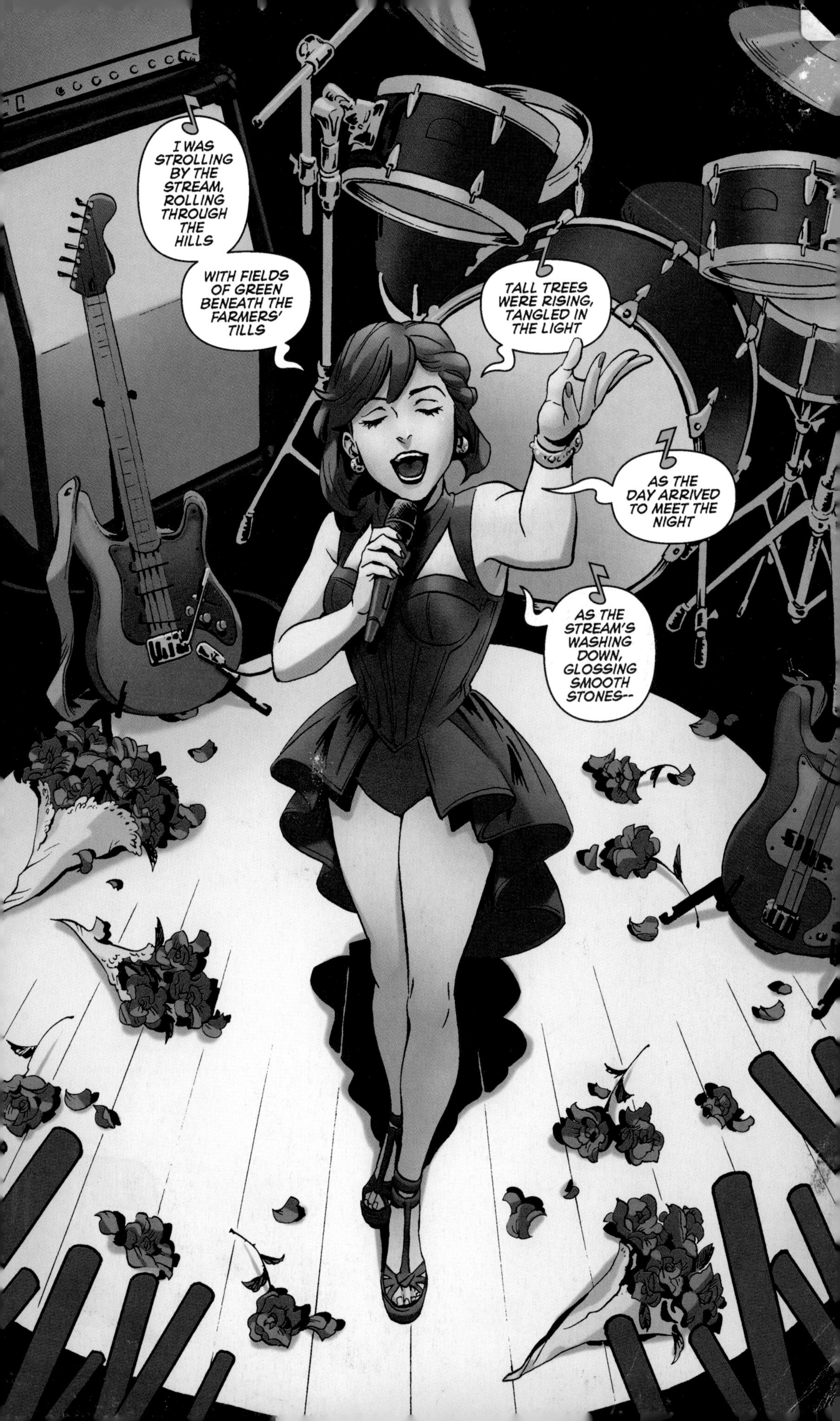
I WAS STROLLING BY THE STREAM, ROLLING THROUGH THE HILLS
WITH FIELDS OF GREEN BENEATH THE FARMERS' TILLS
TALL TREES WERE RISING, TANGLED IN THE LIGHT
AS THE DAY ARRIVED TO MEET THE NIGHT
AS THE STREAM'S WASHING DOWN, GLOSSING SMOOTH STONES--

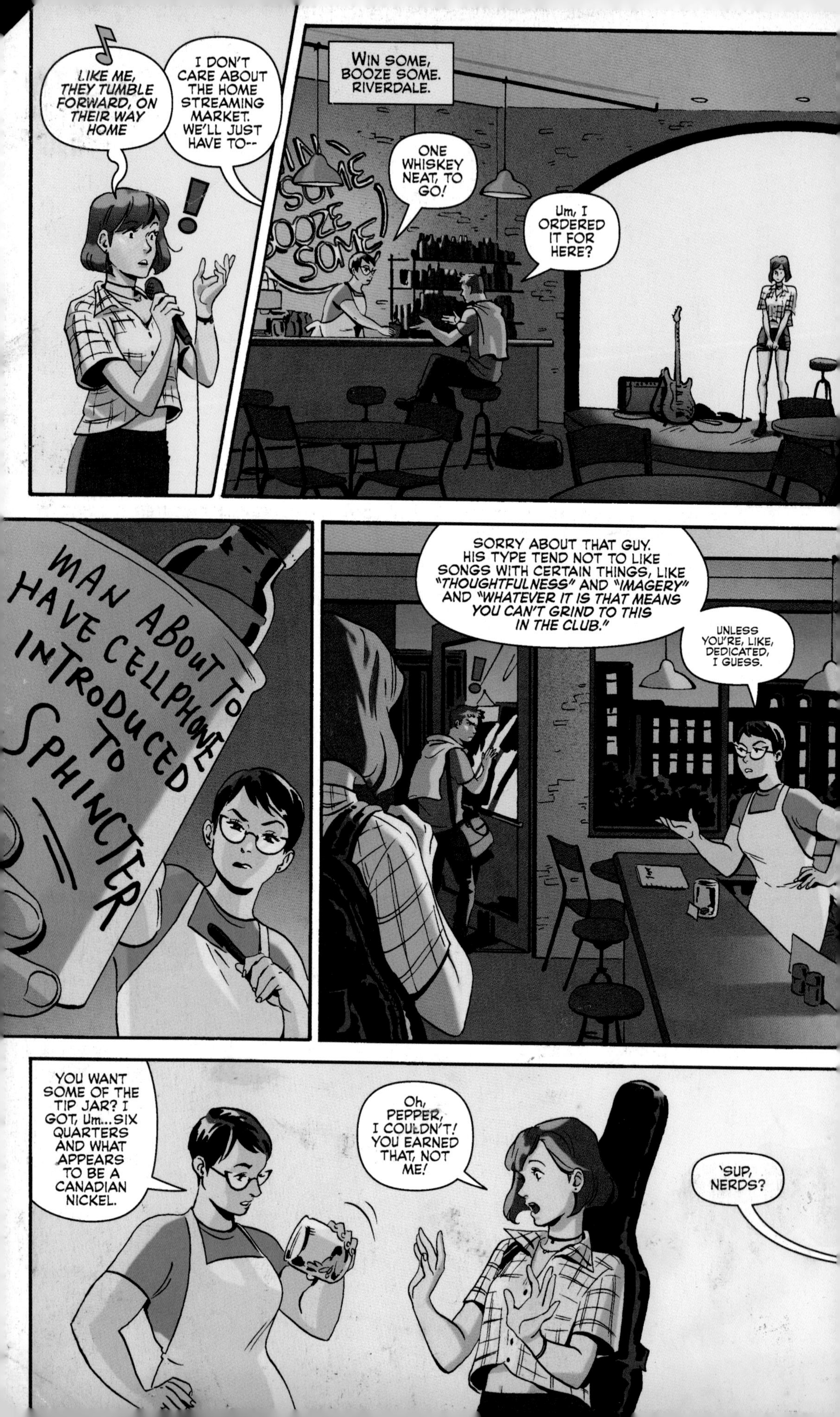
LIKE ME, THEY TUMBLE FORWARD, ON THEIR WAY HOME
I DON'T CARE ABOUT THE HOME STREAMING MARKET. WE'LL JUST HAVE TO--
!
WIN SOME, BOOZE SOME. RIVERDALE.
BOOZE SOME
ONE WHISKEY NEAT, TO GO!
Um, I ORDERED IT FOR HERE?
MAN ABOUT TO HAVE CELLPHONE INTRODUCED TO SPHINCTER
SORRY ABOUT THAT GUY. HIS TYPE TEND NOT TO LIKE SONGS WITH CERTAIN THINGS, LIKE "THOUGHTFULNESS" AND "IMAGERY" AND "WHATEVER IT IS THAT MEANS YOU CAN'T GRIND TO THIS IN THE CLUB."
UNLESS YOU'RE, LIKE, DEDICATED, I GUESS.
!
YOU WANT SOME OF THE TIP JAR? I GOT, Um...SIX QUARTERS AND WHAT APPEARS TO BE A CANADIAN NICKEL.
Oh, PEPPER, I COULDN'T! YOU EARNED THAT, NOT ME!
'SUP, NERDS?

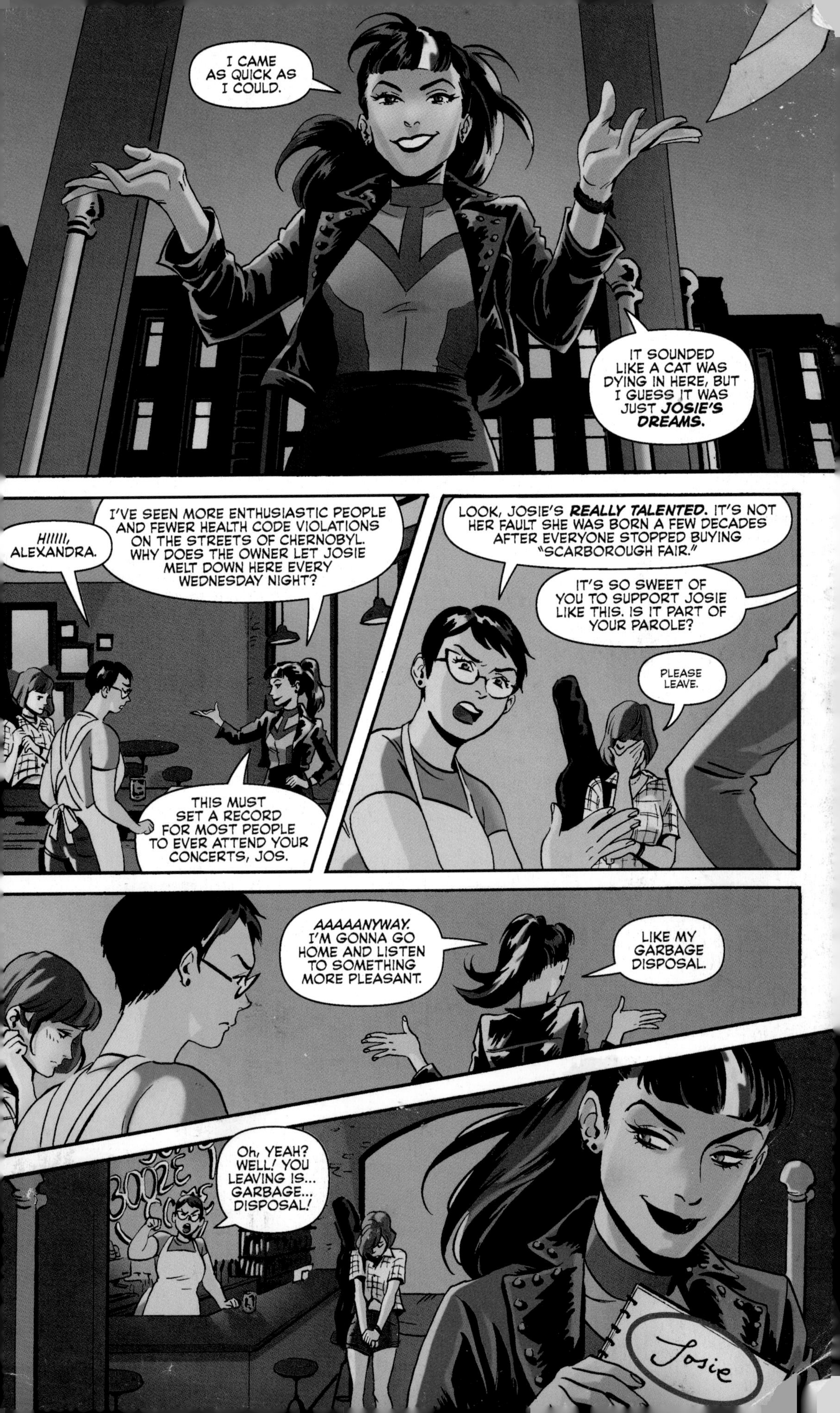

I CAME AS QUICK AS I COULD.
IT SOUNDED LIKE A CAT WAS DYING IN HERE, BUT I GUESS IT WAS JUST JOSIE'S DREAMS.
HIIIII, ALEXANDRA.
I'VE SEEN MORE ENTHUSIASTIC PEOPLE AND FEWER HEALTH CODE VIOLATIONS ON THE STREETS OF CHERNOBYL. WHY DOES THE OWNER LET JOSIE MELT DOWN HERE EVERY WEDNESDAY NIGHT?
THIS MUST SET A RECORD FOR MOST PEOPLE TO EVER ATTEND YOUR CONCERTS, JOS.
LOOK, JOSIE'S REALLY TALENTED. IT'S NOT HER FAULT SHE WAS BORN A FEW DECADES AFTER EVERYONE STOPPED BUYING "SCARBOROUGH FAIR."
IT'S SO SWEET OF YOU TO SUPPORT JOSIE LIKE THIS. IS IT PART OF YOUR PAROLE?
PLEASE LEAVE.
AAAAANYWAY. I'M GONNA GO HOME AND LISTEN TO SOMETHING MORE PLEASANT.
LIKE MY GARBAGE DISPOSAL.
Oh, YEAH? WELL! YOU LEAVING IS... GARBAGE... DISPOSAL!
Josie

UGGGGH. I'M THE WORST.

WHAT *HAPPENED*? YOU GUYS USED TO BE BEST FRIENDS!

YOU PIERCED HER EAR AND SHE CHICKENED OUT BEFORE YOU DID THE SECOND ONE. YOU WERE HER ALIBI THE NIGHT SHE NEARLY GOT CAUGHT TAKING HER DAD'S LEXUS!

YOU GOT SICK ON THE *SAME* KERMIT THE FROG CUPCAKES AT YOUR FIFTH BIRTHDAY!!

YEAH, WELL FRIENDSHIP'S A LOT MORE THAN PUKING TOGETHER, PEPPER.

I DID GREEK WEEK ALL WRONG, THEN.

LOOK, JOSIE. THE RIVERDALE ANIMAL SHELTER IS HAVING A CHARITY CONCERT FOR A FUNDRAISER. THEY NEED VOLUNTEER BANDS.

WANT TO HELP SOME JACKED UP THREE-LEGGED DOGS FIND LOVE? GET THE AFFECTION WE ALL MISSED IN OUR CHILDHOODS?

I *DID* MISS A LOT OF AFFECTION GROWING UP...

HEY. IF A ONE-EYED CAT CAN SING YOU SOME BACK-UP VOCALS, I WOULDN'T TURN UP THAT BUTTON NOSE JUST YET, TOOTS.

AT LEAST THEN I'D GET THE PITY VOTE.

CONCERT TO BENEFIT THE RIVERDALE **ANIMAL SHELTER**

BANDS W— TO PARTI— PLEASE I— AT THE SH—

A GOOD CAUSE MIGHT MOTIVATE SOME FRIENDS TO HELP?

YEAH, WELL. THANKS, PEPPER.

BUT I WOULDN'T WANT TO PUT ANYONE ELSE THROUGH THAT.

CLOSED

MAAAAN, EIGHT YEARS OF ELECTRIC CELLO FOR *NUTHIN'*.

CLOSED

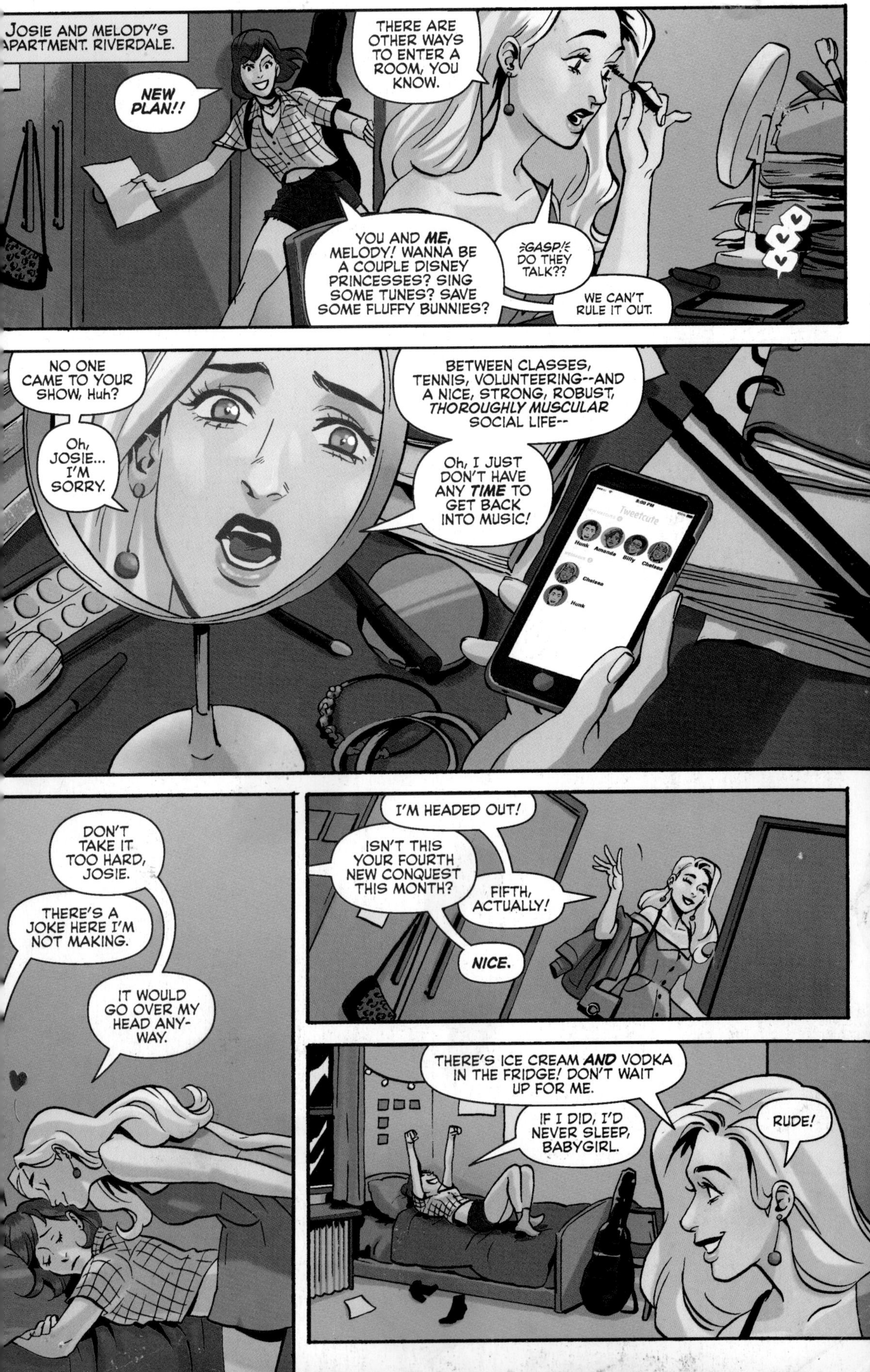

JOSIE AND MELODY'S APARTMENT. RIVERDALE.
NEW PLAN!!
THERE ARE OTHER WAYS TO ENTER A ROOM, YOU KNOW.
YOU AND ME, MELODY! WANNA BE A COUPLE DISNEY PRINCESSES? SING SOME TUNES? SAVE SOME FLUFFY BUNNIES?
GASP! DO THEY TALK??
WE CAN'T RULE IT OUT.
NO ONE CAME TO YOUR SHOW, Huh?
Oh, JOSIE... I'M SORRY.
BETWEEN CLASSES, TENNIS, VOLUNTEERING--AND A NICE, STRONG, ROBUST, THOROUGHLY MUSCULAR SOCIAL LIFE--
Oh, I JUST DON'T HAVE ANY TIME TO GET BACK INTO MUSIC!
Tweetcute
Hunk
Amanda
Billy
Chelsea
Chelsea
Hunk
DON'T TAKE IT TOO HARD, JOSIE.
THERE'S A JOKE HERE I'M NOT MAKING.
IT WOULD GO OVER MY HEAD ANYWAY.
I'M HEADED OUT!
ISN'T THIS YOUR FOURTH NEW CONQUEST THIS MONTH?
FIFTH, ACTUALLY!
NICE.
THERE'S ICE CREAM AND VODKA IN THE FRIDGE! DON'T WAIT UP FOR ME.
IF I DID, I'D NEVER SLEEP, BABYGIRL.
RUDE!

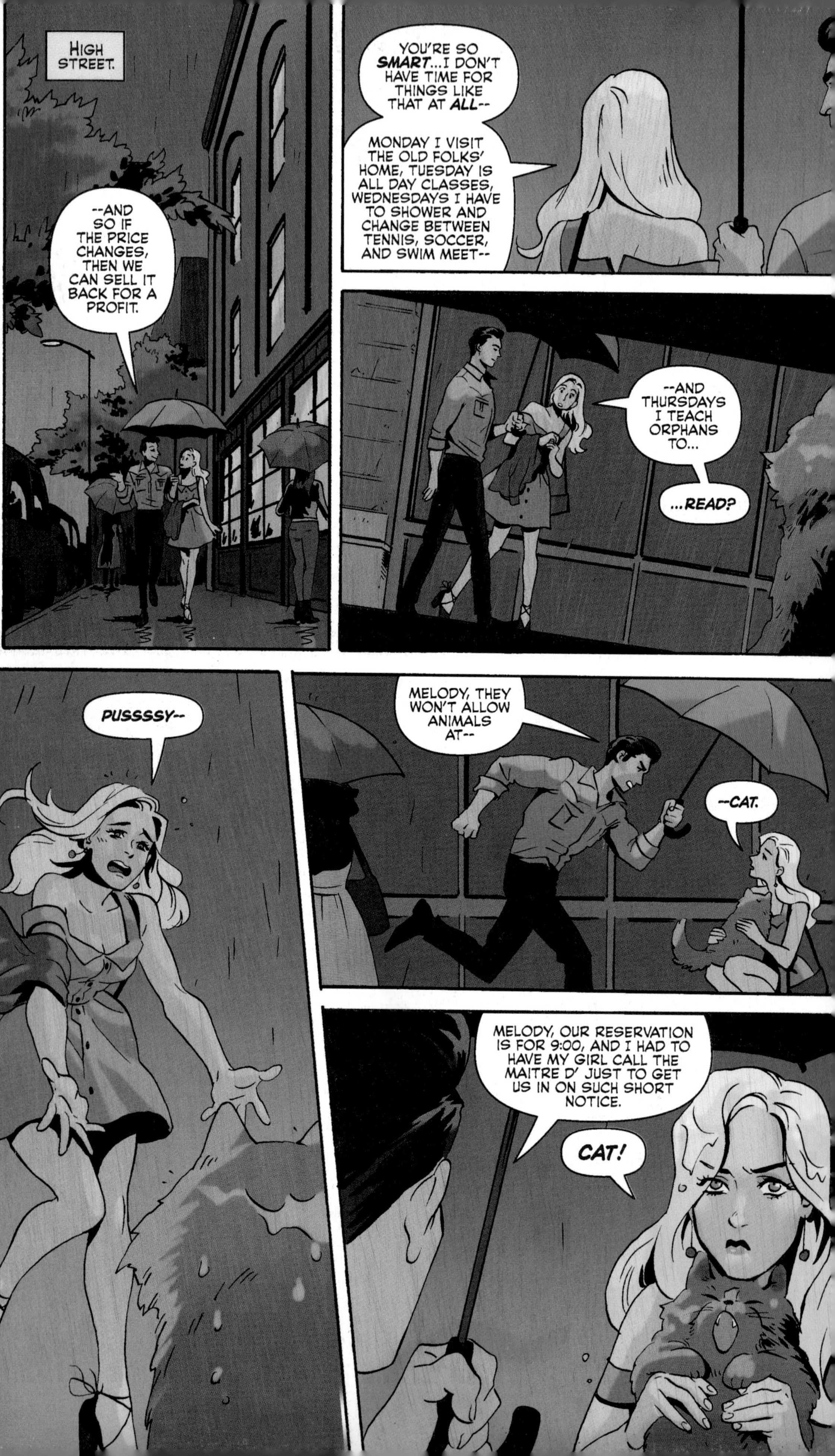
HIGH STREET.
--AND SO IF THE PRICE CHANGES, THEN WE CAN SELL IT BACK FOR A PROFIT.
YOU'RE SO SMART...I DON'T HAVE TIME FOR THINGS LIKE THAT AT ALL--
MONDAY I VISIT THE OLD FOLKS' HOME, TUESDAY IS ALL DAY CLASSES, WEDNESDAYS I HAVE TO SHOWER AND CHANGE BETWEEN TENNIS, SOCCER, AND SWIM MEET--
--AND THURSDAYS I TEACH ORPHANS TO...
...READ?
PUSSSSY--
MELODY, THEY WON'T ALLOW ANIMALS AT--
--CAT.
MELODY, OUR RESERVATION IS FOR 9:00, AND I HAD TO HAVE MY GIRL CALL THE MAITRE D' JUST TO GET US IN ON SUCH SHORT NOTICE.
CAT!

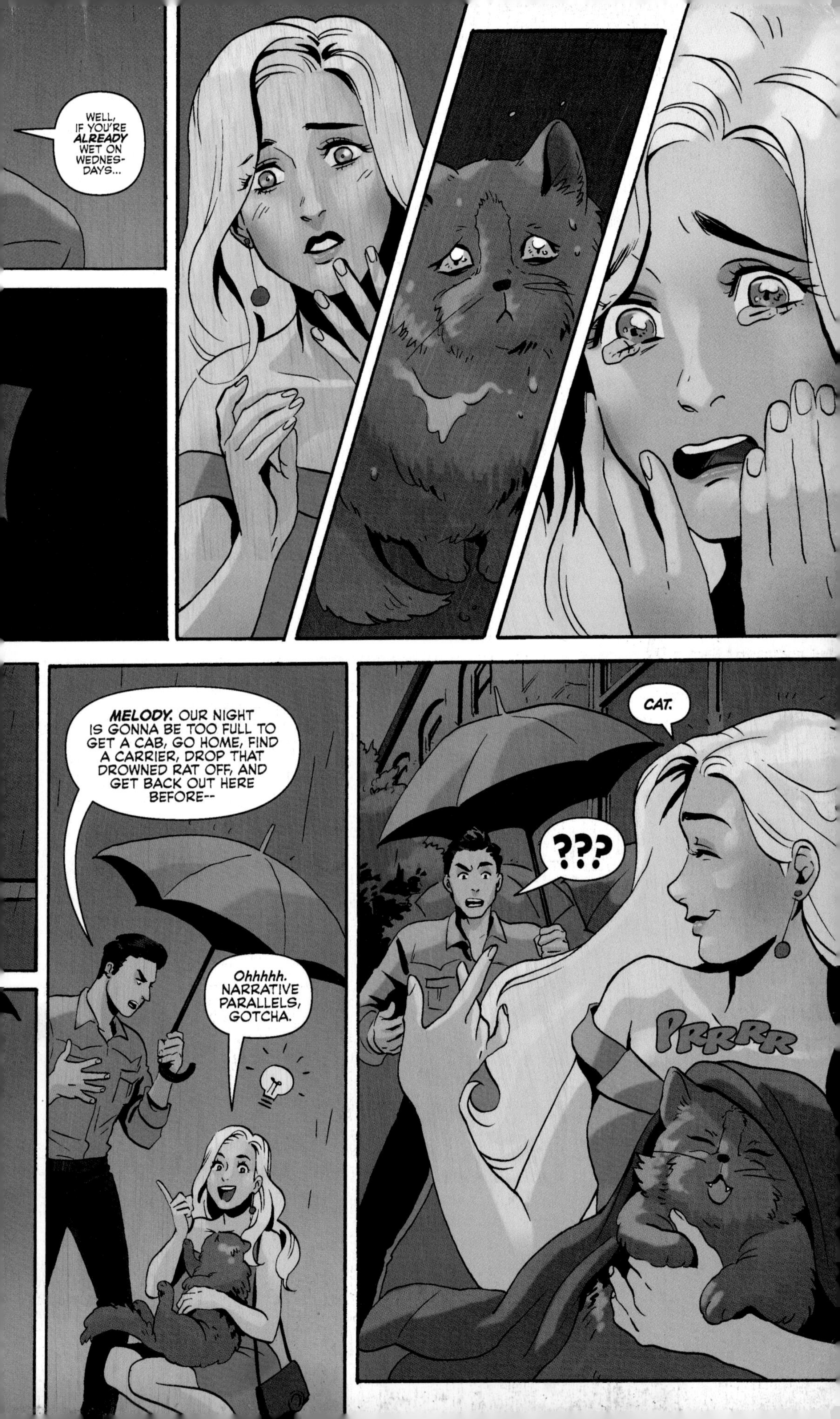
WELL, IF YOU'RE ALREADY WET ON WEDNES-DAYS...
MELODY. OUR NIGHT IS GONNA BE TOO FULL TO GET A CAB, GO HOME, FIND A CARRIER, DROP THAT DROWNED RAT OFF, AND GET BACK OUT HERE BEFORE--
Ohhhhh. NARRATIVE PARALLELS, GOTCHA.
CAT.
???
PRRRR

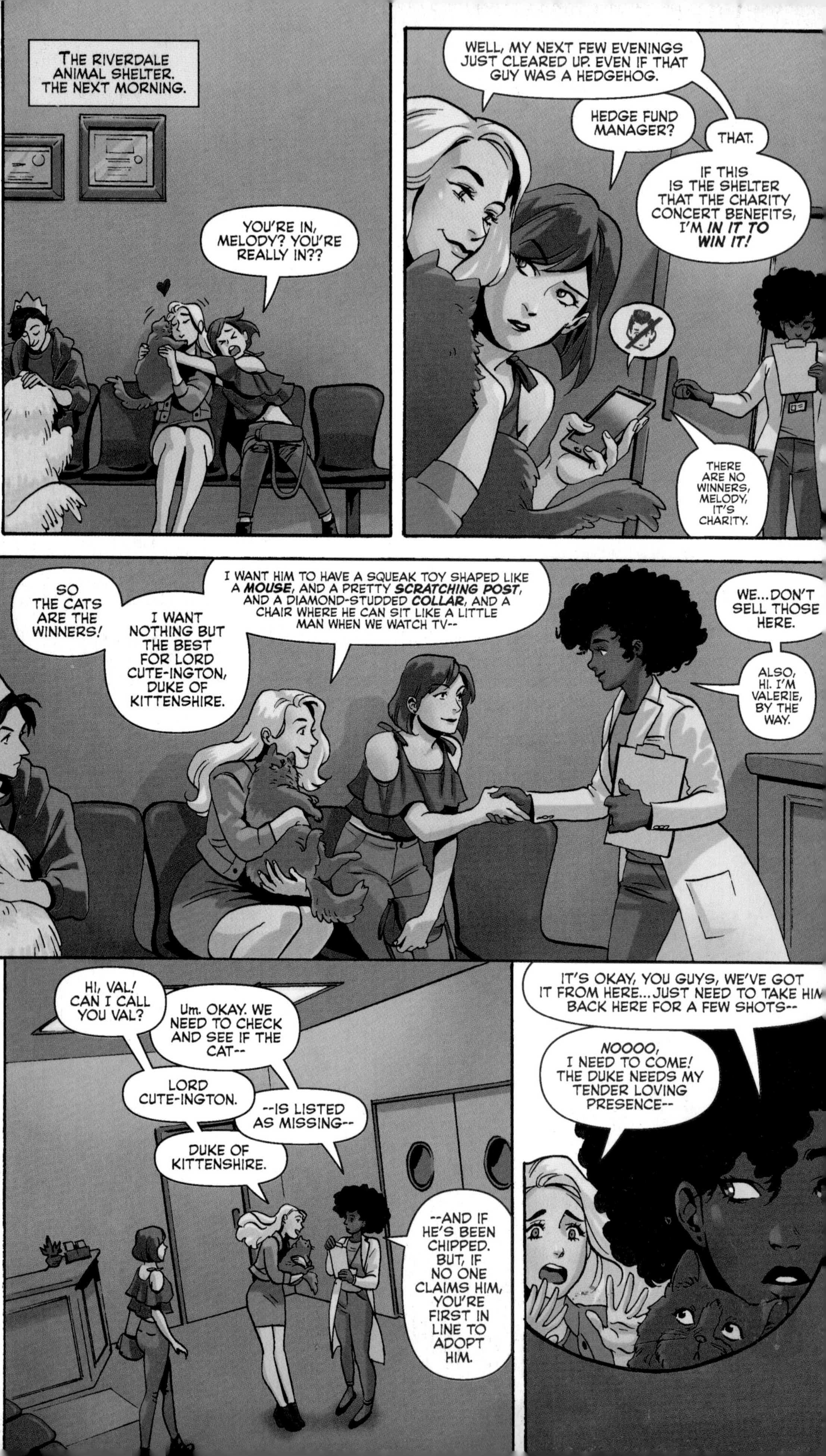
THE RIVERDALE ANIMAL SHELTER. THE NEXT MORNING.
YOU'RE IN, MELODY? YOU'RE REALLY IN??
WELL, MY NEXT FEW EVENINGS JUST CLEARED UP. EVEN IF THAT GUY WAS A HEDGEHOG.
HEDGE FUND MANAGER?
THAT.
IF THIS IS THE SHELTER THAT THE CHARITY CONCERT BENEFITS, I'M ***IN IT TO WIN IT!***
THERE ARE NO WINNERS, MELODY, IT'S CHARITY.
SO THE CATS ARE THE WINNERS!
I WANT NOTHING BUT THE BEST FOR LORD CUTE-INGTON, DUKE OF KITTENSHIRE.
I WANT HIM TO HAVE A SQUEAK TOY SHAPED LIKE A ***MOUSE***, AND A PRETTY ***SCRATCHING POST***, AND A DIAMOND-STUDDED ***COLLAR***, AND A CHAIR WHERE HE CAN SIT LIKE A LITTLE MAN WHEN WE WATCH TV--
WE...DON'T SELL THOSE HERE.
ALSO, HI. I'M VALERIE, BY THE WAY.
HI, VAL! CAN I CALL YOU VAL?
Um. OKAY. WE NEED TO CHECK AND SEE IF THE CAT--
LORD CUTE-INGTON.
--IS LISTED AS MISSING--
DUKE OF KITTENSHIRE.
--AND IF HE'S BEEN CHIPPED. BUT, IF NO ONE CLAIMS HIM, YOU'RE FIRST IN LINE TO ADOPT HIM.
IT'S OKAY, YOU GUYS, WE'VE GOT IT FROM HERE...JUST NEED TO TAKE HIM BACK HERE FOR A FEW SHOTS--
NOOOO, I NEED TO COME! THE DUKE NEEDS MY TENDER LOVING PRESENCE--

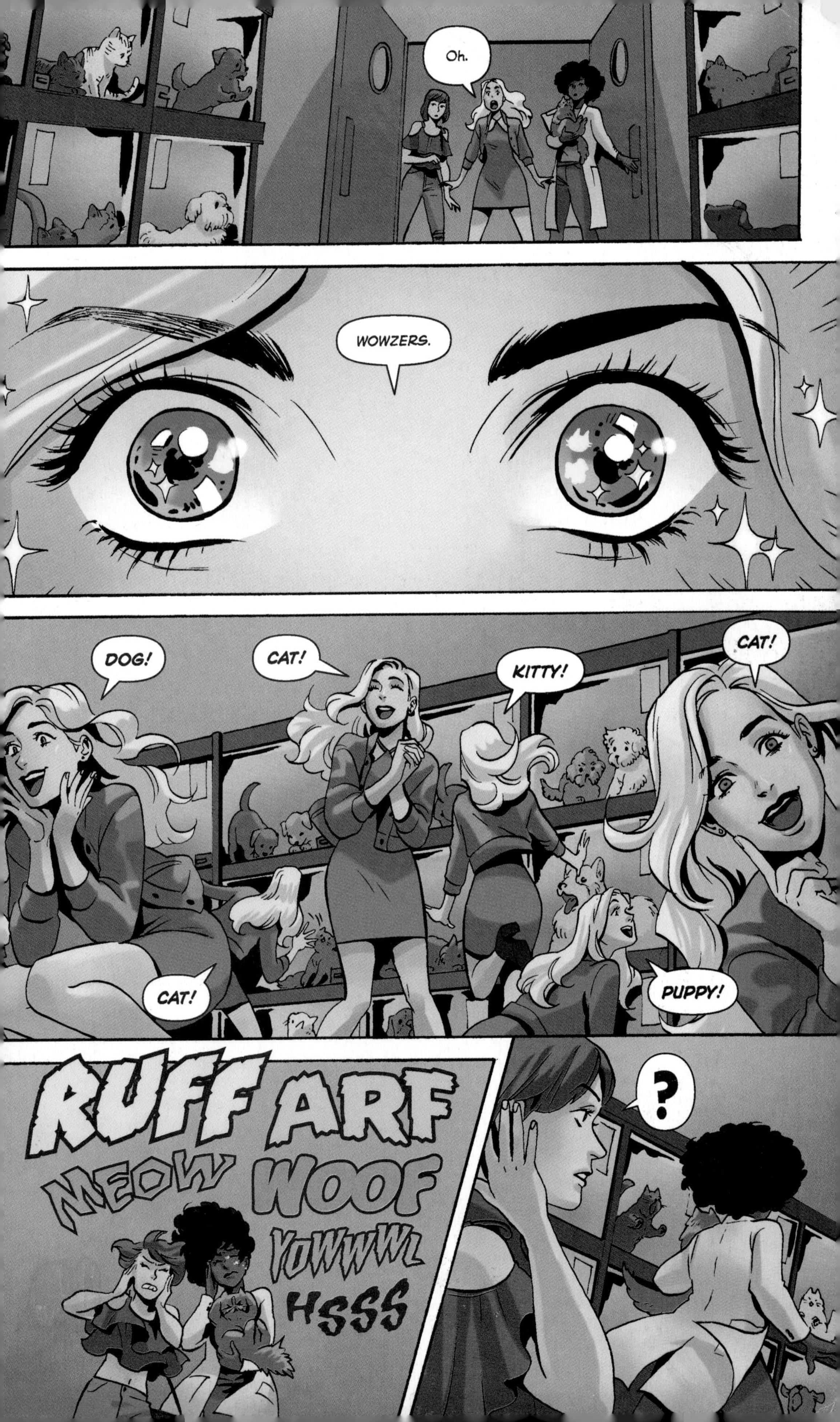
Oh.
WOWZERS.
DOG!
CAT!
KITTY!
CAT!
CAT!
PUPPY!
RUFF ARF
MEOW WOOF
YOWWWL
HSSS
?

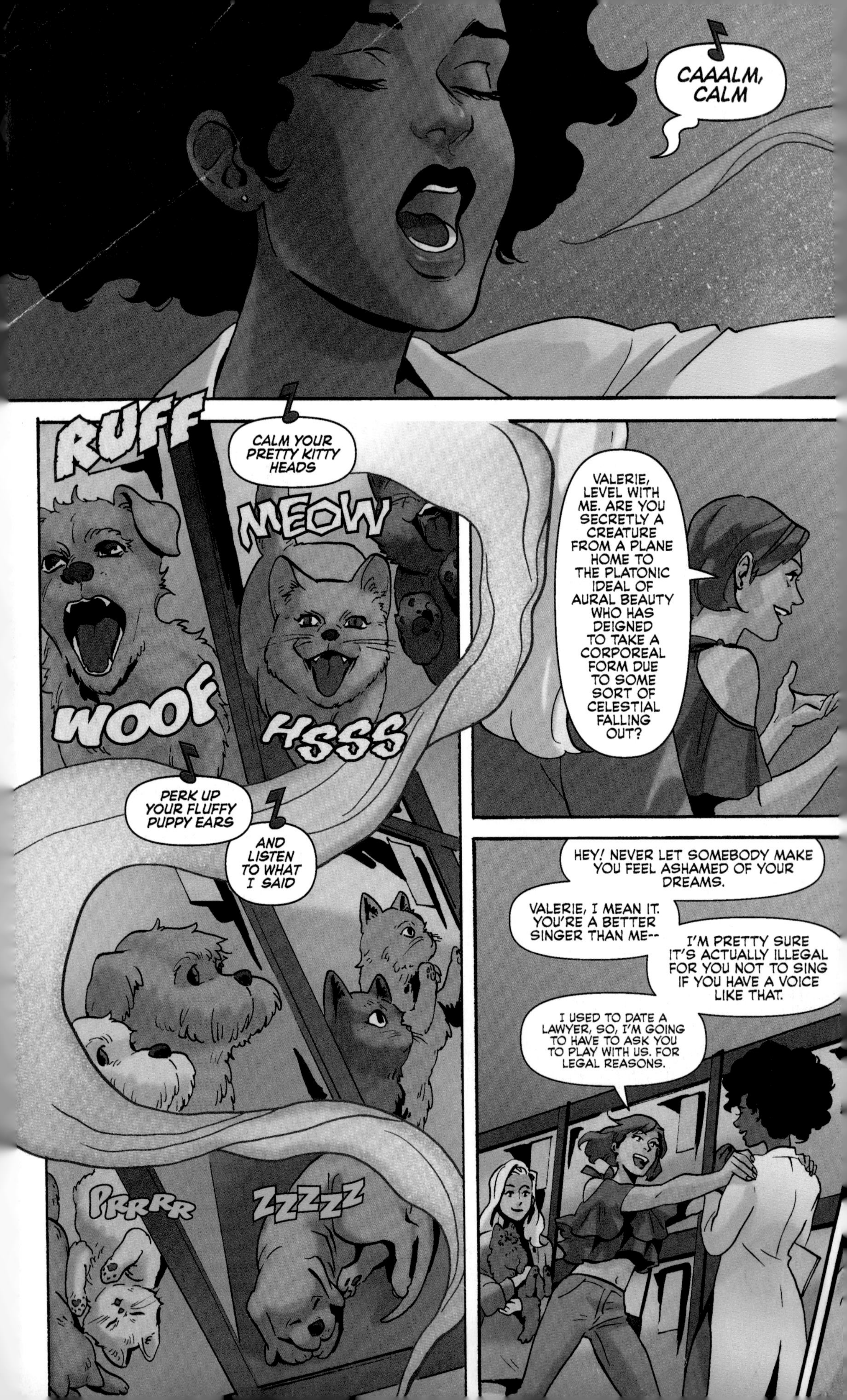
CAAALM, CALM
RUFF
CALM YOUR PRETTY KITTY HEADS
MEOW
WOOF
HSSS
PERK UP YOUR FLUFFY PUPPY EARS
AND LISTEN TO WHAT I SAID
PRRRR
ZZZZZ
VALERIE, LEVEL WITH ME. ARE YOU SECRETLY A CREATURE FROM A PLANE HOME TO THE PLATONIC IDEAL OF AURAL BEAUTY WHO HAS DEIGNED TO TAKE A CORPOREAL FORM DUE TO SOME SORT OF CELESTIAL FALLING OUT?
HEY! NEVER LET SOMEBODY MAKE YOU FEEL ASHAMED OF YOUR DREAMS.
VALERIE, I MEAN IT. YOU'RE A BETTER SINGER THAN ME--
I'M PRETTY SURE IT'S ACTUALLY ILLEGAL FOR YOU NOT TO SING IF YOU HAVE A VOICE LIKE THAT.
I USED TO DATE A LAWYER, SO, I'M GOING TO HAVE TO ASK YOU TO PLAY WITH US. FOR LEGAL REASONS.

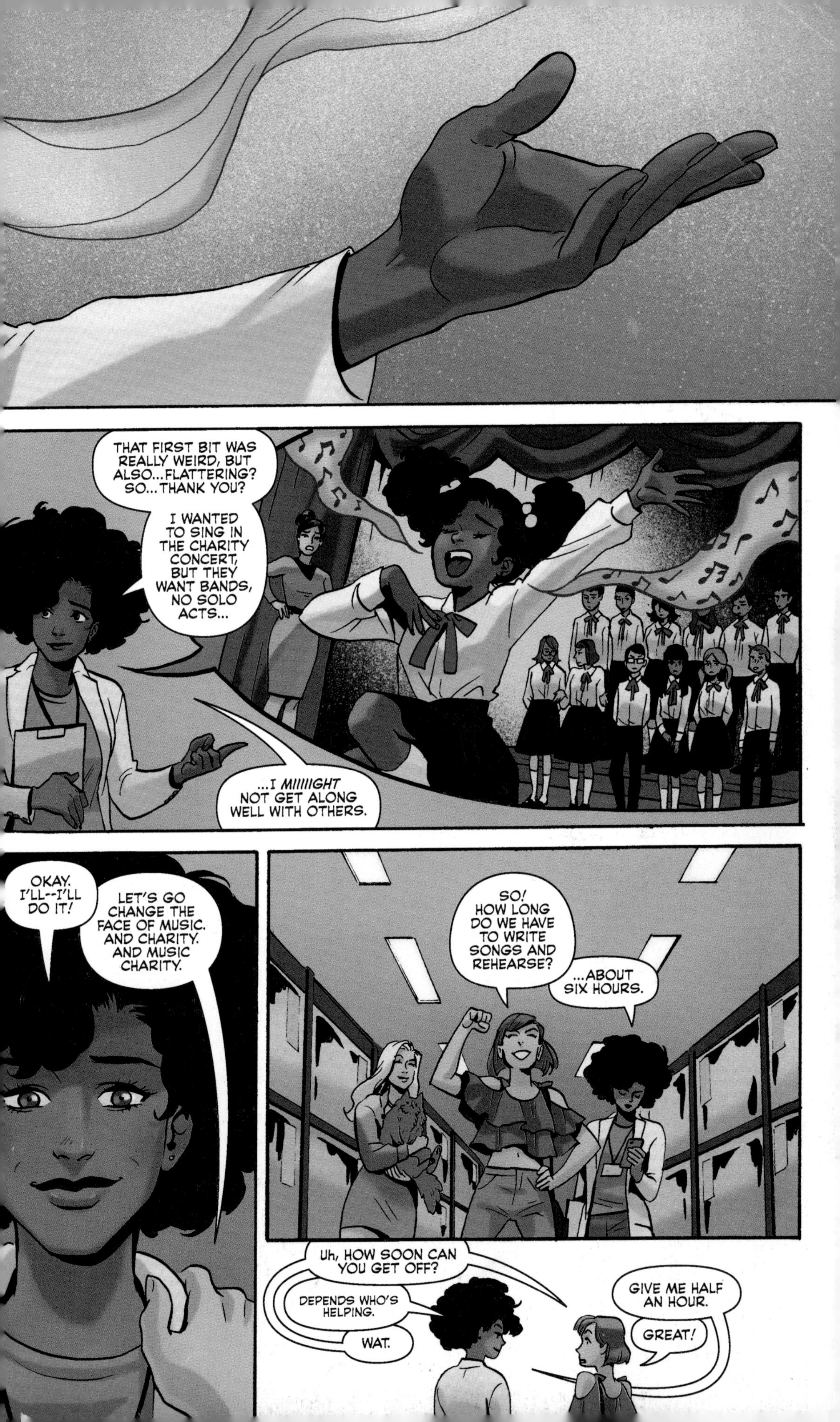
THAT FIRST BIT WAS REALLY WEIRD, BUT ALSO...FLATTERING? SO...THANK YOU?
I WANTED TO SING IN THE CHARITY CONCERT, BUT THEY WANT BANDS, NO SOLO ACTS...
...I MIIIIIGHT NOT GET ALONG WELL WITH OTHERS.
OKAY. I'LL--I'LL DO IT!
LET'S GO CHANGE THE FACE OF MUSIC. AND CHARITY. AND MUSIC CHARITY.
SO! HOW LONG DO WE HAVE TO WRITE SONGS AND REHEARSE?
...ABOUT SIX HOURS.
Uh, HOW SOON CAN YOU GET OFF?
DEPENDS WHO'S HELPING.
WAT.
GIVE ME HALF AN HOUR.
GREAT!

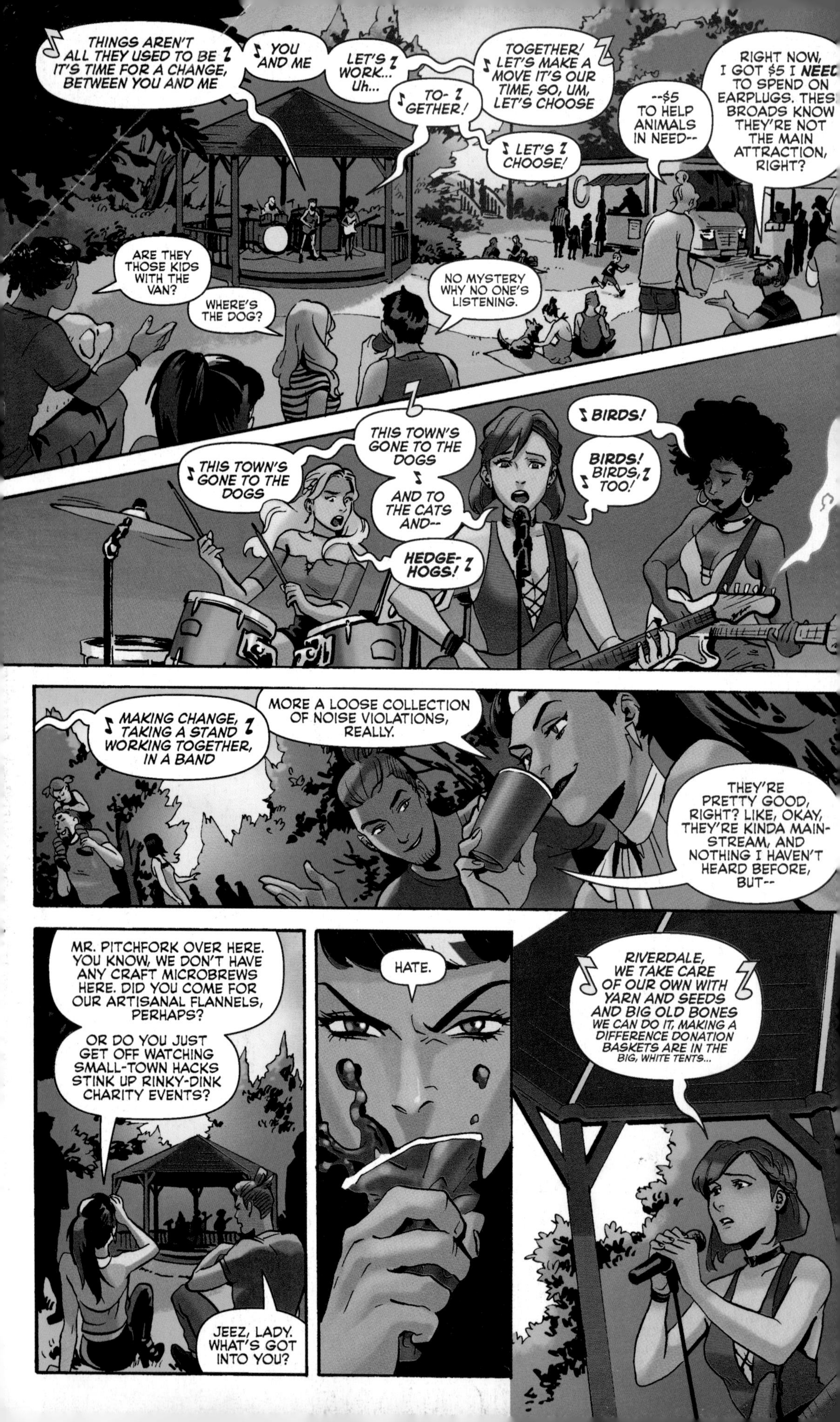
THINGS AREN'T ALL THEY USED TO BE IT'S TIME FOR A CHANGE, BETWEEN YOU AND ME
YOU AND ME
LET'S WORK... Uh...
TO-GETHER!
TOGETHER! LET'S MAKE A MOVE IT'S OUR TIME, SO, UM, LET'S CHOOSE
LET'S CHOOSE!
--$5 TO HELP ANIMALS IN NEED--
RIGHT NOW, I GOT $5 I NEED TO SPEND ON EARPLUGS. THESE BROADS KNOW THEY'RE NOT THE MAIN ATTRACTION, RIGHT?
ARE THEY THOSE KIDS WITH THE VAN?
WHERE'S THE DOG?
NO MYSTERY WHY NO ONE'S LISTENING.
THIS TOWN'S GONE TO THE DOGS
THIS TOWN'S GONE TO THE DOGS
AND TO THE CATS AND--
HEDGE-HOGS!
BIRDS!
BIRDS! BIRDS, TOO!
MAKING CHANGE, TAKING A STAND WORKING TOGETHER, IN A BAND
MORE A LOOSE COLLECTION OF NOISE VIOLATIONS, REALLY.
THEY'RE PRETTY GOOD, RIGHT? LIKE, OKAY, THEY'RE KINDA MAIN-STREAM, AND NOTHING I HAVEN'T HEARD BEFORE, BUT--
MR. PITCHFORK OVER HERE. YOU KNOW, WE DON'T HAVE ANY CRAFT MICROBREWS HERE. DID YOU COME FOR OUR ARTISANAL FLANNELS, PERHAPS?
OR DO YOU JUST GET OFF WATCHING SMALL-TOWN HACKS STINK UP RINKY-DINK CHARITY EVENTS?
JEEZ, LADY. WHAT'S GOT INTO YOU?
HATE.
RIVERDALE, WE TAKE CARE OF OUR OWN WITH YARN AND SEEDS AND BIG OLD BONES WE CAN DO IT, MAKING A DIFFERENCE DONATION BASKETS ARE IN THE BIG, WHITE TENTS...

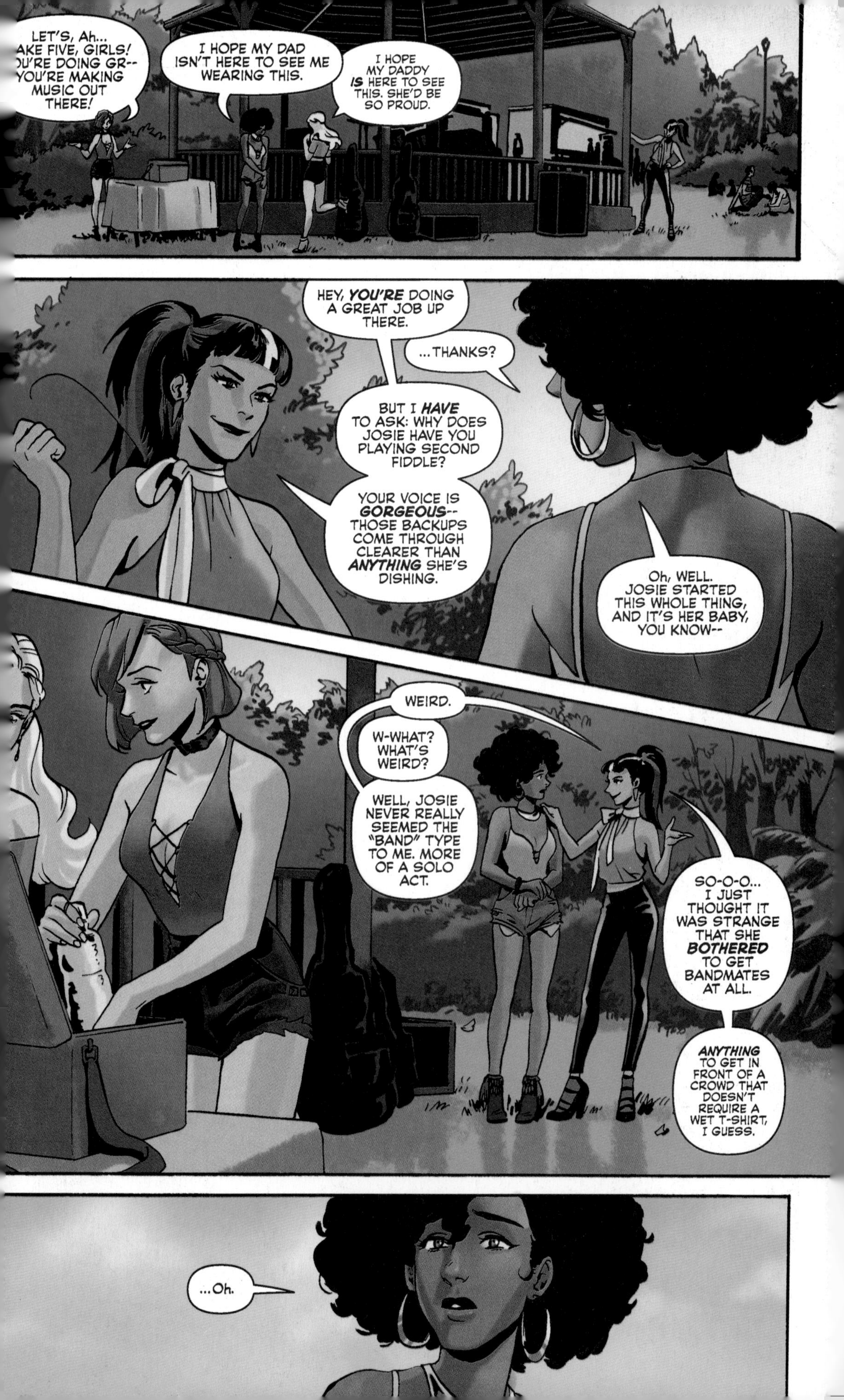
LET'S, AH... AKE FIVE, GIRLS! OU'RE DOING GR-- YOU'RE MAKING MUSIC OUT THERE!
I HOPE MY DAD ISN'T HERE TO SEE ME WEARING THIS.
I HOPE MY DADDY IS HERE TO SEE THIS. SHE'D BE SO PROUD.
HEY, YOU'RE DOING A GREAT JOB UP THERE.
...THANKS?
BUT I HAVE TO ASK: WHY DOES JOSIE HAVE YOU PLAYING SECOND FIDDLE?
YOUR VOICE IS GORGEOUS-- THOSE BACKUPS COME THROUGH CLEARER THAN ANYTHING SHE'S DISHING.
OH, WELL. JOSIE STARTED THIS WHOLE THING, AND IT'S HER BABY, YOU KNOW--
WEIRD.
W-WHAT? WHAT'S WEIRD?
WELL, JOSIE NEVER REALLY SEEMED THE "BAND" TYPE TO ME. MORE OF A SOLO ACT.
SO-O-O... I JUST THOUGHT IT WAS STRANGE THAT SHE BOTHERED TO GET BANDMATES AT ALL.
ANYTHING TO GET IN FRONT OF A CROWD THAT DOESN'T REQUIRE A WET T-SHIRT, I GUESS.
...OH.

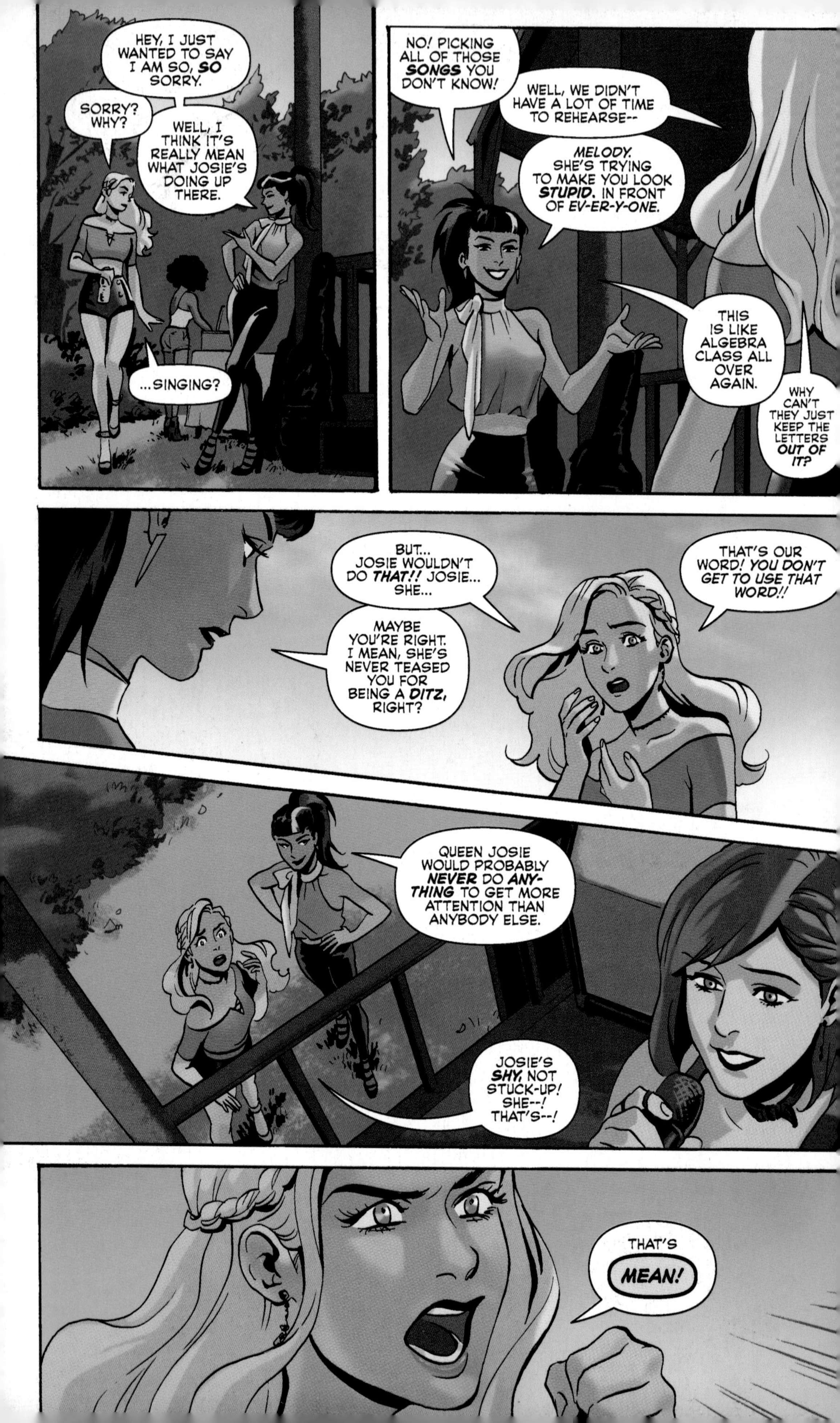
HEY, I JUST WANTED TO SAY I AM SO, **SO** SORRY.
SORRY? WHY?
WELL, I THINK IT'S REALLY MEAN WHAT JOSIE'S DOING UP THERE.
...SINGING?
NO! PICKING ALL OF THOSE **SONGS** YOU DON'T KNOW!
WELL, WE DIDN'T HAVE A LOT OF TIME TO REHEARSE--
MELODY. SHE'S TRYING TO MAKE YOU LOOK **STUPID.** IN FRONT OF *EV-ER-Y-ONE.*
THIS IS LIKE ALGEBRA CLASS ALL OVER AGAIN.
WHY CAN'T THEY JUST KEEP THE LETTERS *OUT OF IT?*
BUT... JOSIE WOULDN'T DO *THAT!!* JOSIE... SHE...
MAYBE YOU'RE RIGHT. I MEAN, SHE'S NEVER TEASED YOU FOR BEING A *DITZ,* RIGHT?
THAT'S OUR WORD! *YOU DON'T GET TO USE THAT WORD!!*
QUEEN JOSIE WOULD PROBABLY ***NEVER*** DO ***ANY-THING*** TO GET MORE ATTENTION THAN ANYBODY ELSE.
JOSIE'S ***SHY,*** NOT STUCK-UP! SHE--! THAT'S--!
THAT'S
MEAN!

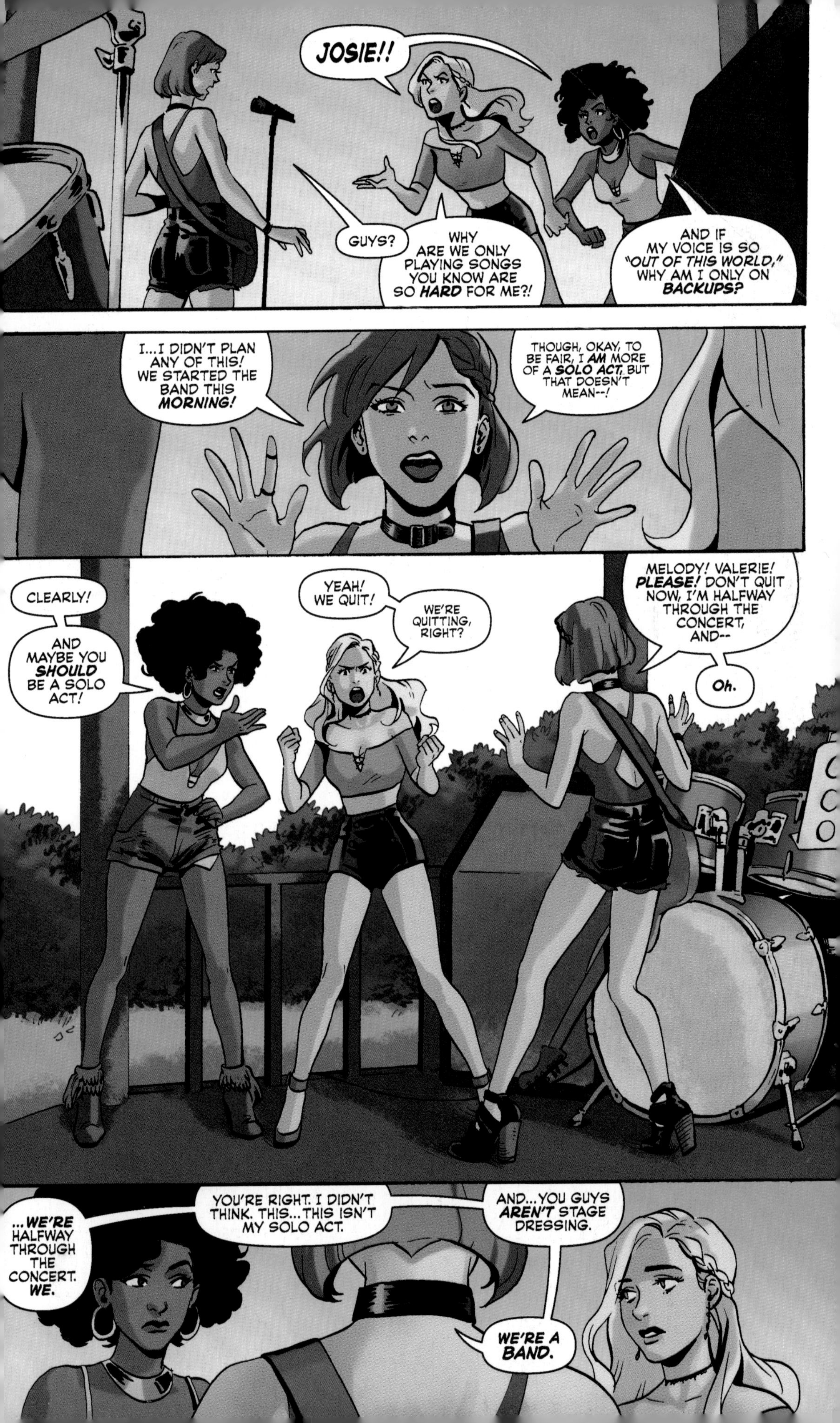
JOSIE!!
GUYS?
WHY ARE WE ONLY PLAYING SONGS YOU KNOW ARE SO HARD FOR ME?!
AND IF MY VOICE IS SO "OUT OF THIS WORLD," WHY AM I ONLY ON BACKUPS?
I...I DIDN'T PLAN ANY OF THIS! WE STARTED THE BAND THIS MORNING!
THOUGH, OKAY, TO BE FAIR, I AM MORE OF A SOLO ACT, BUT THAT DOESN'T MEAN--!
CLEARLY!
AND MAYBE YOU SHOULD BE A SOLO ACT!
YEAH! WE QUIT!
WE'RE QUITTING, RIGHT?
MELODY! VALERIE! PLEASE! DON'T QUIT NOW, I'M HALFWAY THROUGH THE CONCERT, AND--
Oh.
...WE'RE HALFWAY THROUGH THE CONCERT. WE.
YOU'RE RIGHT. I DIDN'T THINK. THIS...THIS ISN'T MY SOLO ACT.
AND...YOU GUYS AREN'T STAGE DRESSING.
WE'RE A BAND.

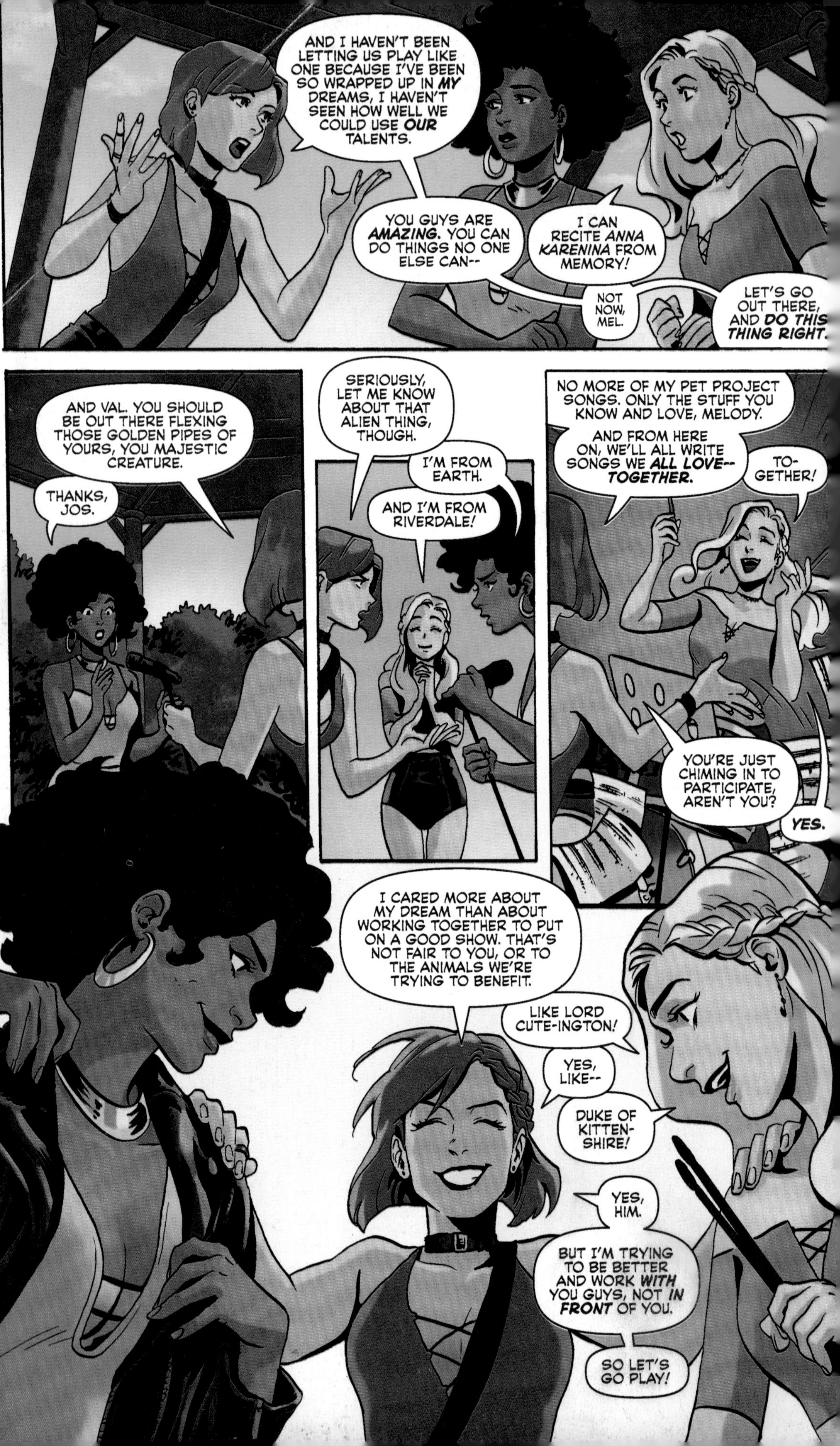
AND I HAVEN'T BEEN LETTING US PLAY LIKE ONE BECAUSE I'VE BEEN SO WRAPPED UP IN *MY* DREAMS, I HAVEN'T SEEN HOW WELL WE COULD USE *OUR* TALENTS.
YOU GUYS ARE **AMAZING.** YOU CAN DO THINGS NO ONE ELSE CAN--
I CAN RECITE *ANNA KARENINA* FROM MEMORY!
NOT NOW, MEL.
LET'S GO OUT THERE, AND **DO THIS THING RIGHT.**
AND VAL. YOU SHOULD BE OUT THERE FLEXING THOSE GOLDEN PIPES OF YOURS, YOU MAJESTIC CREATURE.
THANKS, JOS.
SERIOUSLY, LET ME KNOW ABOUT THAT ALIEN THING, THOUGH.
I'M FROM EARTH.
AND I'M FROM RIVERDALE!
NO MORE OF MY PET PROJECT SONGS. ONLY THE STUFF YOU KNOW AND LOVE, MELODY.
AND FROM HERE ON, WE'LL ALL WRITE SONGS WE **ALL LOVE-- TOGETHER.**
TO-GETHER!
YOU'RE JUST CHIMING IN TO PARTICIPATE, AREN'T YOU?
YES.
I CARED MORE ABOUT MY DREAM THAN ABOUT WORKING TOGETHER TO PUT ON A GOOD SHOW. THAT'S NOT FAIR TO YOU, OR TO THE ANIMALS WE'RE TRYING TO BENEFIT.
LIKE LORD CUTE-INGTON!
YES, LIKE--
DUKE OF KITTEN-SHIRE!
YES, HIM.
BUT I'M TRYING TO BE BETTER AND WORK *WITH* YOU GUYS, NOT *IN FRONT* OF YOU.
SO LET'S GO PLAY!

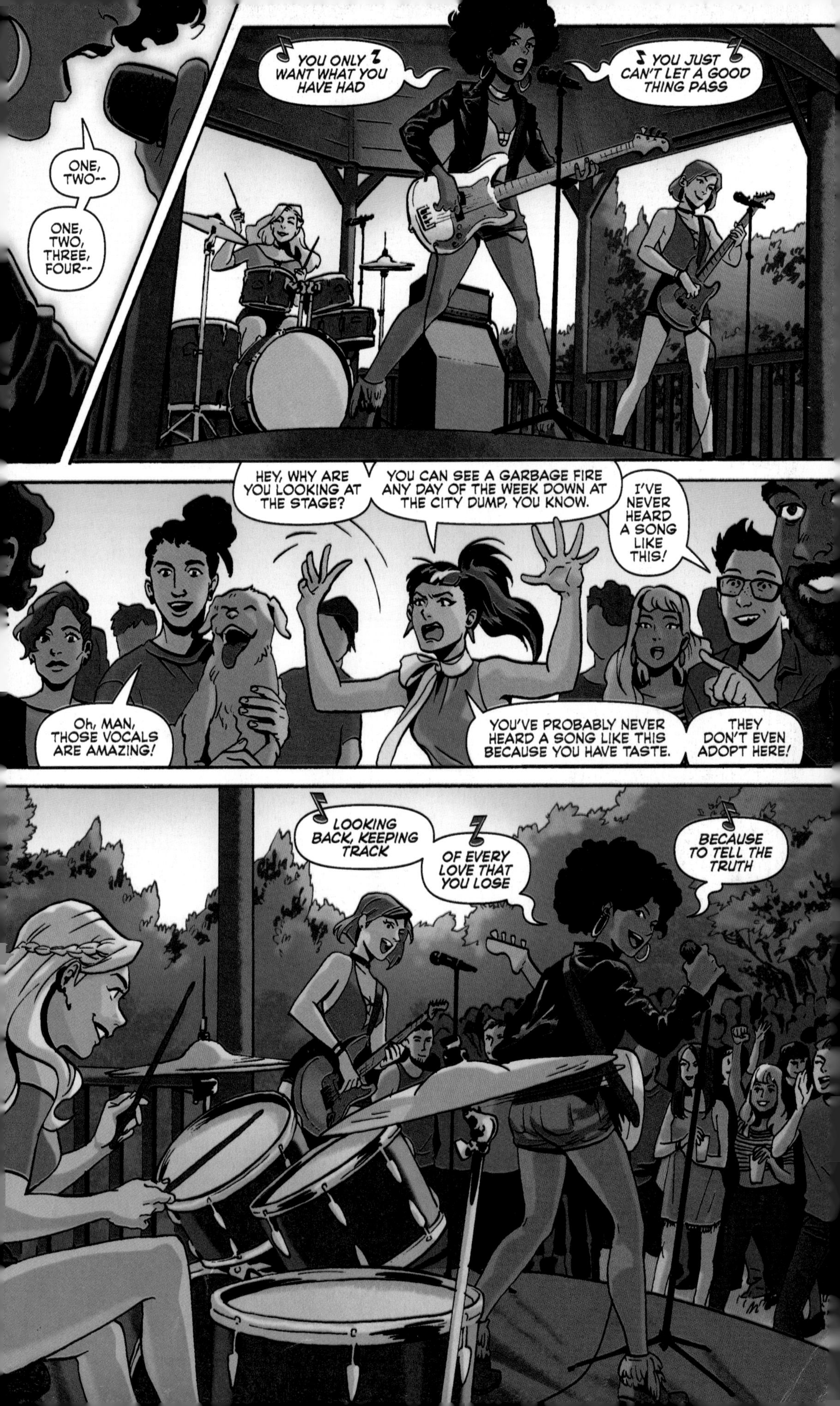
ONE, TWO--
ONE, TWO, THREE, FOUR--
YOU ONLY WANT WHAT YOU HAVE HAD
YOU JUST CAN'T LET A GOOD THING PASS
HEY, WHY ARE YOU LOOKING AT THE STAGE?
YOU CAN SEE A GARBAGE FIRE ANY DAY OF THE WEEK DOWN AT THE CITY DUMP, YOU KNOW.
I'VE NEVER HEARD A SONG LIKE THIS!
Oh, MAN, THOSE VOCALS ARE AMAZING!
YOU'VE PROBABLY NEVER HEARD A SONG LIKE THIS BECAUSE YOU HAVE TASTE.
THEY DON'T EVEN ADOPT HERE!
LOOKING BACK, KEEPING TRACK
OF EVERY LOVE THAT YOU LOSE
BECAUSE TO TELL THE TRUTH

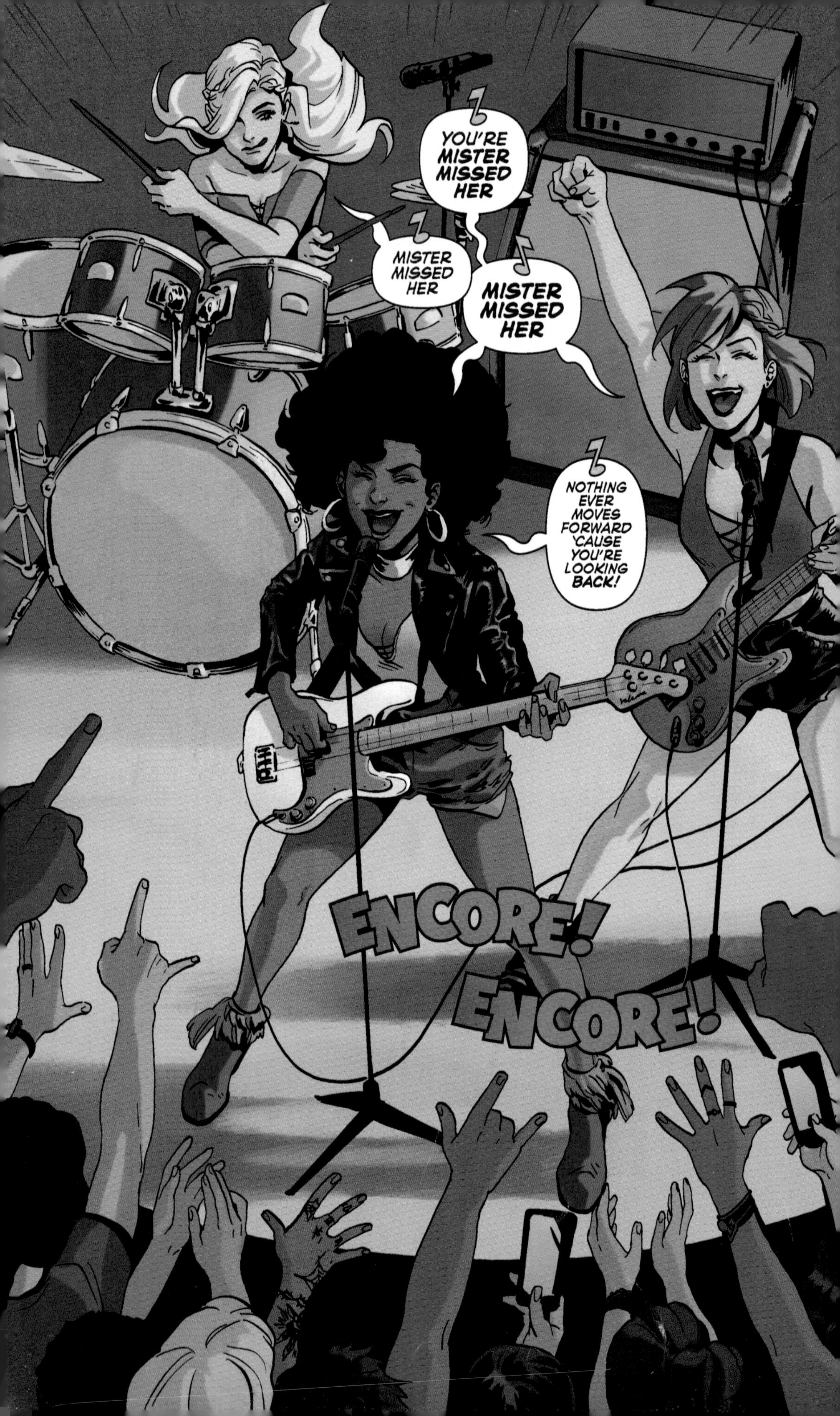
YOU'RE MISTER MISSED HER
MISTER MISSED HER
MISTER MISSED HER
NOTHING EVER MOVES FORWARD 'CAUSE YOU'RE LOOKING BACK!
ENCORE!
ENCORE!

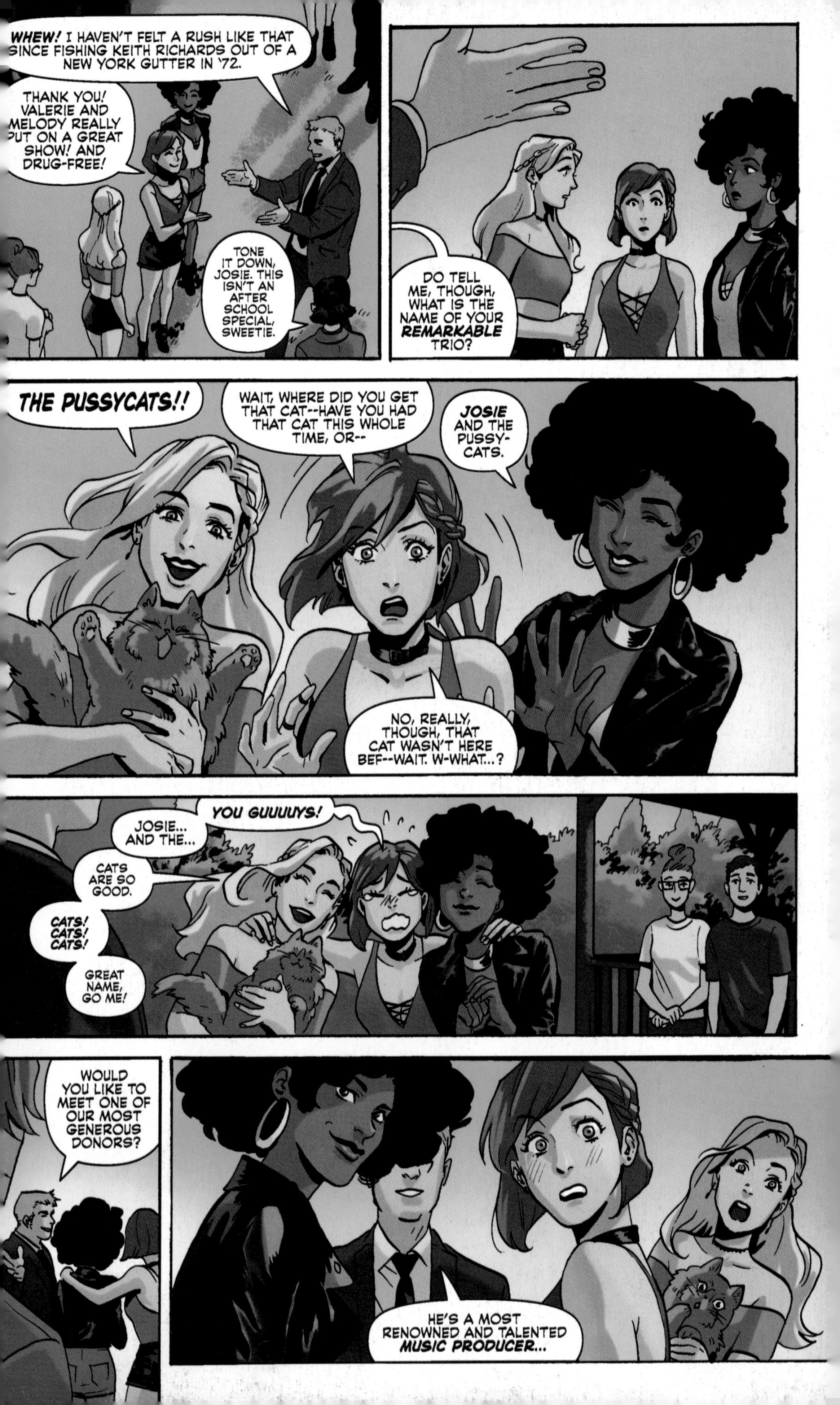
WHEW! I HAVEN'T FELT A RUSH LIKE THAT SINCE FISHING KEITH RICHARDS OUT OF A NEW YORK GUTTER IN '72.
THANK YOU! VALERIE AND MELODY REALLY PUT ON A GREAT SHOW! AND DRUG-FREE!
TONE IT DOWN, JOSIE. THIS ISN'T AN AFTER SCHOOL SPECIAL, SWEETIE.
DO TELL ME, THOUGH, WHAT IS THE NAME OF YOUR REMARKABLE TRIO?
THE PUSSYCATS!!
WAIT, WHERE DID YOU GET THAT CAT--HAVE YOU HAD THAT CAT THIS WHOLE TIME, OR--
JOSIE AND THE PUSSY-CATS.
NO, REALLY, THOUGH, THAT CAT WASN'T HERE BEF--WAIT. W-WHAT...?
JOSIE... AND THE...
YOU GUUUUYS!
CATS ARE SO GOOD.
CATS! CATS! CATS!
GREAT NAME, GO ME!
WOULD YOU LIKE TO MEET ONE OF OUR MOST GENEROUS DONORS?
HE'S A MOST RENOWNED AND TALENTED MUSIC PRODUCER...

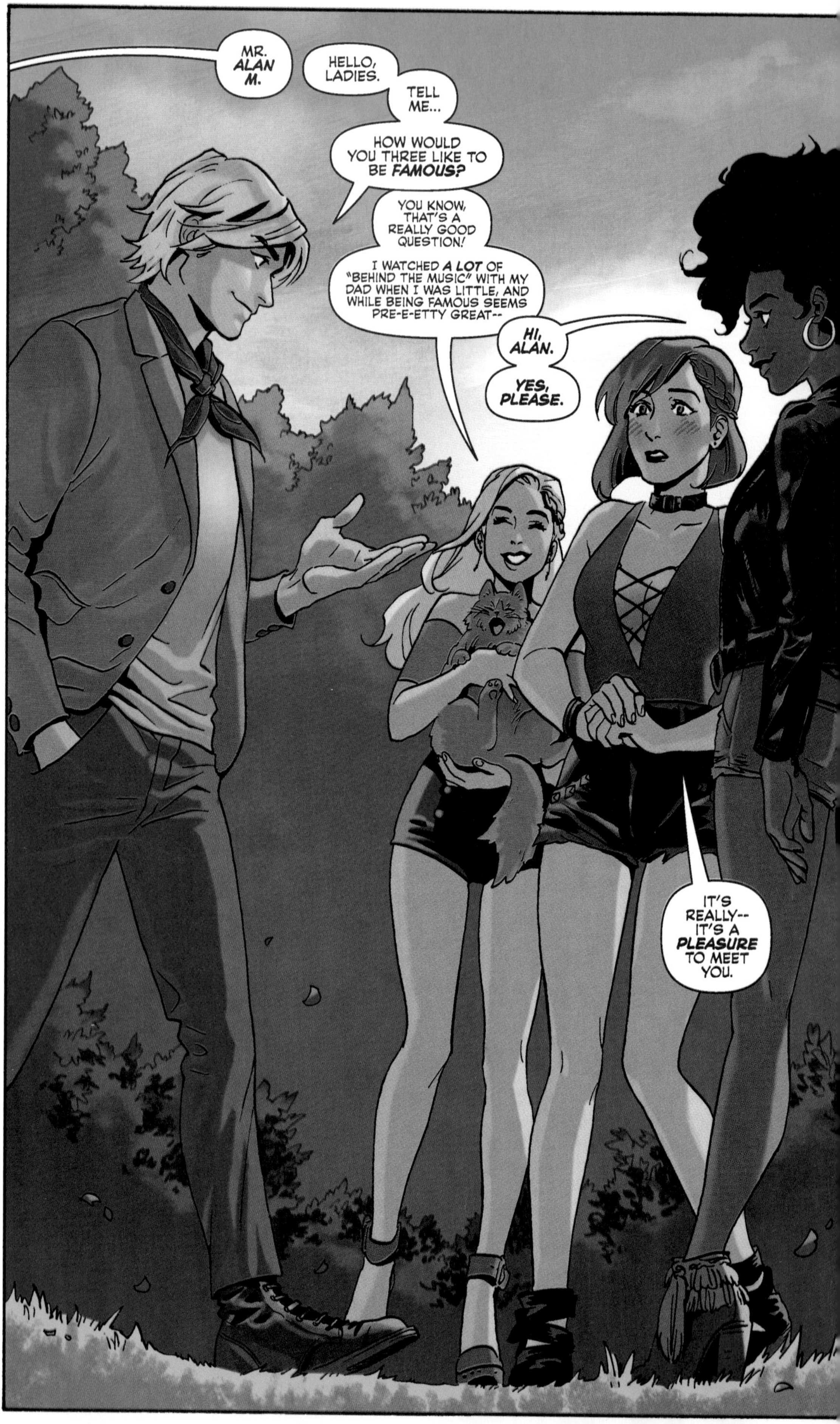
MR. ALAN M.
HELLO, LADIES.
TELL ME...
HOW WOULD YOU THREE LIKE TO BE FAMOUS?
YOU KNOW, THAT'S A REALLY GOOD QUESTION!
I WATCHED A LOT OF "BEHIND THE MUSIC" WITH MY DAD WHEN I WAS LITTLE, AND WHILE BEING FAMOUS SEEMS PRE-E-ETTY GREAT--
HI, ALAN.
YES, PLEASE.
IT'S REALLY-- IT'S A PLEASURE TO MEET YOU.

TO BE CONTINUED...

ISSUE TWO

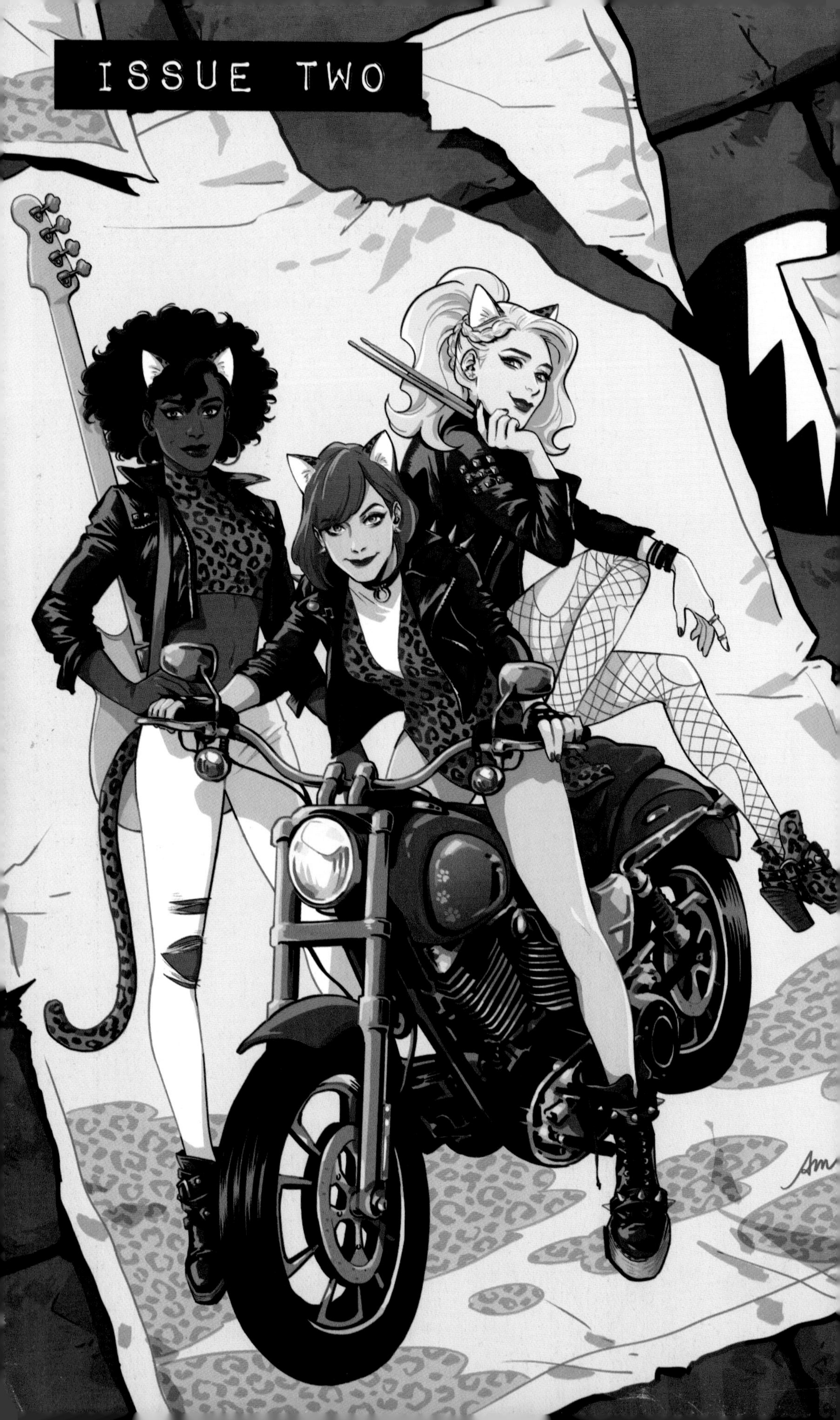

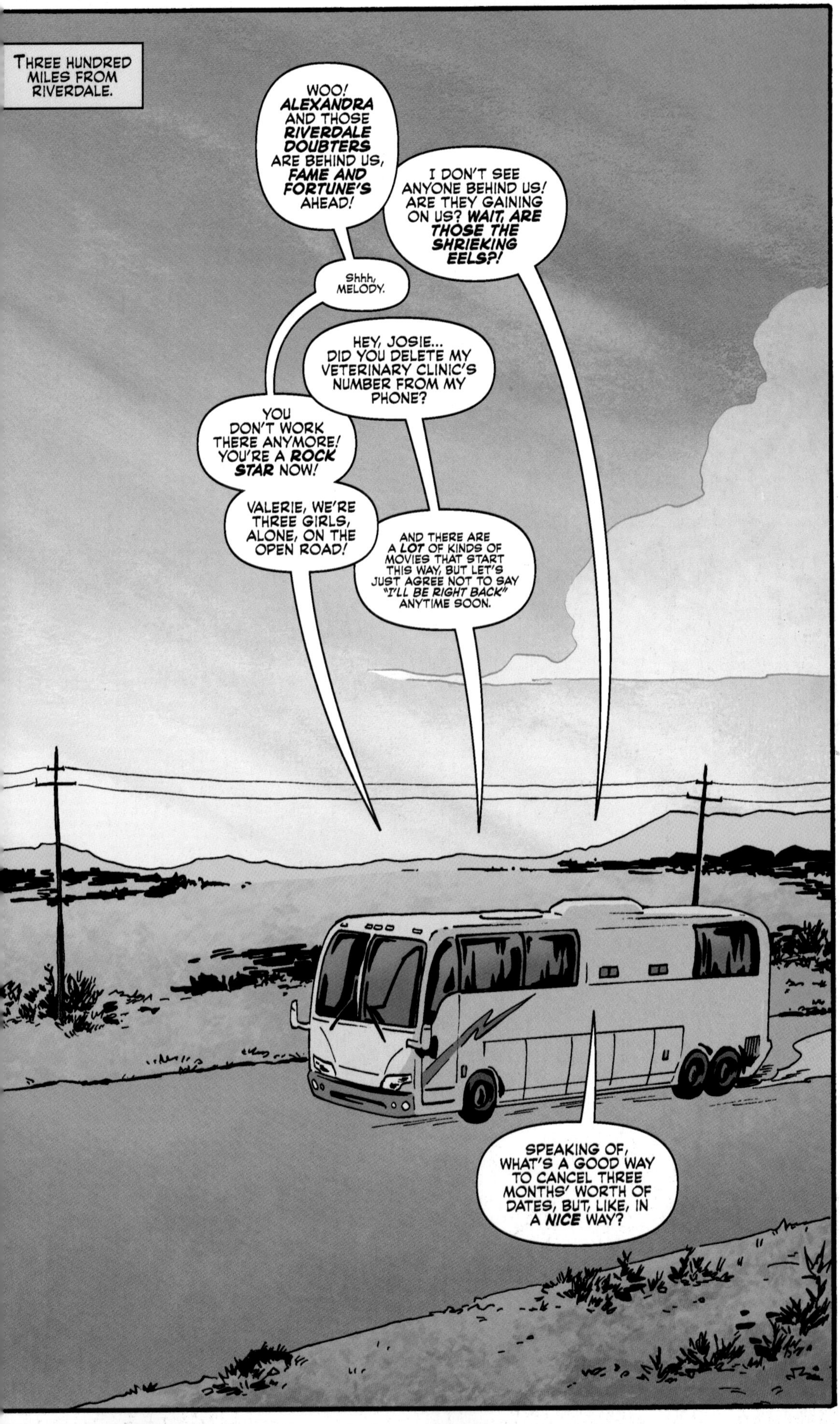
THREE HUNDRED MILES FROM RIVERDALE.
WOO! ALEXANDRA AND THOSE RIVERDALE DOUBTERS ARE BEHIND US, FAME AND FORTUNE'S AHEAD!
I DON'T SEE ANYONE BEHIND US! ARE THEY GAINING ON US? WAIT, ARE THOSE THE SHRIEKING EELS?!
Shhh, MELODY.
HEY, JOSIE... DID YOU DELETE MY VETERINARY CLINIC'S NUMBER FROM MY PHONE?
YOU DON'T WORK THERE ANYMORE! YOU'RE A ROCK STAR NOW!
VALERIE, WE'RE THREE GIRLS, ALONE, ON THE OPEN ROAD!
AND THERE ARE A LOT OF KINDS OF MOVIES THAT START THIS WAY, BUT LET'S JUST AGREE NOT TO SAY "I'LL BE RIGHT BACK" ANYTIME SOON.
SPEAKING OF, WHAT'S A GOOD WAY TO CANCEL THREE MONTHS' WORTH OF DATES, BUT, LIKE, IN A NICE WAY?

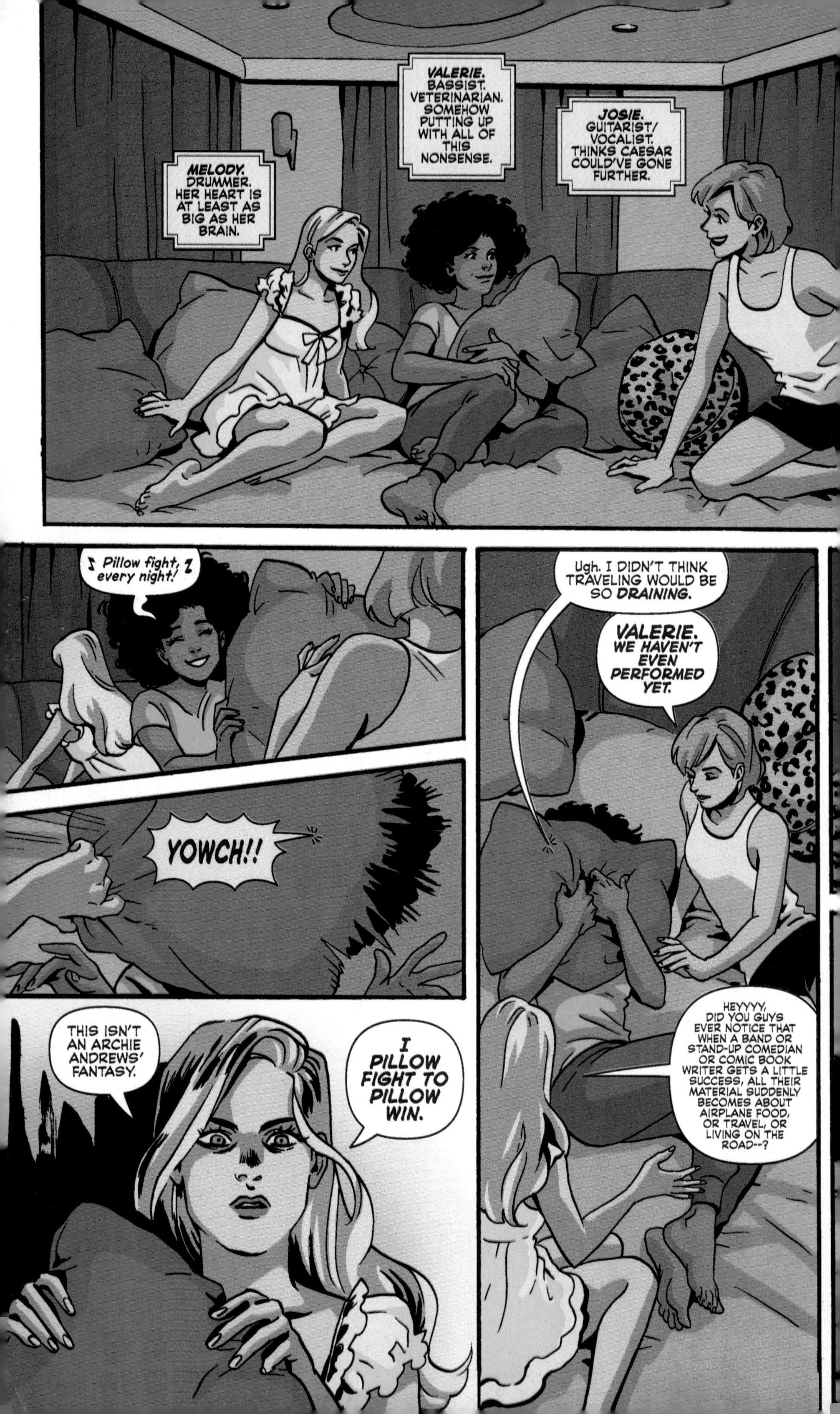

MELODY. DRUMMER. HER HEART IS AT LEAST AS BIG AS HER BRAIN.
VALERIE. BASSIST. VETERINARIAN. SOMEHOW PUTTING UP WITH ALL OF THIS NONSENSE.
JOSIE. GUITARIST/ VOCALIST. THINKS CAESAR COULD'VE GONE FURTHER.
♪ Pillow fight, every night! ♪
YOWCH!!
THIS ISN'T AN ARCHIE ANDREWS' FANTASY.
I PILLOW FIGHT TO PILLOW WIN.
Ugh. I DIDN'T THINK TRAVELING WOULD BE SO DRAINING.
VALERIE. WE HAVEN'T EVEN PERFORMED YET.
HEYYYY, DID YOU GUYS EVER NOTICE THAT WHEN A BAND OR STAND-UP COMEDIAN OR COMIC BOOK WRITER GETS A LITTLE SUCCESS, ALL THEIR MATERIAL SUDDENLY BECOMES ABOUT AIRPLANE FOOD, OR TRAVEL, OR LIVING ON THE ROAD--?

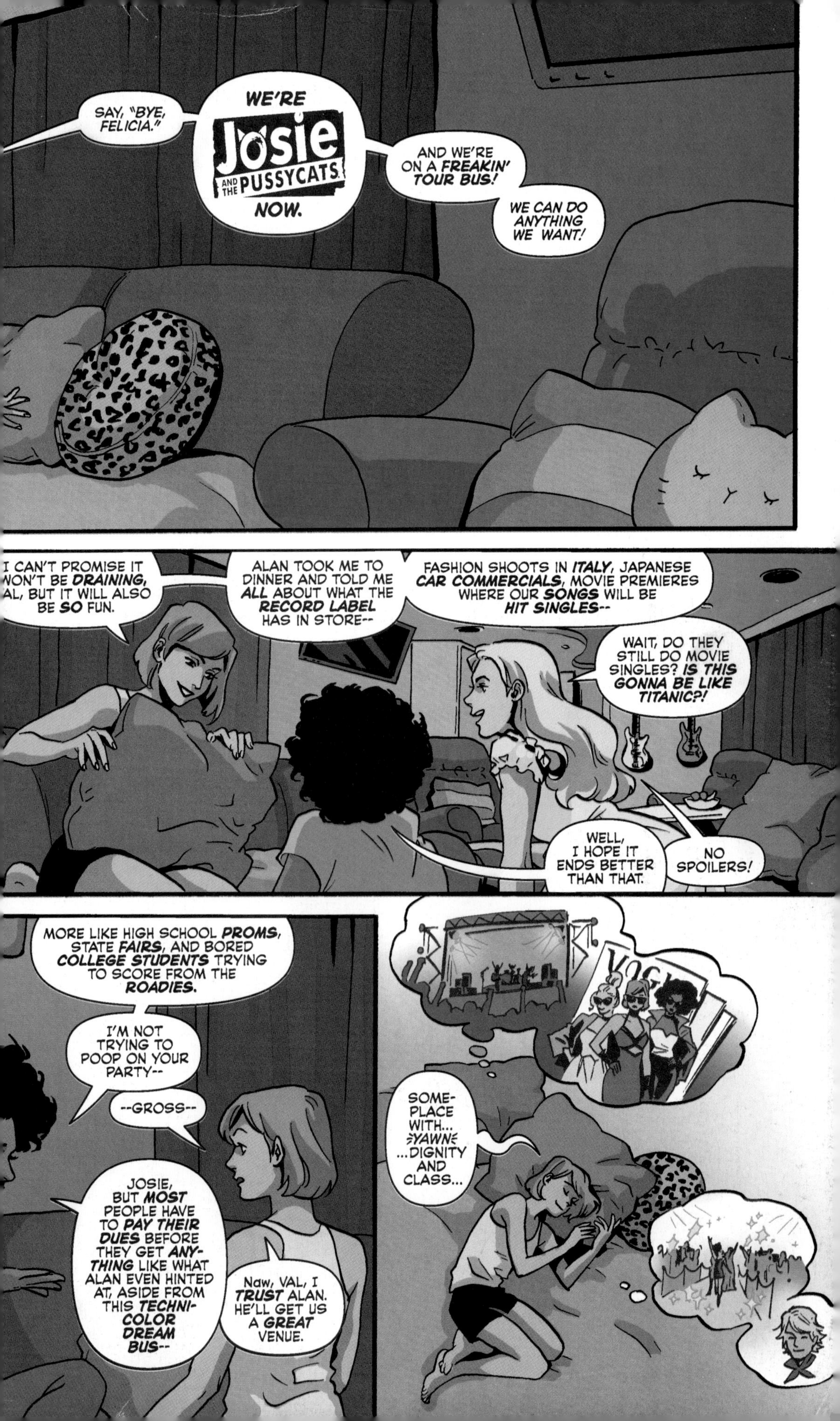
SAY, "BYE, FELICIA."
WE'RE JOSIE AND THE PUSSYCATS NOW.
AND WE'RE ON A FREAKIN' TOUR BUS!
WE CAN DO ANYTHING WE WANT!
I CAN'T PROMISE IT WON'T BE DRAINING, VAL, BUT IT WILL ALSO BE SO FUN.
ALAN TOOK ME TO DINNER AND TOLD ME ALL ABOUT WHAT THE RECORD LABEL HAS IN STORE--
FASHION SHOOTS IN ITALY, JAPANESE CAR COMMERCIALS, MOVIE PREMIERES WHERE OUR SONGS WILL BE HIT SINGLES--
WAIT, DO THEY STILL DO MOVIE SINGLES? IS THIS GONNA BE LIKE TITANIC?!
WELL, I HOPE IT ENDS BETTER THAN THAT.
NO SPOILERS!
MORE LIKE HIGH SCHOOL PROMS, STATE FAIRS, AND BORED COLLEGE STUDENTS TRYING TO SCORE FROM THE ROADIES.
I'M NOT TRYING TO POOP ON YOUR PARTY--
--GROSS--
JOSIE, BUT MOST PEOPLE HAVE TO PAY THEIR DUES BEFORE THEY GET ANYTHING LIKE WHAT ALAN EVEN HINTED AT, ASIDE FROM THIS TECHNICOLOR DREAM BUS--
Naw, VAL, I TRUST ALAN. HE'LL GET US A GREAT VENUE.
SOMEPLACE WITH... YAWN ...DIGNITY AND CLASS...

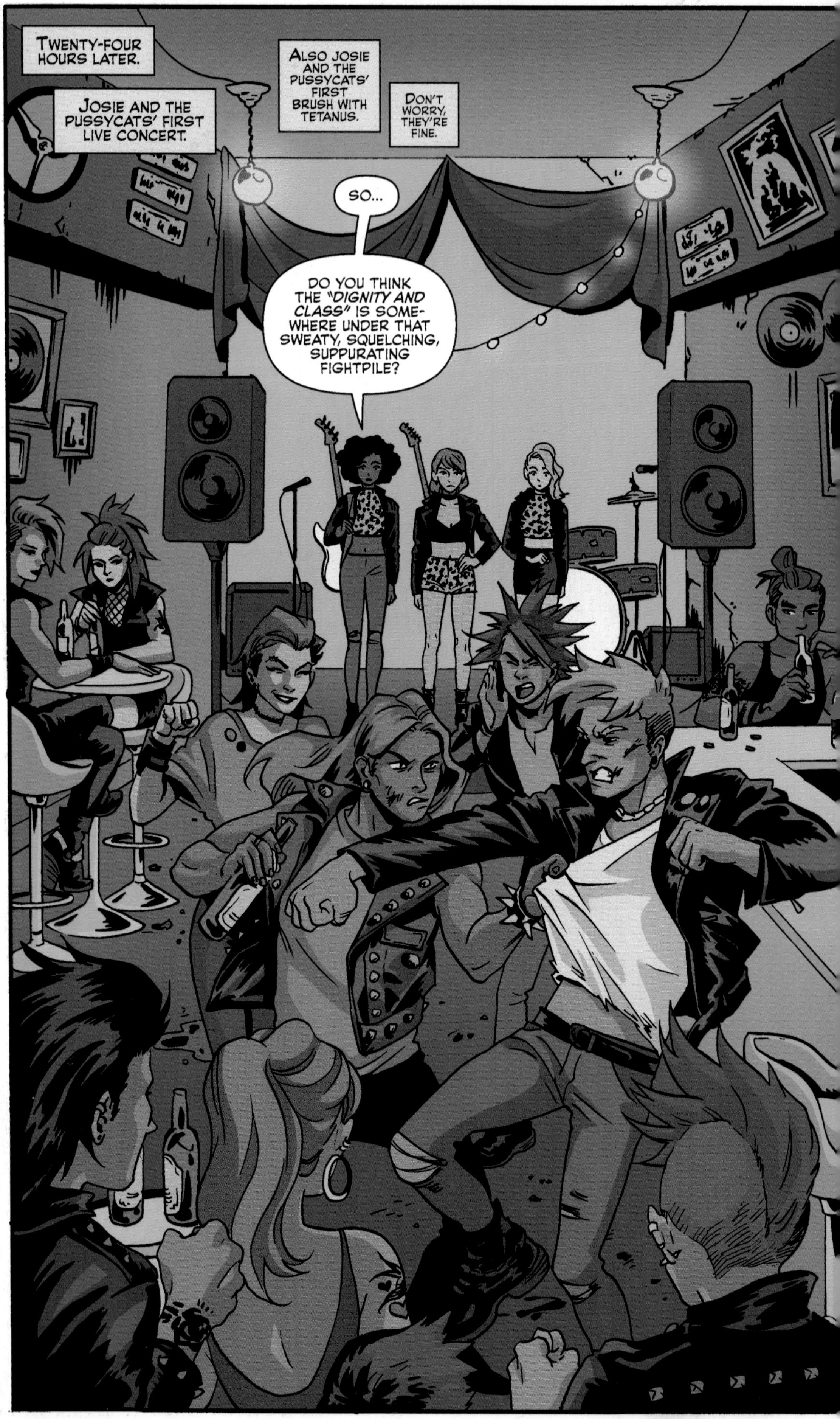
TWENTY-FOUR HOURS LATER.
JOSIE AND THE PUSSYCATS' FIRST LIVE CONCERT.
ALSO JOSIE AND THE PUSSYCATS' FIRST BRUSH WITH TETANUS.
DON'T WORRY, THEY'RE FINE.
SO...
DO YOU THINK THE "DIGNITY AND CLASS" IS SOMEWHERE UNDER THAT SWEATY, SQUELCHING, SUPPURATING FIGHTPILE?

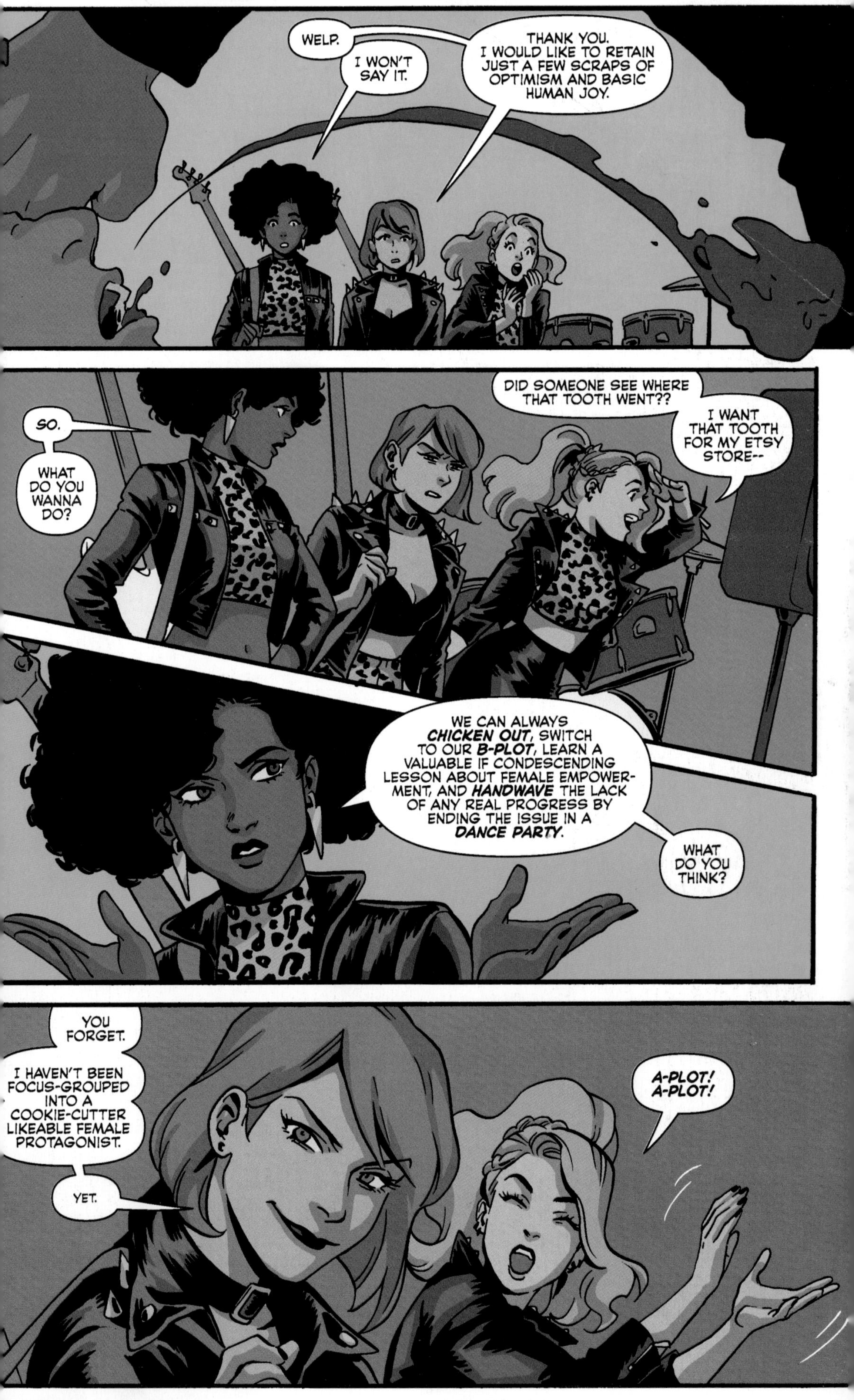

WELP.
I WON'T SAY IT.
THANK YOU. I WOULD LIKE TO RETAIN JUST A FEW SCRAPS OF OPTIMISM AND BASIC HUMAN JOY.
SO.
WHAT DO YOU WANNA DO?
DID SOMEONE SEE WHERE THAT TOOTH WENT??
I WANT THAT TOOTH FOR MY ETSY STORE--
WE CAN ALWAYS CHICKEN OUT, SWITCH TO OUR B-PLOT, LEARN A VALUABLE IF CONDESCENDING LESSON ABOUT FEMALE EMPOWERMENT, AND HANDWAVE THE LACK OF ANY REAL PROGRESS BY ENDING THE ISSUE IN A DANCE PARTY.
WHAT DO YOU THINK?
YOU FORGET.
I HAVEN'T BEEN FOCUS-GROUPED INTO A COOKIE-CUTTER LIKEABLE FEMALE PROTAGONIST.
YET.
A-PLOT! A-PLOT!

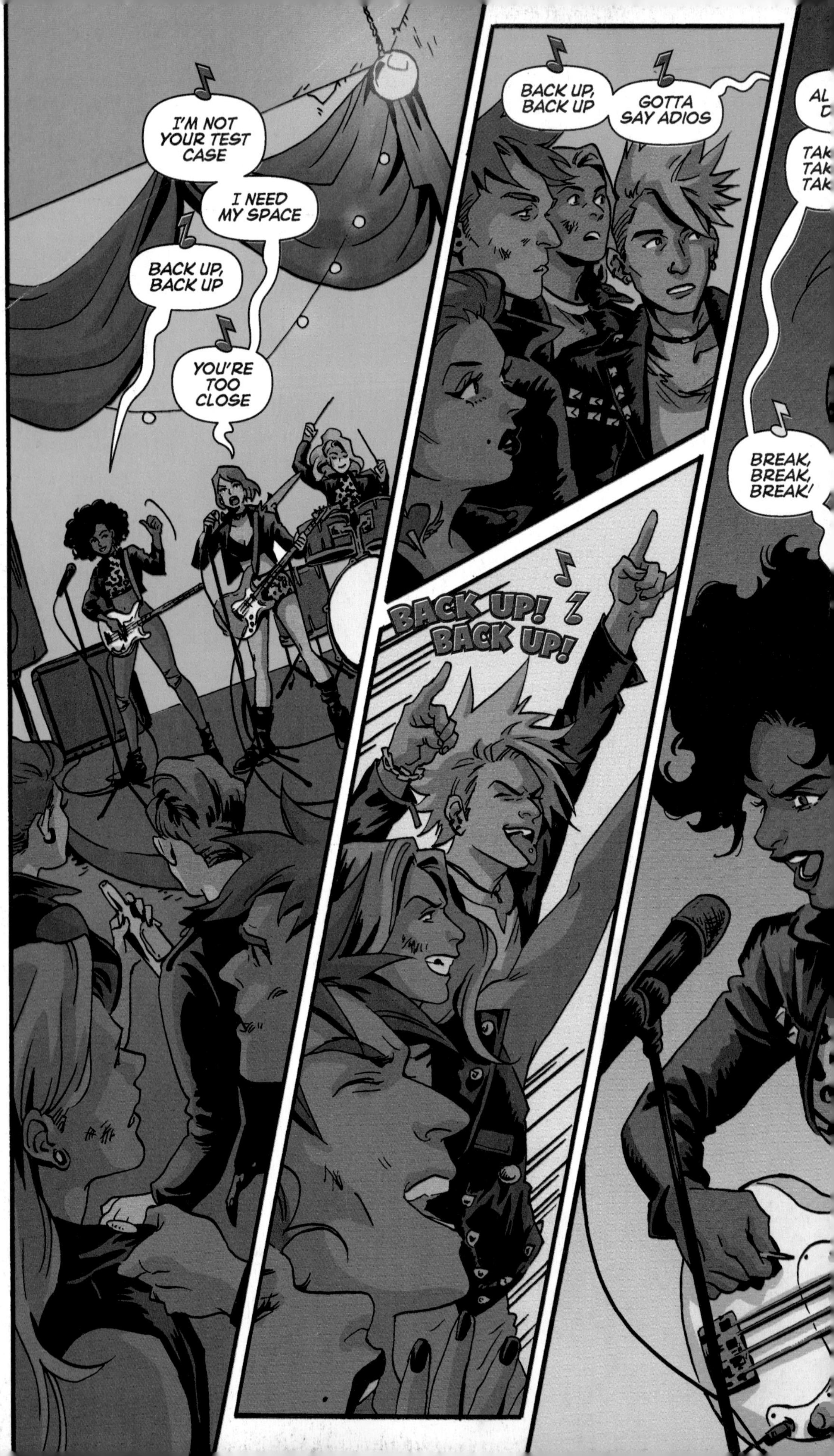
I'M NOT YOUR TEST CASE
I NEED MY SPACE
BACK UP, BACK UP
YOU'RE TOO CLOSE
BACK UP, BACK UP
GOTTA SAY ADIOS
BACK UP! BACK UP!
BREAK, BREAK, BREAK!

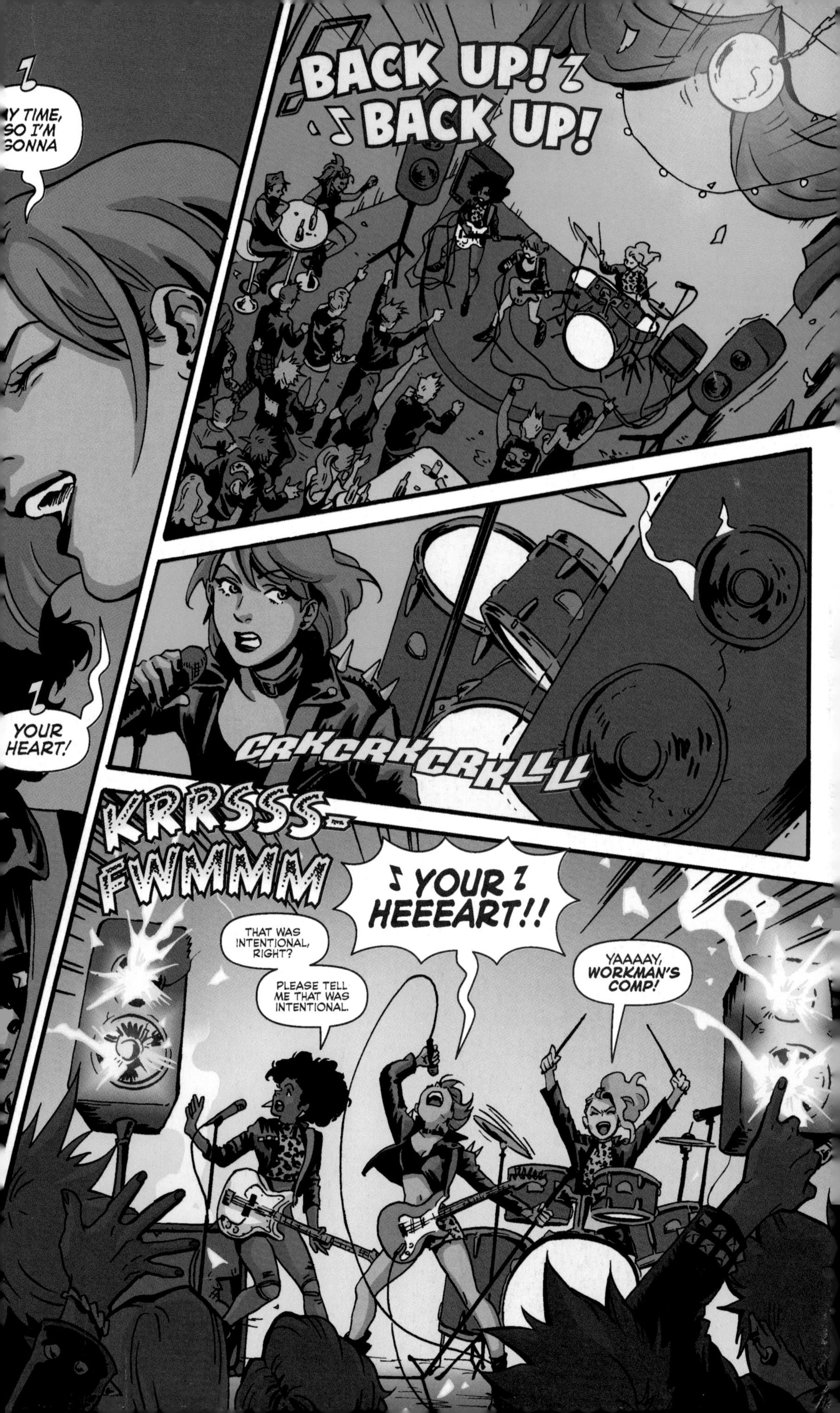

Y TIME, SO I'M GONNA
BACK UP! BACK UP!
CRKCRKCRKLLL
YOUR HEART!
KRRSSS-FWMMM
YOUR HEEEART!!
THAT WAS INTENTIONAL, RIGHT?
PLEASE TELL ME THAT WAS INTENTIONAL.
YAAAAY, WORKMAN'S COMP!

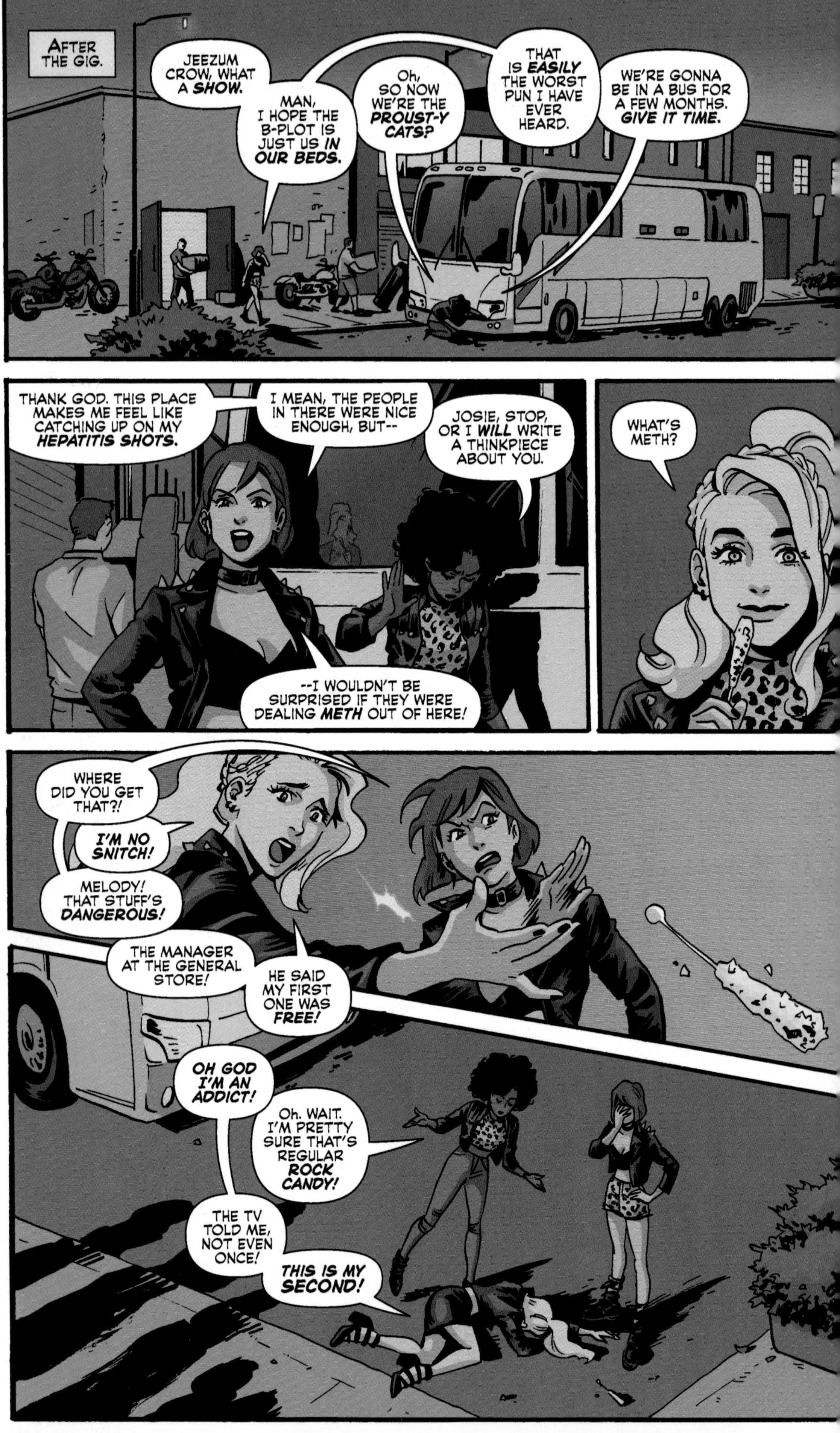
AFTER THE GIG.
JEEZUM CROW, WHAT A SHOW.
MAN, I HOPE THE B-PLOT IS JUST US IN OUR BEDS.
Oh, SO NOW WE'RE THE PROUST-Y CATS?
THAT IS EASILY THE WORST PUN I HAVE EVER HEARD.
WE'RE GONNA BE IN A BUS FOR A FEW MONTHS. GIVE IT TIME.
THANK GOD. THIS PLACE MAKES ME FEEL LIKE CATCHING UP ON MY HEPATITIS SHOTS.
I MEAN, THE PEOPLE IN THERE WERE NICE ENOUGH, BUT--
JOSIE, STOP, OR I WILL WRITE A THINKPIECE ABOUT YOU.
--I WOULDN'T BE SURPRISED IF THEY WERE DEALING METH OUT OF HERE!
WHAT'S METH?
WHERE DID YOU GET THAT?!
I'M NO SNITCH!
MELODY! THAT STUFF'S DANGEROUS!
THE MANAGER AT THE GENERAL STORE!
HE SAID MY FIRST ONE WAS FREE!
OH GOD I'M AN ADDICT!
Oh. WAIT. I'M PRETTY SURE THAT'S REGULAR ROCK CANDY!
THE TV TOLD ME, NOT EVEN ONCE!
THIS IS MY SECOND!

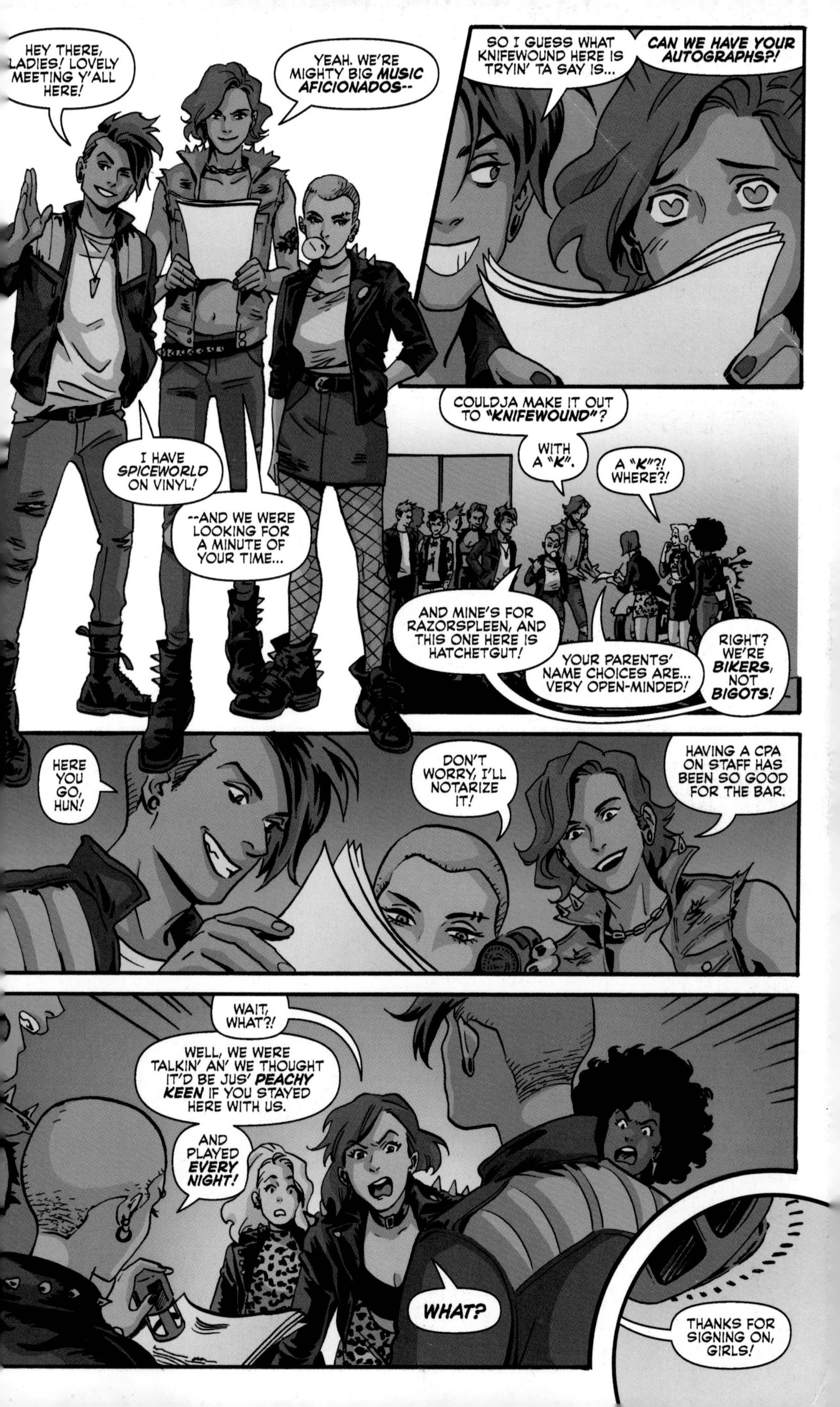
HEY THERE, LADIES! LOVELY MEETING Y'ALL HERE!
YEAH. WE'RE MIGHTY BIG **MUSIC AFICIONADOS**--
I HAVE **SPICEWORLD** ON VINYL!
--AND WE WERE LOOKING FOR A MINUTE OF YOUR TIME...
SO I GUESS WHAT KNIFEWOUND HERE IS TRYIN' TA SAY IS...
CAN WE HAVE YOUR AUTOGRAPHS?!
COULDJA MAKE IT OUT TO **"KNIFEWOUND"**?
WITH A **"K"**.
A **"K"**?! WHERE?!
AND MINE'S FOR RAZORSPLEEN, AND THIS ONE HERE IS HATCHETGUT!
YOUR PARENTS' NAME CHOICES ARE... VERY OPEN-MINDED!
RIGHT? WE'RE **BIKERS**, NOT **BIGOTS**!
HERE YOU GO, HUN!
DON'T WORRY, I'LL NOTARIZE IT!
HAVING A CPA ON STAFF HAS BEEN SO GOOD FOR THE BAR.
WAIT, WHAT?!
WELL, WE WERE TALKIN' AN' WE THOUGHT IT'D BE JUS' **PEACHY KEEN** IF YOU STAYED HERE WITH US.
AND PLAYED **EVERY NIGHT!**
WHAT?
THANKS FOR SIGNING ON, GIRLS!

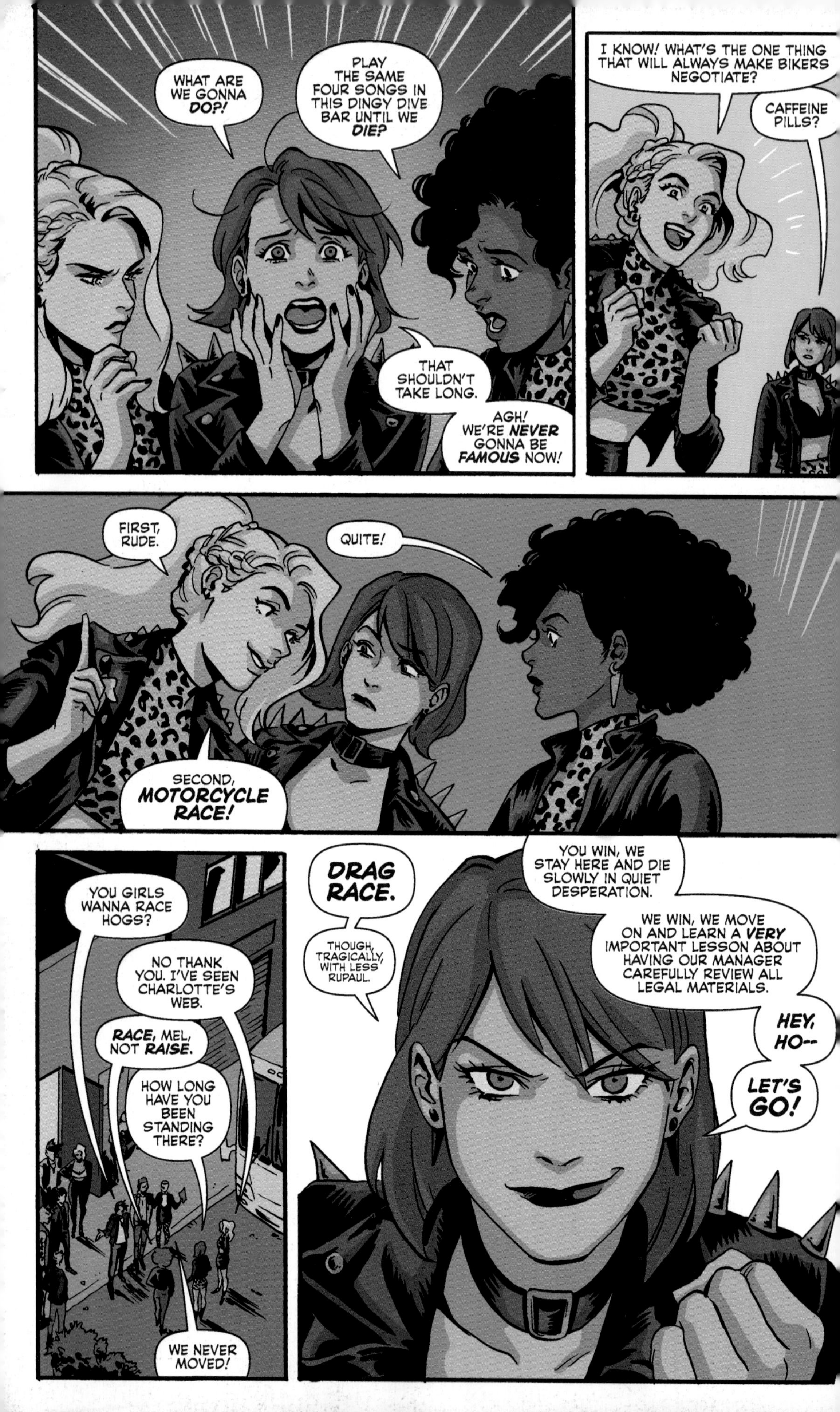
WHAT ARE WE GONNA DO?!
PLAY THE SAME FOUR SONGS IN THIS DINGY DIVE BAR UNTIL WE DIE?
THAT SHOULDN'T TAKE LONG.
AGH! WE'RE NEVER GONNA BE FAMOUS NOW!
I KNOW! WHAT'S THE ONE THING THAT WILL ALWAYS MAKE BIKERS NEGOTIATE?
CAFFEINE PILLS?
FIRST, RUDE.
QUITE!
SECOND, MOTORCYCLE RACE!
YOU GIRLS WANNA RACE HOGS?
NO THANK YOU. I'VE SEEN CHARLOTTE'S WEB.
RACE, MEL, NOT RAISE.
HOW LONG HAVE YOU BEEN STANDING THERE?
WE NEVER MOVED!
DRAG RACE.
THOUGH, TRAGICALLY, WITH LESS RUPAUL.
YOU WIN, WE STAY HERE AND DIE SLOWLY IN QUIET DESPERATION.
WE WIN, WE MOVE ON AND LEARN A VERY IMPORTANT LESSON ABOUT HAVING OUR MANAGER CAREFULLY REVIEW ALL LEGAL MATERIALS.
HEY, HO--
LET'S GO!

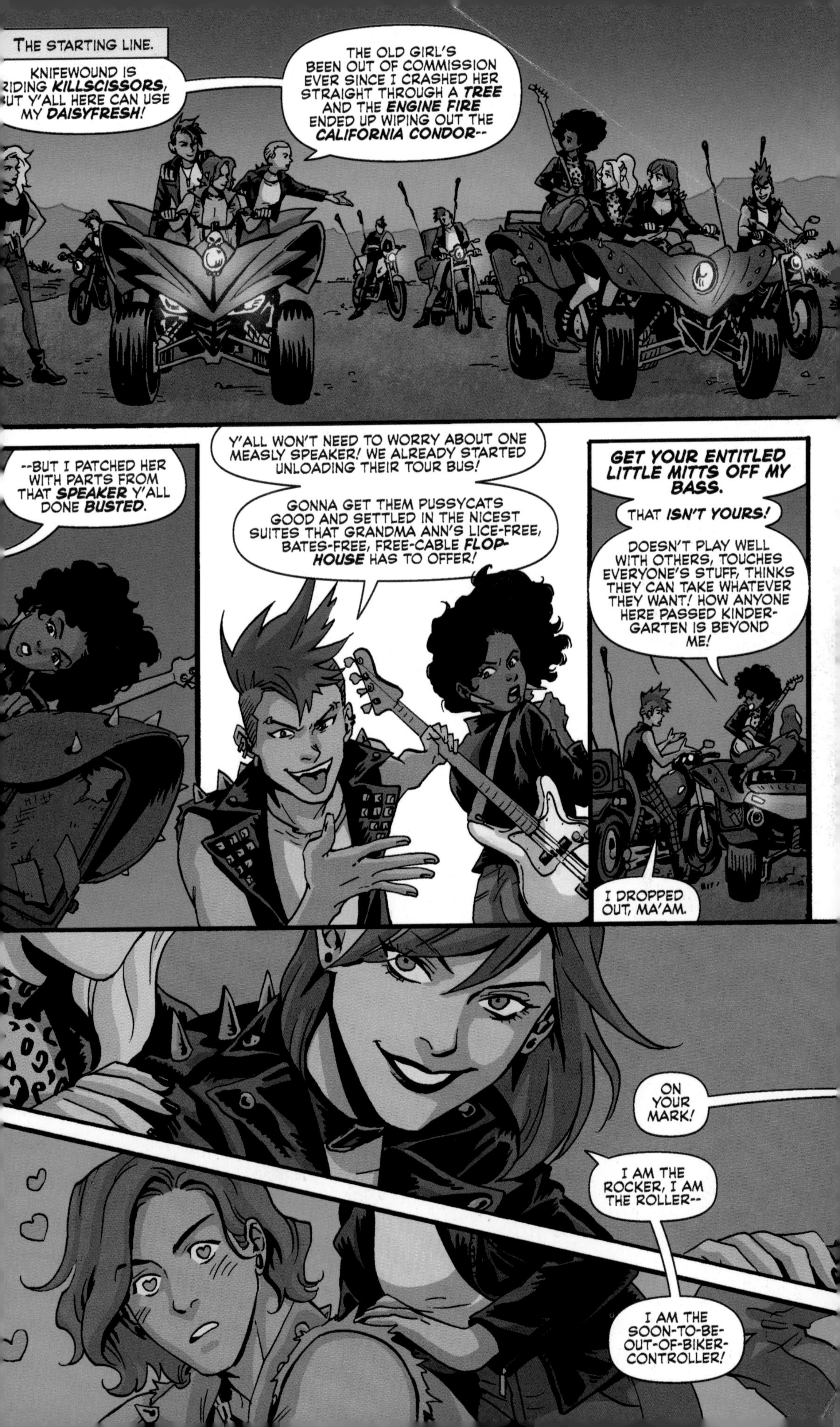
THE STARTING LINE.
KNIFEWOUND IS RIDING KILLSCISSORS, BUT Y'ALL HERE CAN USE MY DAISYFRESH!
THE OLD GIRL'S BEEN OUT OF COMMISSION EVER SINCE I CRASHED HER STRAIGHT THROUGH A TREE AND THE ENGINE FIRE ENDED UP WIPING OUT THE CALIFORNIA CONDOR--
--BUT I PATCHED HER WITH PARTS FROM THAT SPEAKER Y'ALL DONE BUSTED.
Y'ALL WON'T NEED TO WORRY ABOUT ONE MEASLY SPEAKER! WE ALREADY STARTED UNLOADING THEIR TOUR BUS!
GONNA GET THEM PUSSYCATS GOOD AND SETTLED IN THE NICEST SUITES THAT GRANDMA ANN'S LICE-FREE, BATES-FREE, FREE-CABLE FLOPHOUSE HAS TO OFFER!
GET YOUR ENTITLED LITTLE MITTS OFF MY BASS.
THAT ISN'T YOURS!
DOESN'T PLAY WELL WITH OTHERS, TOUCHES EVERYONE'S STUFF, THINKS THEY CAN TAKE WHATEVER THEY WANT! HOW ANYONE HERE PASSED KINDERGARTEN IS BEYOND ME!
I DROPPED OUT, MA'AM.
ON YOUR MARK!
I AM THE ROCKER, I AM THE ROLLER--
I AM THE SOON-TO-BE-OUT-OF-BIKER-CONTROLLER!

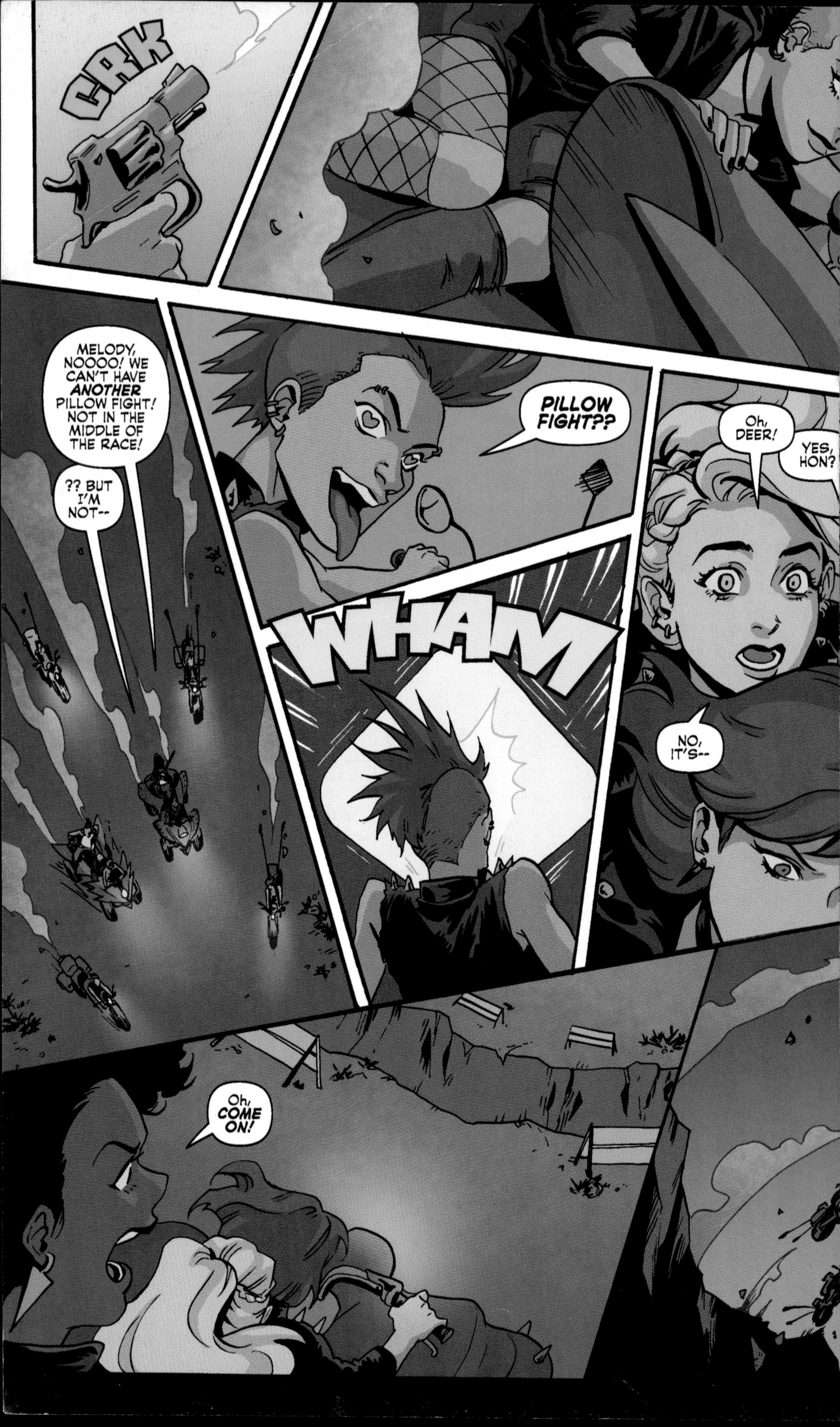

CRK
MELODY, NOOOO! WE CAN'T HAVE ANOTHER PILLOW FIGHT! NOT IN THE MIDDLE OF THE RACE!
?? BUT I'M NOT--
PILLOW FIGHT??
Oh, DEER!
YES, HON?
WHAM
NO, IT'S--
Oh, COME ON!

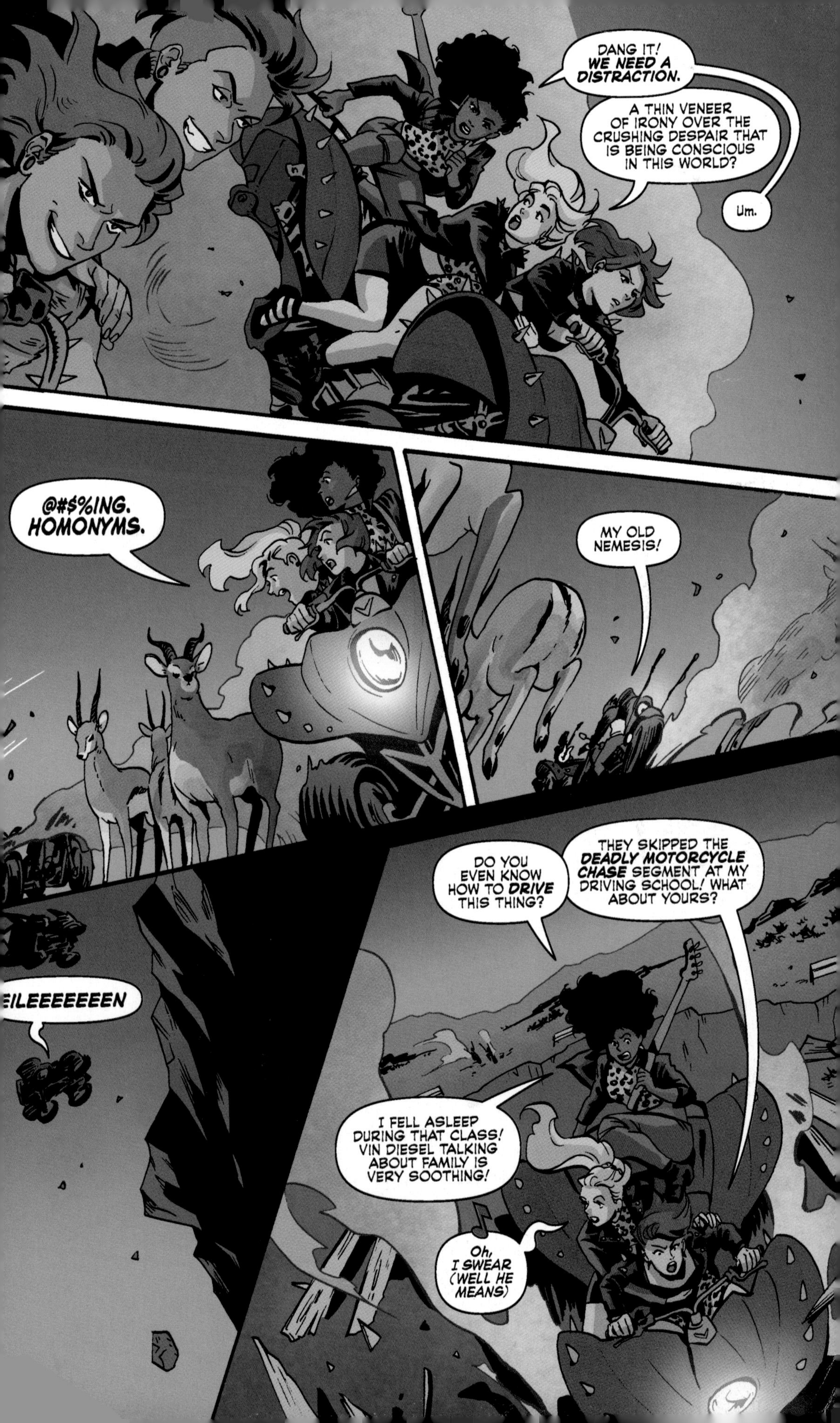
DANG IT! WE NEED A DISTRACTION.
A THIN VENEER OF IRONY OVER THE CRUSHING DESPAIR THAT IS BEING CONSCIOUS IN THIS WORLD?
Um.
@#$%ING. HOMONYMS.
MY OLD NEMESIS!
EILEEEEEEEN
DO YOU EVEN KNOW HOW TO DRIVE THIS THING?
THEY SKIPPED THE DEADLY MOTORCYCLE CHASE SEGMENT AT MY DRIVING SCHOOL! WHAT ABOUT YOURS?
I FELL ASLEEP DURING THAT CLASS! VIN DIESEL TALKING ABOUT FAMILY IS VERY SOOTHING!
Oh, I SWEAR (WELL HE MEANS)

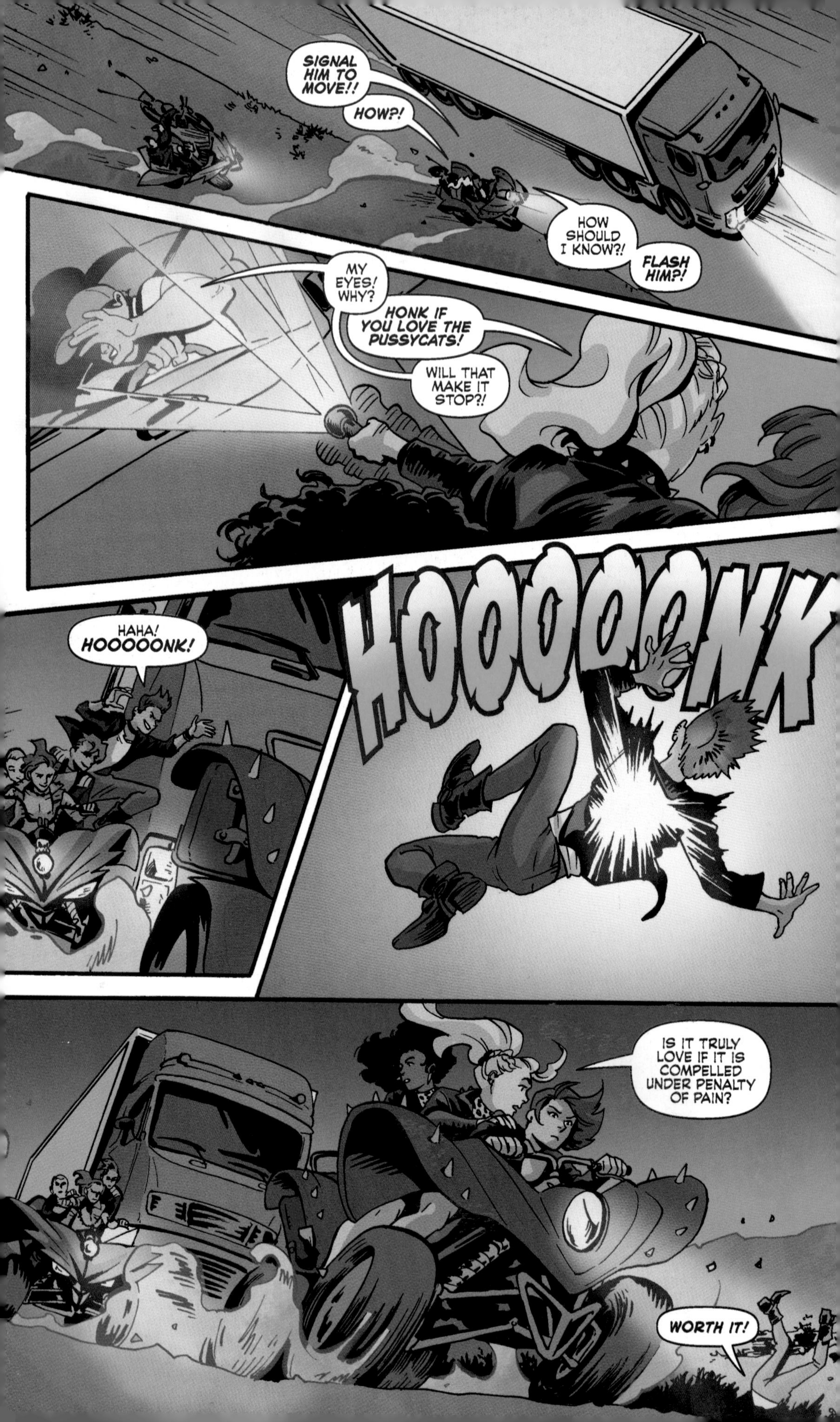
SIGNAL HIM TO MOVE!!
HOW?!
HOW SHOULD I KNOW?!
FLASH HIM?!
MY EYES! WHY?
HONK IF YOU LOVE THE PUSSYCATS!
WILL THAT MAKE IT STOP?!
HAHA! HOOOOONK!
HOOOOONK
IS IT TRULY LOVE IF IT IS COMPELLED UNDER PENALTY OF PAIN?
WORTH IT!

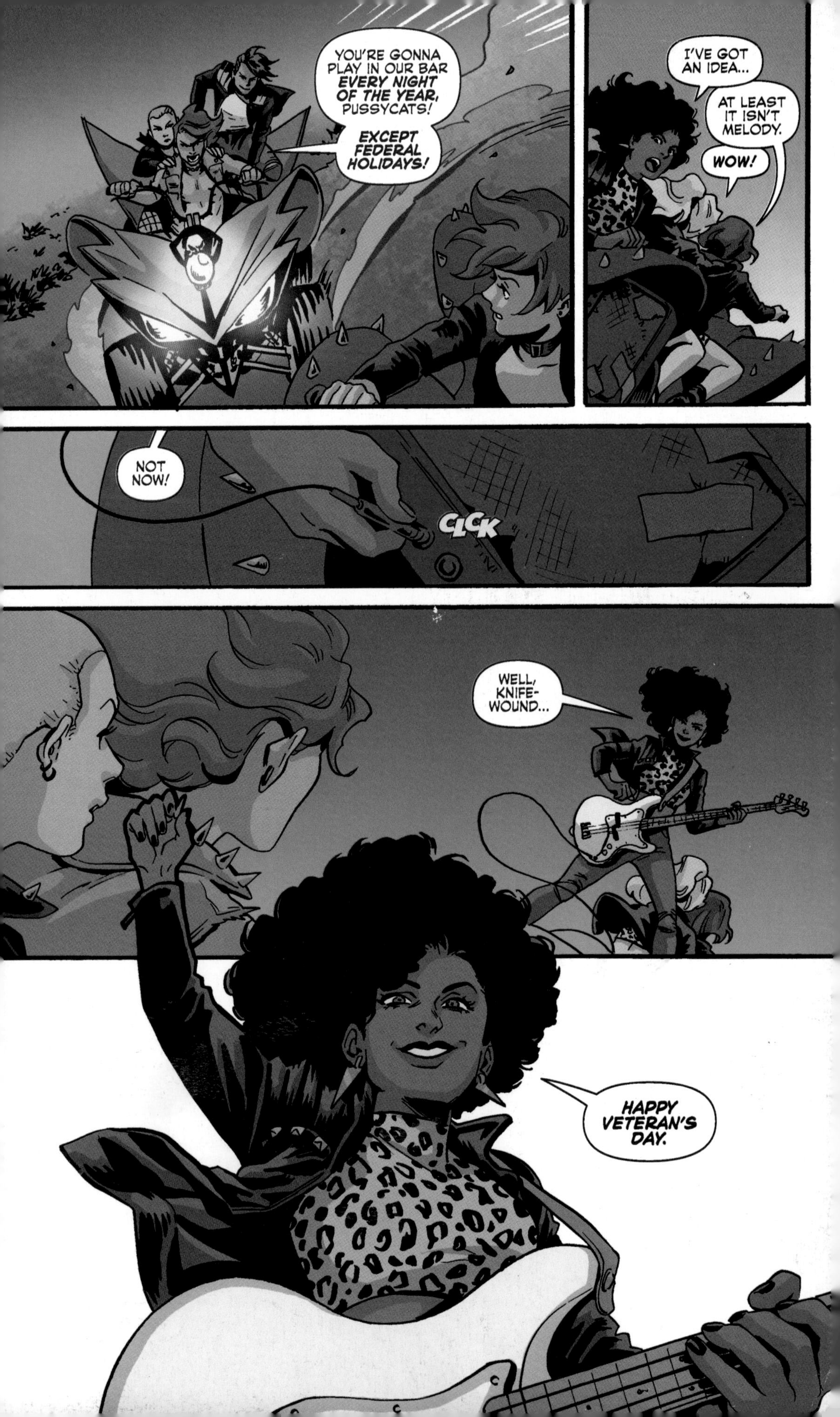

YOU'RE GONNA PLAY IN OUR BAR EVERY NIGHT OF THE YEAR, PUSSYCATS!
EXCEPT FEDERAL HOLIDAYS!
I'VE GOT AN IDEA...
AT LEAST IT ISN'T MELODY.
WOW!
NOT NOW!
CLCK
WELL, KNIFE-WOUND...
HAPPY VETERAN'S DAY.

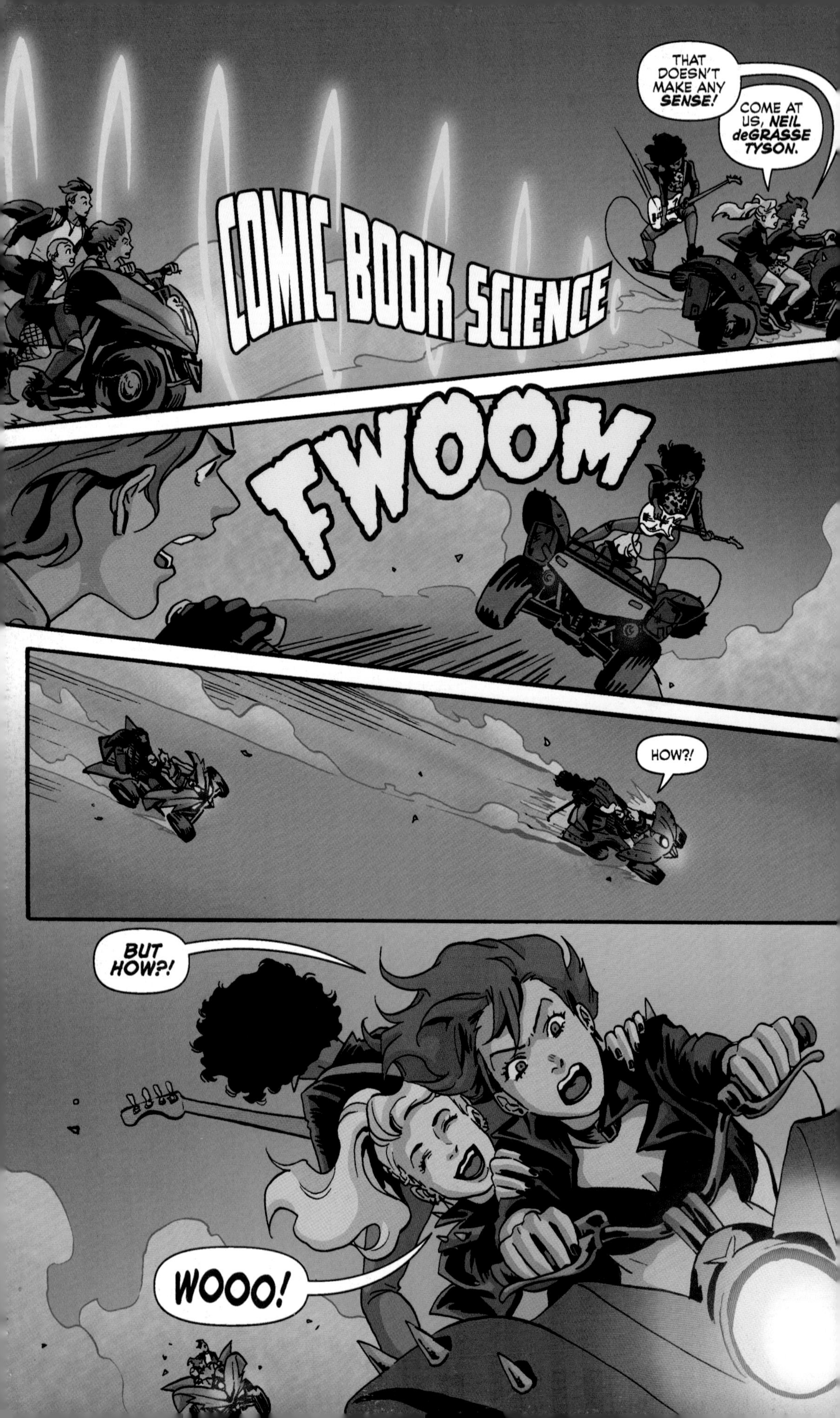
THAT DOESN'T MAKE ANY SENSE!
COME AT US, NEIL deGRASSE TYSON.
COMIC BOOK SCIENCE
FWOOM
HOW?!
BUT HOW?!
WOOO!

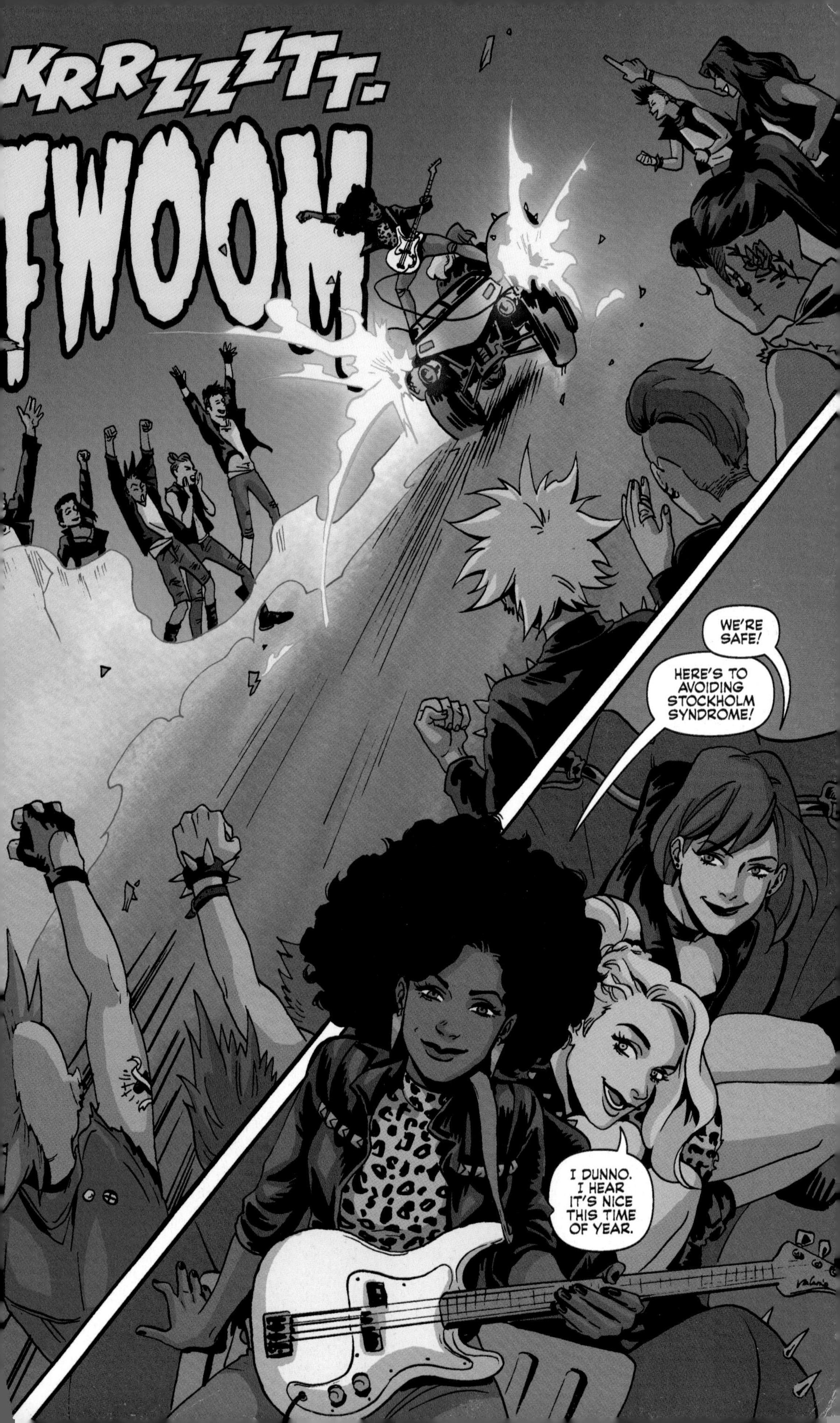
KRRZZZTT-
TWOOM
WE'RE SAFE!
HERE'S TO AVOIDING STOCKHOLM SYNDROME!
I DUNNO. I HEAR IT'S NICE THIS TIME OF YEAR.

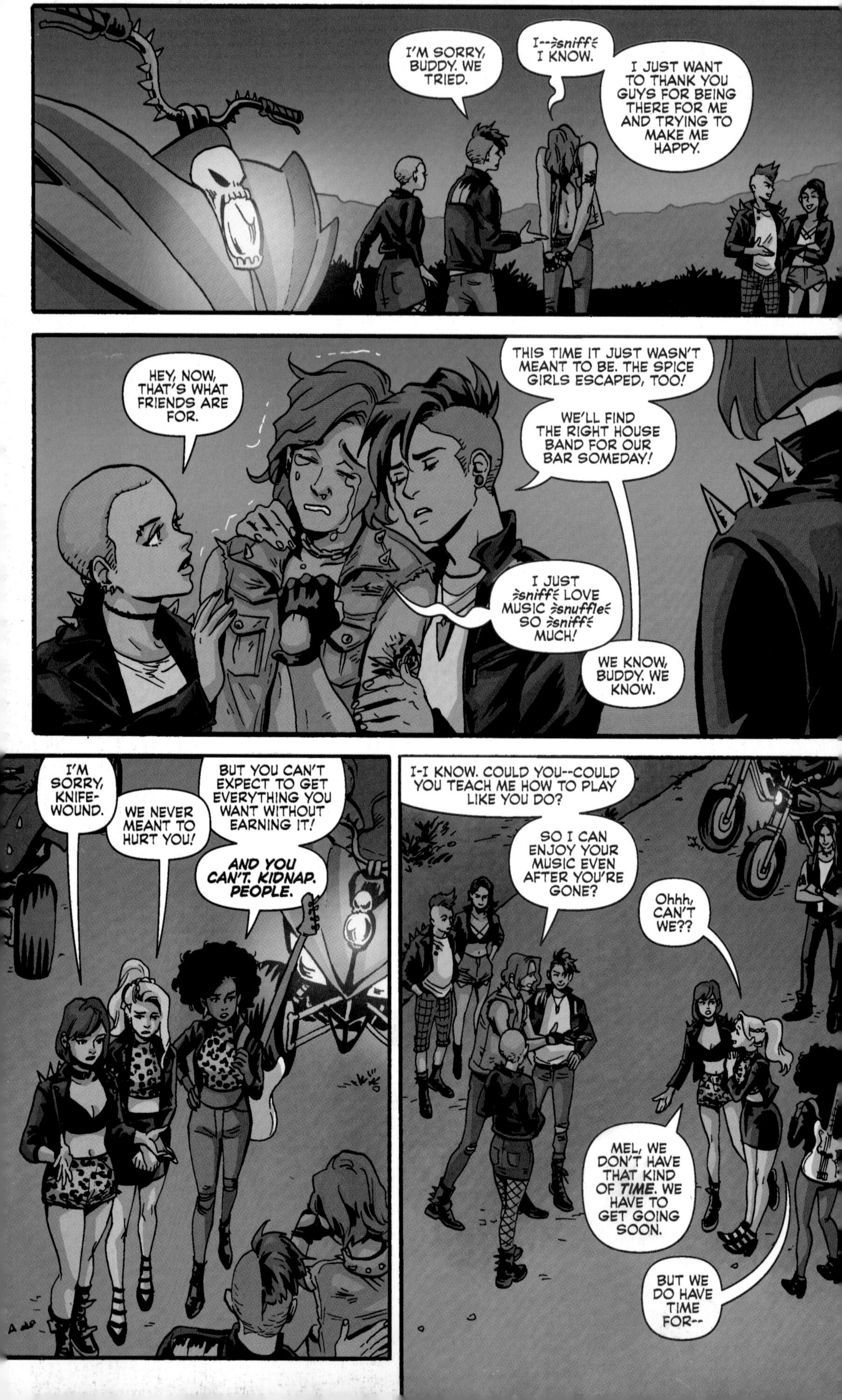
I'M SORRY, BUDDY. WE TRIED.
I--⸗sniff⸗ I KNOW.
I JUST WANT TO THANK YOU GUYS FOR BEING THERE FOR ME AND TRYING TO MAKE ME HAPPY.
HEY, NOW, THAT'S WHAT FRIENDS ARE FOR.
THIS TIME IT JUST WASN'T MEANT TO BE. THE SPICE GIRLS ESCAPED, TOO!
WE'LL FIND THE RIGHT HOUSE BAND FOR OUR BAR SOMEDAY!
I JUST ⸗sniff⸗ LOVE MUSIC ⸗snuffle⸗ SO ⸗sniff⸗ MUCH!
WE KNOW, BUDDY. WE KNOW.
I'M SORRY, KNIFE-WOUND.
WE NEVER MEANT TO HURT YOU!
BUT YOU CAN'T EXPECT TO GET EVERYTHING YOU WANT WITHOUT EARNING IT!
AND YOU CAN'T. KIDNAP. PEOPLE.
I-I KNOW. COULD YOU--COULD YOU TEACH ME HOW TO PLAY LIKE YOU DO?
SO I CAN ENJOY YOUR MUSIC EVEN AFTER YOU'RE GONE?
Ohhh, CAN'T WE??
MEL, WE DON'T HAVE THAT KIND OF *TIME*. WE HAVE TO GET GOING SOON.
BUT WE DO HAVE TIME FOR--

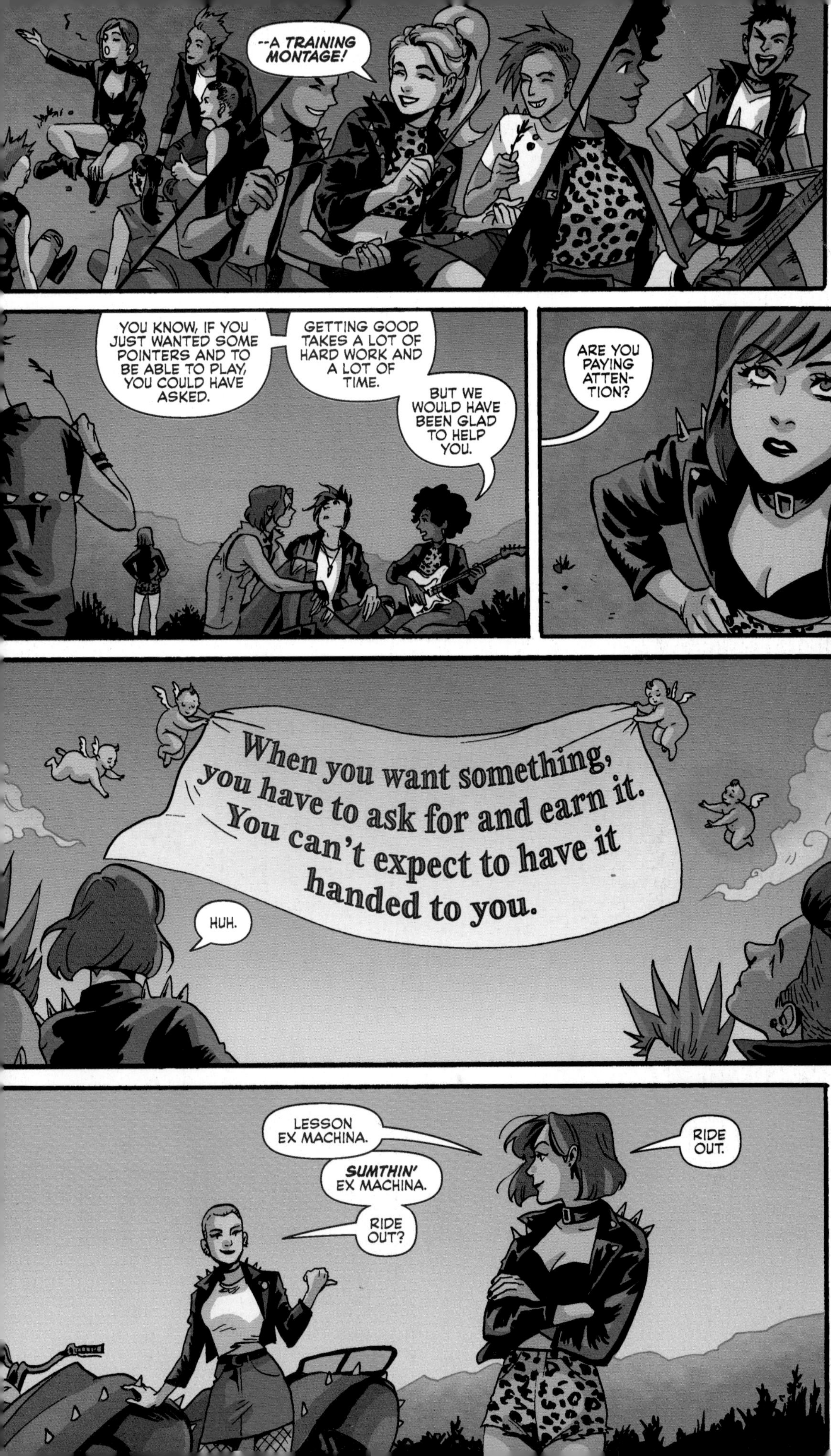
--A *TRAINING MONTAGE!*
YOU KNOW, IF YOU JUST WANTED SOME POINTERS AND TO BE ABLE TO PLAY, YOU COULD HAVE ASKED.
GETTING GOOD TAKES A LOT OF HARD WORK AND A LOT OF TIME.
BUT WE WOULD HAVE BEEN GLAD TO HELP YOU.
ARE YOU PAYING ATTEN-TION?
When you want something, you have to ask for and earn it. You can't expect to have it handed to you.
HUH.
LESSON EX MACHINA.
SUMTHIN' EX MACHINA.
RIDE OUT?
RIDE OUT.

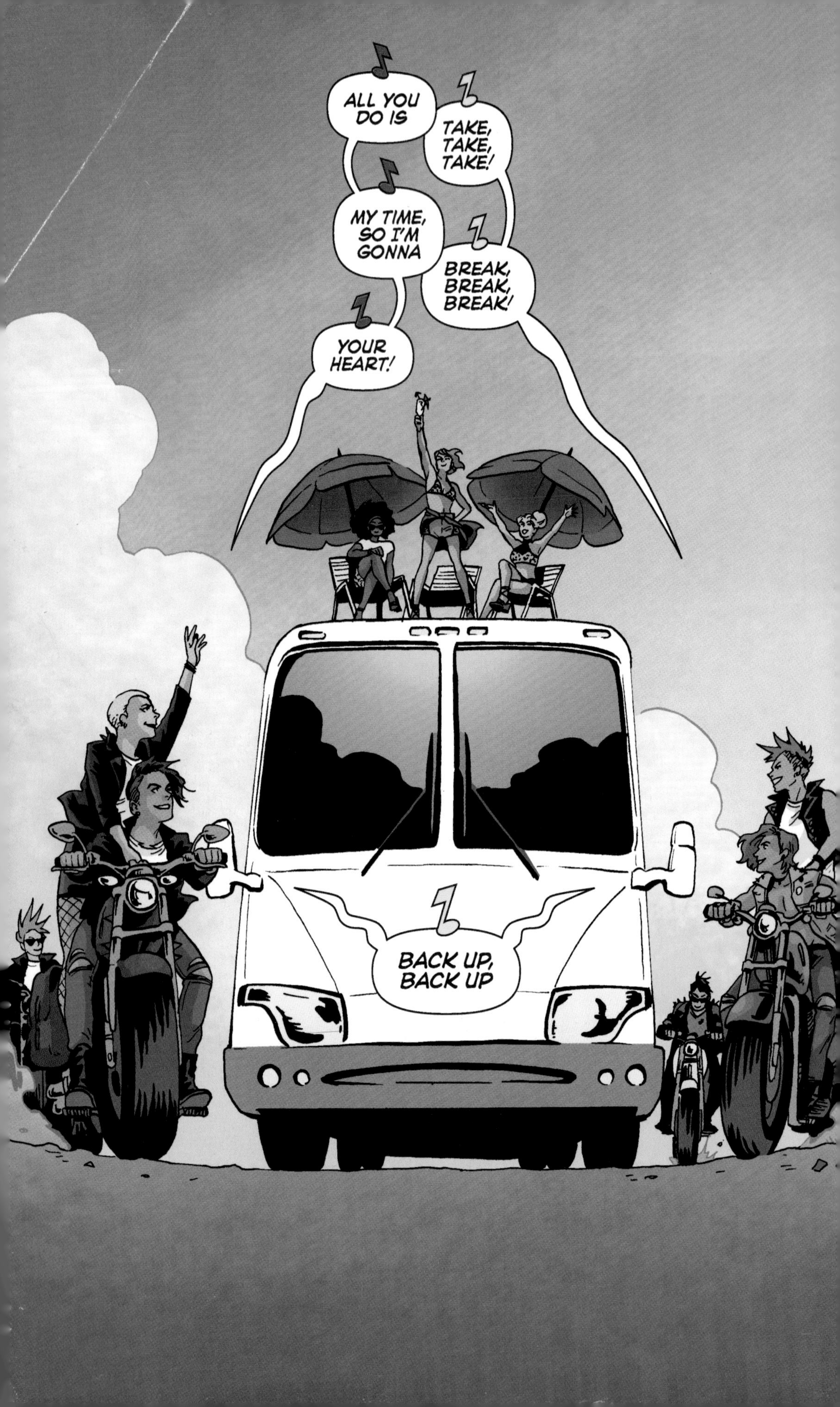
ALL YOU DO IS
TAKE, TAKE, TAKE!
MY TIME, SO I'M GONNA
BREAK, BREAK, BREAK!
YOUR HEART!
BACK UP, BACK UP

TO BE
CONTINUED...

ISSUE THREE

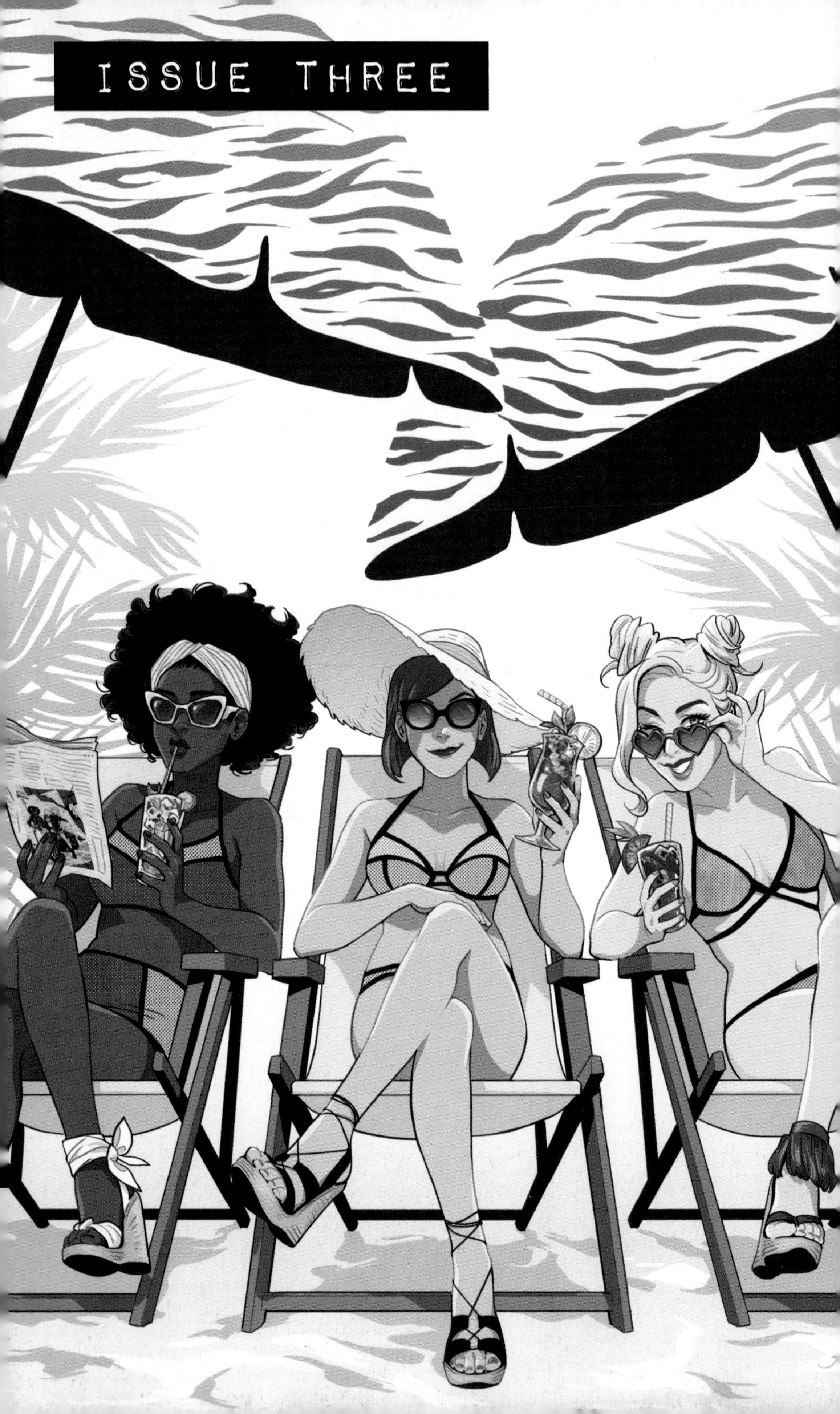

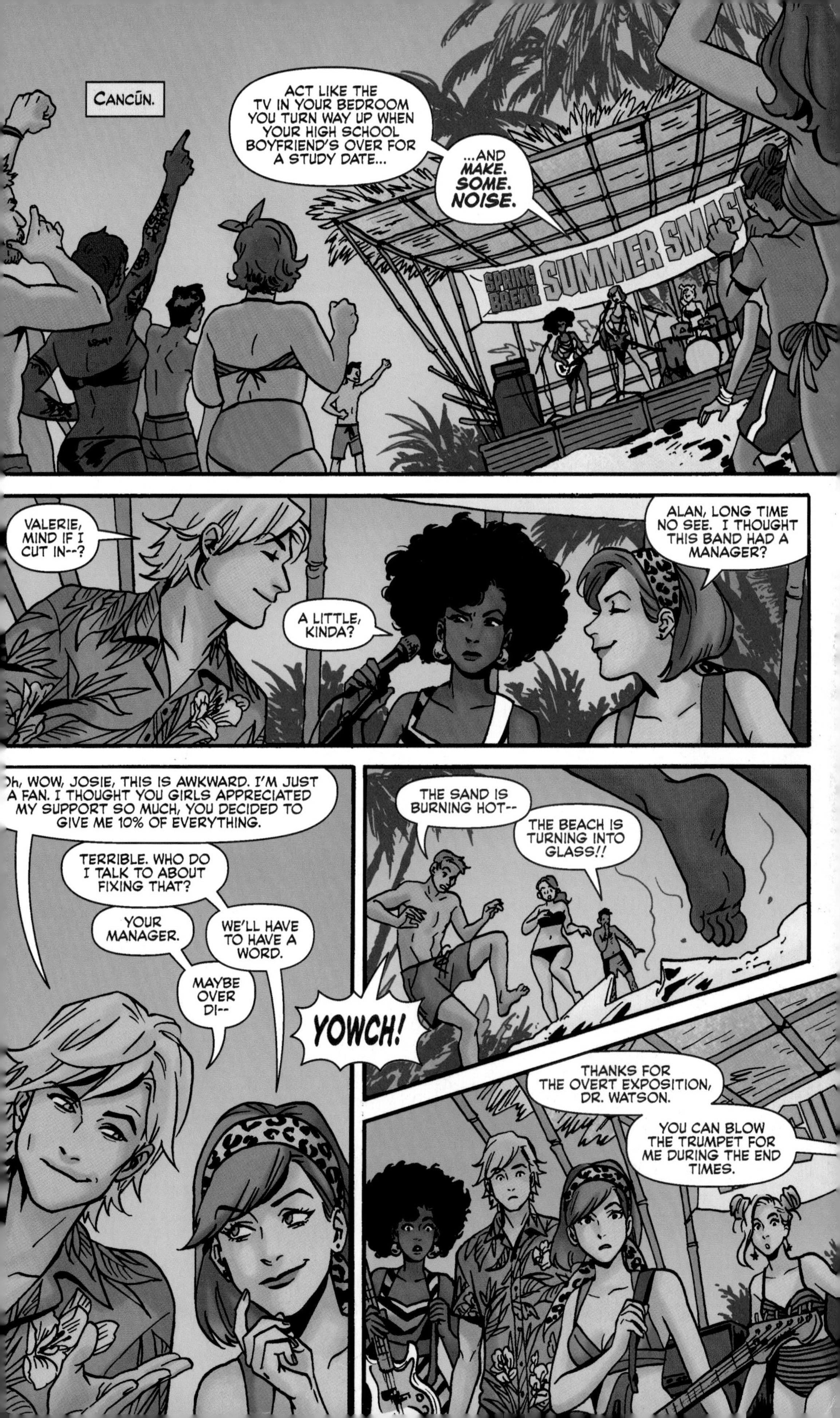
CANCÚN.
ACT LIKE THE TV IN YOUR BEDROOM YOU TURN WAY UP WHEN YOUR HIGH SCHOOL BOYFRIEND'S OVER FOR A STUDY DATE...
...AND MAKE. SOME. NOISE.
SPRING BREAK SUMMER SMAS
VALERIE, MIND IF I CUT IN--?
A LITTLE, KINDA?
ALAN, LONG TIME NO SEE. I THOUGHT THIS BAND HAD A MANAGER?
OH, WOW, JOSIE, THIS IS AWKWARD. I'M JUST A FAN. I THOUGHT YOU GIRLS APPRECIATED MY SUPPORT SO MUCH, YOU DECIDED TO GIVE ME 10% OF EVERYTHING.
TERRIBLE. WHO DO I TALK TO ABOUT FIXING THAT?
YOUR MANAGER.
WE'LL HAVE TO HAVE A WORD.
MAYBE OVER DI--
YOWCH!
THE SAND IS BURNING HOT--
THE BEACH IS TURNING INTO GLASS!!
THANKS FOR THE OVERT EXPOSITION, DR. WATSON.
YOU CAN BLOW THE TRUMPET FOR ME DURING THE END TIMES.

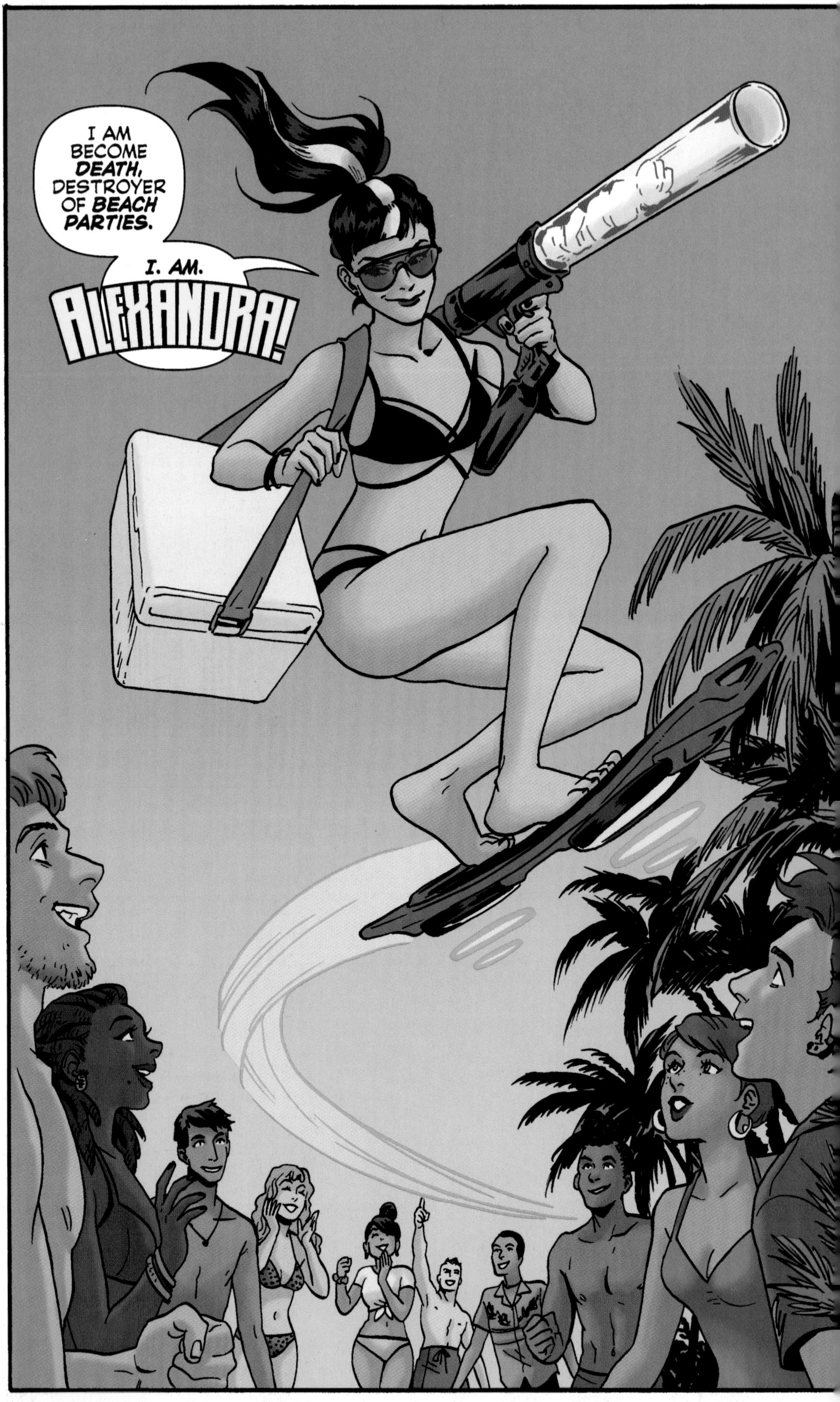
I AM BECOME DEATH, DESTROYER OF BEACH PARTIES.
I. AM. ALEXANDRA!

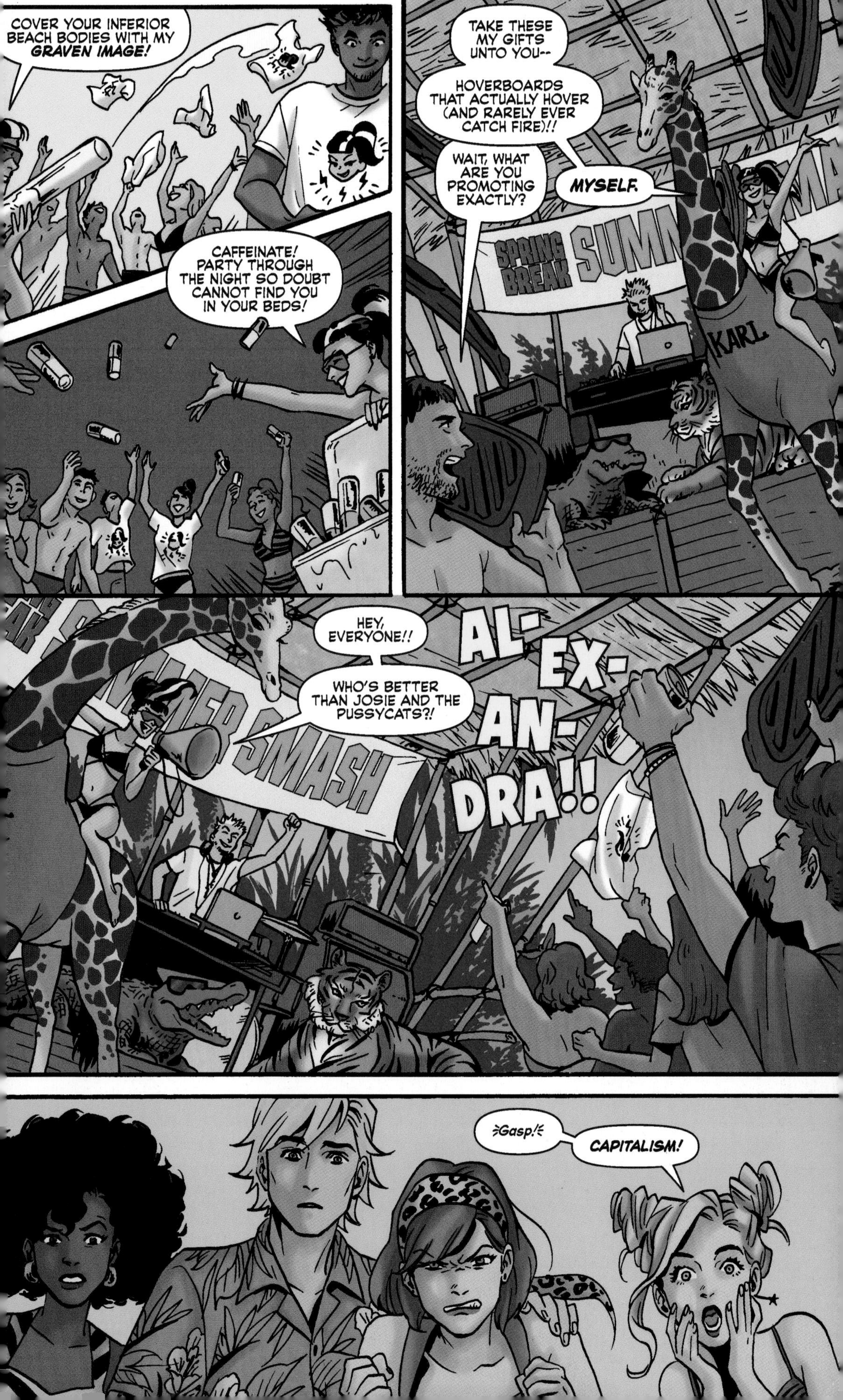

COVER YOUR INFERIOR BEACH BODIES WITH MY *GRAVEN IMAGE!*
CAFFEINATE! PARTY THROUGH THE NIGHT SO DOUBT CANNOT FIND YOU IN YOUR BEDS!
TAKE THESE MY GIFTS UNTO YOU--
HOVERBOARDS THAT ACTUALLY HOVER (AND RARELY EVER CATCH FIRE)!!
WAIT, WHAT ARE YOU PROMOTING EXACTLY?
MYSELF.
SPRING BREAK SUMM
KARL
HEY, EVERYONE!!
WHO'S BETTER THAN JOSIE AND THE PUSSYCATS?!
AL-EX-AN-DRA!!
SMASH
Gasp!
CAPITALISM!

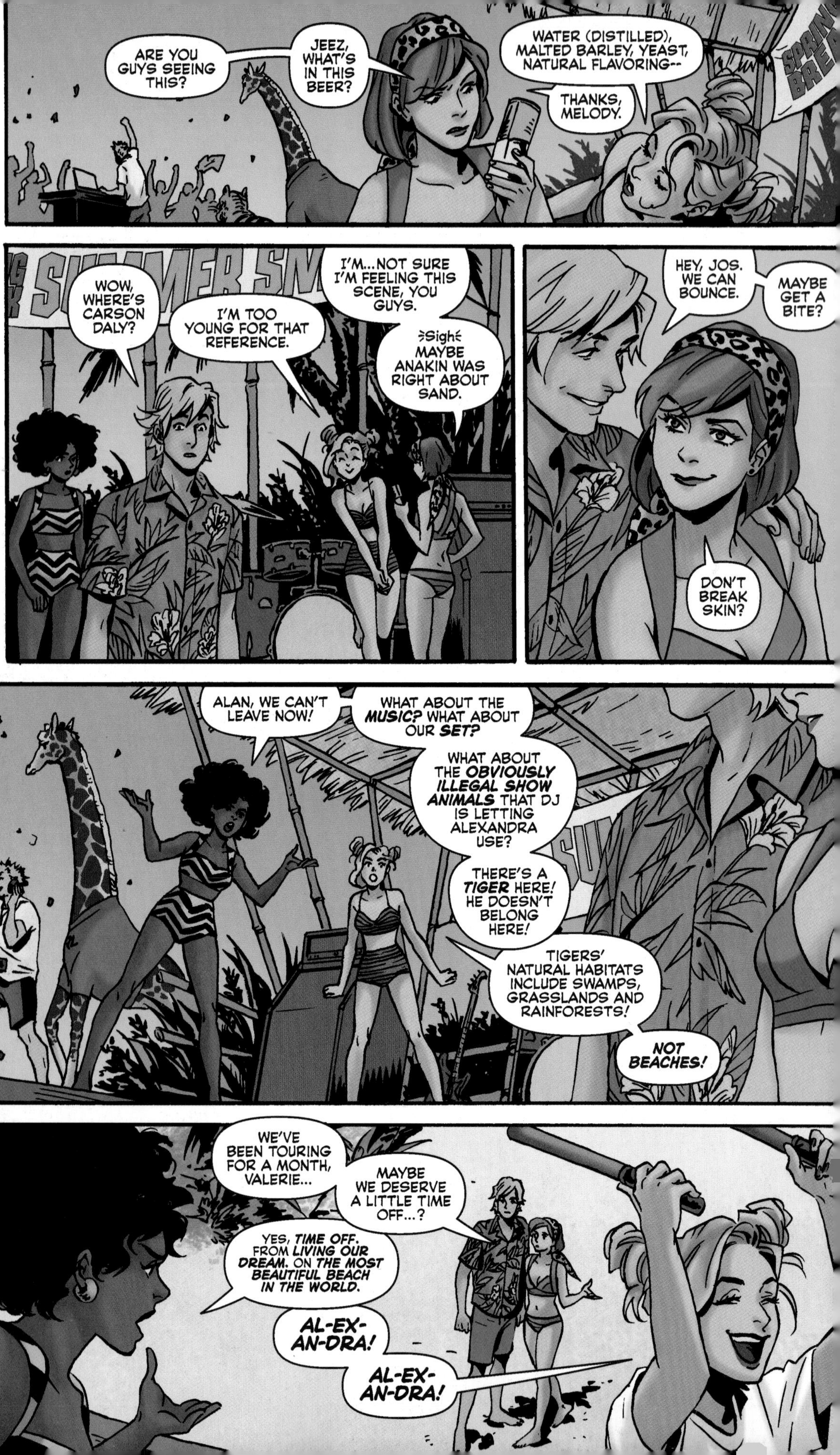
ARE YOU GUYS SEEING THIS?
JEEZ, WHAT'S IN THIS BEER?
WATER (DISTILLED), MALTED BARLEY, YEAST, NATURAL FLAVORING--
THANKS, MELODY.
SPRING BRE
SUMMER SN
WOW, WHERE'S CARSON DALY?
I'M TOO YOUNG FOR THAT REFERENCE.
I'M...NOT SURE I'M FEELING THIS SCENE, YOU GUYS.
Sigh MAYBE ANAKIN WAS RIGHT ABOUT SAND.
HEY, JOS. WE CAN BOUNCE.
MAYBE GET A BITE?
DON'T BREAK SKIN?
ALAN, WE CAN'T LEAVE NOW!
WHAT ABOUT THE MUSIC? WHAT ABOUT OUR SET?
WHAT ABOUT THE OBVIOUSLY ILLEGAL SHOW ANIMALS THAT DJ IS LETTING ALEXANDRA USE?
THERE'S A TIGER HERE! HE DOESN'T BELONG HERE!
TIGERS' NATURAL HABITATS INCLUDE SWAMPS, GRASSLANDS AND RAINFORESTS!
NOT BEACHES!
WE'VE BEEN TOURING FOR A MONTH, VALERIE...
MAYBE WE DESERVE A LITTLE TIME OFF...?
YES, TIME OFF. FROM LIVING OUR DREAM. ON THE MOST BEAUTIFUL BEACH IN THE WORLD.
AL-EX-AN-DRA!
AL-EX-AN-DRA!

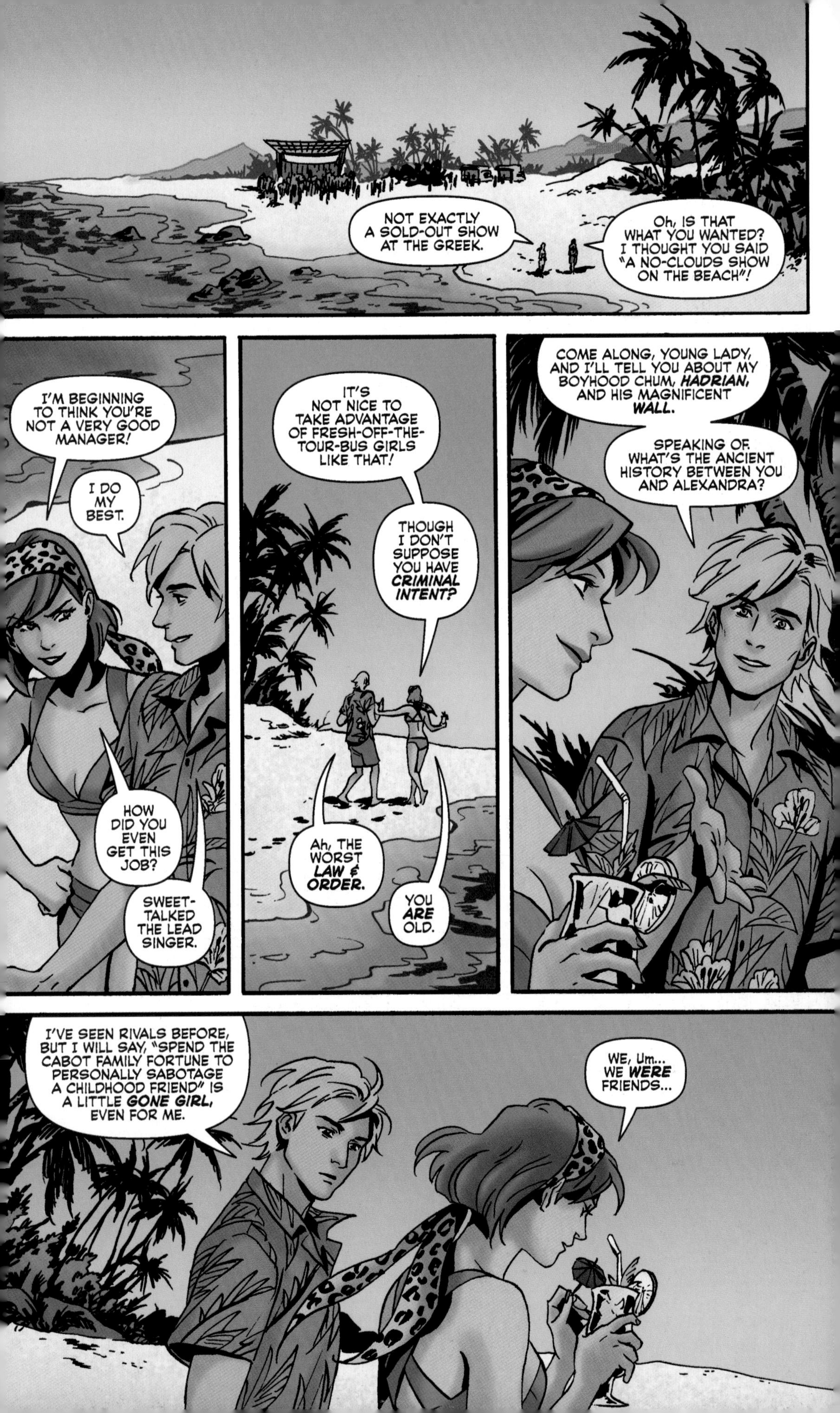

NOT EXACTLY A SOLD-OUT SHOW AT THE GREEK.
Oh, IS THAT WHAT YOU WANTED? I THOUGHT YOU SAID "A NO-CLOUDS SHOW ON THE BEACH"!
I'M BEGINNING TO THINK YOU'RE NOT A VERY GOOD MANAGER!
I DO MY BEST.
HOW DID YOU EVEN GET THIS JOB?
SWEET-TALKED THE LEAD SINGER.
IT'S NOT NICE TO TAKE ADVANTAGE OF FRESH-OFF-THE-TOUR-BUS GIRLS LIKE THAT!
THOUGH I DON'T SUPPOSE YOU HAVE CRIMINAL INTENT?
Ah, THE WORST LAW & ORDER.
YOU ARE OLD.
COME ALONG, YOUNG LADY, AND I'LL TELL YOU ABOUT MY BOYHOOD CHUM, HADRIAN, AND HIS MAGNIFICENT WALL.
SPEAKING OF. WHAT'S THE ANCIENT HISTORY BETWEEN YOU AND ALEXANDRA?
I'VE SEEN RIVALS BEFORE, BUT I WILL SAY, "SPEND THE CABOT FAMILY FORTUNE TO PERSONALLY SABOTAGE A CHILDHOOD FRIEND" IS A LITTLE GONE GIRL, EVEN FOR ME.
WE, Um... WE WERE FRIENDS...

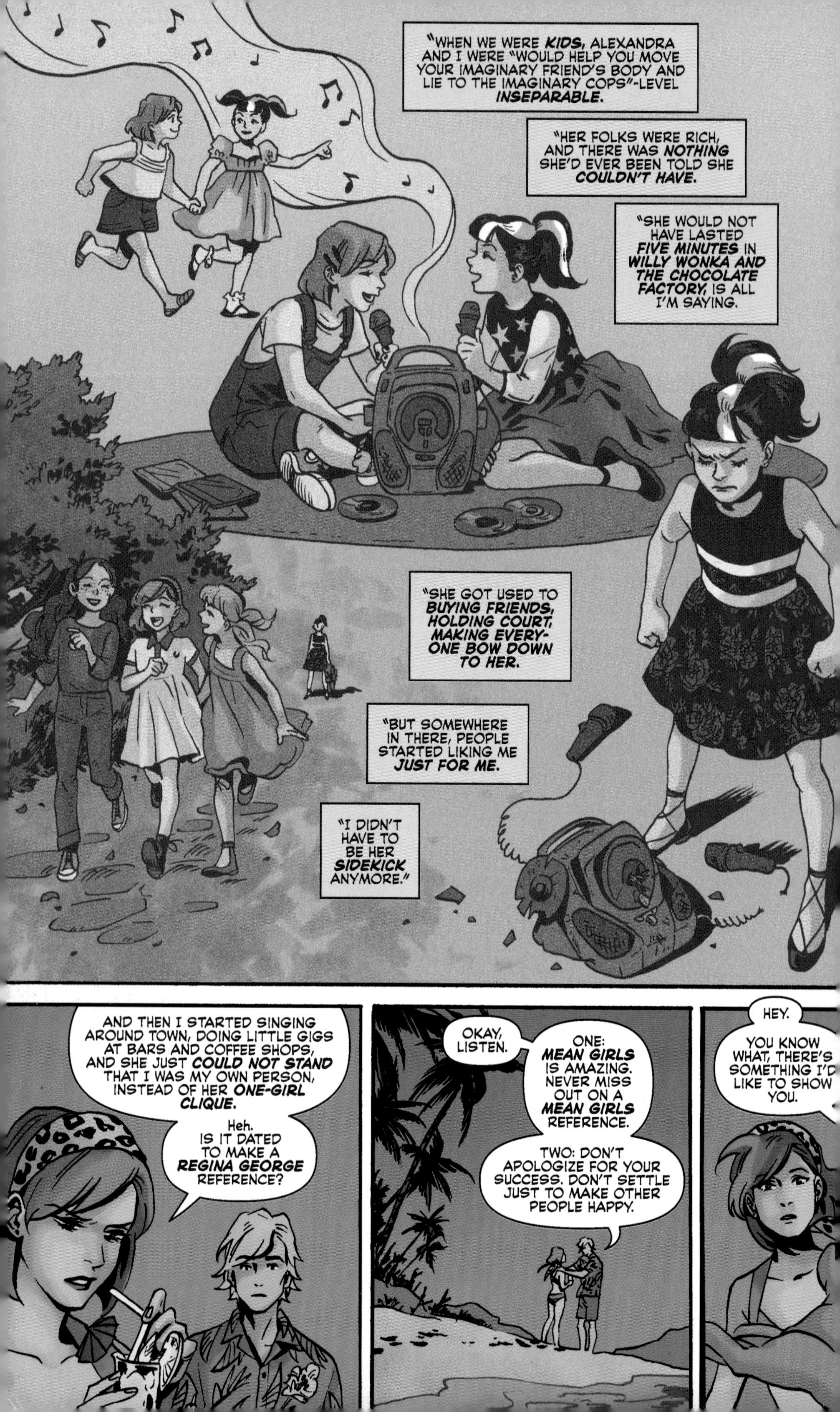
"WHEN WE WERE KIDS, ALEXANDRA AND I WERE "WOULD HELP YOU MOVE YOUR IMAGINARY FRIEND'S BODY AND LIE TO THE IMAGINARY COPS"-LEVEL INSEPARABLE.
"HER FOLKS WERE RICH, AND THERE WAS NOTHING SHE'D EVER BEEN TOLD SHE COULDN'T HAVE.
"SHE WOULD NOT HAVE LASTED FIVE MINUTES IN WILLY WONKA AND THE CHOCOLATE FACTORY, IS ALL I'M SAYING.
"SHE GOT USED TO BUYING FRIENDS, HOLDING COURT, MAKING EVERYONE BOW DOWN TO HER.
"BUT SOMEWHERE IN THERE, PEOPLE STARTED LIKING ME JUST FOR ME.
"I DIDN'T HAVE TO BE HER SIDEKICK ANYMORE."
AND THEN I STARTED SINGING AROUND TOWN, DOING LITTLE GIGS AT BARS AND COFFEE SHOPS, AND SHE JUST COULD NOT STAND THAT I WAS MY OWN PERSON, INSTEAD OF HER ONE-GIRL CLIQUE.
Heh. IS IT DATED TO MAKE A REGINA GEORGE REFERENCE?
OKAY, LISTEN.
ONE: MEAN GIRLS IS AMAZING. NEVER MISS OUT ON A MEAN GIRLS REFERENCE.
TWO: DON'T APOLOGIZE FOR YOUR SUCCESS. DON'T SETTLE JUST TO MAKE OTHER PEOPLE HAPPY.
HEY.
YOU KNOW WHAT, THERE'S SOMETHING I'D LIKE TO SHOW YOU.

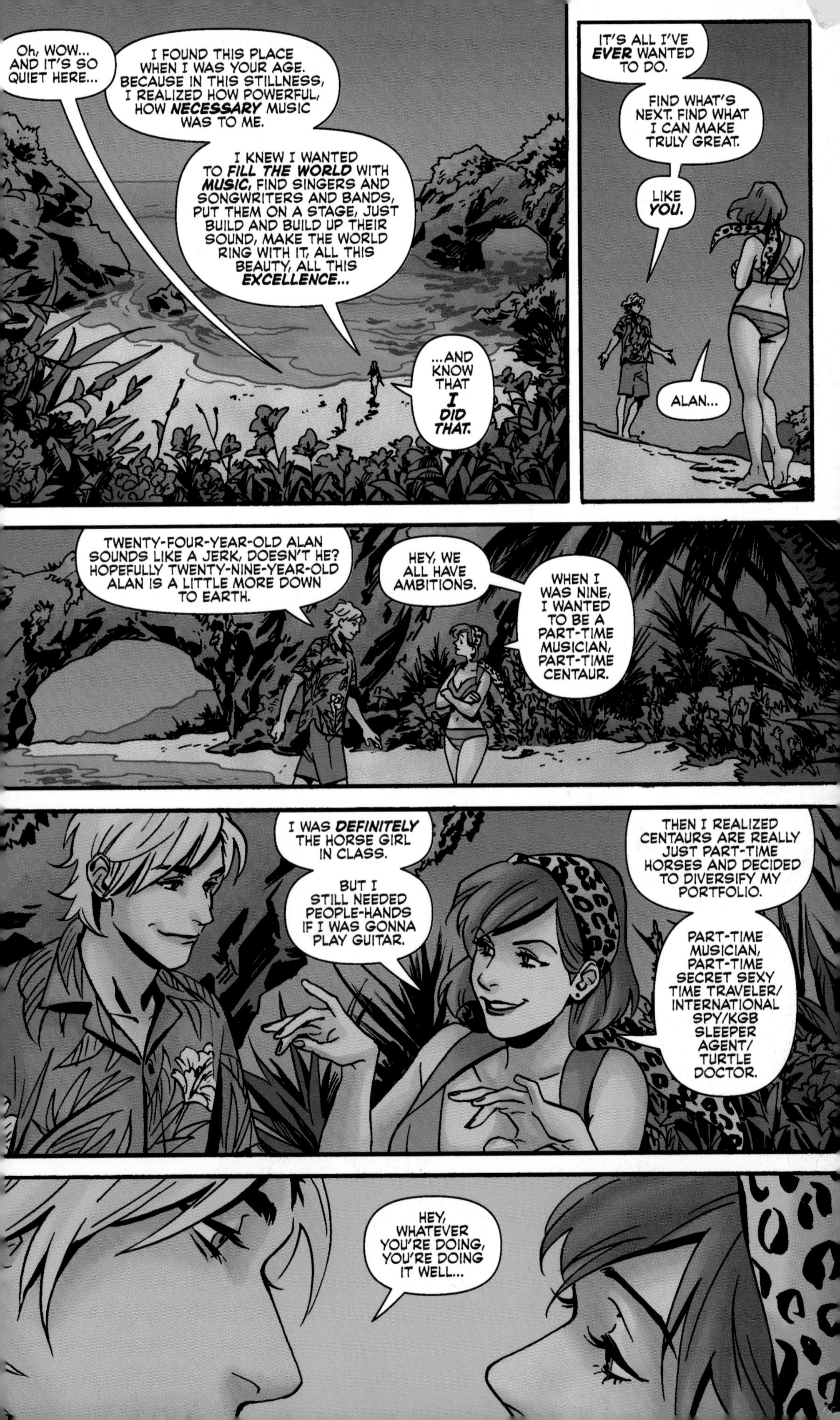

Oh, WOW... AND IT'S SO QUIET HERE...
I FOUND THIS PLACE WHEN I WAS YOUR AGE. BECAUSE IN THIS STILLNESS, I REALIZED HOW POWERFUL, HOW NECESSARY MUSIC WAS TO ME.
I KNEW I WANTED TO FILL THE WORLD WITH MUSIC, FIND SINGERS AND SONGWRITERS AND BANDS, PUT THEM ON A STAGE, JUST BUILD AND BUILD UP THEIR SOUND, MAKE THE WORLD RING WITH IT, ALL THIS BEAUTY, ALL THIS EXCELLENCE...
...AND KNOW THAT I DID THAT.
IT'S ALL I'VE EVER WANTED TO DO.
FIND WHAT'S NEXT. FIND WHAT I CAN MAKE TRULY GREAT.
LIKE YOU.
ALAN...
TWENTY-FOUR-YEAR-OLD ALAN SOUNDS LIKE A JERK, DOESN'T HE? HOPEFULLY TWENTY-NINE-YEAR-OLD ALAN IS A LITTLE MORE DOWN TO EARTH.
HEY, WE ALL HAVE AMBITIONS.
WHEN I WAS NINE, I WANTED TO BE A PART-TIME MUSICIAN, PART-TIME CENTAUR.
I WAS DEFINITELY THE HORSE GIRL IN CLASS.
BUT I STILL NEEDED PEOPLE-HANDS IF I WAS GONNA PLAY GUITAR.
THEN I REALIZED CENTAURS ARE REALLY JUST PART-TIME HORSES AND DECIDED TO DIVERSIFY MY PORTFOLIO.
PART-TIME MUSICIAN, PART-TIME SECRET SEXY TIME TRAVELER/ INTERNATIONAL SPY/KGB SLEEPER AGENT/ TURTLE DOCTOR.
HEY, WHATEVER YOU'RE DOING, YOU'RE DOING IT WELL...

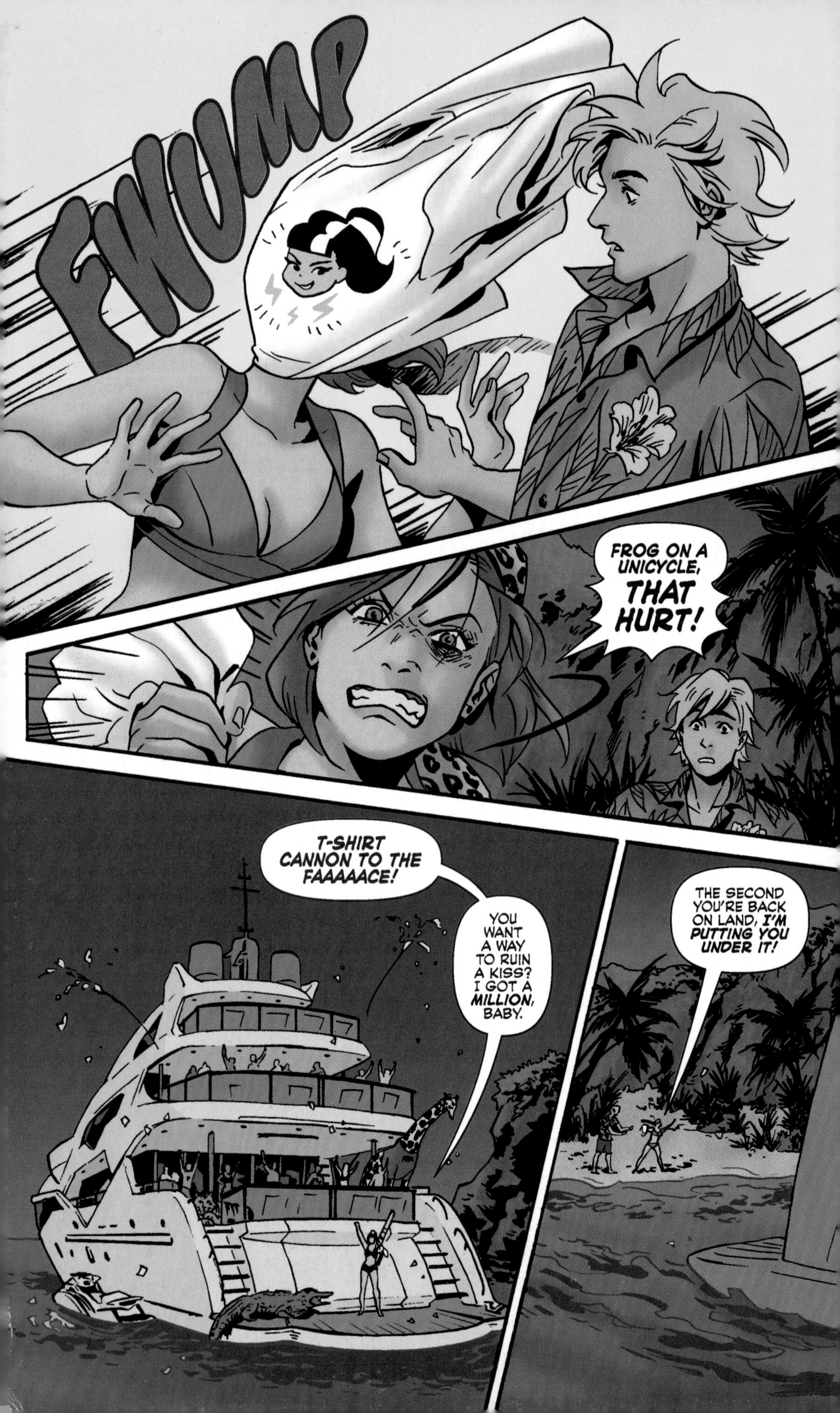
FWUMP
FROG ON A UNICYCLE, THAT HURT!
T-SHIRT CANNON TO THE FAAAAACE!
YOU WANT A WAY TO RUIN A KISS? I GOT A MILLION, BABY.
THE SECOND YOU'RE BACK ON LAND, I'M PUTTING YOU UNDER IT!

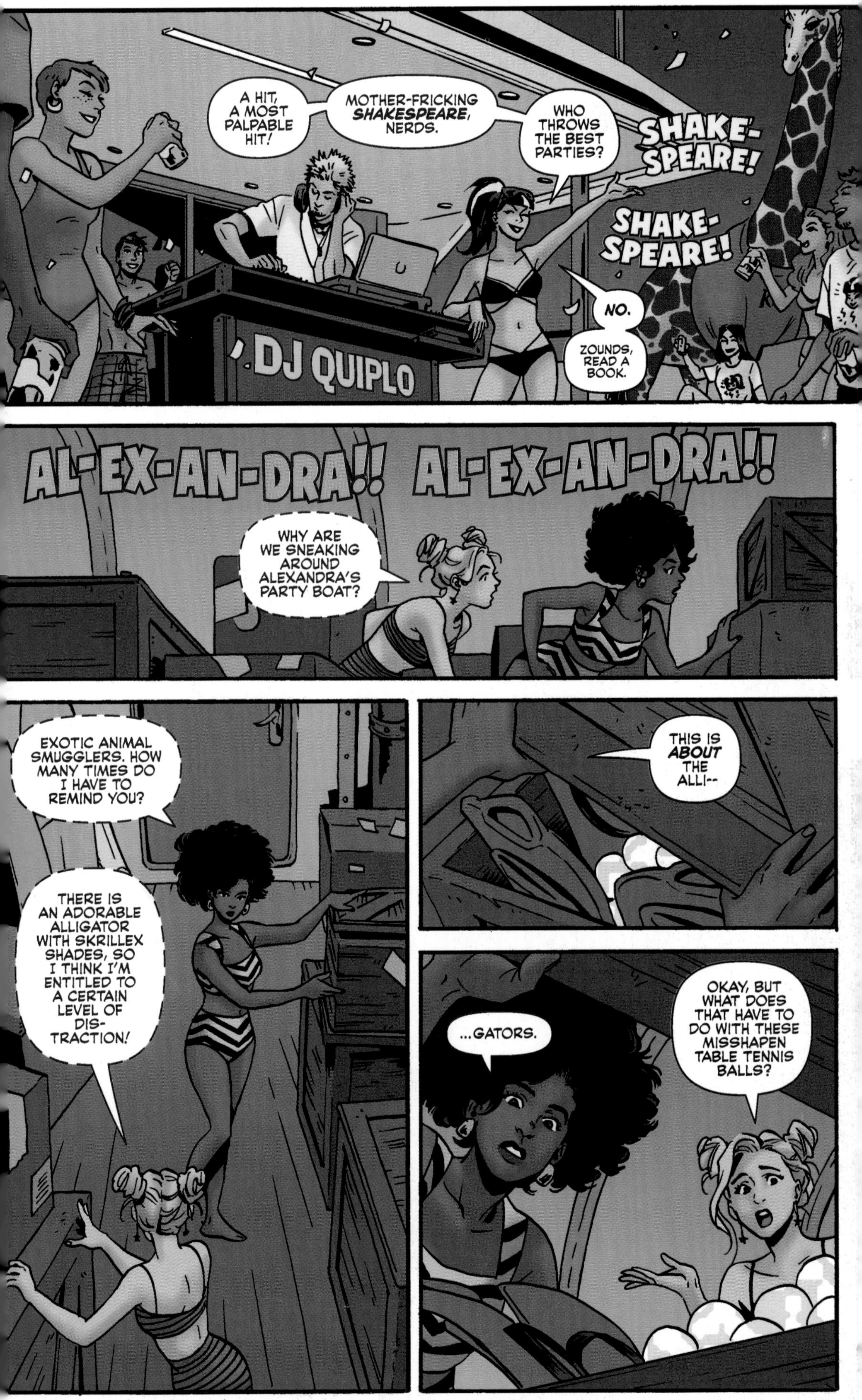
A HIT, A MOST PALPABLE HIT!
MOTHER-FRICKING SHAKESPEARE, NERDS.
WHO THROWS THE BEST PARTIES?
SHAKE-SPEARE!
SHAKE-SPEARE!
NO.
ZOUNDS, READ A BOOK.
DJ QUIPLO
AL-EX-AN-DRA!! AL-EX-AN-DRA!!
WHY ARE WE SNEAKING AROUND ALEXANDRA'S PARTY BOAT?
EXOTIC ANIMAL SMUGGLERS. HOW MANY TIMES DO I HAVE TO REMIND YOU?
THERE IS AN ADORABLE ALLIGATOR WITH SKRILLEX SHADES, SO I THINK I'M ENTITLED TO A CERTAIN LEVEL OF DIS-TRACTION!
THIS IS ABOUT THE ALLI--
...GATORS.
OKAY, BUT WHAT DOES THAT HAVE TO DO WITH THESE MISSHAPEN TABLE TENNIS BALLS?

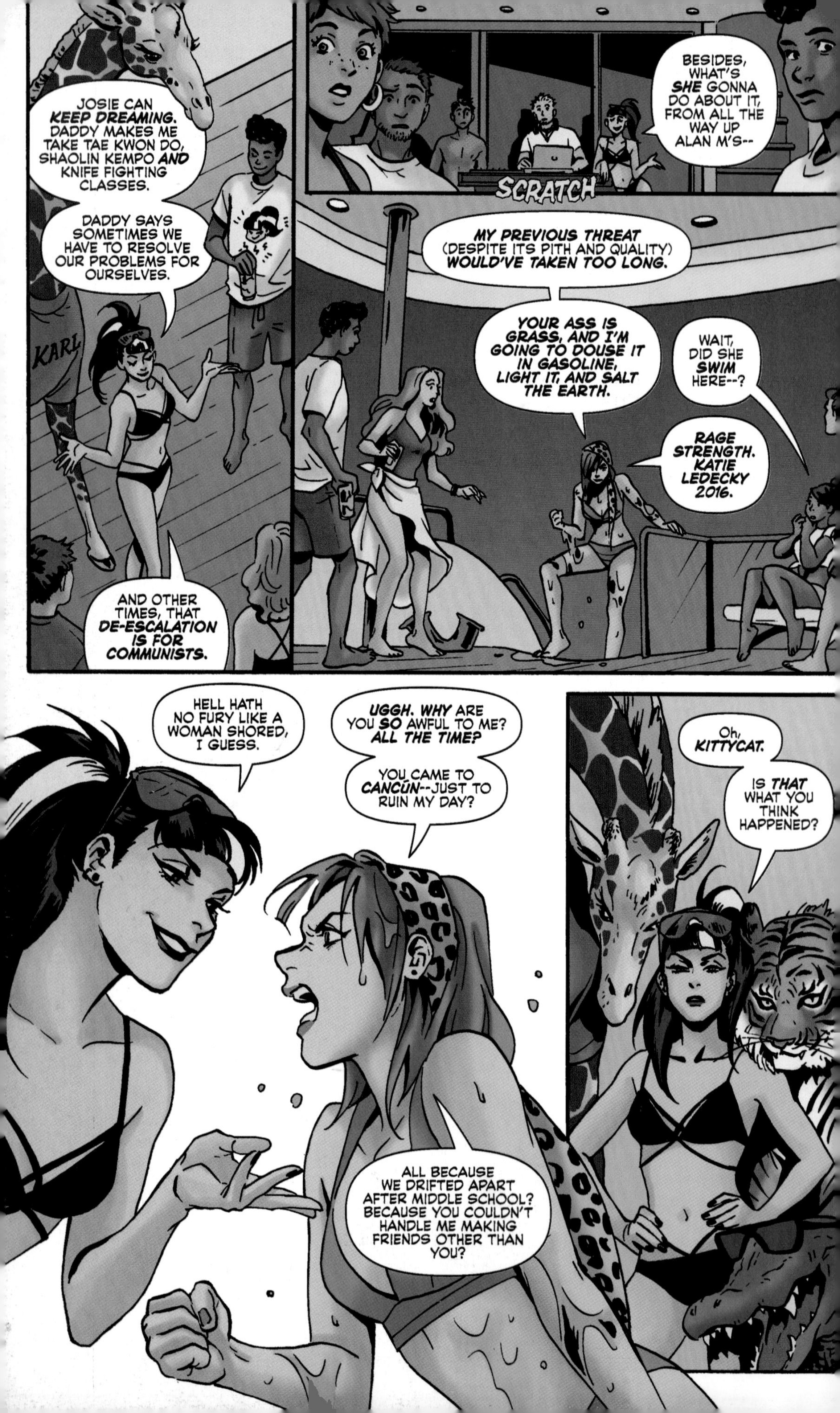
JOSIE CAN **KEEP DREAMING.** DADDY MAKES ME TAKE TAE KWON DO, SHAOLIN KEMPO **AND** KNIFE FIGHTING CLASSES.
DADDY SAYS SOMETIMES WE HAVE TO RESOLVE OUR PROBLEMS FOR OURSELVES.
AND OTHER TIMES, THAT **DE-ESCALATION IS FOR COMMUNISTS.**
BESIDES, WHAT'S **SHE** GONNA DO ABOUT IT, FROM ALL THE WAY UP ALAN M'S--
SCRATCH
MY PREVIOUS THREAT (DESPITE ITS PITH AND QUALITY) **WOULD'VE TAKEN TOO LONG.**
YOUR ASS IS GRASS, AND I'M GOING TO DOUSE IT IN GASOLINE, LIGHT IT, AND SALT THE EARTH.
WAIT, DID SHE **SWIM** HERE--?
RAGE STRENGTH. KATIE LEDECKY 2016.
HELL HATH NO FURY LIKE A WOMAN SHORED, I GUESS.
UGGH. WHY ARE YOU **SO** AWFUL TO ME? **ALL THE TIME?**
YOU CAME TO **CANCÚN**--JUST TO RUIN MY DAY?
ALL BECAUSE WE DRIFTED APART AFTER MIDDLE SCHOOL? BECAUSE YOU COULDN'T HANDLE ME MAKING FRIENDS OTHER THAN YOU?
Oh, **KITTYCAT.**
IS **THAT** WHAT YOU THINK HAPPENED?

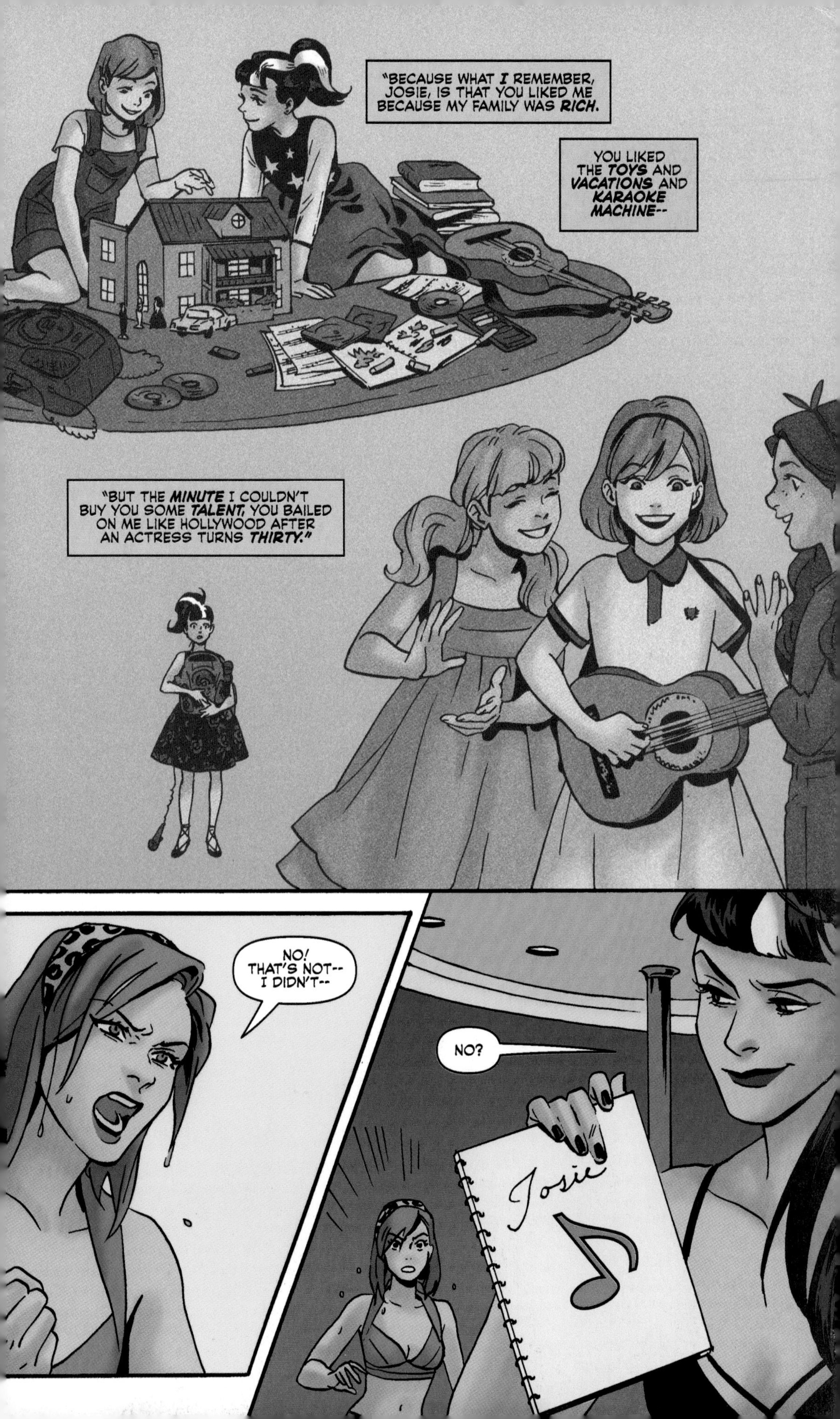
"BECAUSE WHAT I REMEMBER, JOSIE, IS THAT YOU LIKED ME BECAUSE MY FAMILY WAS RICH.
YOU LIKED THE TOYS AND VACATIONS AND KARAOKE MACHINE--
"BUT THE MINUTE I COULDN'T BUY YOU SOME TALENT, YOU BAILED ON ME LIKE HOLLYWOOD AFTER AN ACTRESS TURNS THIRTY."
NO! THAT'S NOT-- I DIDN'T--
NO?
Josie

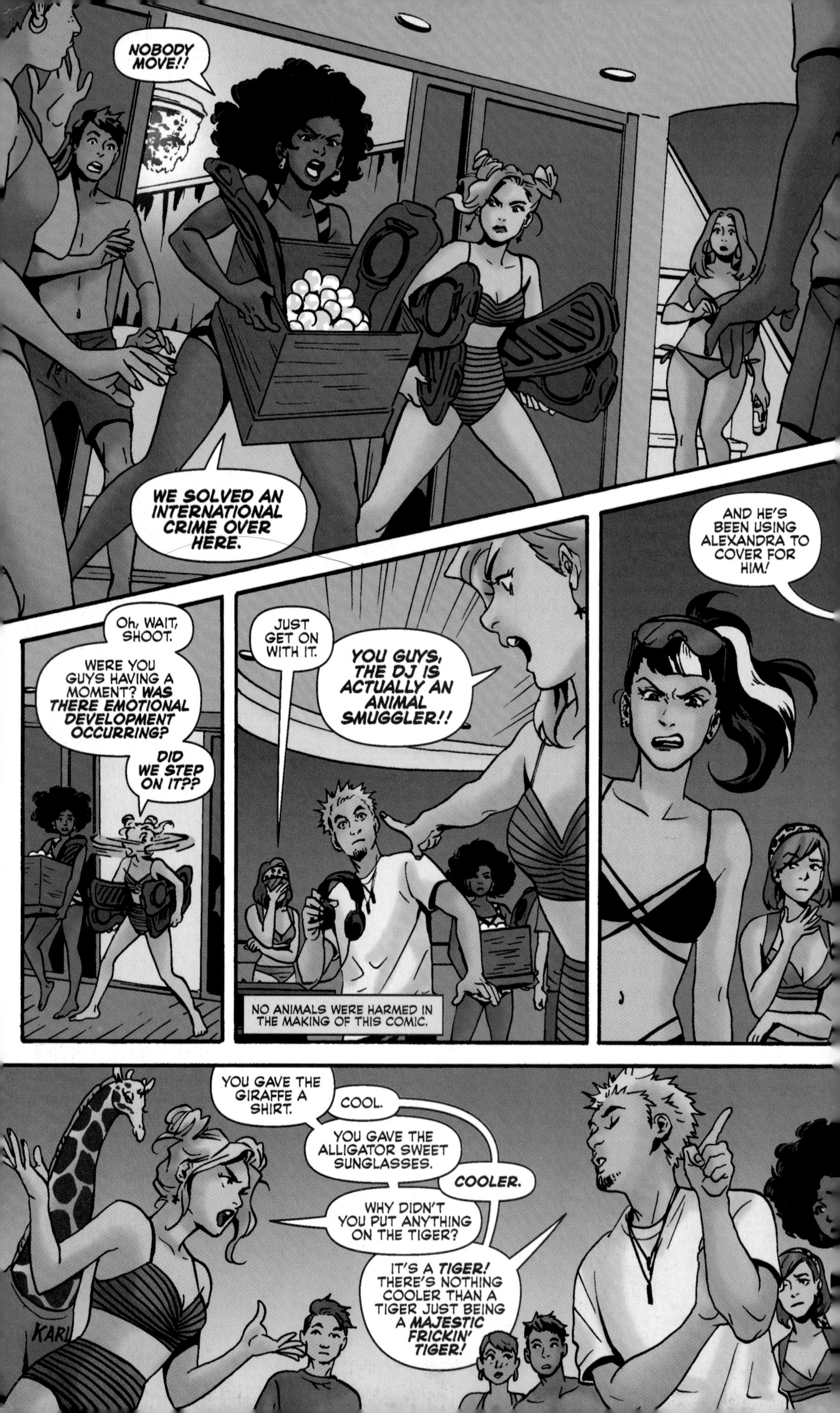
NOBODY MOVE!!
WE SOLVED AN INTERNATIONAL CRIME OVER HERE.
Oh, WAIT, SHOOT.
WERE YOU GUYS HAVING A MOMENT? WAS THERE EMOTIONAL DEVELOPMENT OCCURRING?
DID WE STEP ON IT??
JUST GET ON WITH IT.
YOU GUYS, THE DJ IS ACTUALLY AN ANIMAL SMUGGLER!!
NO ANIMALS WERE HARMED IN THE MAKING OF THIS COMIC.
AND HE'S BEEN USING ALEXANDRA TO COVER FOR HIM!
YOU GAVE THE GIRAFFE A SHIRT.
COOL.
YOU GAVE THE ALLIGATOR SWEET SUNGLASSES.
COOLER.
WHY DIDN'T YOU PUT ANYTHING ON THE TIGER?
IT'S A TIGER! THERE'S NOTHING COOLER THAN A TIGER JUST BEING A MAJESTIC FRICKIN' TIGER!
KARL

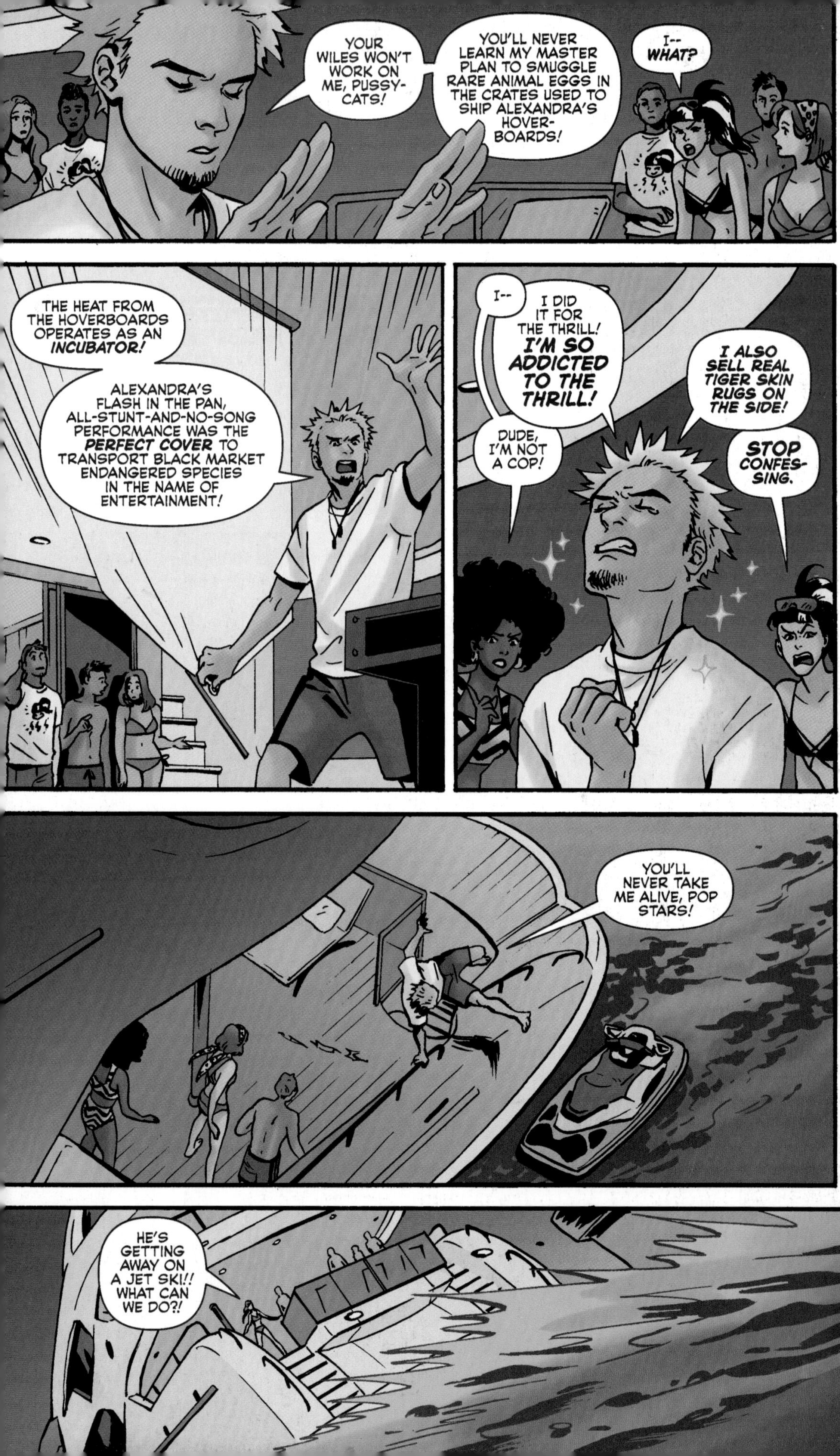
YOUR WILES WON'T WORK ON ME, PUSSY-CATS!
YOU'LL NEVER LEARN MY MASTER PLAN TO SMUGGLE RARE ANIMAL EGGS IN THE CRATES USED TO SHIP ALEXANDRA'S HOVER-BOARDS!
I-- WHAT?
THE HEAT FROM THE HOVERBOARDS OPERATES AS AN INCUBATOR!
ALEXANDRA'S FLASH IN THE PAN, ALL-STUNT-AND-NO-SONG PERFORMANCE WAS THE PERFECT COVER TO TRANSPORT BLACK MARKET ENDANGERED SPECIES IN THE NAME OF ENTERTAINMENT!
I--
I DID IT FOR THE THRILL! I'M SO ADDICTED TO THE THRILL!
DUDE, I'M NOT A COP!
I ALSO SELL REAL TIGER SKIN RUGS ON THE SIDE!
STOP CONFES-SING.
YOU'LL NEVER TAKE ME ALIVE, POP STARS!
HE'S GETTING AWAY ON A JET SKI!! WHAT CAN WE DO?!

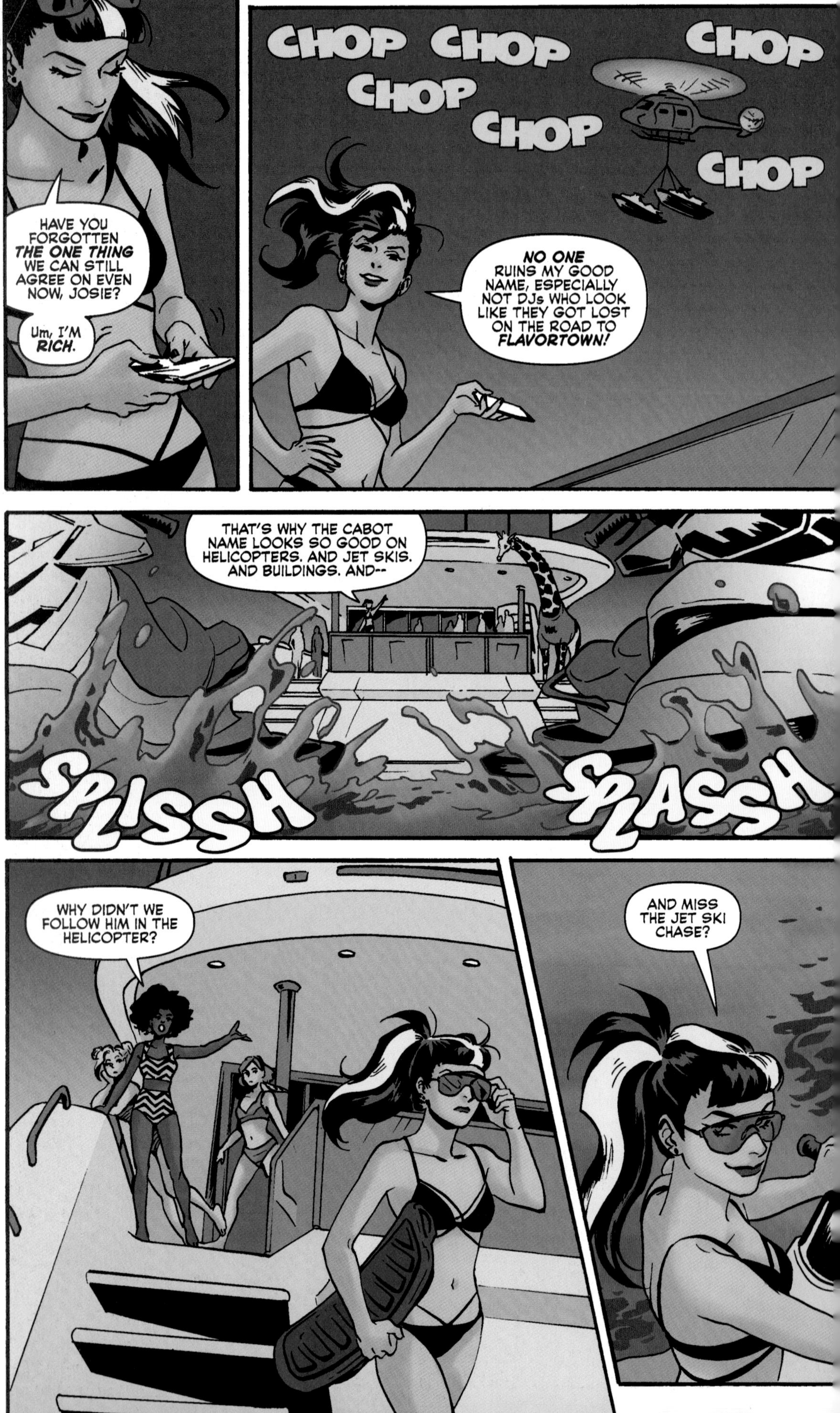

HAVE YOU FORGOTTEN ***THE ONE THING*** WE CAN STILL AGREE ON EVEN NOW, JOSIE?
Um, I'M ***RICH***.
CHOP CHOP
CHOP
CHOP
CHOP
CHOP
NO ONE RUINS MY GOOD NAME, ESPECIALLY NOT DJs WHO LOOK LIKE THEY GOT LOST ON THE ROAD TO ***FLAVORTOWN!***
THAT'S WHY THE CABOT NAME LOOKS SO GOOD ON HELICOPTERS. AND JET SKIS. AND BUILDINGS. AND--
SPLISSH
SPLASSH
WHY DIDN'T WE FOLLOW HIM IN THE HELICOPTER?
AND MISS THE JET SKI CHASE?

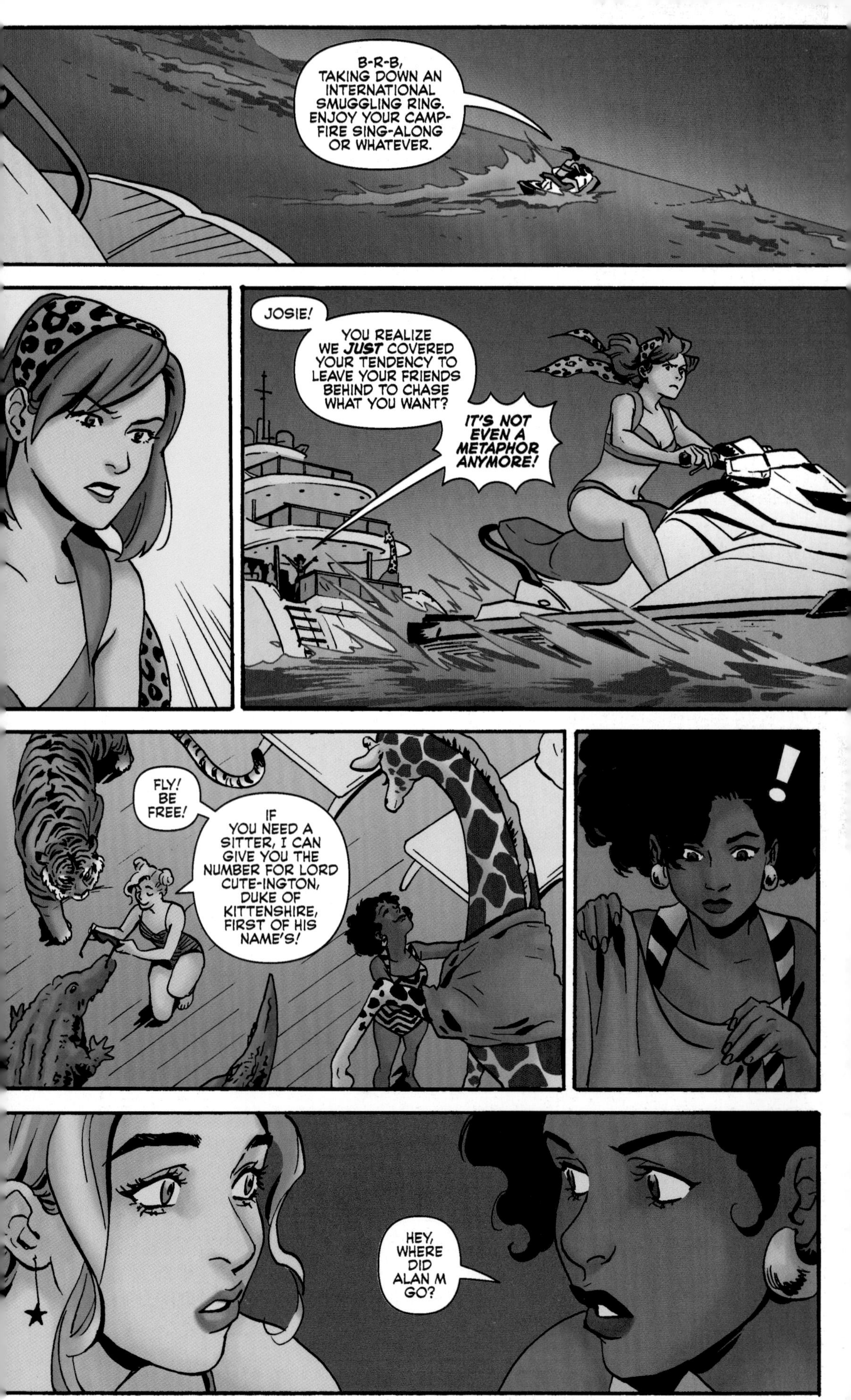

B-R-B, TAKING DOWN AN INTERNATIONAL SMUGGLING RING. ENJOY YOUR CAMP-FIRE SING-ALONG OR WHATEVER.
JOSIE!
YOU REALIZE WE JUST COVERED YOUR TENDENCY TO LEAVE YOUR FRIENDS BEHIND TO CHASE WHAT YOU WANT?
IT'S NOT EVEN A METAPHOR ANYMORE!
FLY! BE FREE!
IF YOU NEED A SITTER, I CAN GIVE YOU THE NUMBER FOR LORD CUTE-INGTON, DUKE OF KITTENSHIRE, FIRST OF HIS NAME'S!
!
HEY, WHERE DID ALAN M GO?

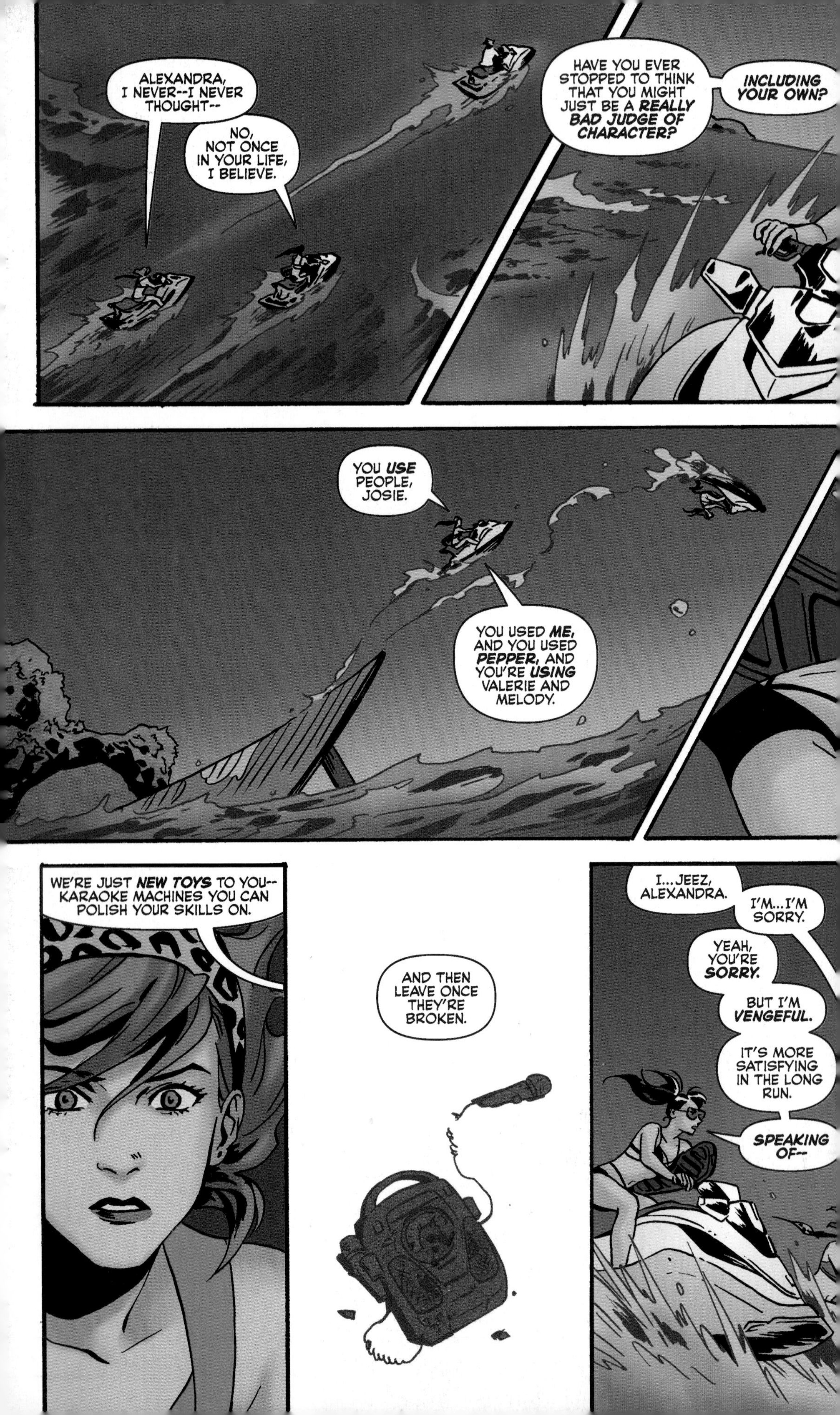

ALEXANDRA, I NEVER--I NEVER THOUGHT--
NO, NOT ONCE IN YOUR LIFE, I BELIEVE.
HAVE YOU EVER STOPPED TO THINK THAT YOU MIGHT JUST BE A REALLY BAD JUDGE OF CHARACTER?
INCLUDING YOUR OWN?
YOU USE PEOPLE, JOSIE.
YOU USED ME, AND YOU USED PEPPER, AND YOU'RE USING VALERIE AND MELODY.
WE'RE JUST NEW TOYS TO YOU--KARAOKE MACHINES YOU CAN POLISH YOUR SKILLS ON.
AND THEN LEAVE ONCE THEY'RE BROKEN.
I...JEEZ, ALEXANDRA.
I'M...I'M SORRY.
YEAH, YOU'RE SORRY.
BUT I'M VENGEFUL.
IT'S MORE SATISFYING IN THE LONG RUN.
SPEAKING OF--

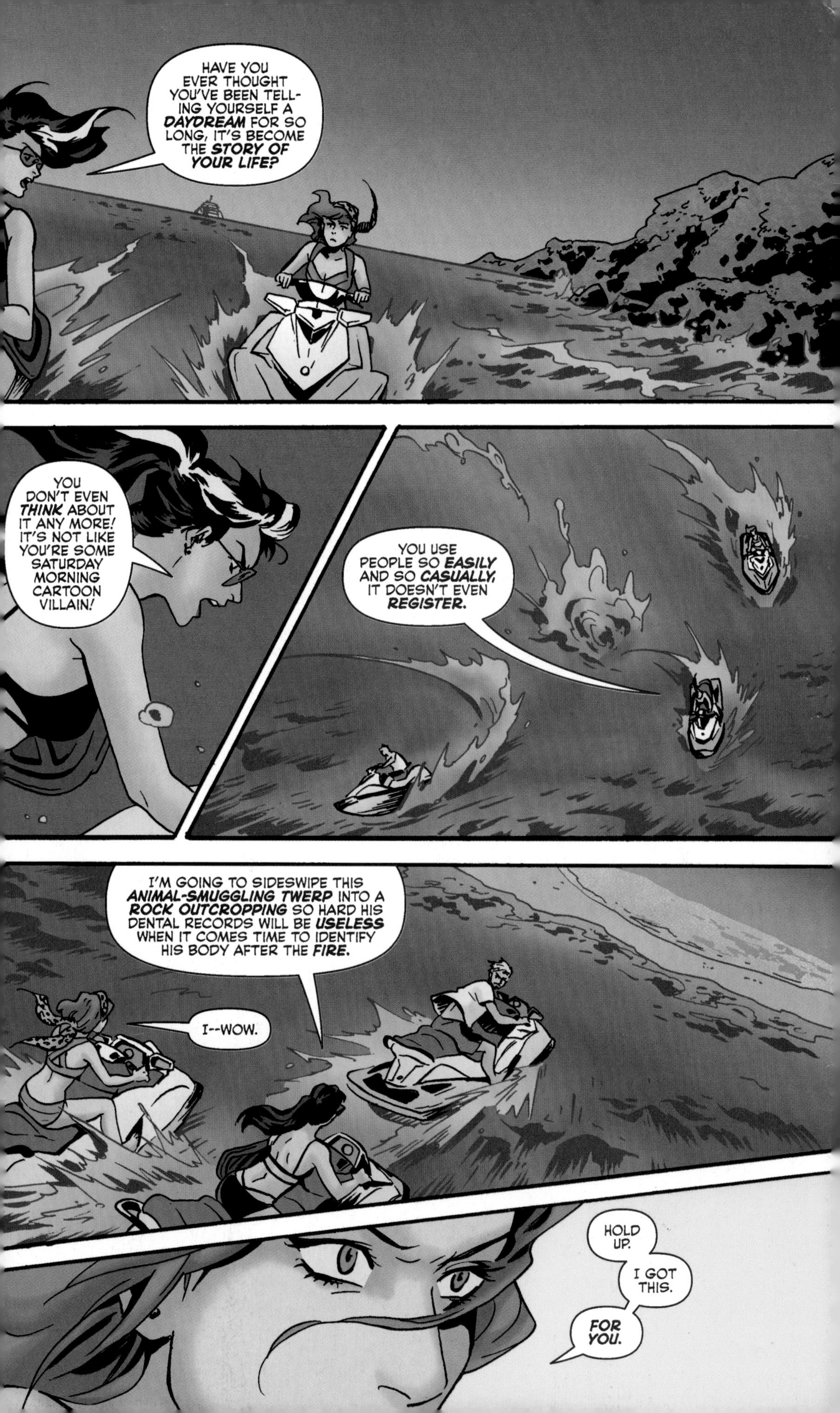
HAVE YOU EVER THOUGHT YOU'VE BEEN TELLING YOURSELF A DAYDREAM FOR SO LONG, IT'S BECOME THE STORY OF YOUR LIFE?
YOU DON'T EVEN THINK ABOUT IT ANY MORE! IT'S NOT LIKE YOU'RE SOME SATURDAY MORNING CARTOON VILLAIN!
YOU USE PEOPLE SO EASILY AND SO CASUALLY, IT DOESN'T EVEN REGISTER.
I'M GOING TO SIDESWIPE THIS ANIMAL-SMUGGLING TWERP INTO A ROCK OUTCROPPING SO HARD HIS DENTAL RECORDS WILL BE USELESS WHEN IT COMES TIME TO IDENTIFY HIS BODY AFTER THE FIRE.
I--WOW.
HOLD UP.
I GOT THIS.
FOR YOU.

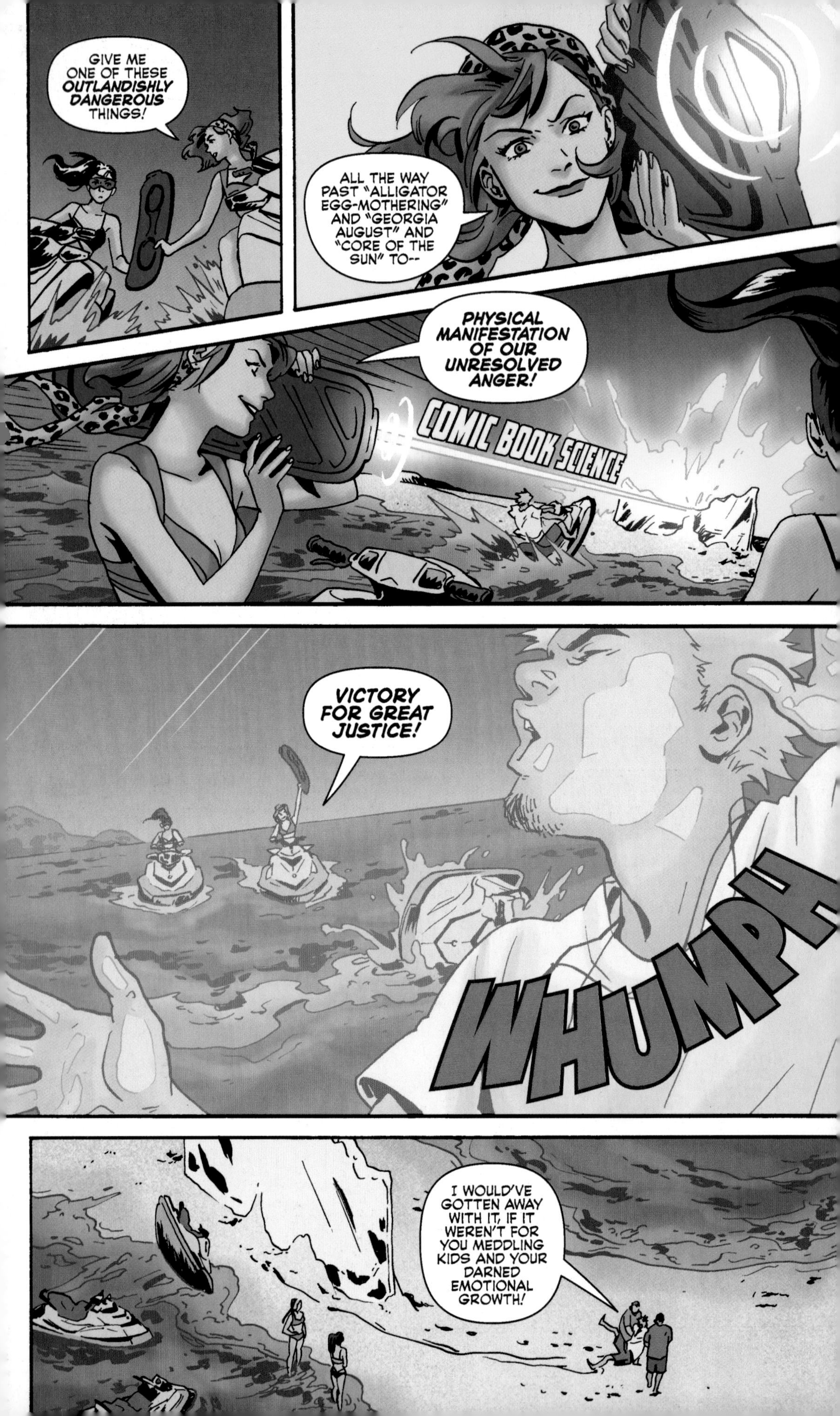
GIVE ME ONE OF THESE OUTLANDISHLY DANGEROUS THINGS!
ALL THE WAY PAST "ALLIGATOR EGG-MOTHERING" AND "GEORGIA AUGUST" AND "CORE OF THE SUN" TO--
PHYSICAL MANIFESTATION OF OUR UNRESOLVED ANGER!
COMIC BOOK SCIENCE
VICTORY FOR GREAT JUSTICE!
WHUMPH
I WOULD'VE GOTTEN AWAY WITH IT, IF IT WEREN'T FOR YOU MEDDLING KIDS AND YOUR DARNED EMOTIONAL GROWTH!

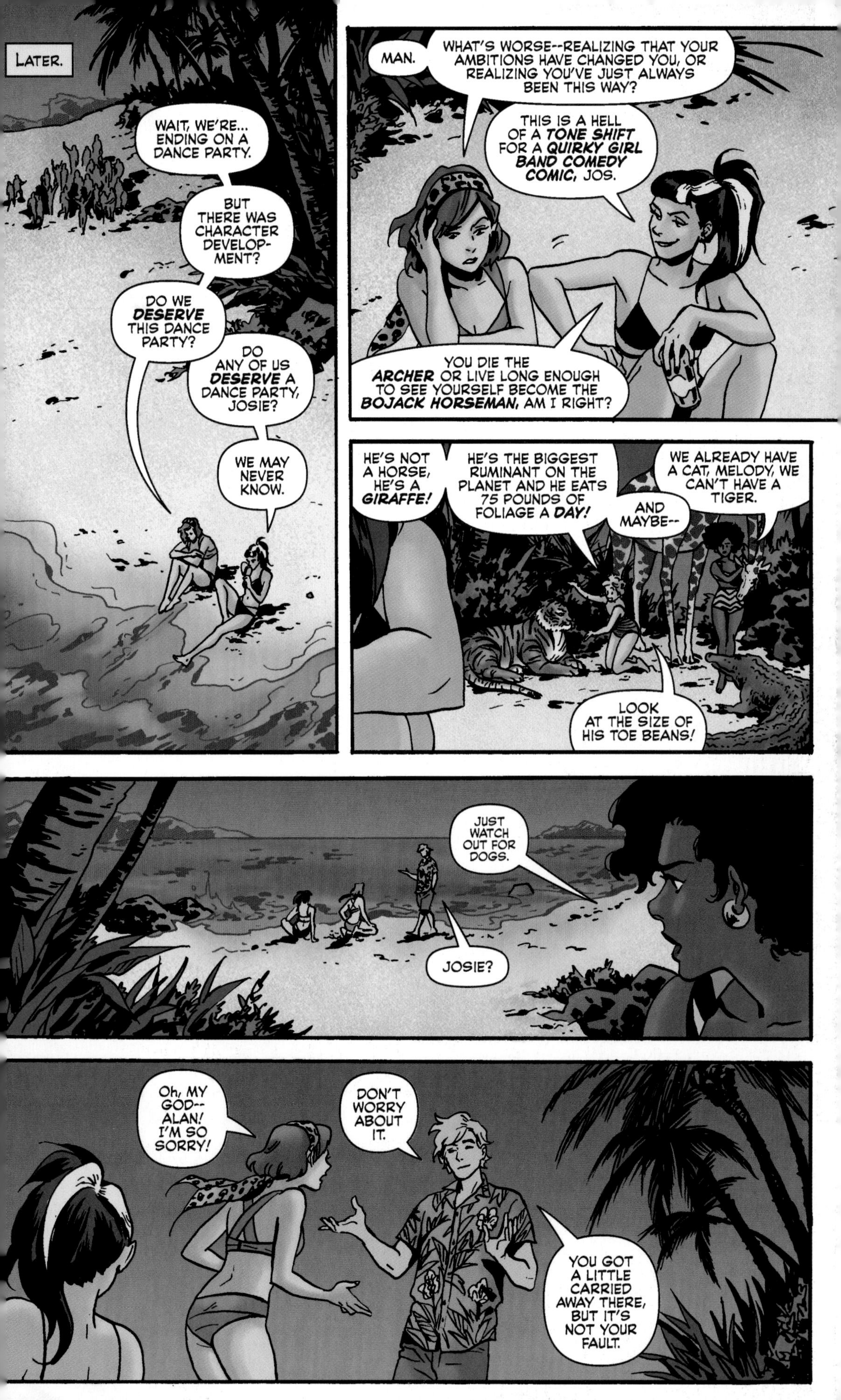
LATER.
WAIT, WE'RE... ENDING ON A DANCE PARTY.
BUT THERE WAS CHARACTER DEVELOP-MENT?
DO WE DESERVE THIS DANCE PARTY?
DO ANY OF US DESERVE A DANCE PARTY, JOSIE?
WE MAY NEVER KNOW.
MAN.
WHAT'S WORSE--REALIZING THAT YOUR AMBITIONS HAVE CHANGED YOU, OR REALIZING YOU'VE JUST ALWAYS BEEN THIS WAY?
THIS IS A HELL OF A TONE SHIFT FOR A QUIRKY GIRL BAND COMEDY COMIC, JOS.
YOU DIE THE ARCHER OR LIVE LONG ENOUGH TO SEE YOURSELF BECOME THE BOJACK HORSEMAN, AM I RIGHT?
HE'S NOT A HORSE, HE'S A GIRAFFE!
HE'S THE BIGGEST RUMINANT ON THE PLANET AND HE EATS 75 POUNDS OF FOLIAGE A DAY!
AND MAYBE--
WE ALREADY HAVE A CAT, MELODY, WE CAN'T HAVE A TIGER.
LOOK AT THE SIZE OF HIS TOE BEANS!
JUST WATCH OUT FOR DOGS.
JOSIE?
Oh, MY GOD-- ALAN! I'M SO SORRY!
DON'T WORRY ABOUT IT.
YOU GOT A LITTLE CARRIED AWAY THERE, BUT IT'S NOT YOUR FAULT.

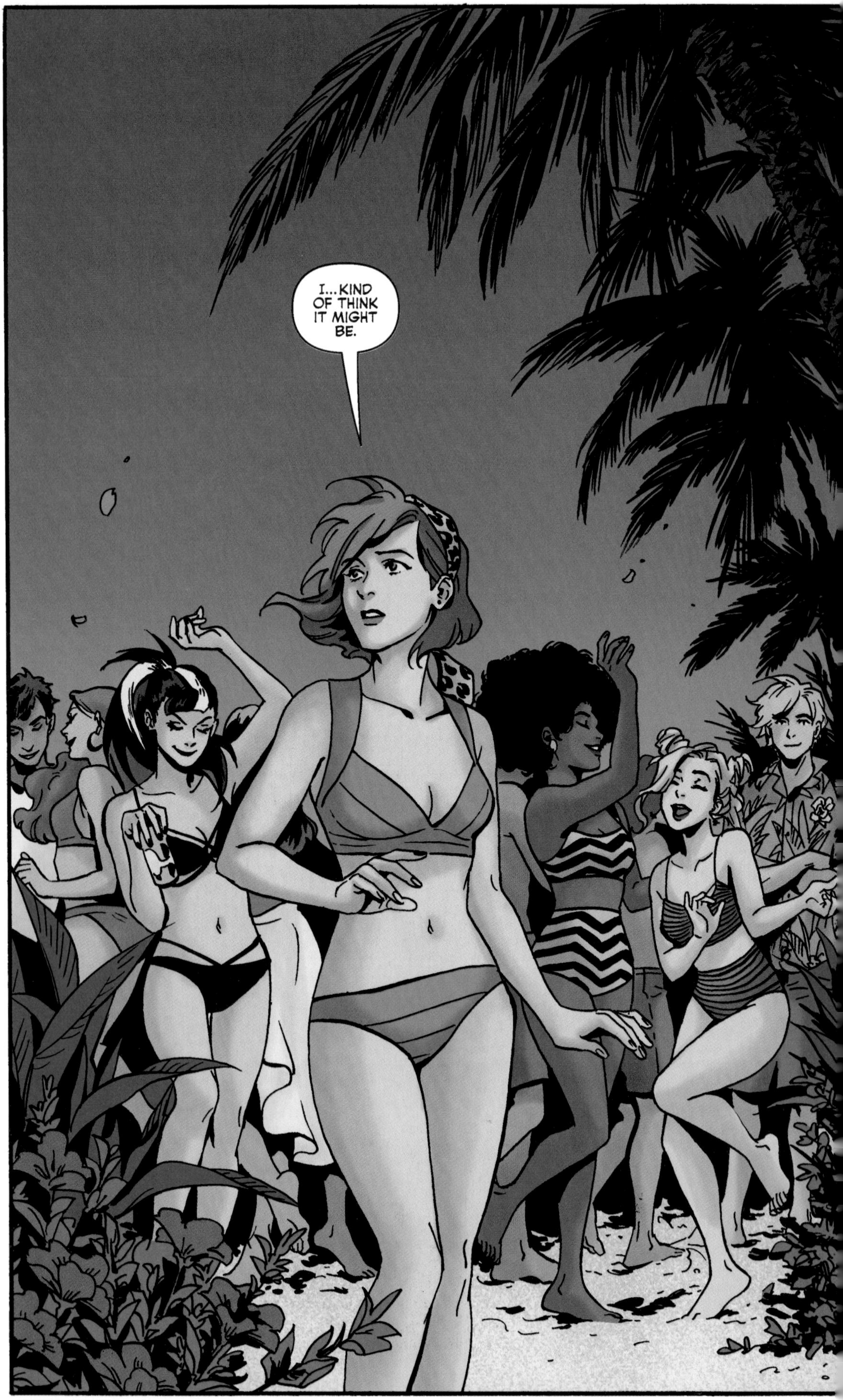
I...KIND OF THINK IT MIGHT BE.

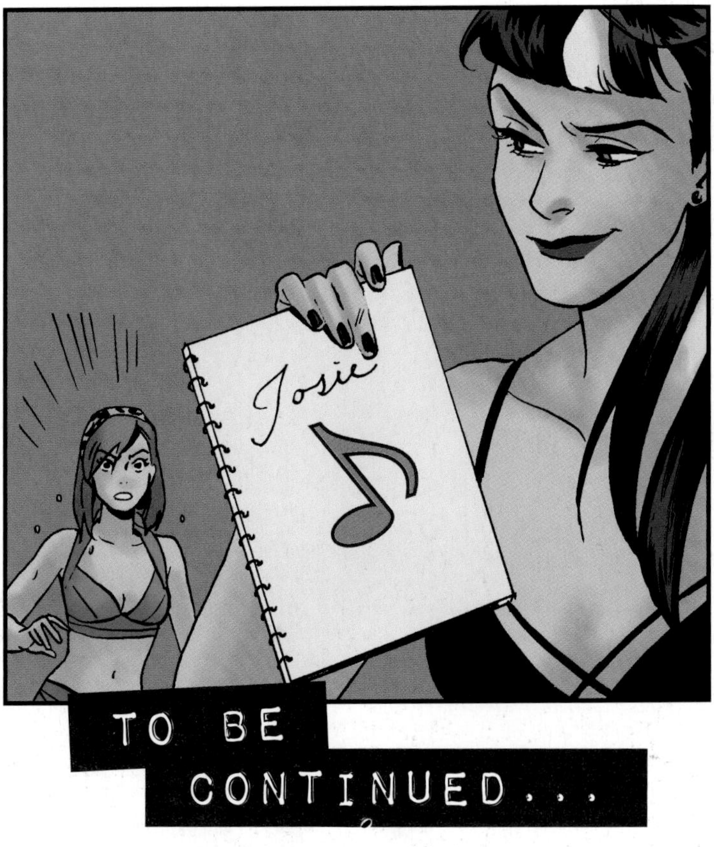
Josie
TO BE
CONTINUED...

ISSUE FOUR

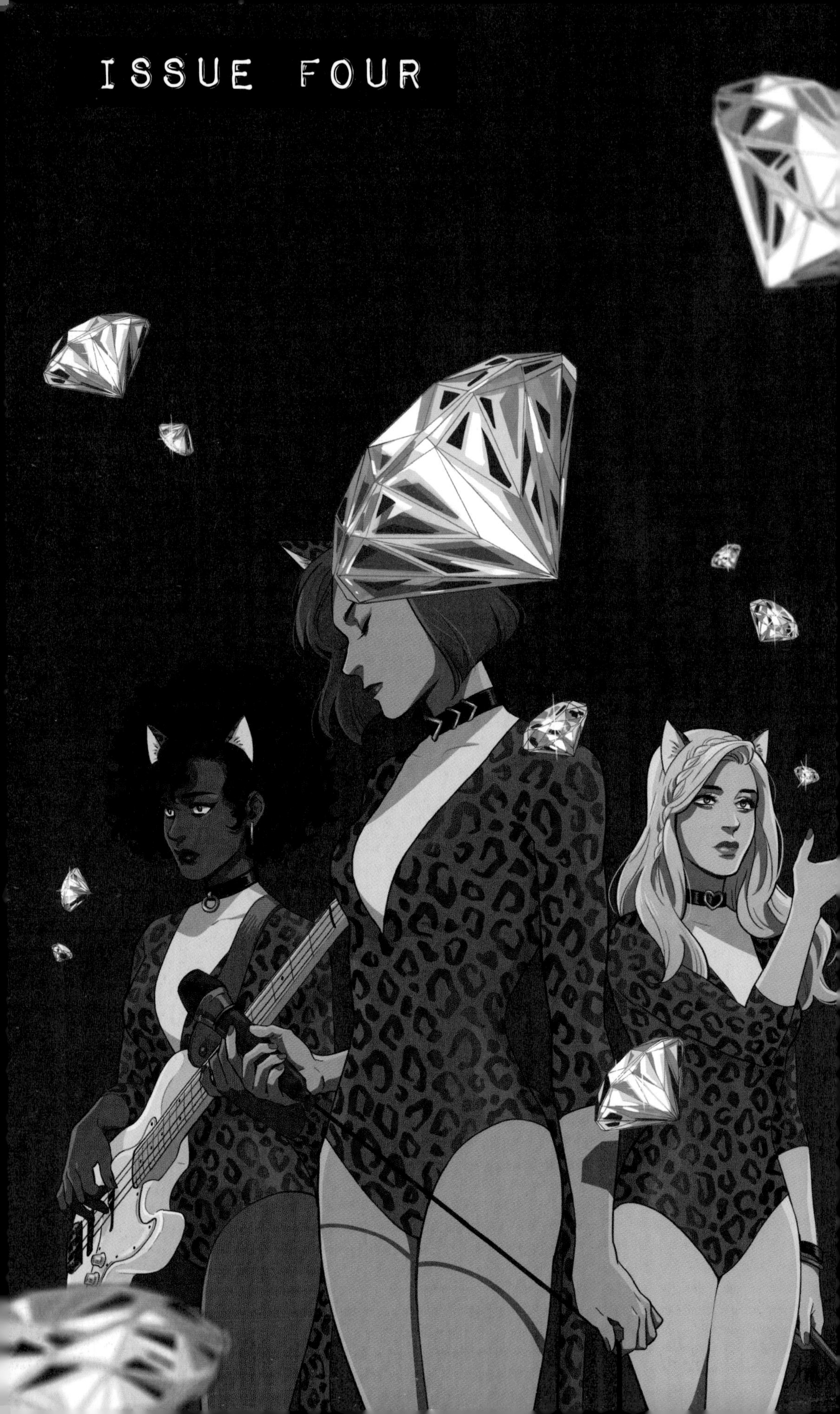

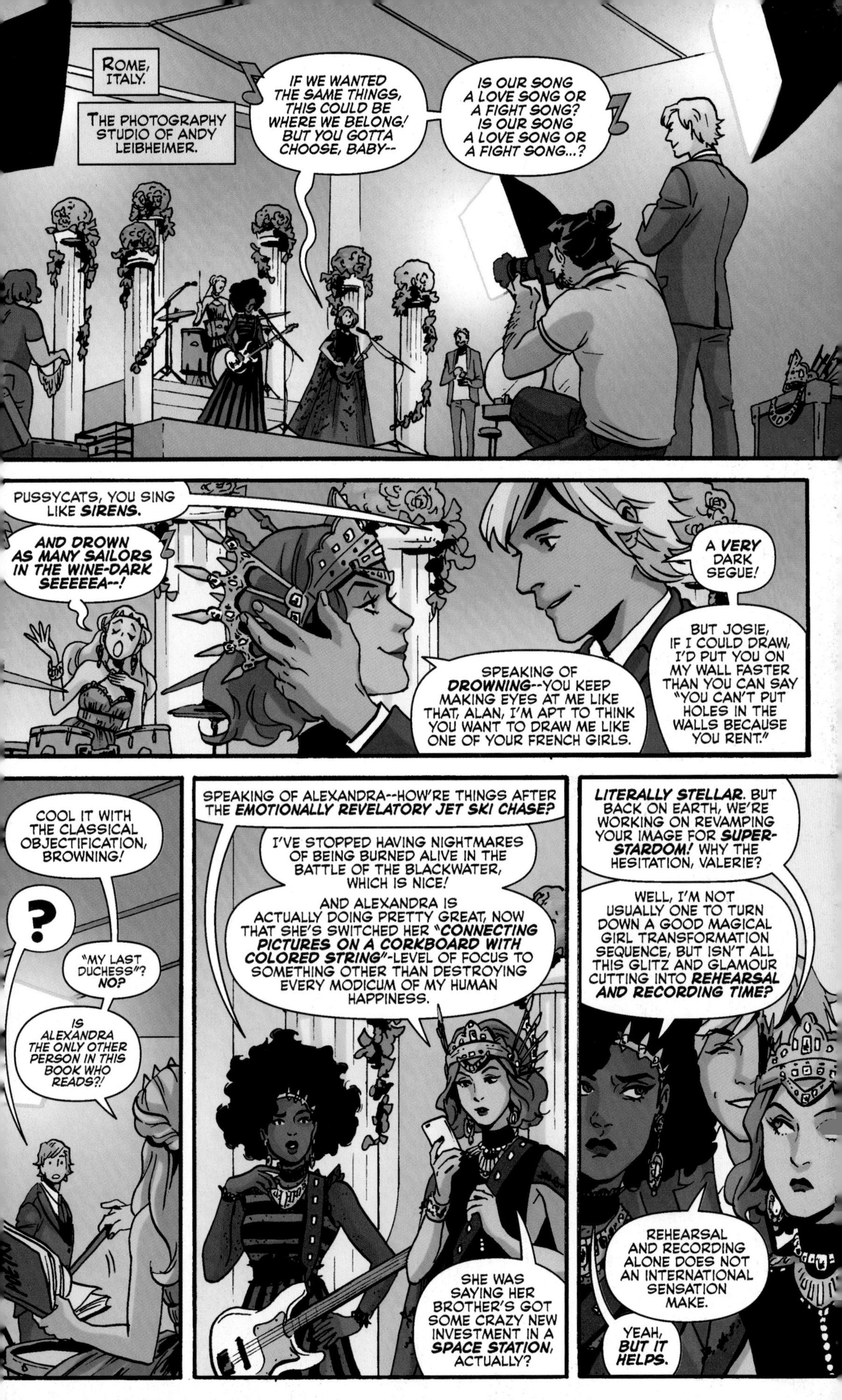
ROME, ITALY.
THE PHOTOGRAPHY STUDIO OF ANDY LEIBHEIMER.
IF WE WANTED THE SAME THINGS, THIS COULD BE WHERE WE BELONG! BUT YOU GOTTA CHOOSE, BABY--
IS OUR SONG A LOVE SONG OR A FIGHT SONG? IS OUR SONG A LOVE SONG OR A FIGHT SONG...?
PUSSYCATS, YOU SING LIKE SIRENS.
AND DROWN AS MANY SAILORS IN THE WINE-DARK SEEEEEA--!
A VERY DARK SEGUE!
SPEAKING OF DROWNING--YOU KEEP MAKING EYES AT ME LIKE THAT, ALAN, I'M APT TO THINK YOU WANT TO DRAW ME LIKE ONE OF YOUR FRENCH GIRLS.
BUT JOSIE, IF I COULD DRAW, I'D PUT YOU ON MY WALL FASTER THAN YOU CAN SAY "YOU CAN'T PUT HOLES IN THE WALLS BECAUSE YOU RENT."
COOL IT WITH THE CLASSICAL OBJECTIFICATION, BROWNING!
?
"MY LAST DUCHESS"? NO?
IS ALEXANDRA THE ONLY OTHER PERSON IN THIS BOOK WHO READS?!
SPEAKING OF ALEXANDRA--HOW'RE THINGS AFTER THE EMOTIONALLY REVELATORY JET SKI CHASE?
I'VE STOPPED HAVING NIGHTMARES OF BEING BURNED ALIVE IN THE BATTLE OF THE BLACKWATER, WHICH IS NICE!
AND ALEXANDRA IS ACTUALLY DOING PRETTY GREAT, NOW THAT SHE'S SWITCHED HER "CONNECTING PICTURES ON A CORKBOARD WITH COLORED STRING"-LEVEL OF FOCUS TO SOMETHING OTHER THAN DESTROYING EVERY MODICUM OF MY HUMAN HAPPINESS.
SHE WAS SAYING HER BROTHER'S GOT SOME CRAZY NEW INVESTMENT IN A SPACE STATION, ACTUALLY?
LITERALLY STELLAR. BUT BACK ON EARTH, WE'RE WORKING ON REVAMPING YOUR IMAGE FOR SUPER-STARDOM! WHY THE HESITATION, VALERIE?
WELL, I'M NOT USUALLY ONE TO TURN DOWN A GOOD MAGICAL GIRL TRANSFORMATION SEQUENCE, BUT ISN'T ALL THIS GLITZ AND GLAMOUR CUTTING INTO REHEARSAL AND RECORDING TIME?
REHEARSAL AND RECORDING ALONE DOES NOT AN INTERNATIONAL SENSATION MAKE.
YEAH, BUT IT HELPS.

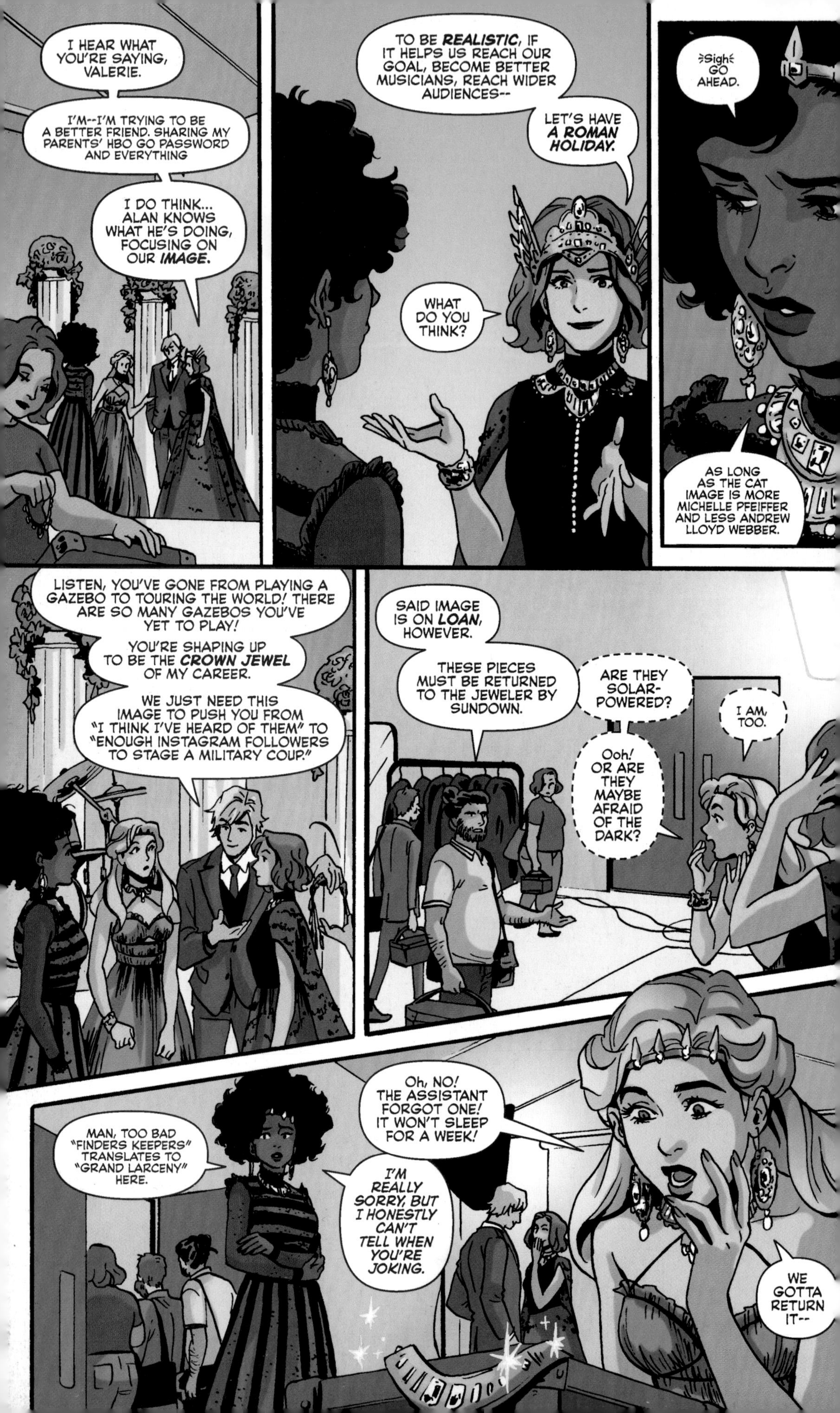
I HEAR WHAT YOU'RE SAYING, VALERIE.
I'M--I'M TRYING TO BE A BETTER FRIEND. SHARING MY PARENTS' HBO GO PASSWORD AND EVERYTHING
I DO THINK... ALAN KNOWS WHAT HE'S DOING, FOCUSING ON OUR IMAGE.
TO BE REALISTIC, IF IT HELPS US REACH OUR GOAL, BECOME BETTER MUSICIANS, REACH WIDER AUDIENCES--
LET'S HAVE A ROMAN HOLIDAY.
WHAT DO YOU THINK?
Sigh GO AHEAD.
AS LONG AS THE CAT IMAGE IS MORE MICHELLE PFEIFFER AND LESS ANDREW LLOYD WEBBER.
LISTEN, YOU'VE GONE FROM PLAYING A GAZEBO TO TOURING THE WORLD! THERE ARE SO MANY GAZEBOS YOU'VE YET TO PLAY!
YOU'RE SHAPING UP TO BE THE CROWN JEWEL OF MY CAREER.
WE JUST NEED THIS IMAGE TO PUSH YOU FROM "I THINK I'VE HEARD OF THEM" TO "ENOUGH INSTAGRAM FOLLOWERS TO STAGE A MILITARY COUP."
SAID IMAGE IS ON LOAN, HOWEVER.
THESE PIECES MUST BE RETURNED TO THE JEWELER BY SUNDOWN.
ARE THEY SOLAR-POWERED?
Ooh! OR ARE THEY MAYBE AFRAID OF THE DARK?
I AM, TOO.
MAN, TOO BAD "FINDERS KEEPERS" TRANSLATES TO "GRAND LARCENY" HERE.
I'M REALLY SORRY, BUT I HONESTLY CAN'T TELL WHEN YOU'RE JOKING.
Oh, NO! THE ASSISTANT FORGOT ONE! IT WON'T SLEEP FOR A WEEK!
WE GOTTA RETURN IT--

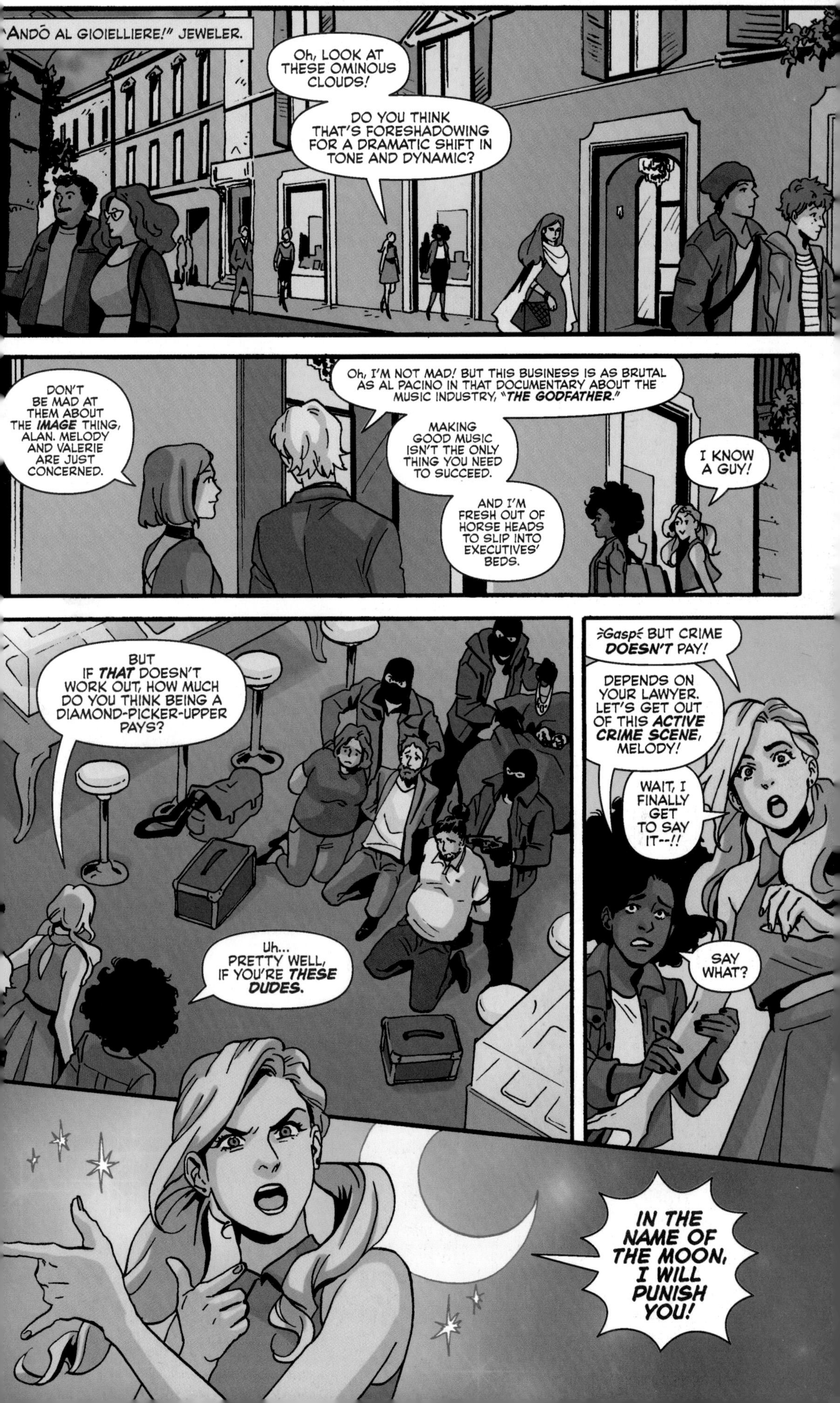
ANDÓ AL GIOIELLIERE!" JEWELER.
Oh, LOOK AT THESE OMINOUS CLOUDS!
DO YOU THINK THAT'S FORESHADOWING FOR A DRAMATIC SHIFT IN TONE AND DYNAMIC?
DON'T BE MAD AT THEM ABOUT THE IMAGE THING, ALAN. MELODY AND VALERIE ARE JUST CONCERNED.
Oh, I'M NOT MAD! BUT THIS BUSINESS IS AS BRUTAL AS AL PACINO IN THAT DOCUMENTARY ABOUT THE MUSIC INDUSTRY, "THE GODFATHER."
MAKING GOOD MUSIC ISN'T THE ONLY THING YOU NEED TO SUCCEED.
AND I'M FRESH OUT OF HORSE HEADS TO SLIP INTO EXECUTIVES' BEDS.
I KNOW A GUY!
BUT IF THAT DOESN'T WORK OUT, HOW MUCH DO YOU THINK BEING A DIAMOND-PICKER-UPPER PAYS?
Uh... PRETTY WELL, IF YOU'RE THESE DUDES.
Gasp BUT CRIME DOESN'T PAY!
DEPENDS ON YOUR LAWYER. LET'S GET OUT OF THIS ACTIVE CRIME SCENE, MELODY!
WAIT, I FINALLY GET TO SAY IT--!!
SAY WHAT?
IN THE NAME OF THE MOON, I WILL PUNISH YOU!

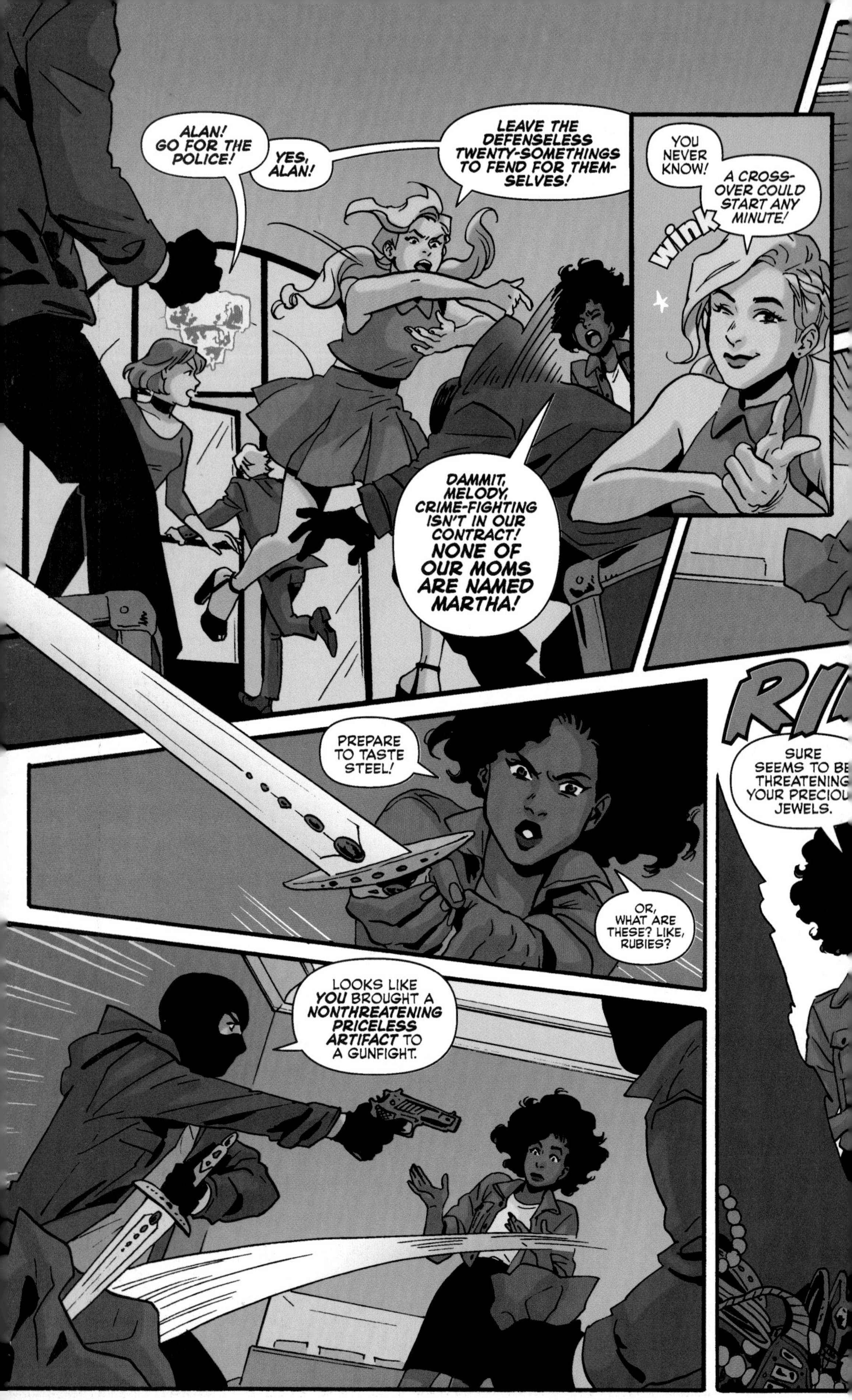
ALAN! GO FOR THE POLICE!
YES, ALAN!
LEAVE THE DEFENSELESS TWENTY-SOMETHINGS TO FEND FOR THEM-SELVES!
YOU NEVER KNOW!
A CROSS-OVER COULD START ANY MINUTE!
wink
DAMMIT, MELODY, CRIME-FIGHTING ISN'T IN OUR CONTRACT! NONE OF OUR MOMS ARE NAMED MARTHA!
PREPARE TO TASTE STEEL!
SURE SEEMS TO BE THREATENING YOUR PRECIOU JEWELS.
OR, WHAT ARE THESE? LIKE, RUBIES?
LOOKS LIKE YOU BROUGHT A NONTHREATENING PRICELESS ARTIFACT TO A GUNFIGHT.

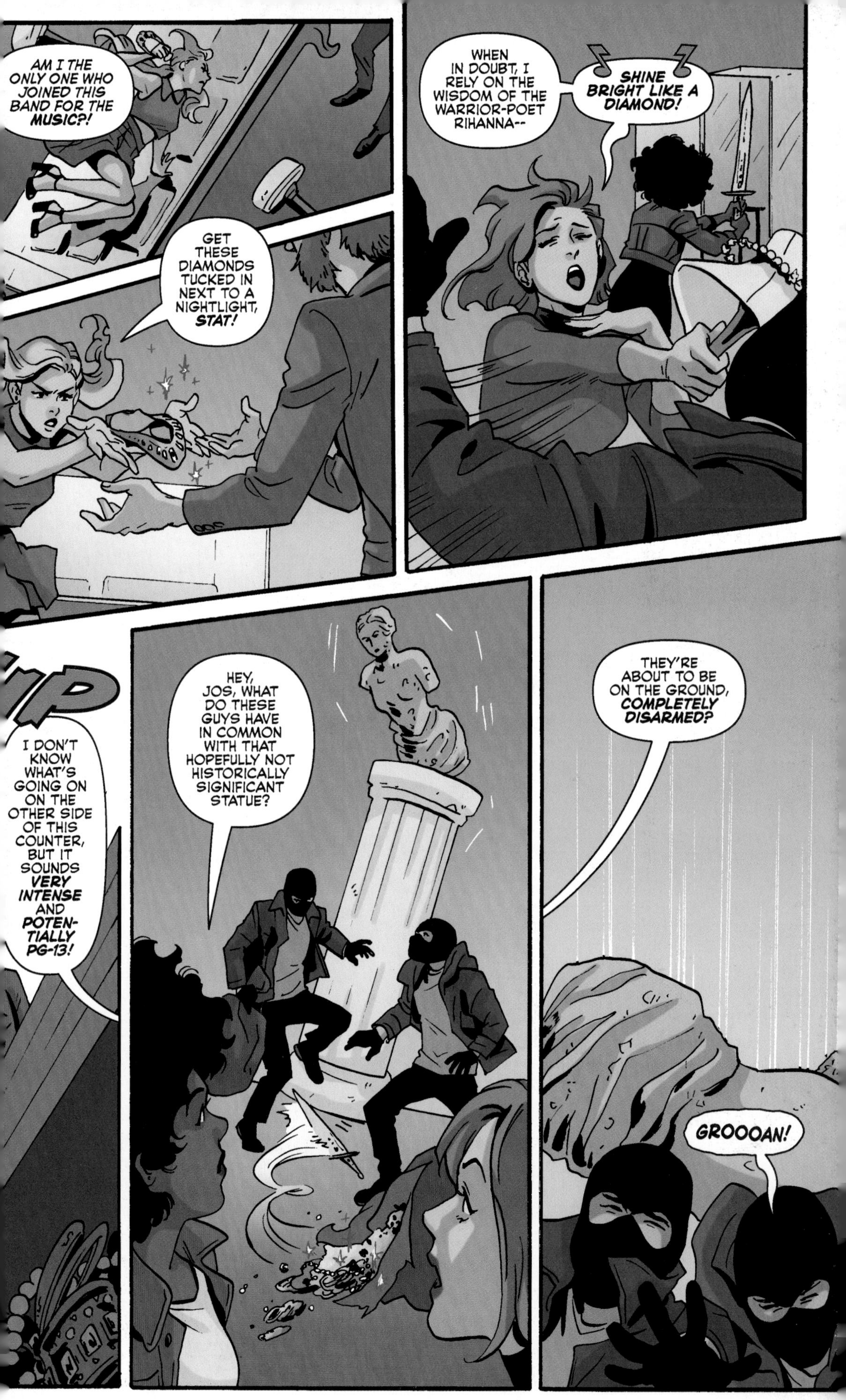
AM I THE ONLY ONE WHO JOINED THIS BAND FOR THE MUSIC?!
GET THESE DIAMONDS TUCKED IN NEXT TO A NIGHTLIGHT, STAT!
WHEN IN DOUBT, I RELY ON THE WISDOM OF THE WARRIOR-POET RIHANNA--
SHINE BRIGHT LIKE A DIAMOND!
I DON'T KNOW WHAT'S GOING ON ON THE OTHER SIDE OF THIS COUNTER, BUT IT SOUNDS VERY INTENSE AND POTEN-TIALLY PG-13!
HEY, JOS, WHAT DO THESE GUYS HAVE IN COMMON WITH THAT HOPEFULLY NOT HISTORICALLY SIGNIFICANT STATUE?
THEY'RE ABOUT TO BE ON THE GROUND, COMPLETELY DISARMED?
GROOOAN!

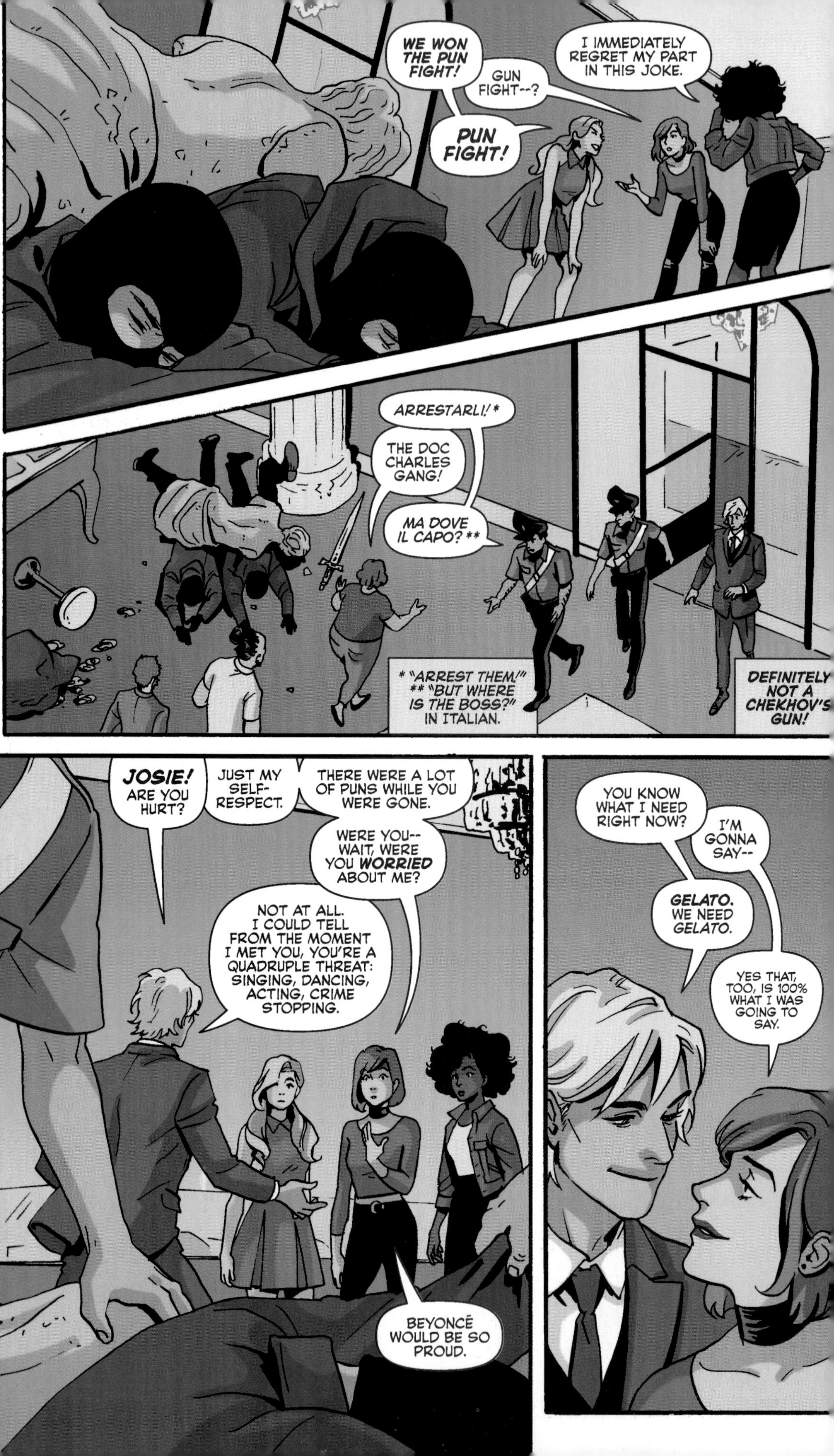
WE WON THE PUN FIGHT!
GUN FIGHT--?
PUN FIGHT!
I IMMEDIATELY REGRET MY PART IN THIS JOKE.
ARRESTARLI!*
THE DOC CHARLES GANG!
MA DOVE IL CAPO?**
* "ARREST THEM!" ** "BUT WHERE IS THE BOSS?" IN ITALIAN.
DEFINITELY NOT A CHEKHOV'S GUN!
JOSIE! ARE YOU HURT?
JUST MY SELF-RESPECT.
THERE WERE A LOT OF PUNS WHILE YOU WERE GONE.
WERE YOU-- WAIT, WERE YOU WORRIED ABOUT ME?
NOT AT ALL. I COULD TELL FROM THE MOMENT I MET YOU, YOU'RE A QUADRUPLE THREAT: SINGING, DANCING, ACTING, CRIME STOPPING.
BEYONCÉ WOULD BE SO PROUD.
YOU KNOW WHAT I NEED RIGHT NOW?
I'M GONNA SAY--
GELATO. WE NEED GELATO.
YES THAT, TOO, IS 100% WHAT I WAS GOING TO SAY.

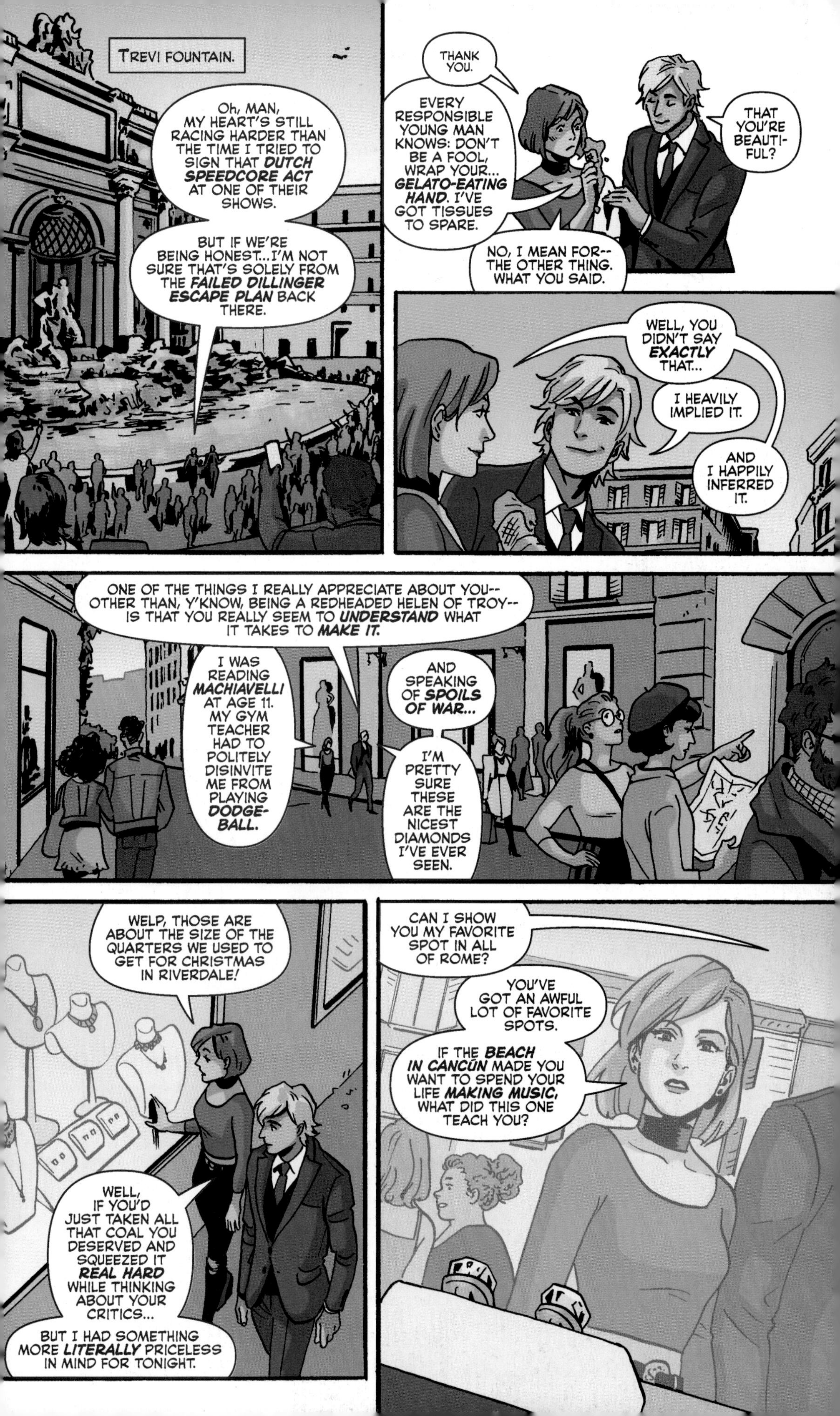
TREVI FOUNTAIN.
Oh, MAN, MY HEART'S STILL RACING HARDER THAN THE TIME I TRIED TO SIGN THAT DUTCH SPEEDCORE ACT AT ONE OF THEIR SHOWS.
BUT IF WE'RE BEING HONEST...I'M NOT SURE THAT'S SOLELY FROM THE FAILED DILLINGER ESCAPE PLAN BACK THERE.
THANK YOU.
EVERY RESPONSIBLE YOUNG MAN KNOWS: DON'T BE A FOOL, WRAP YOUR... GELATO-EATING HAND. I'VE GOT TISSUES TO SPARE.
NO, I MEAN FOR-- THE OTHER THING. WHAT YOU SAID.
THAT YOU'RE BEAUTI-FUL?
WELL, YOU DIDN'T SAY EXACTLY THAT...
I HEAVILY IMPLIED IT.
AND I HAPPILY INFERRED IT.
ONE OF THE THINGS I REALLY APPRECIATE ABOUT YOU-- OTHER THAN, Y'KNOW, BEING A REDHEADED HELEN OF TROY-- IS THAT YOU REALLY SEEM TO UNDERSTAND WHAT IT TAKES TO MAKE IT.
I WAS READING MACHIAVELLI AT AGE 11. MY GYM TEACHER HAD TO POLITELY DISINVITE ME FROM PLAYING DODGE-BALL.
AND SPEAKING OF SPOILS OF WAR...
I'M PRETTY SURE THESE ARE THE NICEST DIAMONDS I'VE EVER SEEN.
WELP, THOSE ARE ABOUT THE SIZE OF THE QUARTERS WE USED TO GET FOR CHRISTMAS IN RIVERDALE!
WELL, IF YOU'D JUST TAKEN ALL THAT COAL YOU DESERVED AND SQUEEZED IT REAL HARD WHILE THINKING ABOUT YOUR CRITICS...
BUT I HAD SOMETHING MORE LITERALLY PRICELESS IN MIND FOR TONIGHT.
CAN I SHOW YOU MY FAVORITE SPOT IN ALL OF ROME?
YOU'VE GOT AN AWFUL LOT OF FAVORITE SPOTS.
IF THE BEACH IN CANCÚN MADE YOU WANT TO SPEND YOUR LIFE MAKING MUSIC, WHAT DID THIS ONE TEACH YOU?

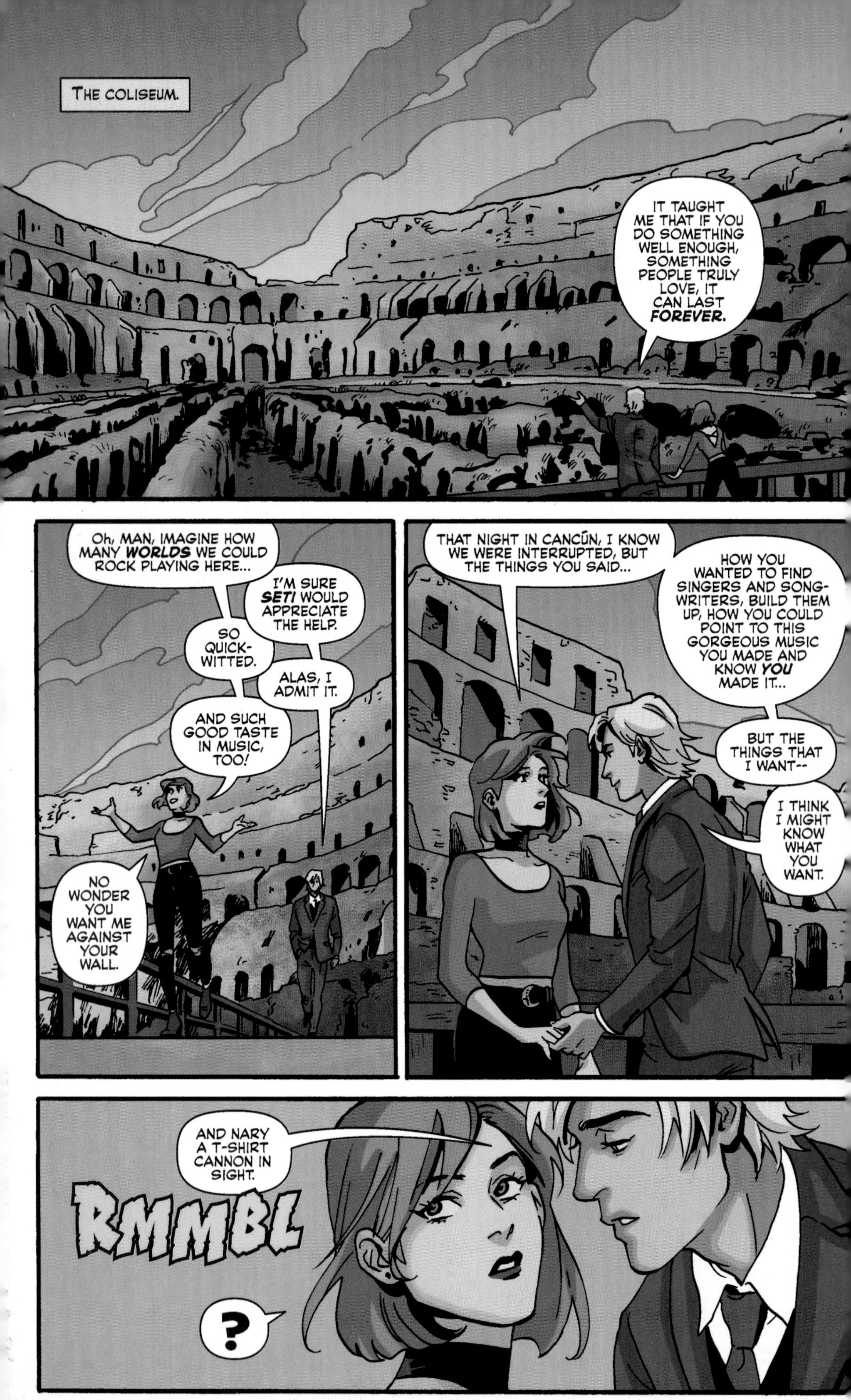
THE COLISEUM.
IT TAUGHT ME THAT IF YOU DO SOMETHING WELL ENOUGH, SOMETHING PEOPLE TRULY LOVE, IT CAN LAST FOREVER.
Oh, MAN, IMAGINE HOW MANY WORLDS WE COULD ROCK PLAYING HERE...
I'M SURE SETI WOULD APPRECIATE THE HELP.
SO QUICK-WITTED.
ALAS, I ADMIT IT.
AND SUCH GOOD TASTE IN MUSIC, TOO!
NO WONDER YOU WANT ME AGAINST YOUR WALL.
THAT NIGHT IN CANCÚN, I KNOW WE WERE INTERRUPTED, BUT THE THINGS YOU SAID...
HOW YOU WANTED TO FIND SINGERS AND SONG-WRITERS, BUILD THEM UP, HOW YOU COULD POINT TO THIS GORGEOUS MUSIC YOU MADE AND KNOW YOU MADE IT...
BUT THE THINGS THAT I WANT--
I THINK I MIGHT KNOW WHAT YOU WANT.
AND NARY A T-SHIRT CANNON IN SIGHT.
RMMBL
?

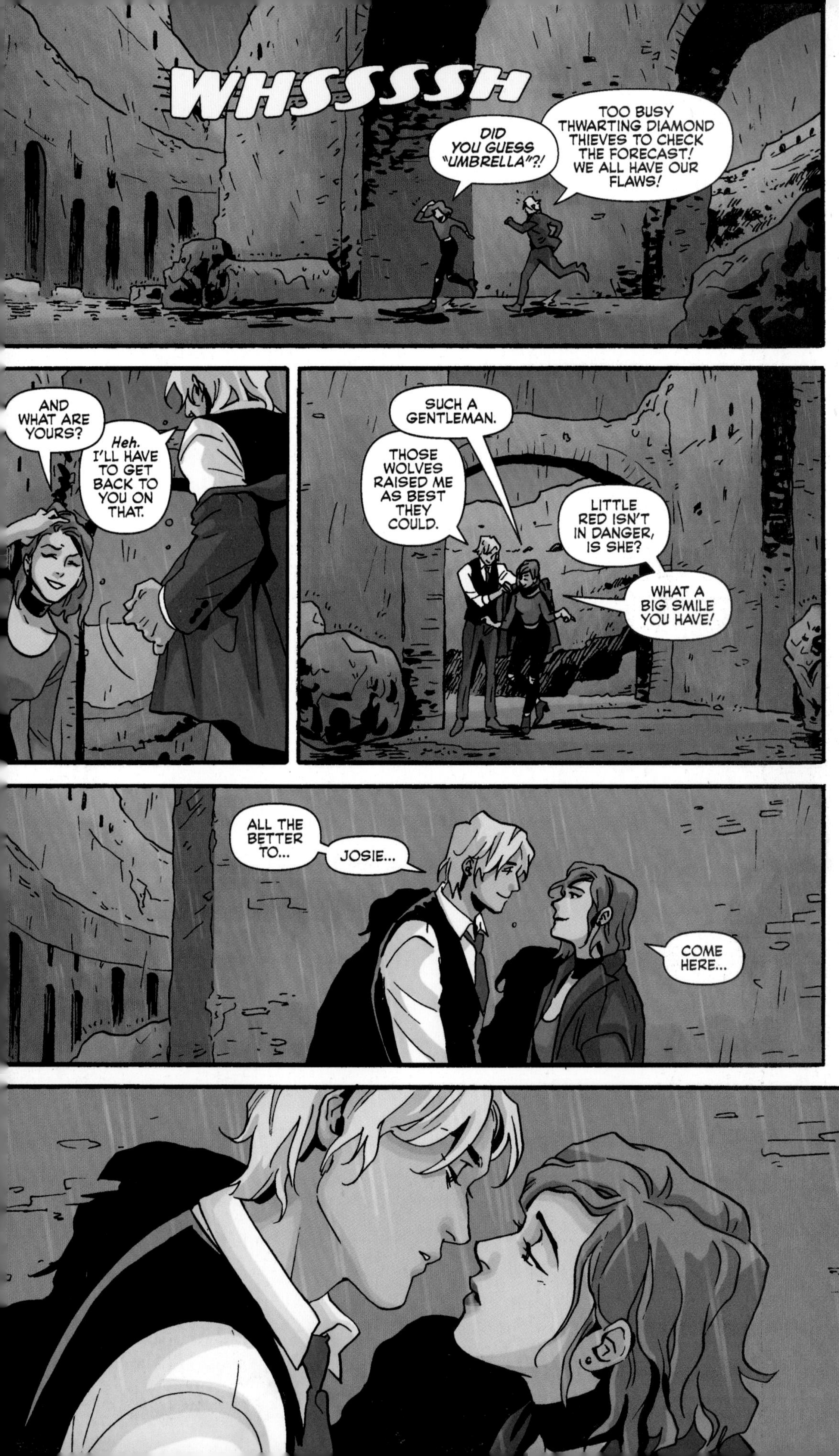
WHSSSSH
DID YOU GUESS "UMBRELLA"?!
TOO BUSY THWARTING DIAMOND THIEVES TO CHECK THE FORECAST! WE ALL HAVE OUR FLAWS!
AND WHAT ARE YOURS?
Heh. I'LL HAVE TO GET BACK TO YOU ON THAT.
SUCH A GENTLEMAN.
THOSE WOLVES RAISED ME AS BEST THEY COULD.
LITTLE RED ISN'T IN DANGER, IS SHE?
WHAT A BIG SMILE YOU HAVE!
ALL THE BETTER TO...
JOSIE...
COME HERE...

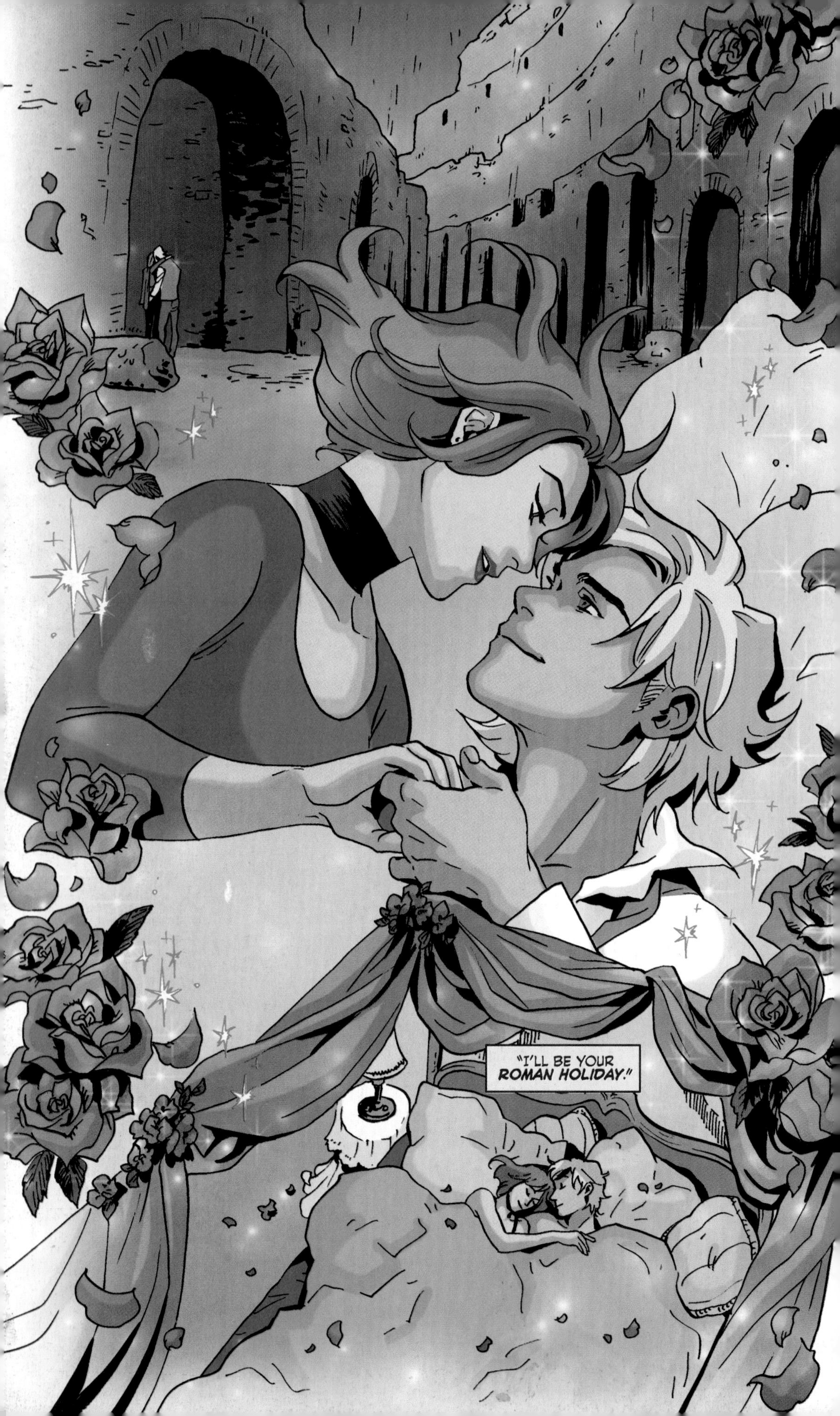
"I'LL BE YOUR ROMAN HOLIDAY."

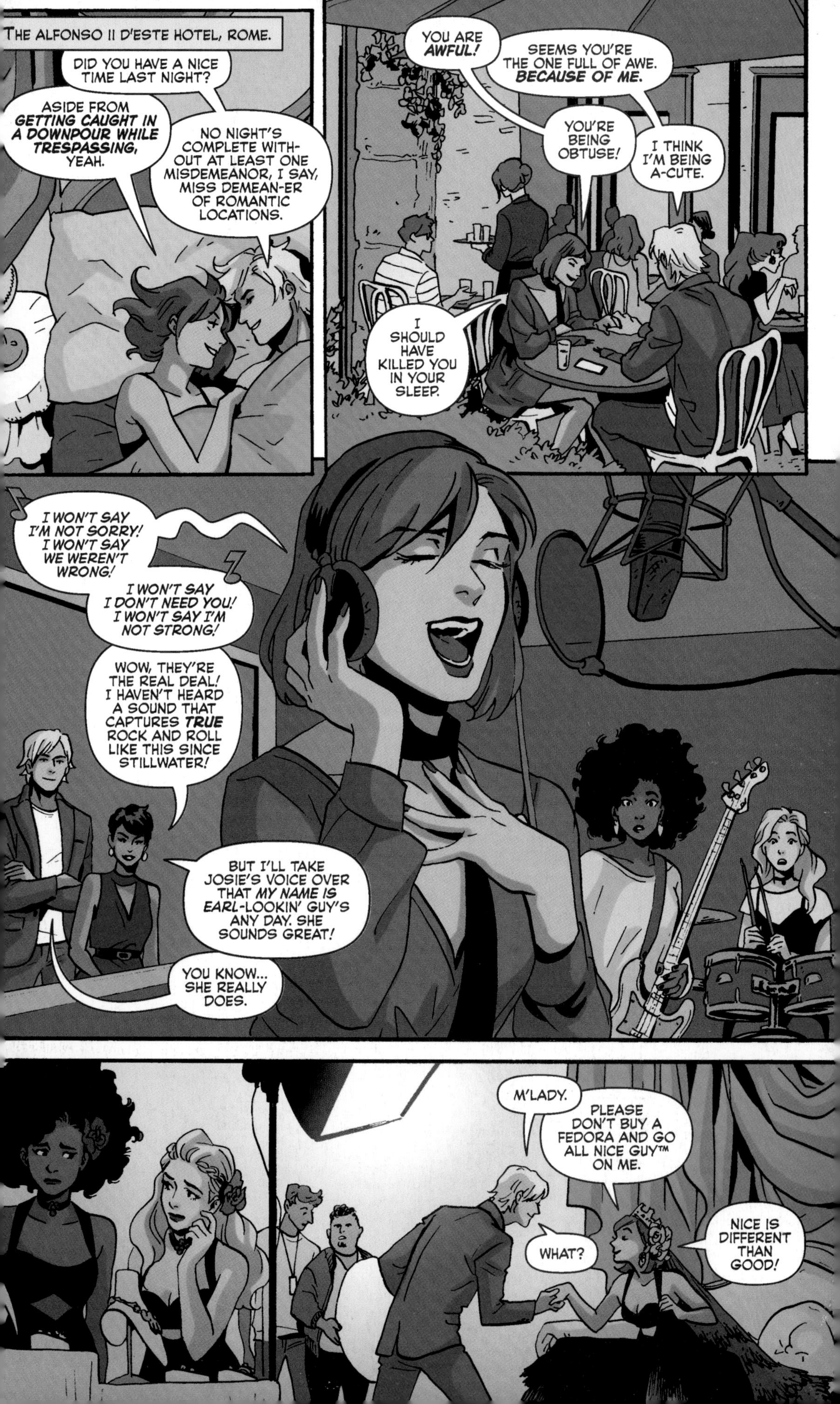
THE ALFONSO II D'ESTE HOTEL, ROME.
DID YOU HAVE A NICE TIME LAST NIGHT?
ASIDE FROM GETTING CAUGHT IN A DOWNPOUR WHILE TRESPASSING, YEAH.
NO NIGHT'S COMPLETE WITH-OUT AT LEAST ONE MISDEMEANOR, I SAY, MISS DEMEAN-ER OF ROMANTIC LOCATIONS.
YOU ARE AWFUL!
SEEMS YOU'RE THE ONE FULL OF AWE. BECAUSE OF ME.
YOU'RE BEING OBTUSE!
I THINK I'M BEING A-CUTE.
I SHOULD HAVE KILLED YOU IN YOUR SLEEP.
I WON'T SAY I'M NOT SORRY! I WON'T SAY WE WEREN'T WRONG!
I WON'T SAY I DON'T NEED YOU! I WON'T SAY I'M NOT STRONG!
WOW, THEY'RE THE REAL DEAL! I HAVEN'T HEARD A SOUND THAT CAPTURES TRUE ROCK AND ROLL LIKE THIS SINCE STILLWATER!
BUT I'LL TAKE JOSIE'S VOICE OVER THAT MY NAME IS EARL-LOOKIN' GUY'S ANY DAY. SHE SOUNDS GREAT!
YOU KNOW... SHE REALLY DOES.
M'LADY.
PLEASE DON'T BUY A FEDORA AND GO ALL NICE GUY™ ON ME.
WHAT?
NICE IS DIFFERENT THAN GOOD!

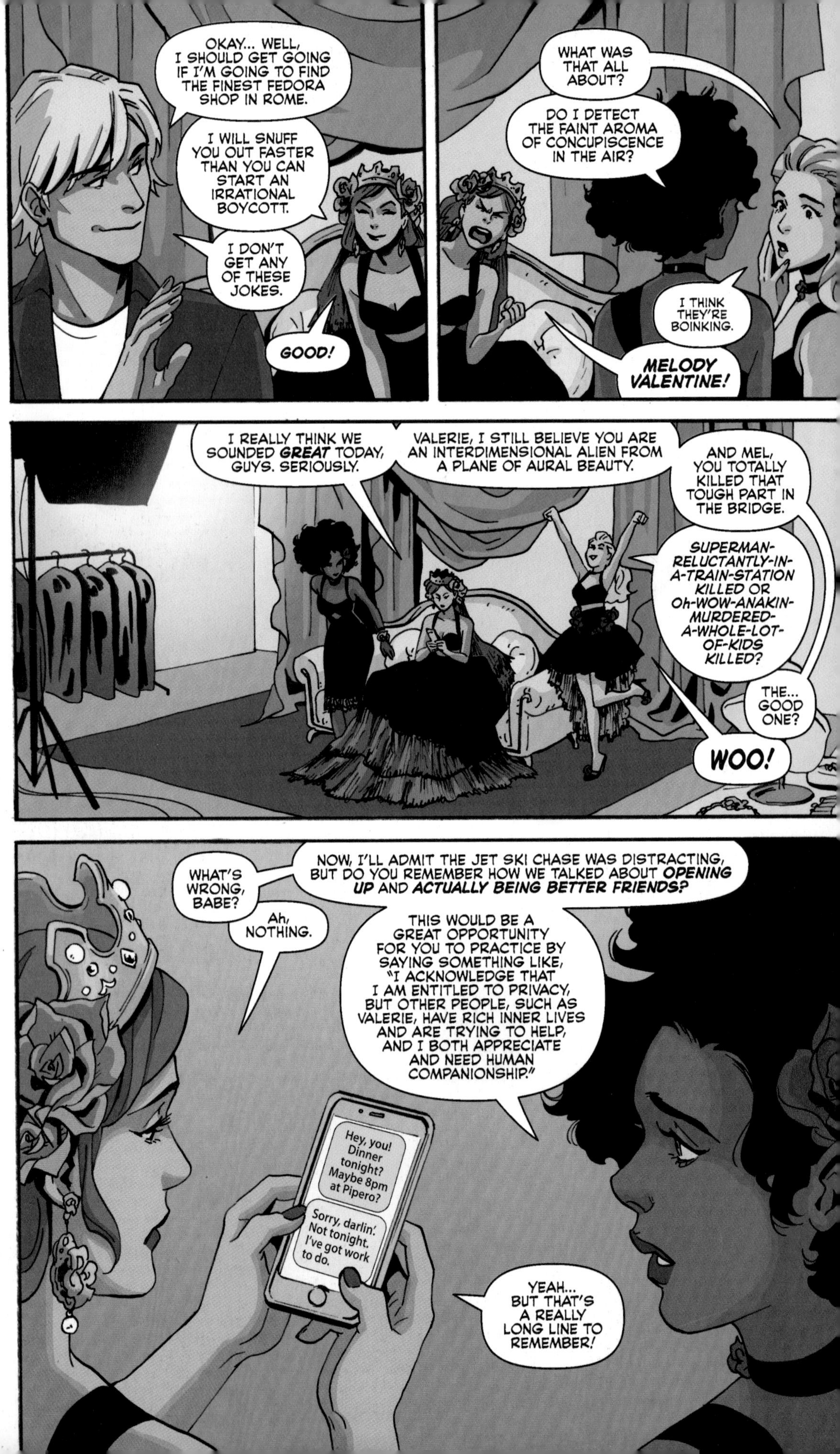
OKAY... WELL, I SHOULD GET GOING IF I'M GOING TO FIND THE FINEST FEDORA SHOP IN ROME.
I WILL SNUFF YOU OUT FASTER THAN YOU CAN START AN IRRATIONAL BOYCOTT.
I DON'T GET ANY OF THESE JOKES.
GOOD!
WHAT WAS THAT ALL ABOUT?
DO I DETECT THE FAINT AROMA OF CONCUPISCENCE IN THE AIR?
I THINK THEY'RE BOINKING.
MELODY VALENTINE!
I REALLY THINK WE SOUNDED GREAT TODAY, GUYS. SERIOUSLY.
VALERIE, I STILL BELIEVE YOU ARE AN INTERDIMENSIONAL ALIEN FROM A PLANE OF AURAL BEAUTY.
AND MEL, YOU TOTALLY KILLED THAT TOUGH PART IN THE BRIDGE.
SUPERMAN-RELUCTANTLY-IN-A-TRAIN-STATION KILLED OR Oh-WOW-ANAKIN-MURDERED-A-WHOLE-LOT-OF-KIDS KILLED?
THE... GOOD ONE?
WOO!
WHAT'S WRONG, BABE?
Ah, NOTHING.
NOW, I'LL ADMIT THE JET SKI CHASE WAS DISTRACTING, BUT DO YOU REMEMBER HOW WE TALKED ABOUT OPENING UP AND ACTUALLY BEING BETTER FRIENDS?
THIS WOULD BE A GREAT OPPORTUNITY FOR YOU TO PRACTICE BY SAYING SOMETHING LIKE, "I ACKNOWLEDGE THAT I AM ENTITLED TO PRIVACY, BUT OTHER PEOPLE, SUCH AS VALERIE, HAVE RICH INNER LIVES AND ARE TRYING TO HELP, AND I BOTH APPRECIATE AND NEED HUMAN COMPANIONSHIP."
Hey, you! Dinner tonight? Maybe 8pm at Pipero?
Sorry, darlin'. Not tonight. I've got work to do.
YEAH... BUT THAT'S A REALLY LONG LINE TO REMEMBER!

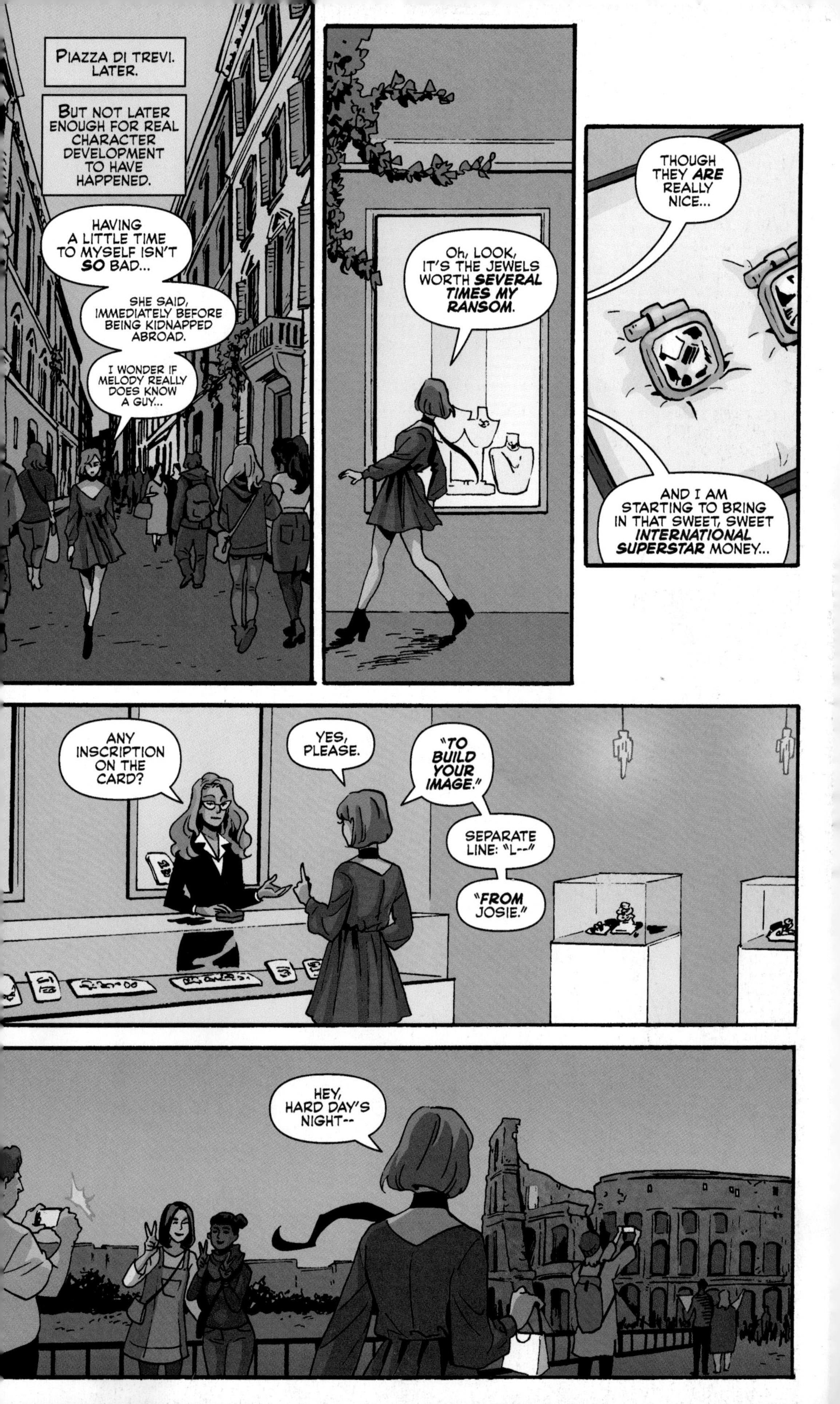
Piazza di trevi. Later.
But not later enough for real character development to have happened.
Having a little time to myself isn't so bad...
She said, immediately before being kidnapped abroad.
I wonder if Melody really does know a guy...
Oh, look, it's the jewels worth several times my ransom.
Though they are really nice...
And I am starting to bring in that sweet, sweet international superstar money...
Any inscription on the card?
Yes, please.
"To build your image."
Separate line: "L--"
"From Josie."
Hey, Hard Day's Night--

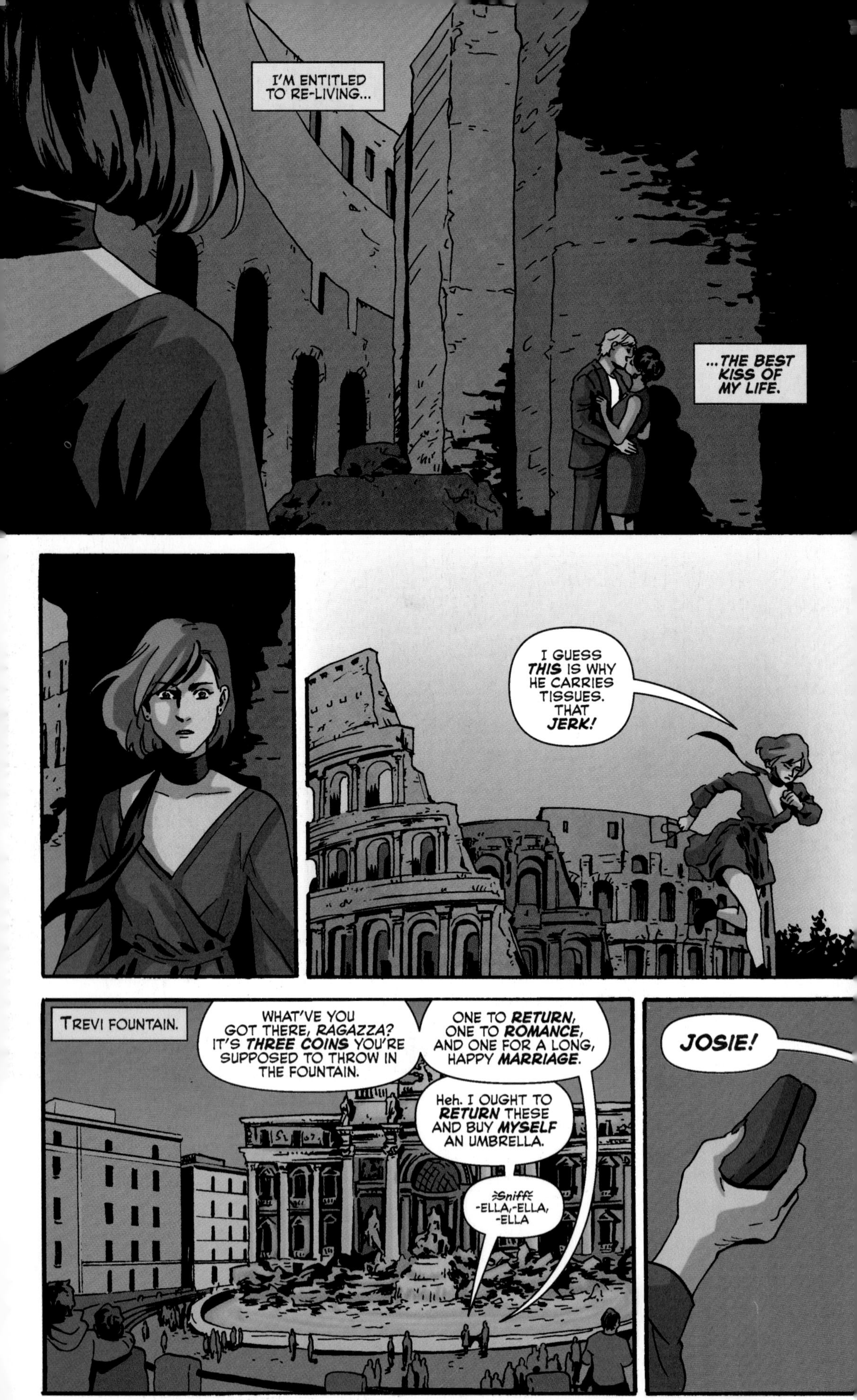
I'M ENTITLED TO RE-LIVING...
...THE BEST KISS OF MY LIFE.
I GUESS THIS IS WHY HE CARRIES TISSUES. THAT JERK!
TREVI FOUNTAIN.
WHAT'VE YOU GOT THERE, RAGAZZA? IT'S THREE COINS YOU'RE SUPPOSED TO THROW IN THE FOUNTAIN.
ONE TO RETURN, ONE TO ROMANCE, AND ONE FOR A LONG, HAPPY MARRIAGE.
Heh. I OUGHT TO RETURN THESE AND BUY MYSELF AN UMBRELLA.
Sniff -ELLA,-ELLA, -ELLA
JOSIE!

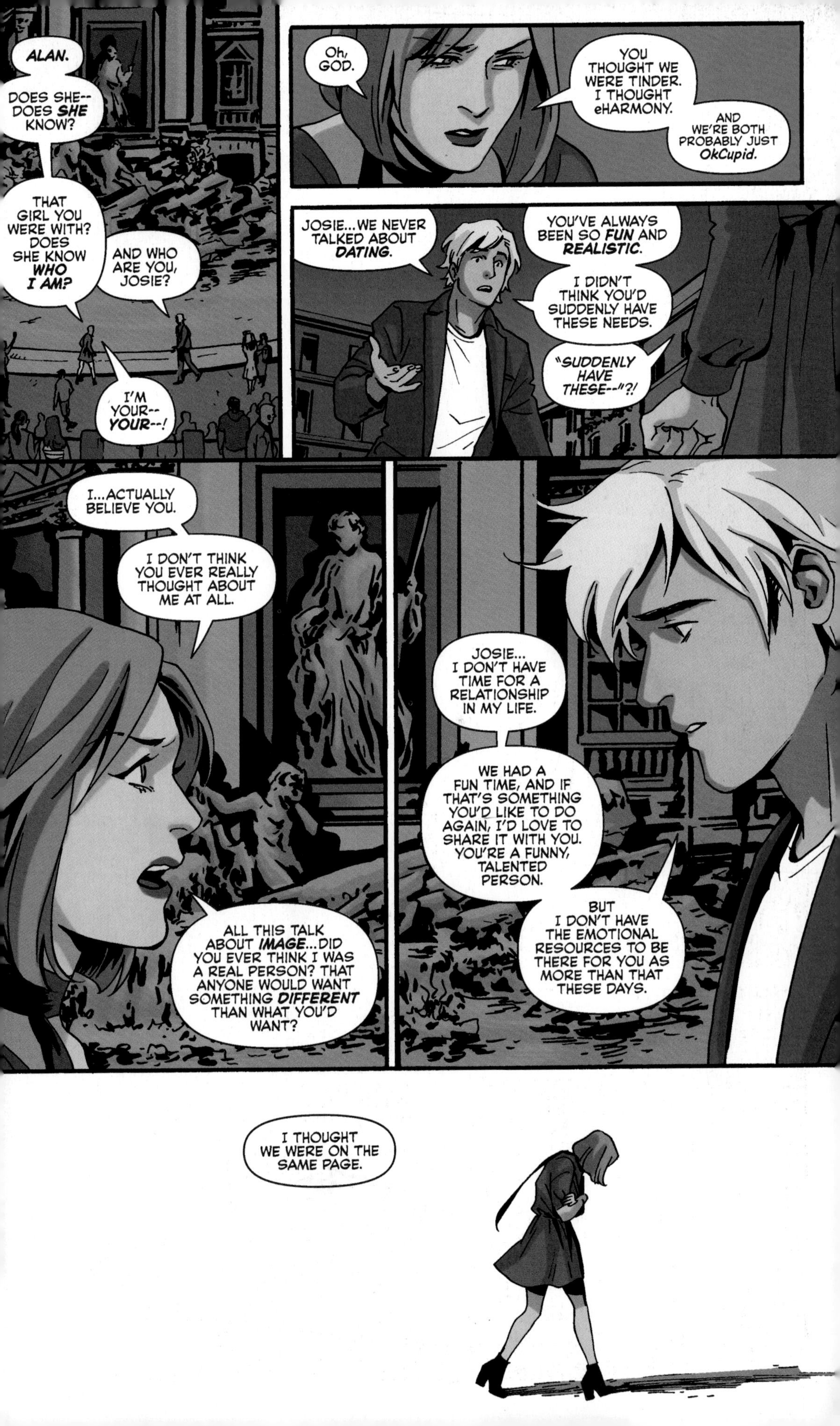
ALAN.
DOES SHE--DOES SHE KNOW?
THAT GIRL YOU WERE WITH? DOES SHE KNOW WHO I AM?
AND WHO ARE YOU, JOSIE?
I'M YOUR--YOUR--!
Oh, GOD.
YOU THOUGHT WE WERE TINDER. I THOUGHT eHARMONY.
AND WE'RE BOTH PROBABLY JUST OkCupid.
JOSIE...WE NEVER TALKED ABOUT DATING.
YOU'VE ALWAYS BEEN SO FUN AND REALISTIC.
I DIDN'T THINK YOU'D SUDDENLY HAVE THESE NEEDS.
"SUDDENLY HAVE THESE--"?!
I...ACTUALLY BELIEVE YOU.
I DON'T THINK YOU EVER REALLY THOUGHT ABOUT ME AT ALL.
ALL THIS TALK ABOUT IMAGE...DID YOU EVER THINK I WAS A REAL PERSON? THAT ANYONE WOULD WANT SOMETHING DIFFERENT THAN WHAT YOU'D WANT?
JOSIE... I DON'T HAVE TIME FOR A RELATIONSHIP IN MY LIFE.
WE HAD A FUN TIME, AND IF THAT'S SOMETHING YOU'D LIKE TO DO AGAIN, I'D LOVE TO SHARE IT WITH YOU. YOU'RE A FUNNY, TALENTED PERSON.
BUT I DON'T HAVE THE EMOTIONAL RESOURCES TO BE THERE FOR YOU AS MORE THAN THAT THESE DAYS.
I THOUGHT WE WERE ON THE SAME PAGE.

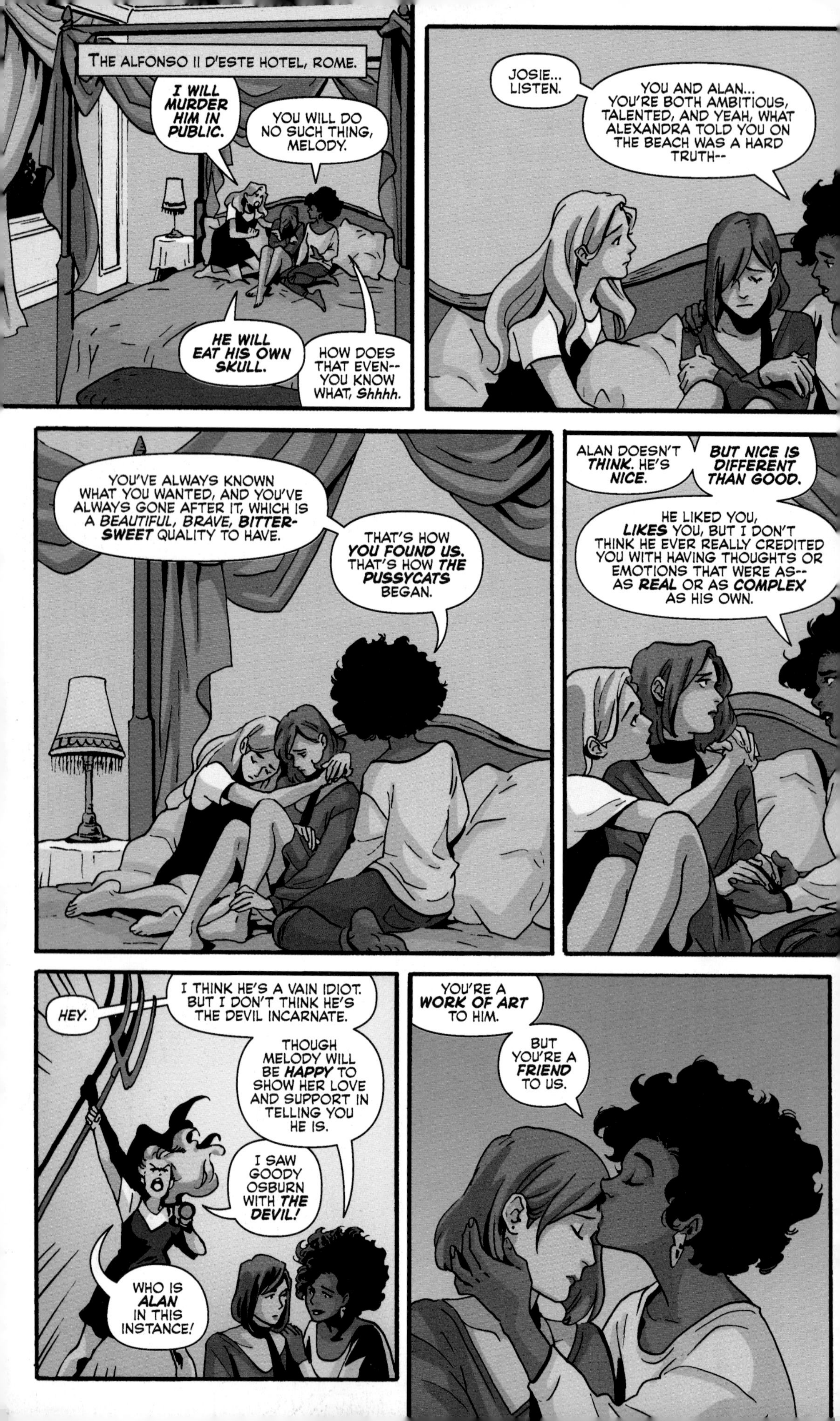

THE ALFONSO II D'ESTE HOTEL, ROME.
I WILL MURDER HIM IN PUBLIC.
YOU WILL DO NO SUCH THING, MELODY.
HE WILL EAT HIS OWN SKULL.
HOW DOES THAT EVEN-- YOU KNOW WHAT, Shhhh.
JOSIE... LISTEN.
YOU AND ALAN... YOU'RE BOTH AMBITIOUS, TALENTED, AND YEAH, WHAT ALEXANDRA TOLD YOU ON THE BEACH WAS A HARD TRUTH--
YOU'VE ALWAYS KNOWN WHAT YOU WANTED, AND YOU'VE ALWAYS GONE AFTER IT, WHICH IS A BEAUTIFUL, BRAVE, BITTER-SWEET QUALITY TO HAVE.
THAT'S HOW YOU FOUND US. THAT'S HOW THE PUSSYCATS BEGAN.
ALAN DOESN'T THINK. HE'S NICE.
BUT NICE IS DIFFERENT THAN GOOD.
HE LIKED YOU, LIKES YOU, BUT I DON'T THINK HE EVER REALLY CREDITED YOU WITH HAVING THOUGHTS OR EMOTIONS THAT WERE AS-- AS REAL OR AS COMPLEX AS HIS OWN.
HEY.
I THINK HE'S A VAIN IDIOT. BUT I DON'T THINK HE'S THE DEVIL INCARNATE.
THOUGH MELODY WILL BE HAPPY TO SHOW HER LOVE AND SUPPORT IN TELLING YOU HE IS.
I SAW GOODY OSBURN WITH THE DEVIL!
WHO IS ALAN IN THIS INSTANCE!
YOU'RE A WORK OF ART TO HIM.
BUT YOU'RE A FRIEND TO US.

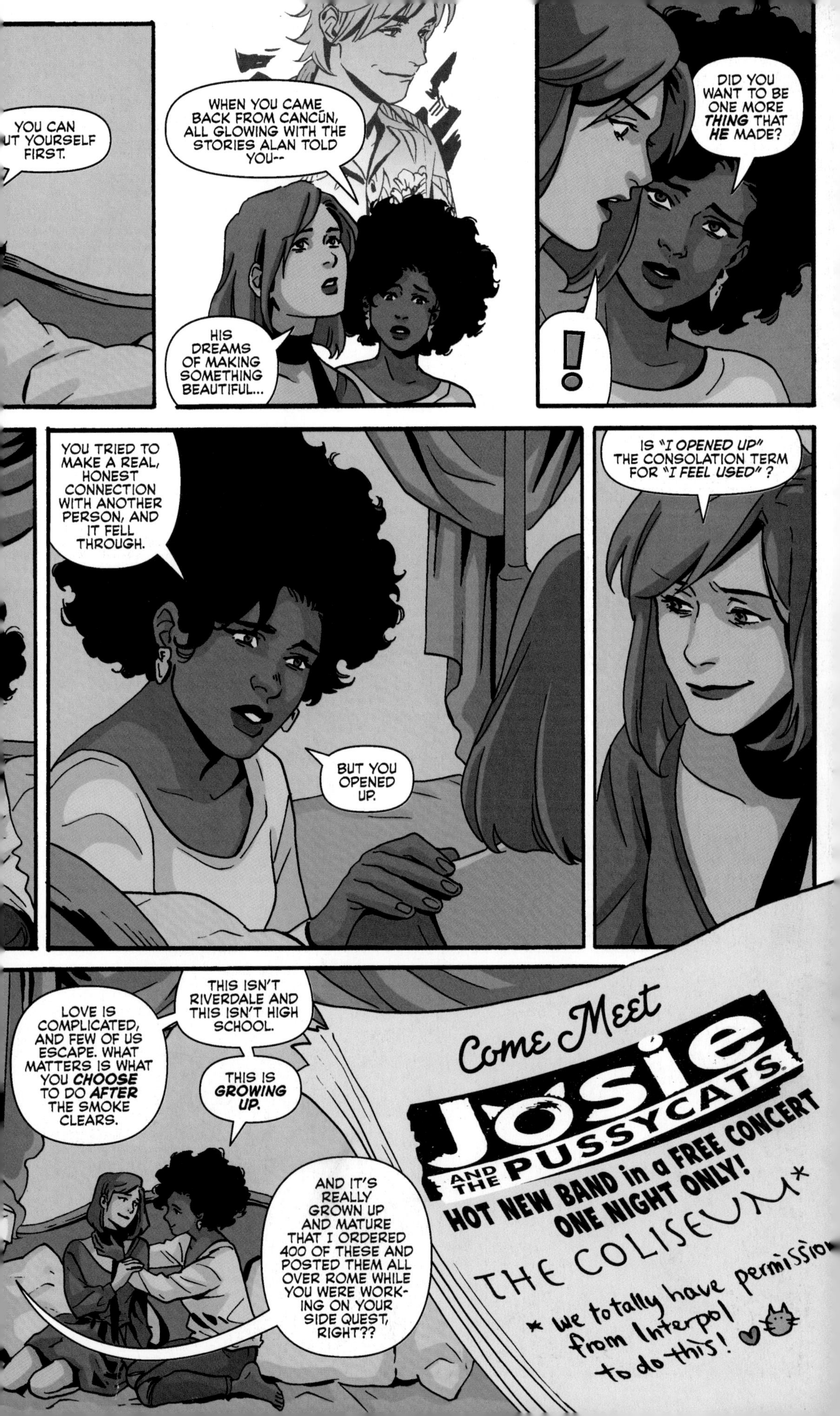
YOU CAN
UT YOURSELF
FIRST.
WHEN YOU CAME BACK FROM CANCÚN, ALL GLOWING WITH THE STORIES ALAN TOLD YOU--
HIS DREAMS OF MAKING SOMETHING BEAUTIFUL...
DID YOU WANT TO BE ONE MORE *THING* THAT *HE* MADE?
!
YOU TRIED TO MAKE A REAL, HONEST CONNECTION WITH ANOTHER PERSON, AND IT FELL THROUGH.
BUT YOU OPENED UP.
IS *"I OPENED UP"* THE CONSOLATION TERM FOR *"I FEEL USED"*?
LOVE IS COMPLICATED, AND FEW OF US ESCAPE. WHAT MATTERS IS WHAT YOU *CHOOSE* TO DO *AFTER* THE SMOKE CLEARS.
THIS ISN'T RIVERDALE AND THIS ISN'T HIGH SCHOOL.
THIS IS *GROWING UP.*
AND IT'S REALLY GROWN UP AND MATURE THAT I ORDERED 400 OF THESE AND POSTED THEM ALL OVER ROME WHILE YOU WERE WORKING ON YOUR SIDE QUEST, RIGHT??
Come Meet
JOSIE AND THE PUSSYCATS
HOT NEW BAND in a FREE CONCERT ONE NIGHT ONLY!
THE COLISEUM*
* we totally have permission from Interpol to do this!

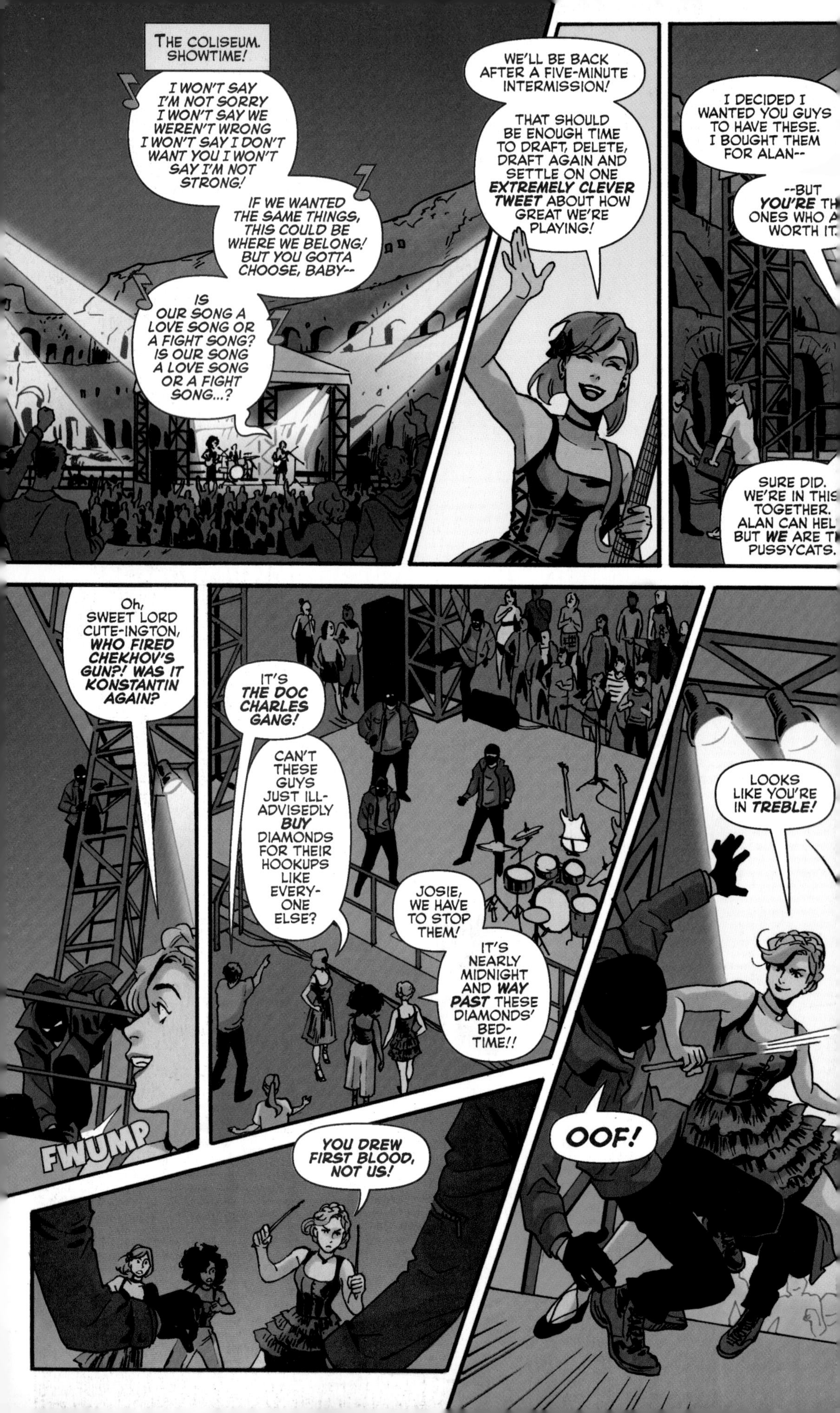
THE COLISEUM. SHOWTIME!
I WON'T SAY I'M NOT SORRY I WON'T SAY WE WEREN'T WRONG I WON'T SAY I DON'T WANT YOU I WON'T SAY I'M NOT STRONG!
IF WE WANTED THE SAME THINGS, THIS COULD BE WHERE WE BELONG! BUT YOU GOTTA CHOOSE, BABY--
IS OUR SONG A LOVE SONG OR A FIGHT SONG? IS OUR SONG A LOVE SONG OR A FIGHT SONG...?
WE'LL BE BACK AFTER A FIVE-MINUTE INTERMISSION!
THAT SHOULD BE ENOUGH TIME TO DRAFT, DELETE, DRAFT AGAIN AND SETTLE ON ONE EXTREMELY CLEVER TWEET ABOUT HOW GREAT WE'RE PLAYING!
I DECIDED I WANTED YOU GUYS TO HAVE THESE. I BOUGHT THEM FOR ALAN--
--BUT YOU'RE TH ONES WHO A WORTH IT.
SURE DID. WE'RE IN THIS TOGETHER. ALAN CAN HEL BUT WE ARE T PUSSYCATS.
Oh, SWEET LORD CUTE-INGTON, WHO FIRED CHEKHOV'S GUN?! WAS IT KONSTANTIN AGAIN?
FWUMP
IT'S THE DOC CHARLES GANG!
CAN'T THESE GUYS JUST ILL-ADVISEDLY BUY DIAMONDS FOR THEIR HOOKUPS LIKE EVERY-ONE ELSE?
JOSIE, WE HAVE TO STOP THEM!
IT'S NEARLY MIDNIGHT AND WAY PAST THESE DIAMONDS' BED-TIME!!
LOOKS LIKE YOU'RE IN TREBLE!
OOF!
YOU DREW FIRST BLOOD, NOT US!

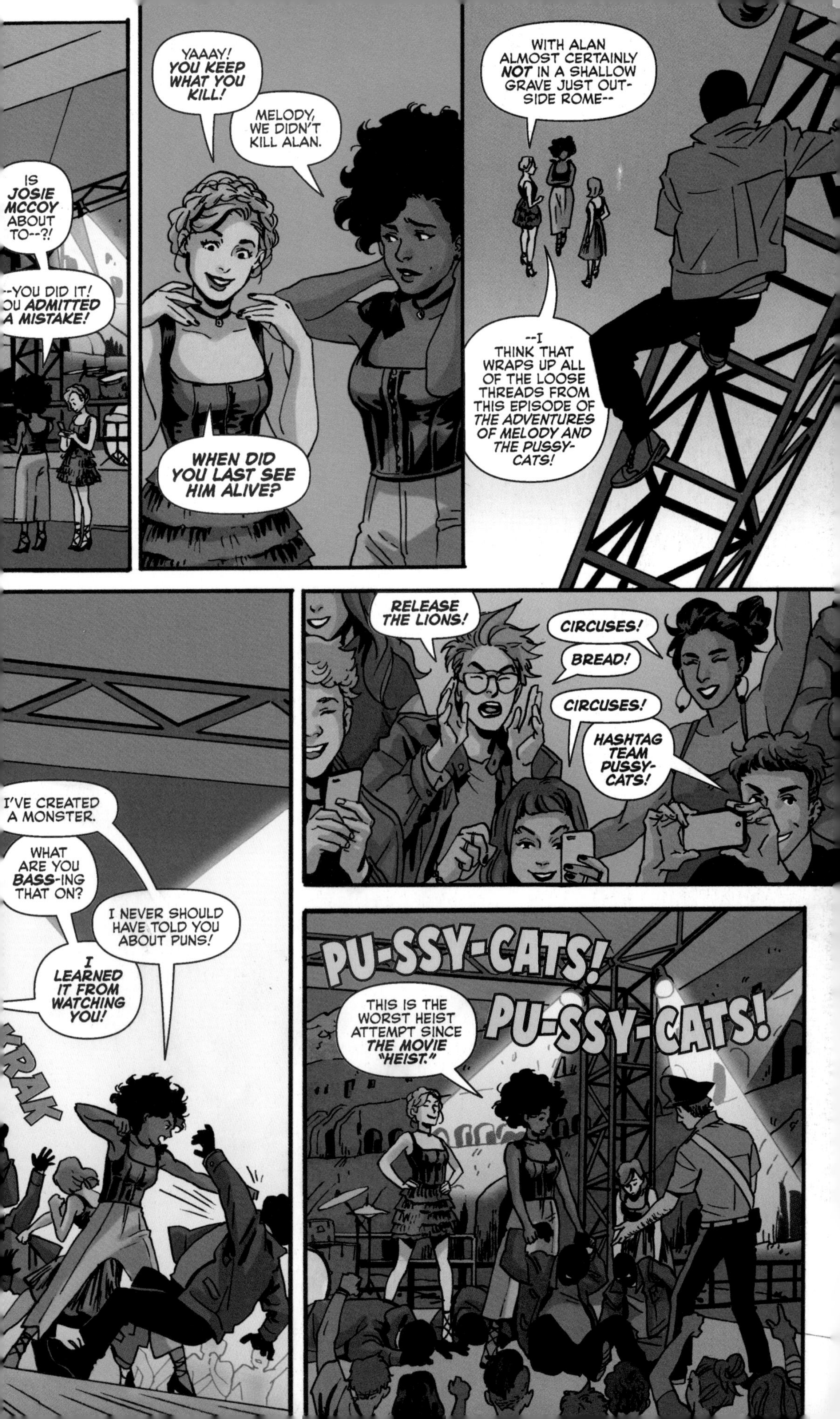

IS JOSIE MCCOY ABOUT TO--?!
--YOU DID IT! OU ADMITTED A MISTAKE!
YAAAY! YOU KEEP WHAT YOU KILL!
MELODY, WE DIDN'T KILL ALAN.
WHEN DID YOU LAST SEE HIM ALIVE?
WITH ALAN ALMOST CERTAINLY NOT IN A SHALLOW GRAVE JUST OUT-SIDE ROME--
--I THINK THAT WRAPS UP ALL OF THE LOOSE THREADS FROM THIS EPISODE OF THE ADVENTURES OF MELODY AND THE PUSSY-CATS!
I'VE CREATED A MONSTER.
WHAT ARE YOU BASS-ING THAT ON?
I NEVER SHOULD HAVE TOLD YOU ABOUT PUNS!
I LEARNED IT FROM WATCHING YOU!
RAK
RELEASE THE LIONS!
CIRCUSES!
BREAD!
CIRCUSES!
HASHTAG TEAM PUSSY-CATS!
PU-SSY-CATS!
PU-SSY-CATS!
THIS IS THE WORST HEIST ATTEMPT SINCE THE MOVIE "HEIST."

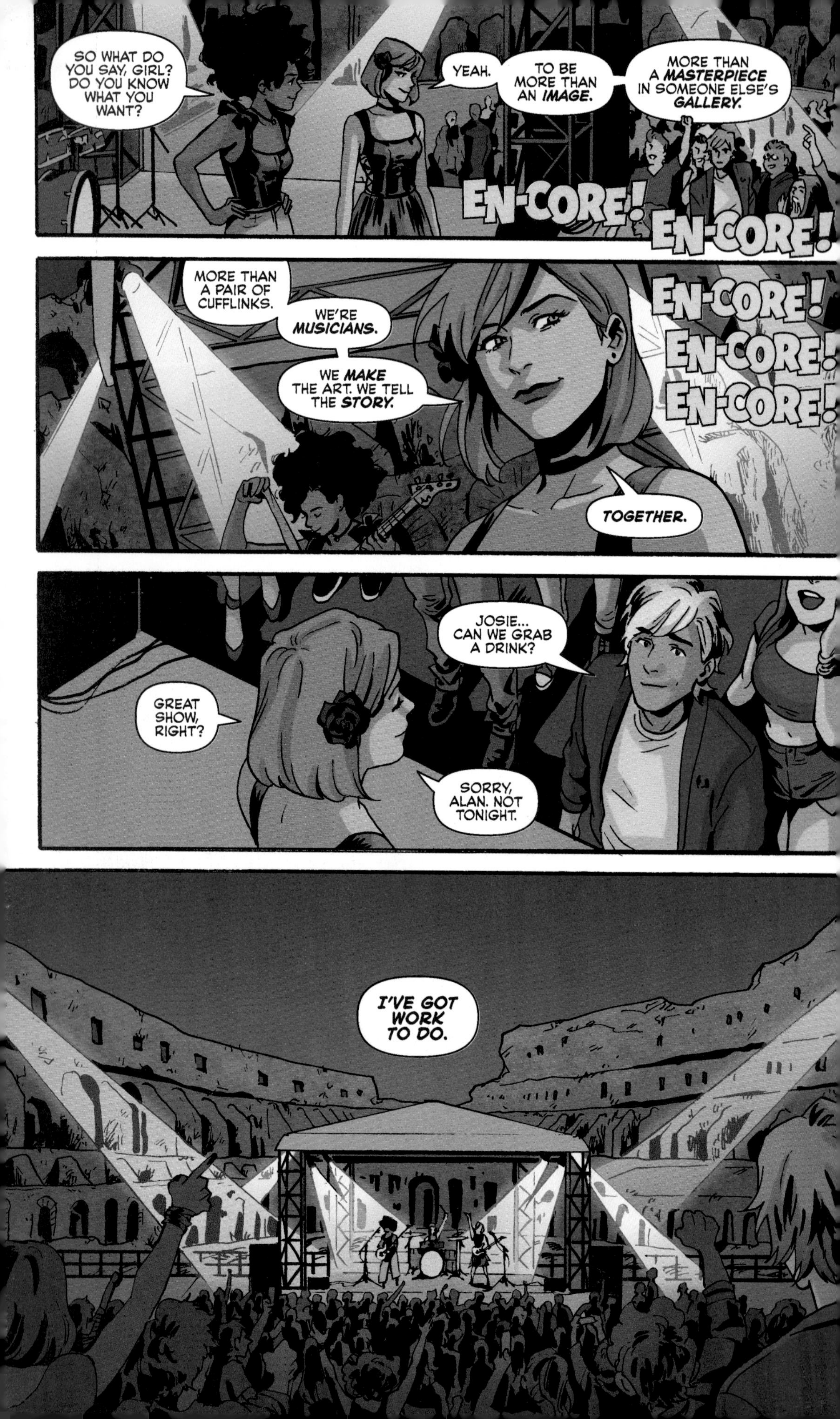
SO WHAT DO YOU SAY, GIRL? DO YOU KNOW WHAT YOU WANT?
YEAH.
TO BE MORE THAN AN *IMAGE.*
MORE THAN A *MASTERPIECE* IN SOMEONE ELSE'S *GALLERY.*
EN-CORE! EN-CORE!
MORE THAN A PAIR OF CUFFLINKS.
WE'RE *MUSICIANS.*
WE *MAKE* THE ART. WE TELL THE *STORY.*
EN-CORE! EN-CORE! EN-CORE!
TOGETHER.
GREAT SHOW, RIGHT?
JOSIE... CAN WE GRAB A DRINK?
SORRY, ALAN. NOT TONIGHT.
I'VE GOT WORK TO DO.

TO BE
CONTINUED...

ISSUE FIVE

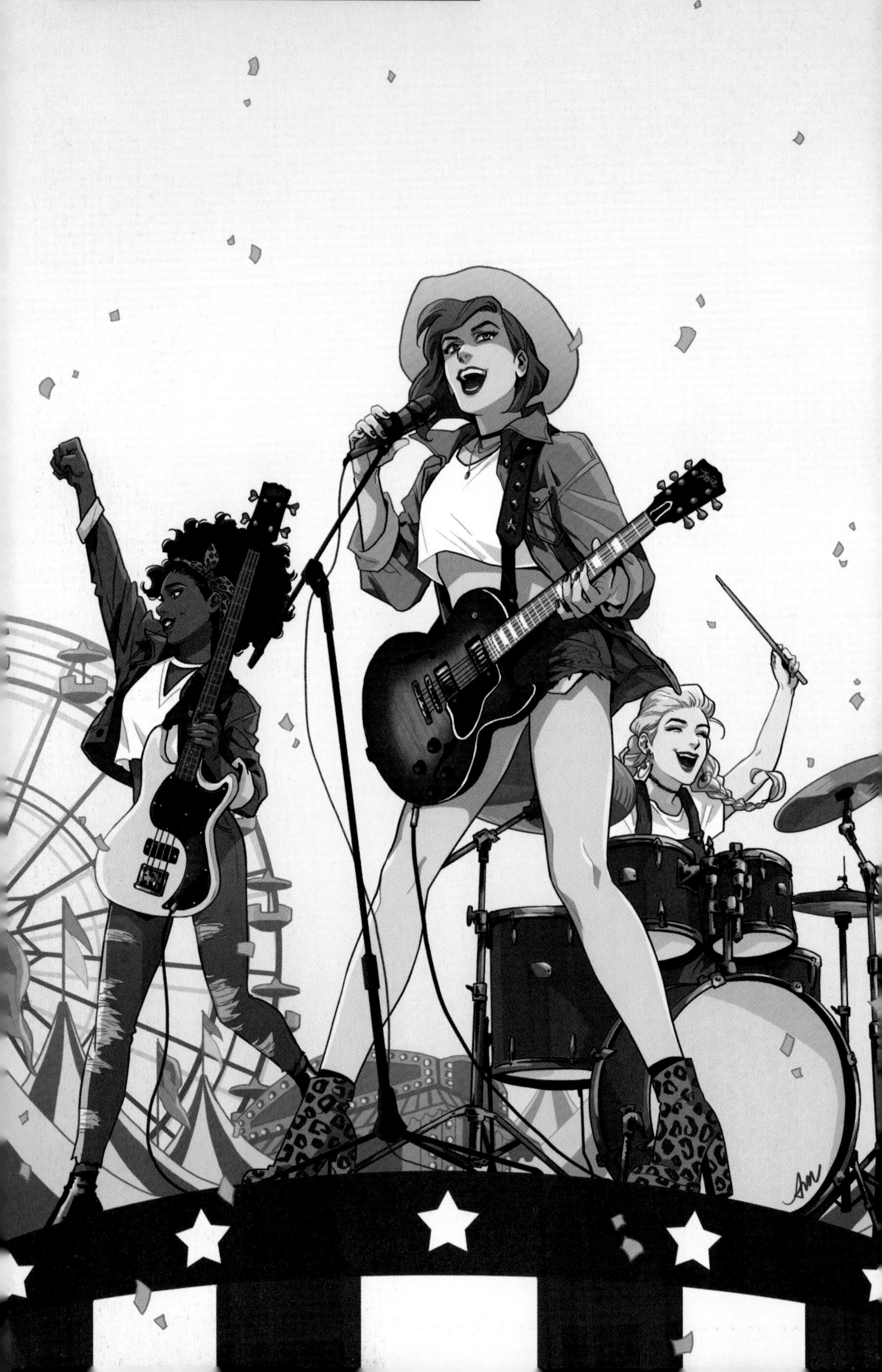

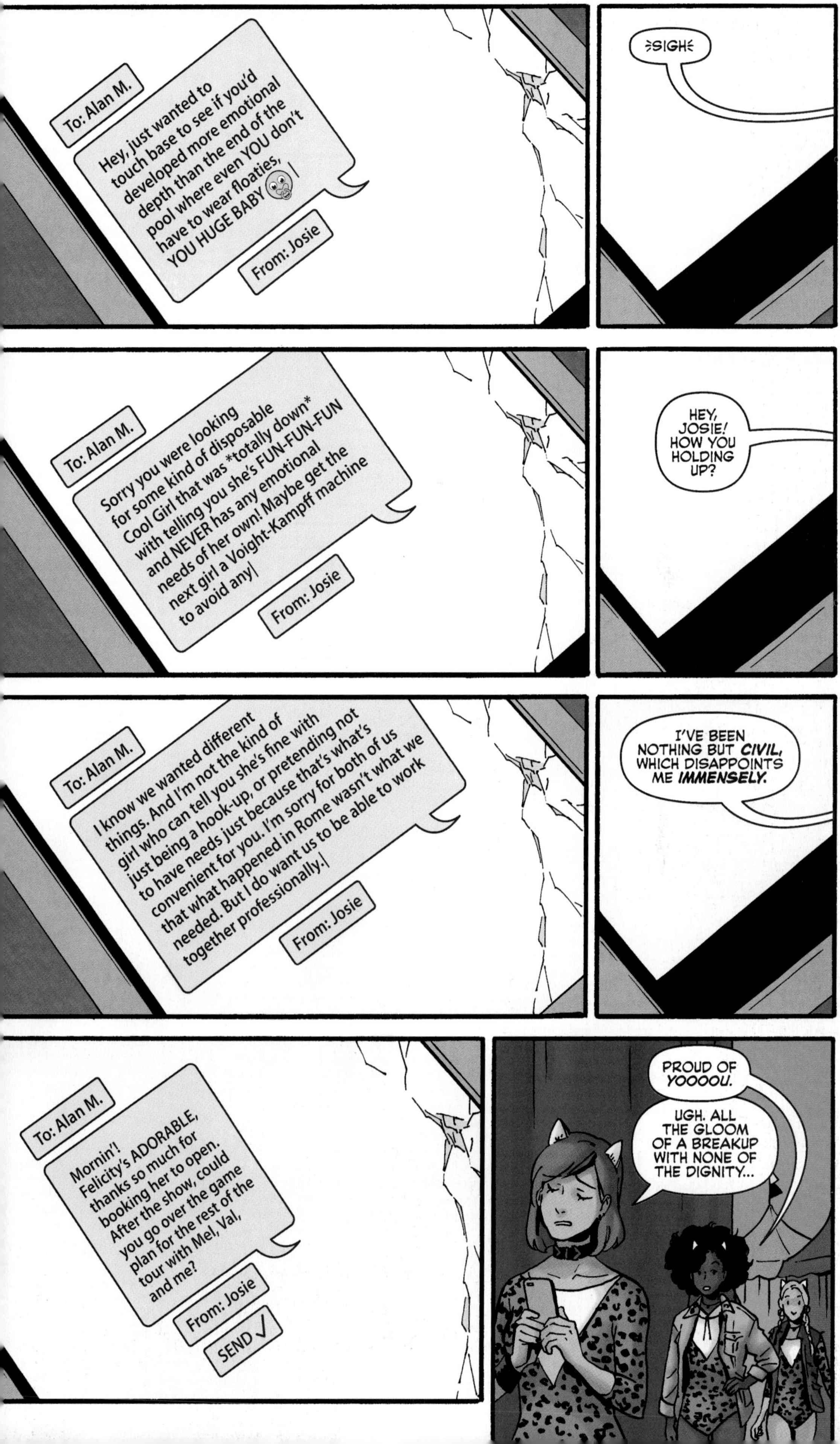
To: Alan M.
Hey, just wanted to touch base to see if you'd developed more emotional depth than the end of the pool where even YOU don't have to wear floaties, YOU HUGE BABY
From: Josie
SIGH
To: Alan M.
Sorry you were looking for some kind of disposable Cool Girl that was *totally down* with telling you she's FUN-FUN-FUN and NEVER has any emotional needs of her own! Maybe get the next girl a Voight-Kampff machine to avoid any
From: Josie
HEY, JOSIE! HOW YOU HOLDING UP?
To: Alan M.
I know we wanted different things. And I'm not the kind of girl who can tell you she's fine with just being a hook-up, or pretending not to have needs just because that's what's convenient for you. I'm sorry for both of us that what happened in Rome wasn't what we needed. But I do want us to be able to work together professionally.
From: Josie
I'VE BEEN NOTHING BUT CIVIL, WHICH DISAPPOINTS ME IMMENSELY.
To: Alan M.
Mornin'! Felicity's ADORABLE, thanks so much for booking her to open. After the show, could you go over the game plan for the rest of the tour with Mel, Val, and me?
From: Josie
SEND ✓
PROUD OF YOOOOU.
UGH. ALL THE GLOOM OF A BREAKUP WITH NONE OF THE DIGNITY...

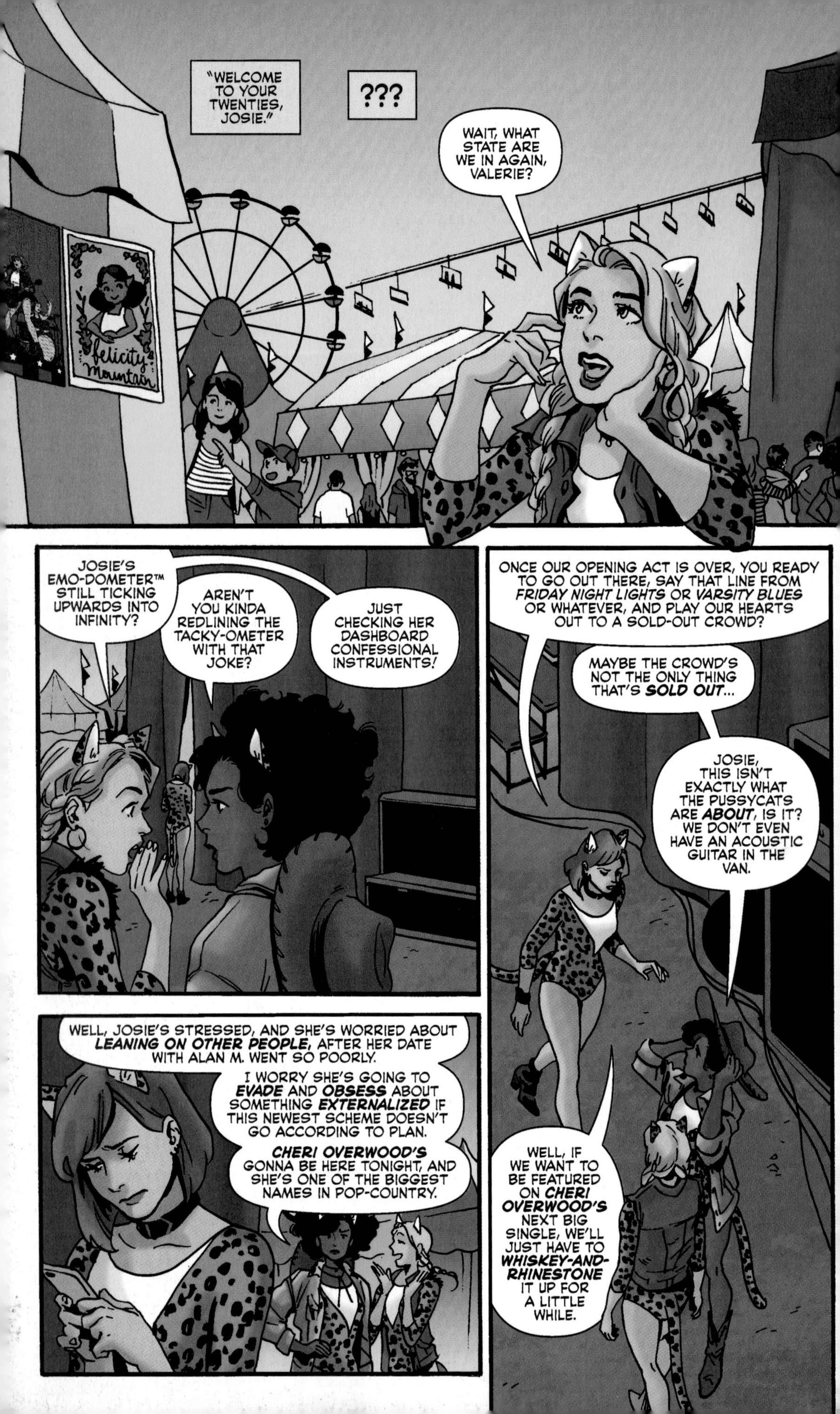
"WELCOME TO YOUR TWENTIES, JOSIE."
???
WAIT, WHAT STATE ARE WE IN AGAIN, VALERIE?
felicity Mountain
JOSIE'S EMO-DOMETER™ STILL TICKING UPWARDS INTO INFINITY?
AREN'T YOU KINDA REDLINING THE TACKY-OMETER WITH THAT JOKE?
JUST CHECKING HER DASHBOARD CONFESSIONAL INSTRUMENTS!
WELL, JOSIE'S STRESSED, AND SHE'S WORRIED ABOUT LEANING ON OTHER PEOPLE, AFTER HER DATE WITH ALAN M. WENT SO POORLY.
I WORRY SHE'S GOING TO EVADE AND OBSESS ABOUT SOMETHING EXTERNALIZED IF THIS NEWEST SCHEME DOESN'T GO ACCORDING TO PLAN.
CHERI OVERWOOD'S GONNA BE HERE TONIGHT, AND SHE'S ONE OF THE BIGGEST NAMES IN POP-COUNTRY.
ONCE OUR OPENING ACT IS OVER, YOU READY TO GO OUT THERE, SAY THAT LINE FROM FRIDAY NIGHT LIGHTS OR VARSITY BLUES OR WHATEVER, AND PLAY OUR HEARTS OUT TO A SOLD-OUT CROWD?
MAYBE THE CROWD'S NOT THE ONLY THING THAT'S SOLD OUT...
JOSIE, THIS ISN'T EXACTLY WHAT THE PUSSYCATS ARE ABOUT, IS IT? WE DON'T EVEN HAVE AN ACOUSTIC GUITAR IN THE VAN.
WELL, IF WE WANT TO BE FEATURED ON CHERI OVERWOOD'S NEXT BIG SINGLE, WE'LL JUST HAVE TO WHISKEY-AND-RHINESTONE IT UP FOR A LITTLE WHILE.

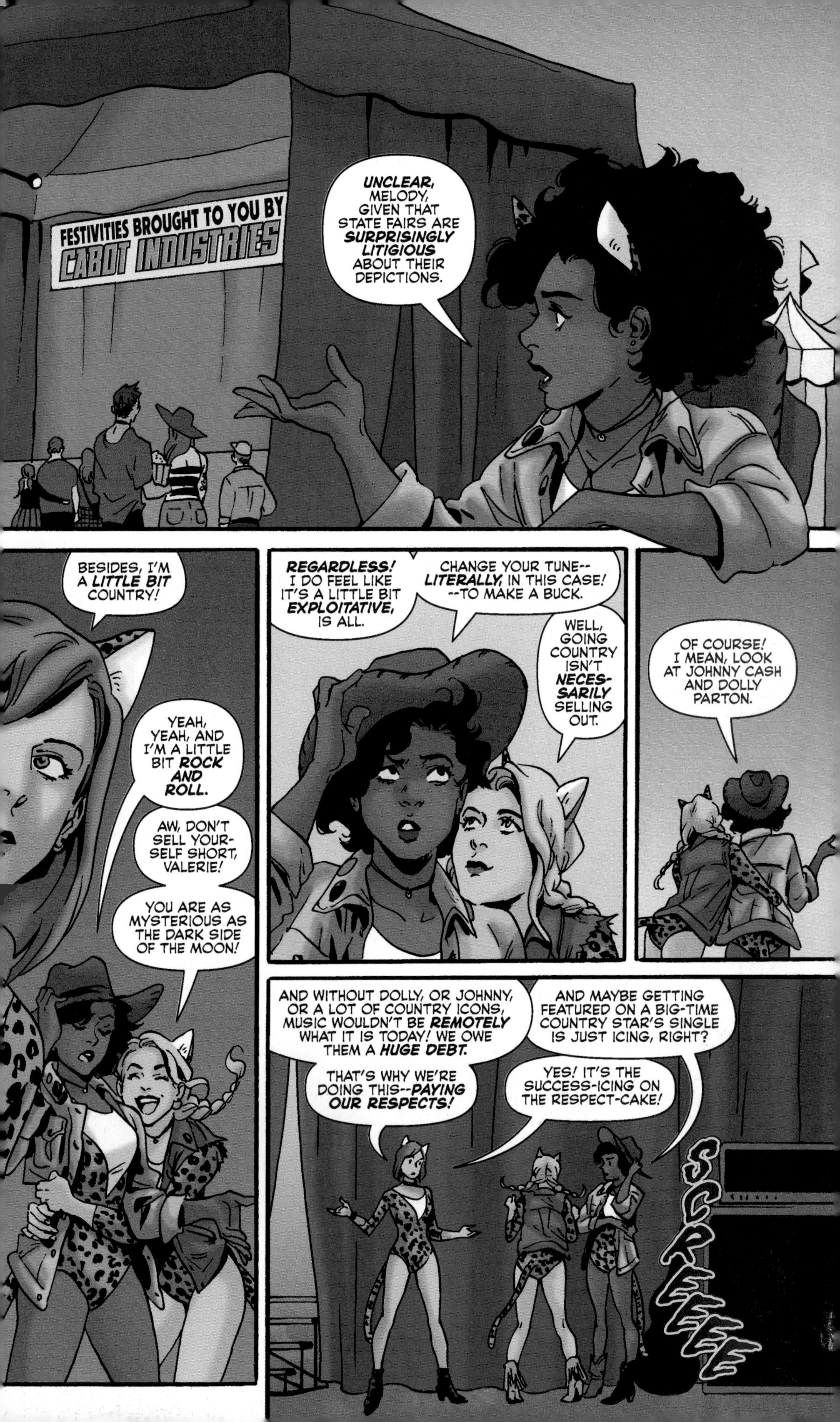
FESTIVITIES BROUGHT TO YOU BY CABOT INDUSTRIES
UNCLEAR, MELODY, GIVEN THAT STATE FAIRS ARE SURPRISINGLY LITIGIOUS ABOUT THEIR DEPICTIONS.
BESIDES, I'M A LITTLE BIT COUNTRY!
YEAH, YEAH, AND I'M A LITTLE BIT ROCK AND ROLL.
AW, DON'T SELL YOURSELF SHORT, VALERIE!
YOU ARE AS MYSTERIOUS AS THE DARK SIDE OF THE MOON!
REGARDLESS! I DO FEEL LIKE IT'S A LITTLE BIT EXPLOITATIVE, IS ALL.
CHANGE YOUR TUNE-- LITERALLY, IN THIS CASE! --TO MAKE A BUCK.
WELL, GOING COUNTRY ISN'T NECESSARILY SELLING OUT.
OF COURSE! I MEAN, LOOK AT JOHNNY CASH AND DOLLY PARTON.
AND WITHOUT DOLLY, OR JOHNNY, OR A LOT OF COUNTRY ICONS, MUSIC WOULDN'T BE REMOTELY WHAT IT IS TODAY! WE OWE THEM A HUGE DEBT.
THAT'S WHY WE'RE DOING THIS--PAYING OUR RESPECTS!
AND MAYBE GETTING FEATURED ON A BIG-TIME COUNTRY STAR'S SINGLE IS JUST ICING, RIGHT?
YES! IT'S THE SUCCESS-ICING ON THE RESPECT-CAKE!
SCREEEE

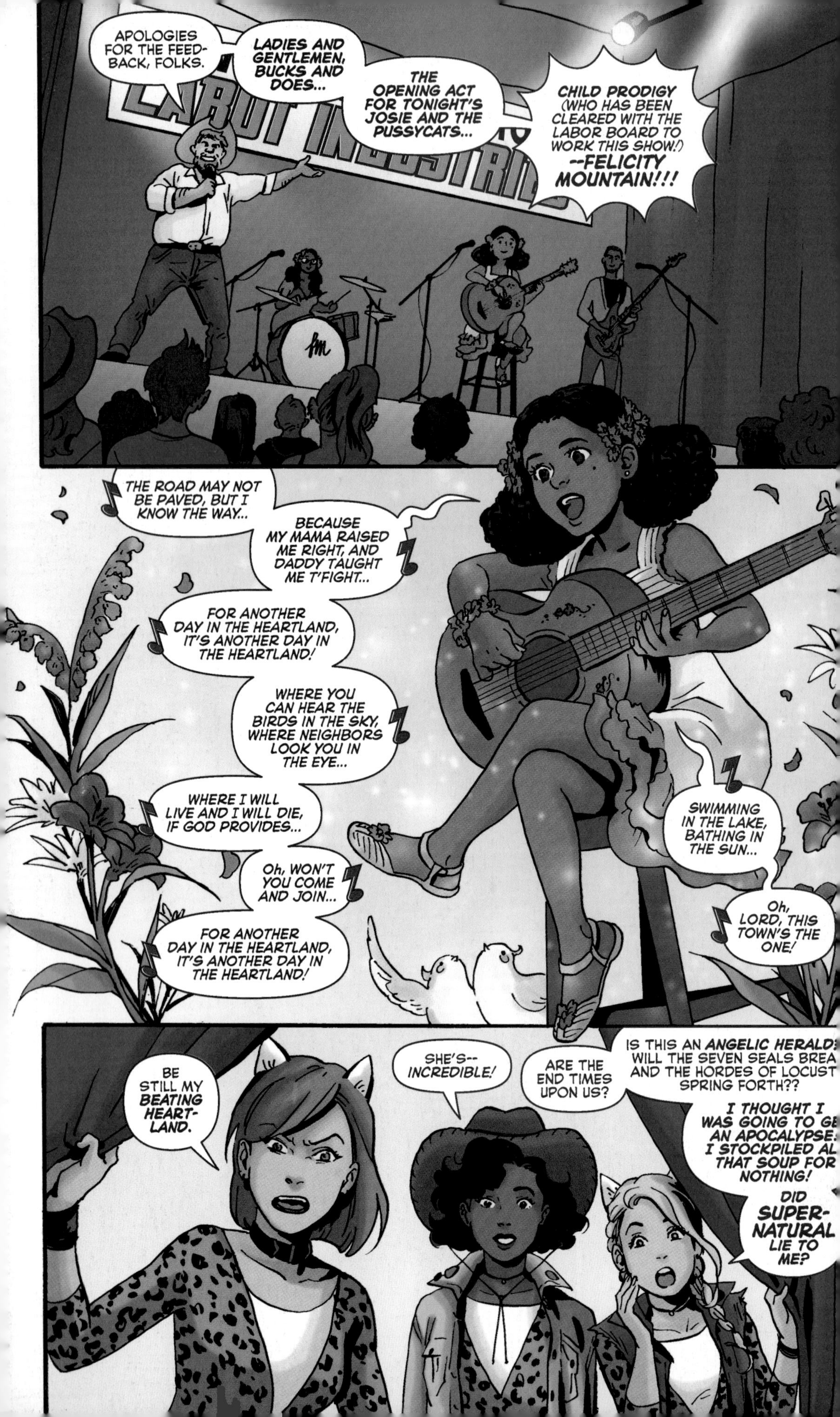
APOLOGIES FOR THE FEED-BACK, FOLKS.
LADIES AND GENTLEMEN, BUCKS AND DOES...
THE OPENING ACT FOR TONIGHT'S JOSIE AND THE PUSSYCATS...
CHILD PRODIGY (WHO HAS BEEN CLEARED WITH THE LABOR BOARD TO WORK THIS SHOW!) --FELICITY MOUNTAIN!!!
THE ROAD MAY NOT BE PAVED, BUT I KNOW THE WAY...
BECAUSE MY MAMA RAISED ME RIGHT, AND DADDY TAUGHT ME T'FIGHT...
FOR ANOTHER DAY IN THE HEARTLAND, IT'S ANOTHER DAY IN THE HEARTLAND!
WHERE YOU CAN HEAR THE BIRDS IN THE SKY, WHERE NEIGHBORS LOOK YOU IN THE EYE...
WHERE I WILL LIVE AND I WILL DIE, IF GOD PROVIDES...
Oh, WON'T YOU COME AND JOIN...
FOR ANOTHER DAY IN THE HEARTLAND, IT'S ANOTHER DAY IN THE HEARTLAND!
SWIMMING IN THE LAKE, BATHING IN THE SUN...
Oh, LORD, THIS TOWN'S THE ONE!
BE STILL MY BEATING HEART-LAND.
SHE'S-- INCREDIBLE!
ARE THE END TIMES UPON US?
IS THIS AN ANGELIC HERALD? WILL THE SEVEN SEALS BREA AND THE HORDES OF LOCUST SPRING FORTH??
I THOUGHT I WAS GOING TO GE AN APOCALYPSE. I STOCKPILED AL THAT SOUP FOR NOTHING!
DID SUPER-NATURAL LIE TO ME?

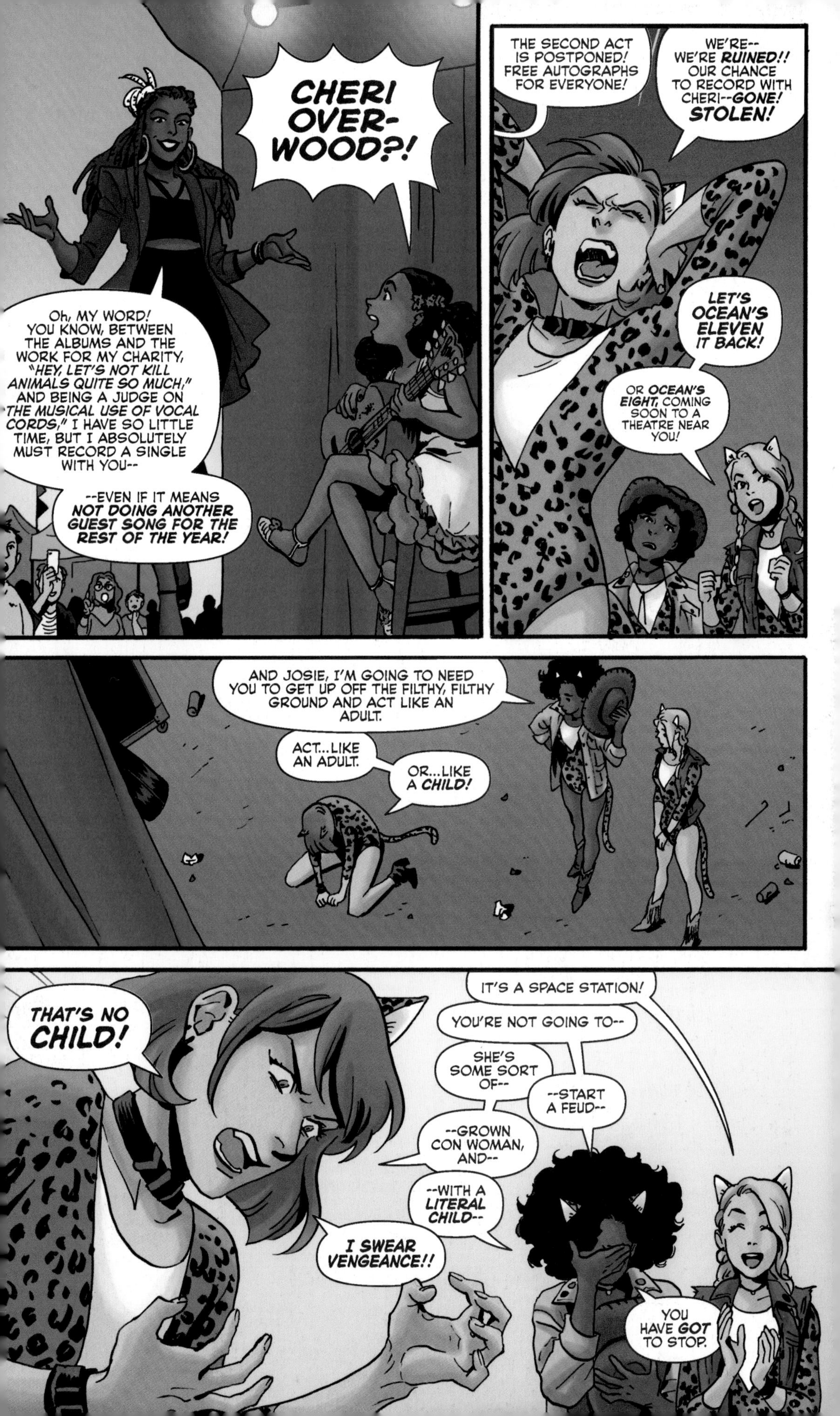
CHERI OVER-WOOD?!
Oh, MY WORD! YOU KNOW, BETWEEN THE ALBUMS AND THE WORK FOR MY CHARITY, "HEY, LET'S NOT KILL ANIMALS QUITE SO MUCH," AND BEING A JUDGE ON "THE MUSICAL USE OF VOCAL CORDS," I HAVE SO LITTLE TIME, BUT I ABSOLUTELY MUST RECORD A SINGLE WITH YOU--
--EVEN IF IT MEANS NOT DOING ANOTHER GUEST SONG FOR THE REST OF THE YEAR!
THE SECOND ACT IS POSTPONED! FREE AUTOGRAPHS FOR EVERYONE!
WE'RE-- WE'RE RUINED!! OUR CHANCE TO RECORD WITH CHERI--GONE! STOLEN!
LET'S OCEAN'S ELEVEN IT BACK!
OR OCEAN'S EIGHT, COMING SOON TO A THEATRE NEAR YOU!
AND JOSIE, I'M GOING TO NEED YOU TO GET UP OFF THE FILTHY, FILTHY GROUND AND ACT LIKE AN ADULT.
ACT...LIKE AN ADULT.
OR...LIKE A CHILD!
THAT'S NO CHILD!
IT'S A SPACE STATION!
YOU'RE NOT GOING TO--
SHE'S SOME SORT OF--
--START A FEUD--
--GROWN CON WOMAN, AND--
--WITH A LITERAL CHILD--
I SWEAR VENGEANCE!!
YOU HAVE GOT TO STOP.

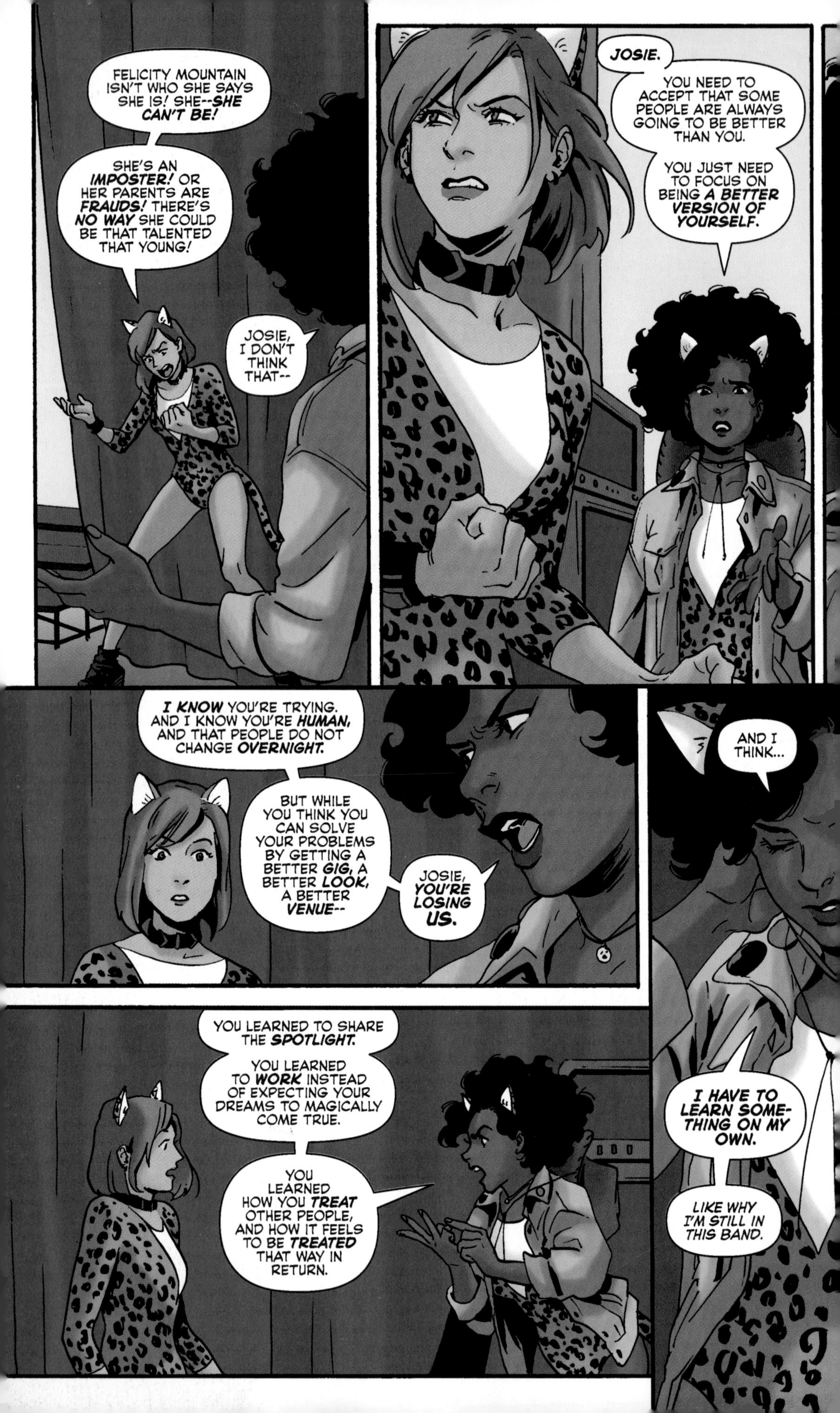

FELICITY MOUNTAIN ISN'T WHO SHE SAYS SHE IS! SHE--SHE CAN'T BE!
SHE'S AN IMPOSTER! OR HER PARENTS ARE FRAUDS! THERE'S NO WAY SHE COULD BE THAT TALENTED THAT YOUNG!
JOSIE, I DON'T THINK THAT--
JOSIE.
YOU NEED TO ACCEPT THAT SOME PEOPLE ARE ALWAYS GOING TO BE BETTER THAN YOU.
YOU JUST NEED TO FOCUS ON BEING A BETTER VERSION OF YOURSELF.
I KNOW YOU'RE TRYING. AND I KNOW YOU'RE HUMAN, AND THAT PEOPLE DO NOT CHANGE OVERNIGHT.
BUT WHILE YOU THINK YOU CAN SOLVE YOUR PROBLEMS BY GETTING A BETTER GIG, A BETTER LOOK, A BETTER VENUE--
JOSIE, YOU'RE LOSING US.
YOU LEARNED TO SHARE THE SPOTLIGHT.
YOU LEARNED TO WORK INSTEAD OF EXPECTING YOUR DREAMS TO MAGICALLY COME TRUE.
YOU LEARNED HOW YOU TREAT OTHER PEOPLE, AND HOW IT FEELS TO BE TREATED THAT WAY IN RETURN.
AND I THINK...
I HAVE TO LEARN SOME-THING ON MY OWN.
LIKE WHY I'M STILL IN THIS BAND.

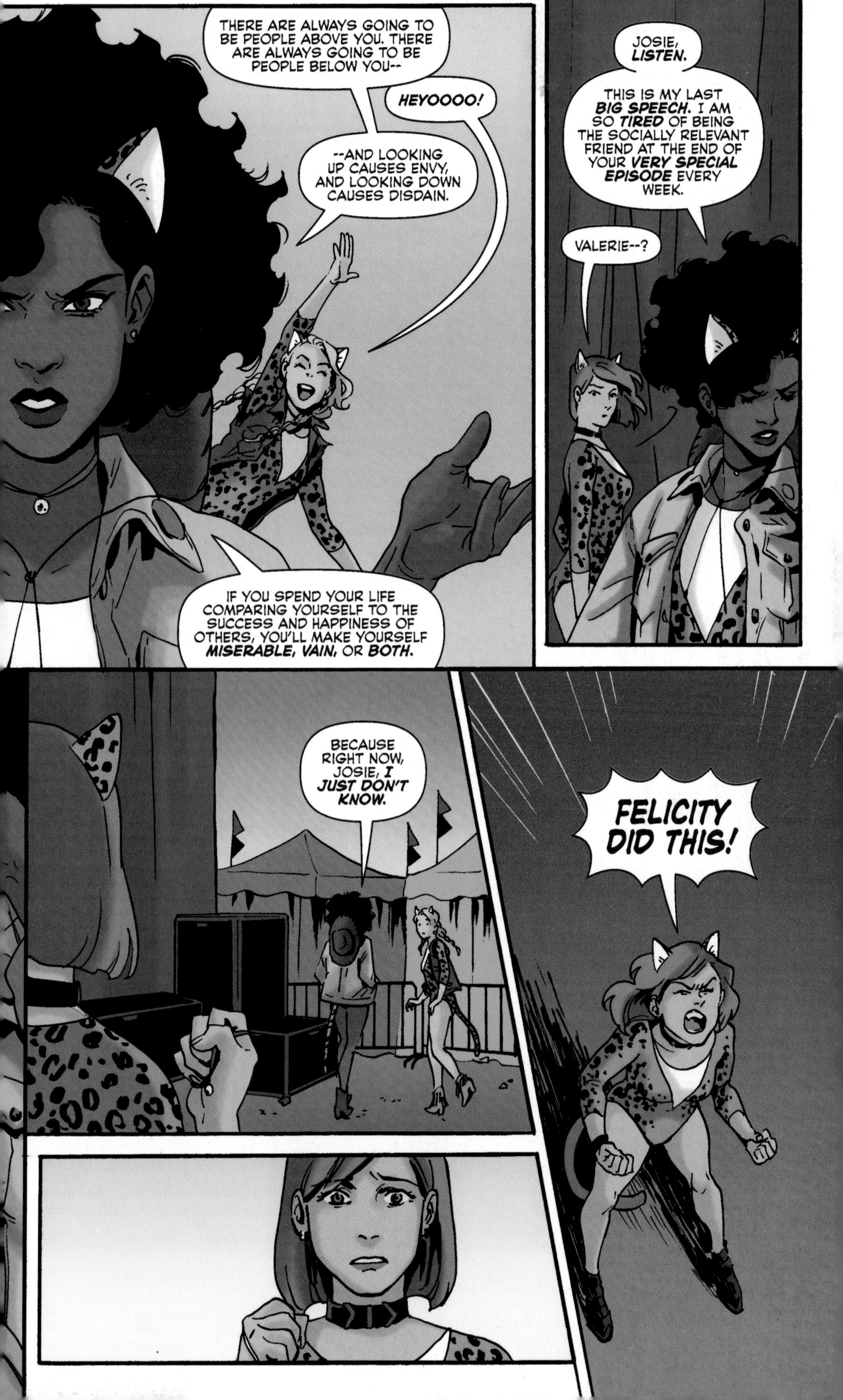
THERE ARE ALWAYS GOING TO BE PEOPLE ABOVE YOU. THERE ARE ALWAYS GOING TO BE PEOPLE BELOW YOU--
HEYOOOO!
--AND LOOKING UP CAUSES ENVY, AND LOOKING DOWN CAUSES DISDAIN.
IF YOU SPEND YOUR LIFE COMPARING YOURSELF TO THE SUCCESS AND HAPPINESS OF OTHERS, YOU'LL MAKE YOURSELF ***MISERABLE, VAIN,*** OR ***BOTH.***
JOSIE, ***LISTEN.***
THIS IS MY LAST ***BIG SPEECH.*** I AM SO ***TIRED*** OF BEING THE SOCIALLY RELEVANT FRIEND AT THE END OF YOUR ***VERY SPECIAL EPISODE*** EVERY WEEK.
VALERIE--?
BECAUSE RIGHT NOW, JOSIE, ***I JUST DON'T KNOW.***
FELICITY DID THIS!

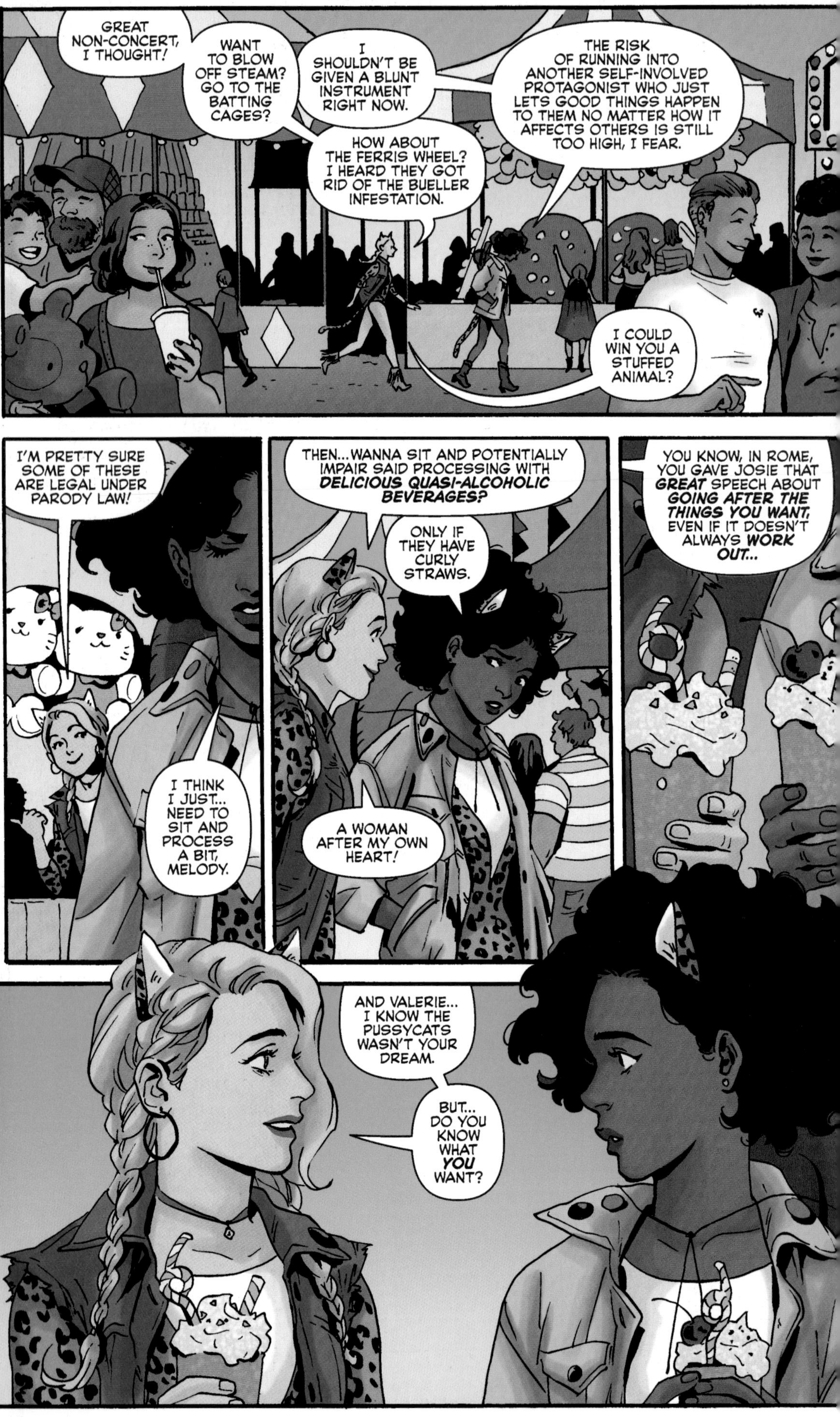

GREAT NON-CONCERT, I THOUGHT!
WANT TO BLOW OFF STEAM? GO TO THE BATTING CAGES?
I SHOULDN'T BE GIVEN A BLUNT INSTRUMENT RIGHT NOW.
HOW ABOUT THE FERRIS WHEEL? I HEARD THEY GOT RID OF THE BUELLER INFESTATION.
THE RISK OF RUNNING INTO ANOTHER SELF-INVOLVED PROTAGONIST WHO JUST LETS GOOD THINGS HAPPEN TO THEM NO MATTER HOW IT AFFECTS OTHERS IS STILL TOO HIGH, I FEAR.
I COULD WIN YOU A STUFFED ANIMAL?
I'M PRETTY SURE SOME OF THESE ARE LEGAL UNDER PARODY LAW!
I THINK I JUST... NEED TO SIT AND PROCESS A BIT, MELODY.
THEN...WANNA SIT AND POTENTIALLY IMPAIR SAID PROCESSING WITH ***DELICIOUS QUASI-ALCOHOLIC BEVERAGES?***
ONLY IF THEY HAVE CURLY STRAWS.
A WOMAN AFTER MY OWN HEART!
YOU KNOW, IN ROME, YOU GAVE JOSIE THAT ***GREAT*** SPEECH ABOUT ***GOING AFTER THE THINGS YOU WANT,*** EVEN IF IT DOESN'T ALWAYS ***WORK OUT...***
AND VALERIE... I KNOW THE PUSSYCATS WASN'T YOUR DREAM.
BUT... DO YOU KNOW WHAT ***YOU*** WANT?

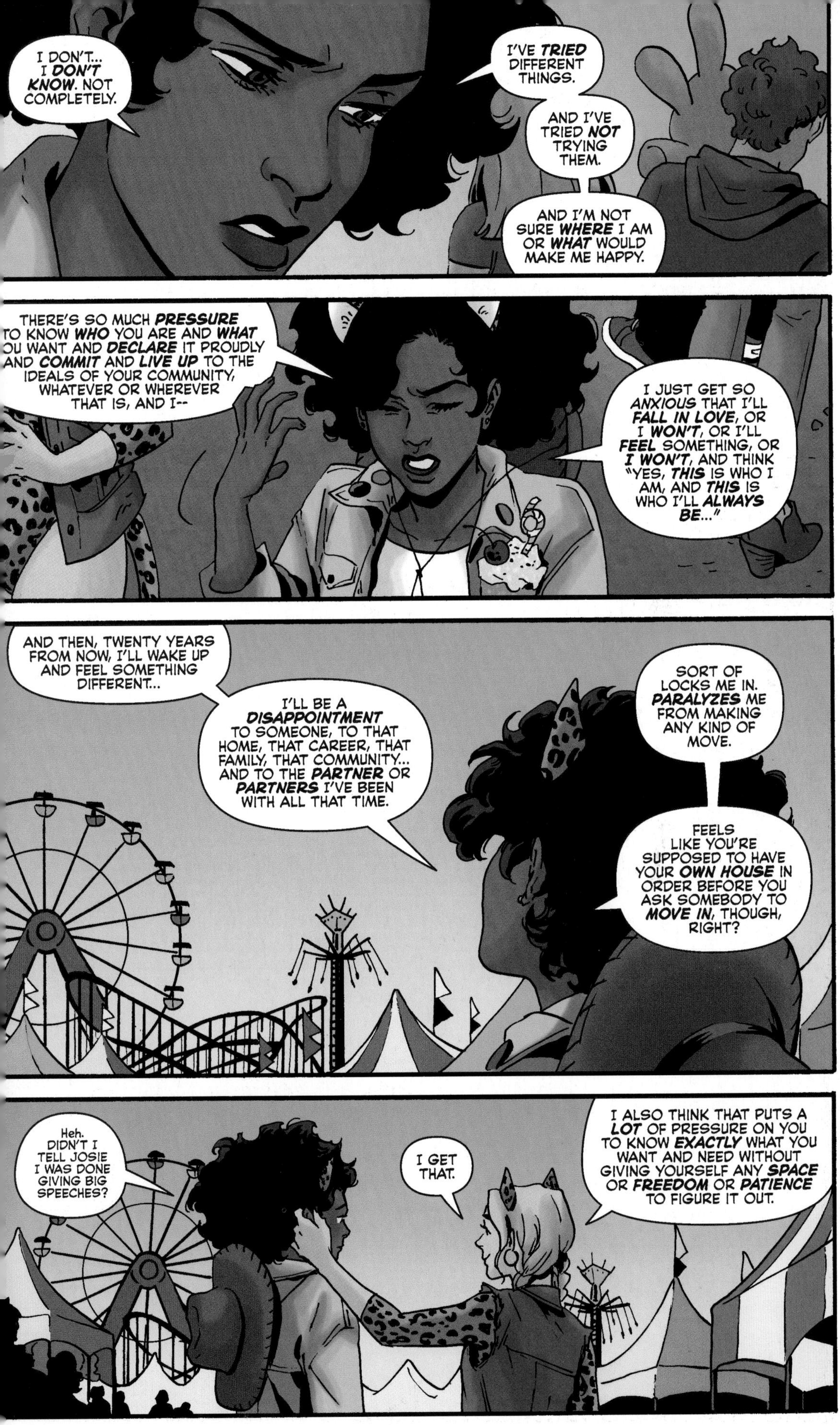
I DON'T... I DON'T KNOW. NOT COMPLETELY.
I'VE TRIED DIFFERENT THINGS.
AND I'VE TRIED NOT TRYING THEM.
AND I'M NOT SURE WHERE I AM OR WHAT WOULD MAKE ME HAPPY.
THERE'S SO MUCH PRESSURE TO KNOW WHO YOU ARE AND WHAT YOU WANT AND DECLARE IT PROUDLY AND COMMIT AND LIVE UP TO THE IDEALS OF YOUR COMMUNITY, WHATEVER OR WHEREVER THAT IS, AND I--
I JUST GET SO ANXIOUS THAT I'LL FALL IN LOVE, OR I WON'T, OR I'LL FEEL SOMETHING, OR I WON'T, AND THINK "YES, THIS IS WHO I AM, AND THIS IS WHO I'LL ALWAYS BE..."
AND THEN, TWENTY YEARS FROM NOW, I'LL WAKE UP AND FEEL SOMETHING DIFFERENT...
I'LL BE A DISAPPOINTMENT TO SOMEONE, TO THAT HOME, THAT CAREER, THAT FAMILY, THAT COMMUNITY... AND TO THE PARTNER OR PARTNERS I'VE BEEN WITH ALL THAT TIME.
SORT OF LOCKS ME IN. PARALYZES ME FROM MAKING ANY KIND OF MOVE.
FEELS LIKE YOU'RE SUPPOSED TO HAVE YOUR OWN HOUSE IN ORDER BEFORE YOU ASK SOMEBODY TO MOVE IN, THOUGH, RIGHT?
I ALSO THINK THAT PUTS A LOT OF PRESSURE ON YOU TO KNOW EXACTLY WHAT YOU WANT AND NEED WITHOUT GIVING YOURSELF ANY SPACE OR FREEDOM OR PATIENCE TO FIGURE IT OUT.
I GET THAT.
Heh. DIDN'T I TELL JOSIE I WAS DONE GIVING BIG SPEECHES?

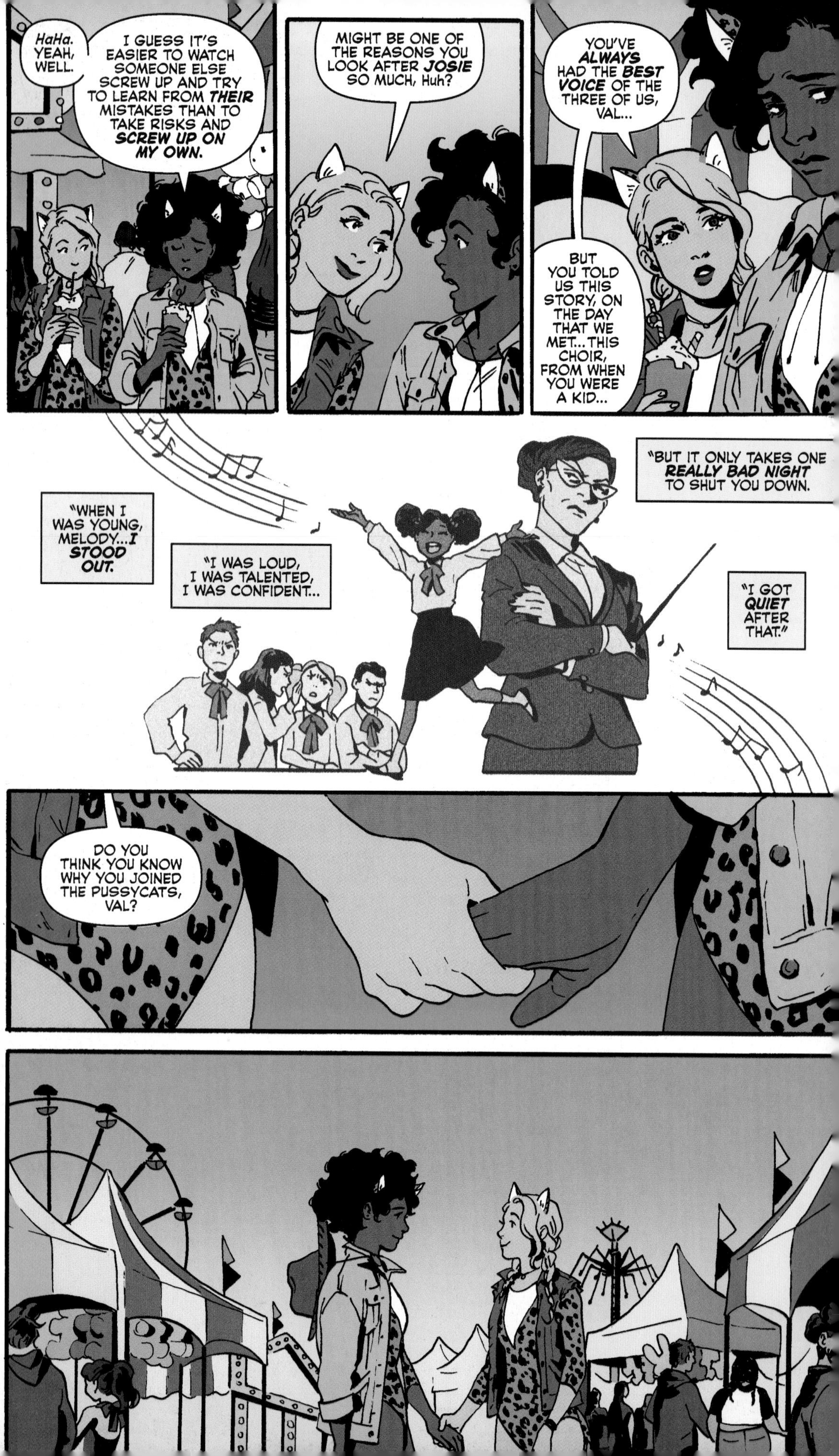

HaHa. YEAH, WELL.
I GUESS IT'S EASIER TO WATCH SOMEONE ELSE SCREW UP AND TRY TO LEARN FROM THEIR MISTAKES THAN TO TAKE RISKS AND SCREW UP ON MY OWN.
MIGHT BE ONE OF THE REASONS YOU LOOK AFTER JOSIE SO MUCH, Huh?
YOU'VE ALWAYS HAD THE BEST VOICE OF THE THREE OF US, VAL...
BUT YOU TOLD US THIS STORY, ON THE DAY THAT WE MET...THIS CHOIR, FROM WHEN YOU WERE A KID...
"WHEN I WAS YOUNG, MELODY...I STOOD OUT.
"I WAS LOUD, I WAS TALENTED, I WAS CONFIDENT...
"BUT IT ONLY TAKES ONE REALLY BAD NIGHT TO SHUT YOU DOWN.
"I GOT QUIET AFTER THAT."
DO YOU THINK YOU KNOW WHY YOU JOINED THE PUSSYCATS, VAL?

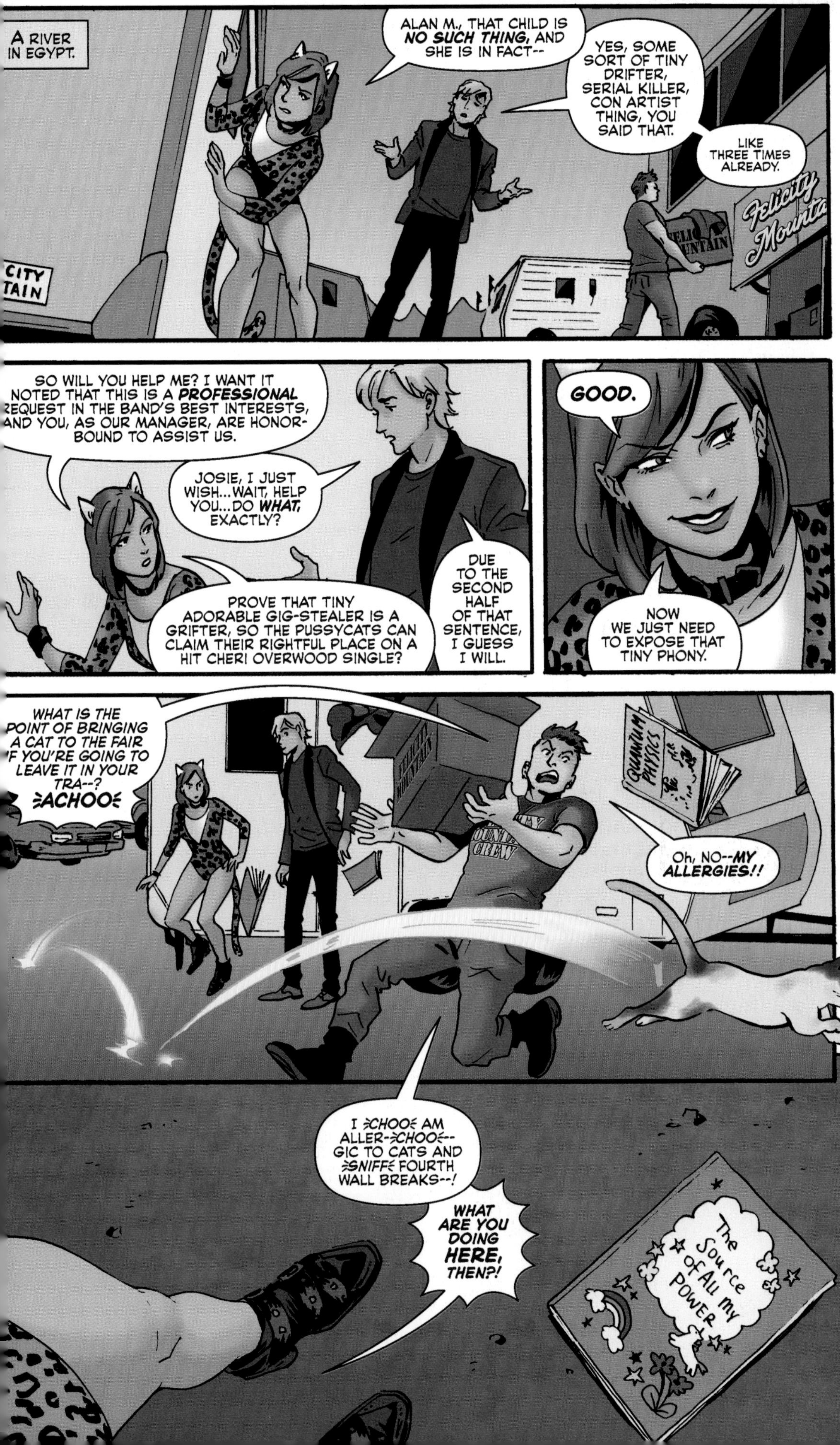
A RIVER IN EGYPT.
ALAN M., THAT CHILD IS NO SUCH THING, AND SHE IS IN FACT--
YES, SOME SORT OF TINY DRIFTER, SERIAL KILLER, CON ARTIST THING, YOU SAID THAT.
LIKE THREE TIMES ALREADY.
Felicity Mounta
CITY TAIN
SO WILL YOU HELP ME? I WANT IT NOTED THAT THIS IS A PROFESSIONAL REQUEST IN THE BAND'S BEST INTERESTS, AND YOU, AS OUR MANAGER, ARE HONOR-BOUND TO ASSIST US.
JOSIE, I JUST WISH...WAIT, HELP YOU...DO WHAT, EXACTLY?
PROVE THAT TINY ADORABLE GIG-STEALER IS A GRIFTER, SO THE PUSSYCATS CAN CLAIM THEIR RIGHTFUL PLACE ON A HIT CHERI OVERWOOD SINGLE?
DUE TO THE SECOND HALF OF THAT SENTENCE, I GUESS I WILL.
GOOD.
NOW WE JUST NEED TO EXPOSE THAT TINY PHONY.
WHAT IS THE POINT OF BRINGING A CAT TO THE FAIR IF YOU'RE GOING TO LEAVE IT IN YOUR TRA--? ACHOO
QUANTUM PHYSICS
Oh, NO--MY ALLERGIES!!
MOUNTAIN CREW
I CHOO AM ALLER-CHOO--GIC TO CATS AND SNIFF FOURTH WALL BREAKS--!
WHAT ARE YOU DOING HERE, THEN?!
The Source of All my POWER

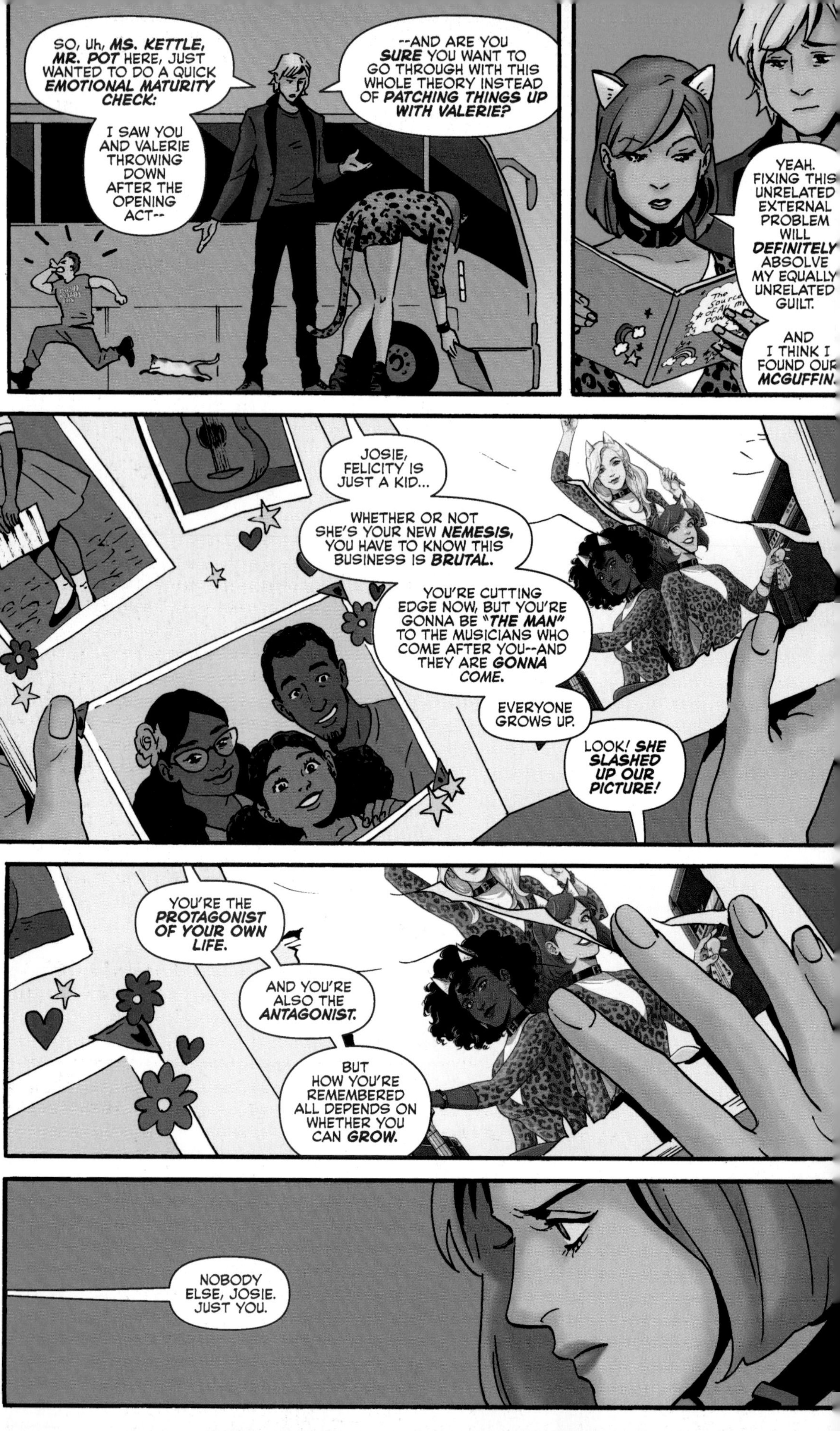
SO, Uh, MS. KETTLE, MR. POT HERE, JUST WANTED TO DO A QUICK EMOTIONAL MATURITY CHECK:
I SAW YOU AND VALERIE THROWING DOWN AFTER THE OPENING ACT--
--AND ARE YOU SURE YOU WANT TO GO THROUGH WITH THIS WHOLE THEORY INSTEAD OF PATCHING THINGS UP WITH VALERIE?
YEAH. FIXING THIS UNRELATED EXTERNAL PROBLEM WILL DEFINITELY ABSOLVE MY EQUALLY UNRELATED GUILT.
AND I THINK I FOUND OUR MCGUFFIN.
JOSIE, FELICITY IS JUST A KID...
WHETHER OR NOT SHE'S YOUR NEW NEMESIS, YOU HAVE TO KNOW THIS BUSINESS IS BRUTAL.
YOU'RE CUTTING EDGE NOW, BUT YOU'RE GONNA BE "THE MAN" TO THE MUSICIANS WHO COME AFTER YOU--AND THEY ARE GONNA COME.
EVERYONE GROWS UP.
LOOK! SHE SLASHED UP OUR PICTURE!
YOU'RE THE PROTAGONIST OF YOUR OWN LIFE.
AND YOU'RE ALSO THE ANTAGONIST.
BUT HOW YOU'RE REMEMBERED ALL DEPENDS ON WHETHER YOU CAN GROW.
NOBODY ELSE, JOSIE. JUST YOU.

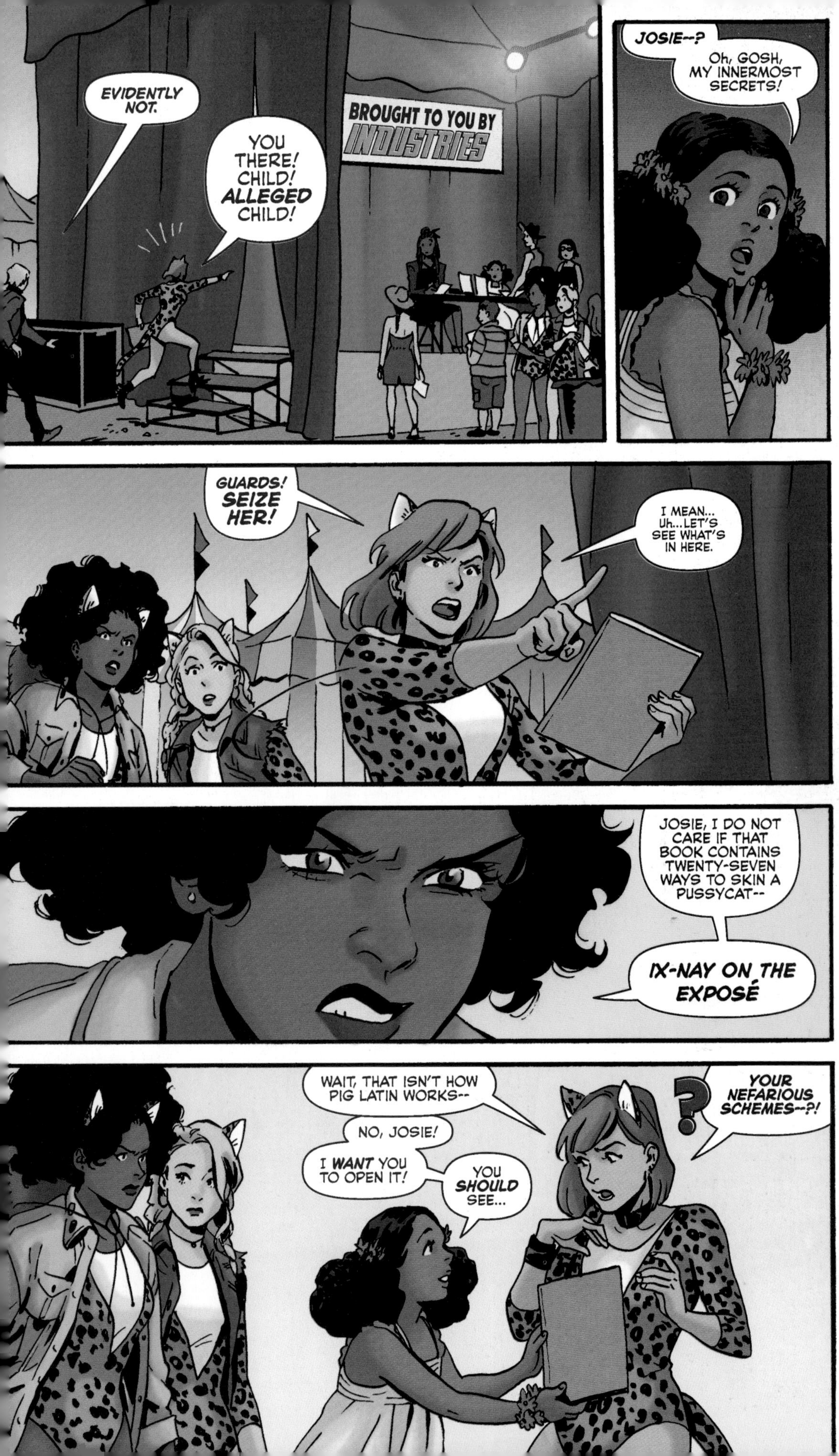
EVIDENTLY NOT.
YOU THERE! CHILD! ALLEGED CHILD!
BROUGHT TO YOU BY INDUSTRIES
JOSIE--?
Oh, GOSH, MY INNERMOST SECRETS!
GUARDS! SEIZE HER!
I MEAN... Uh...LET'S SEE WHAT'S IN HERE.
JOSIE, I DO NOT CARE IF THAT BOOK CONTAINS TWENTY-SEVEN WAYS TO SKIN A PUSSYCAT--
IX-NAY ON THE EXPOSÉ
WAIT, THAT ISN'T HOW PIG LATIN WORKS--
?
YOUR NEFARIOUS SCHEMES--?!
NO, JOSIE!
I WANT YOU TO OPEN IT!
YOU SHOULD SEE...

MY KITTY-CAT GOT AT SOME OF THE MAGAZINES BEFORE I COULD CUT OUT THE PHOTOS, BUT...

I'M...I'M A *REALLY* BIG FAN.

WAIT, AS IN A "MAKE YOUR IDOLS YOUR RIVALS" KINDA WAY?

IN A *SINGLE WHITE FEMALE* WAY??

A TONYA HARDING WAY???

IN A "SOCIETAL CRIMINALIZATION OF FEMININITY THAT URGES WOMEN TO SEPARATE THEM-SELVES FROM AND DISPAR-AGE OTHER WOMEN" WAY?

WE OWE YOU AND THE PUSSYCATS A *HUGE DEBT.*

FELICITY HAS ALWAYS BEEN VERY DRIVEN...

A FEW MONTHS AGO, SHE TOLD US IT WAS HER DREAM TO BE LIKE *YOU THREE*, AND WE WANTED TO MAKE SURE SHE COULD HAVE A *HAPPY* AND *LOVING* TIME ON HER JOURNEY.

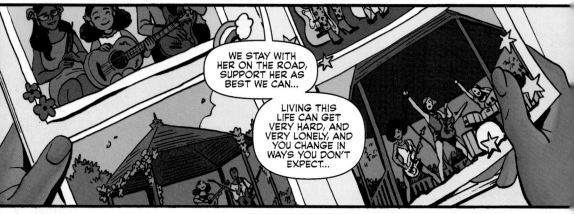

WE STAY WITH HER ON THE ROAD, SUPPORT HER AS BEST WE CAN...

LIVING THIS LIFE CAN GET VERY HARD, AND VERY LONELY, AND YOU CHANGE IN WAYS YOU DON'T EXPECT...

HAVING THEM WITH ME, I KNOW I'M LOVED.

I KNOW I'LL *BE* A BETTER PERSON, BECAUSE OF THEM.

I KNOW I *AM* A BETTER PERSON, BECAUSE OF THEM.

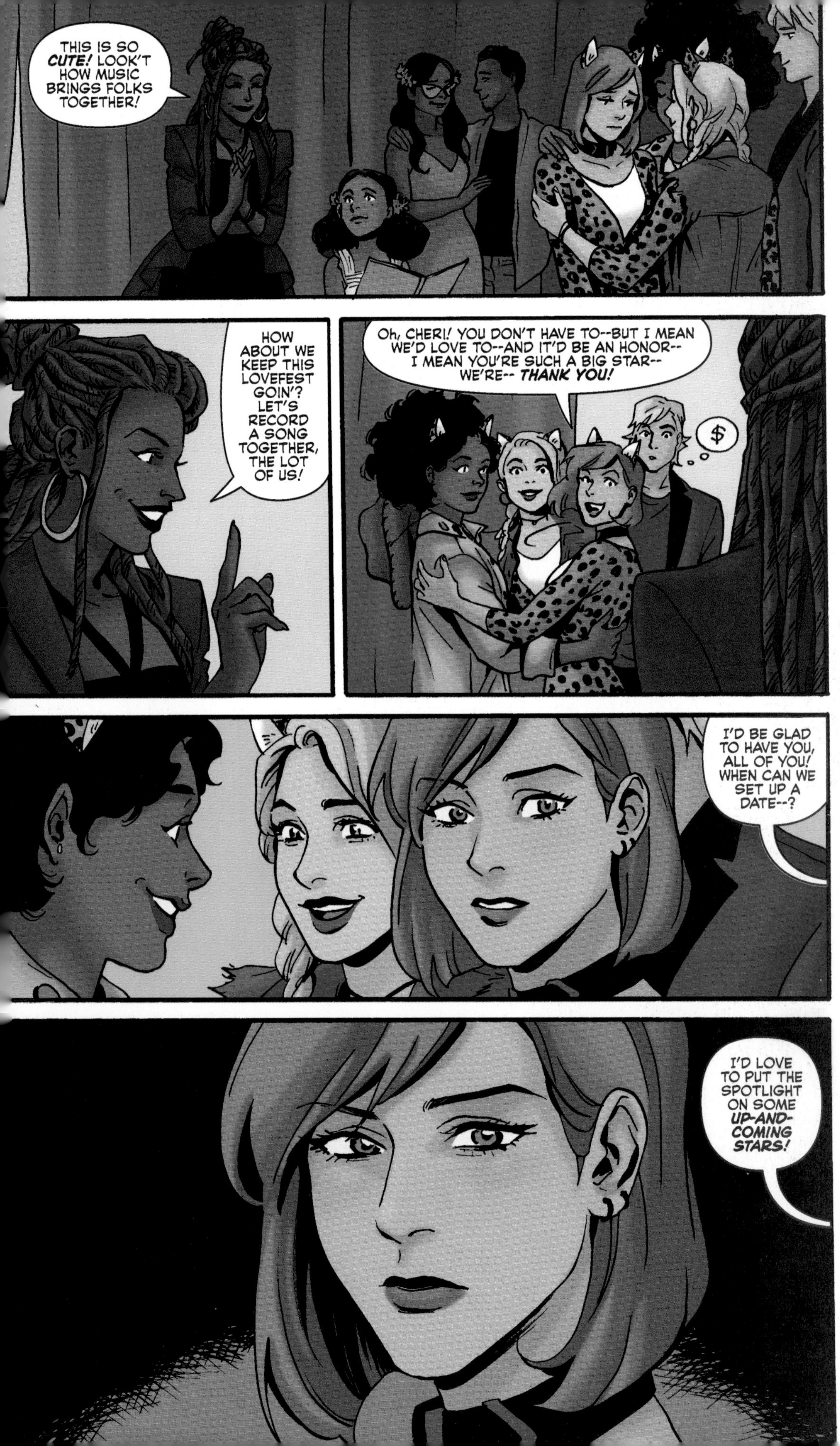
THIS IS SO CUTE! LOOK'T HOW MUSIC BRINGS FOLKS TOGETHER!
HOW ABOUT WE KEEP THIS LOVEFEST GOIN'? LET'S RECORD A SONG TOGETHER, THE LOT OF US!
Oh, CHERI! YOU DON'T HAVE TO--BUT I MEAN WE'D LOVE TO--AND IT'D BE AN HONOR-- I MEAN YOU'RE SUCH A BIG STAR-- WE'RE-- THANK YOU!
$
I'D BE GLAD TO HAVE YOU, ALL OF YOU! WHEN CAN WE SET UP A DATE--?
I'D LOVE TO PUT THE SPOTLIGHT ON SOME UP-AND-COMING STARS!

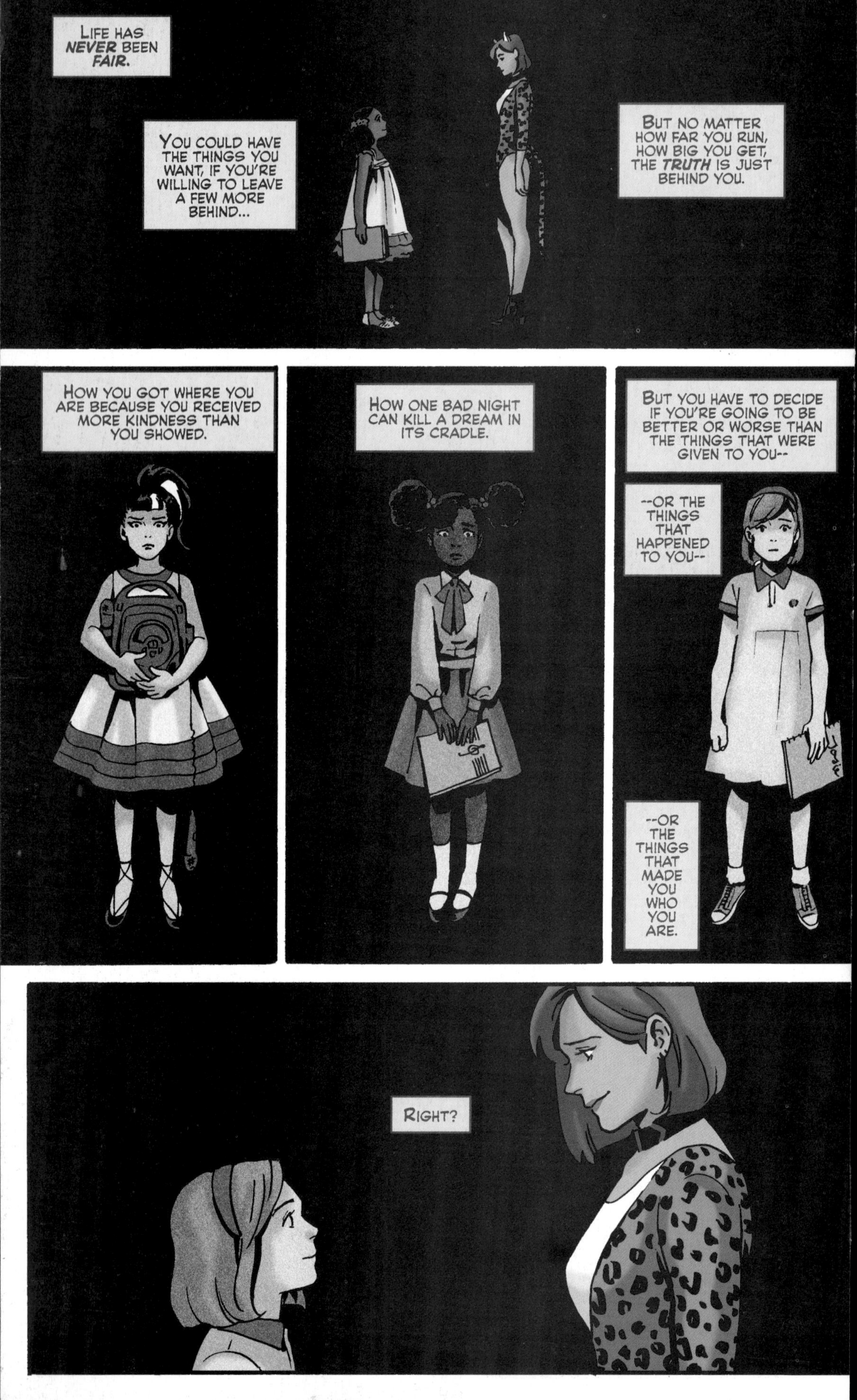
LIFE HAS NEVER BEEN FAIR.
YOU COULD HAVE THE THINGS YOU WANT, IF YOU'RE WILLING TO LEAVE A FEW MORE BEHIND...
BUT NO MATTER HOW FAR YOU RUN, HOW BIG YOU GET, THE TRUTH IS JUST BEHIND YOU.
HOW YOU GOT WHERE YOU ARE BECAUSE YOU RECEIVED MORE KINDNESS THAN YOU SHOWED.
HOW ONE BAD NIGHT CAN KILL A DREAM IN ITS CRADLE.
BUT YOU HAVE TO DECIDE IF YOU'RE GOING TO BE BETTER OR WORSE THAN THE THINGS THAT WERE GIVEN TO YOU--
--OR THE THINGS THAT HAPPENED TO YOU--
--OR THE THINGS THAT MADE YOU WHO YOU ARE.
RIGHT?

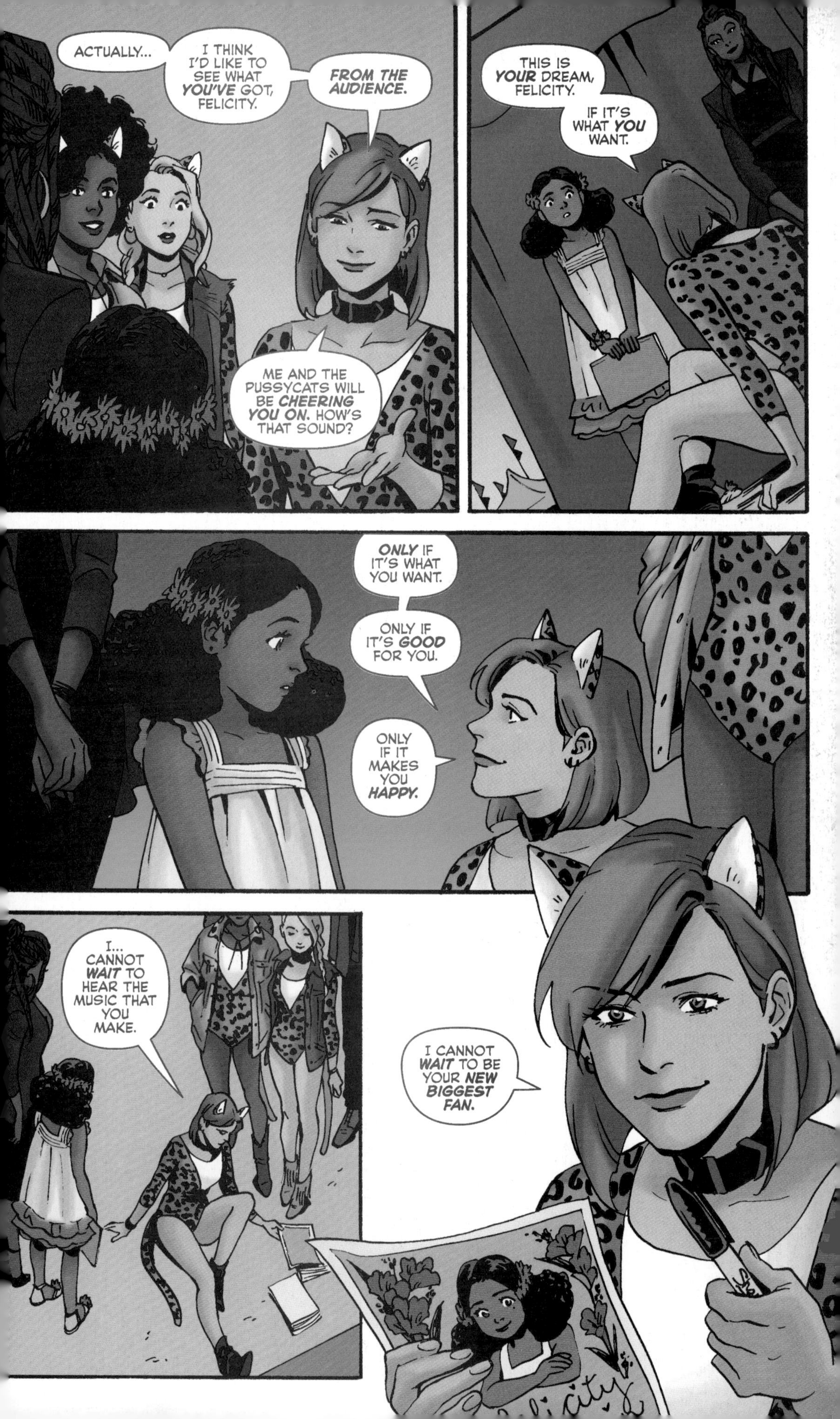
ACTUALLY...
I THINK I'D LIKE TO SEE WHAT YOU'VE GOT, FELICITY.
FROM THE AUDIENCE.
ME AND THE PUSSYCATS WILL BE CHEERING YOU ON. HOW'S THAT SOUND?
THIS IS YOUR DREAM, FELICITY.
IF IT'S WHAT YOU WANT.
ONLY IF IT'S WHAT YOU WANT.
ONLY IF IT'S GOOD FOR YOU.
ONLY IF IT MAKES YOU HAPPY.
I... CANNOT WAIT TO HEAR THE MUSIC THAT YOU MAKE.
I CANNOT WAIT TO BE YOUR NEW BIGGEST FAN.

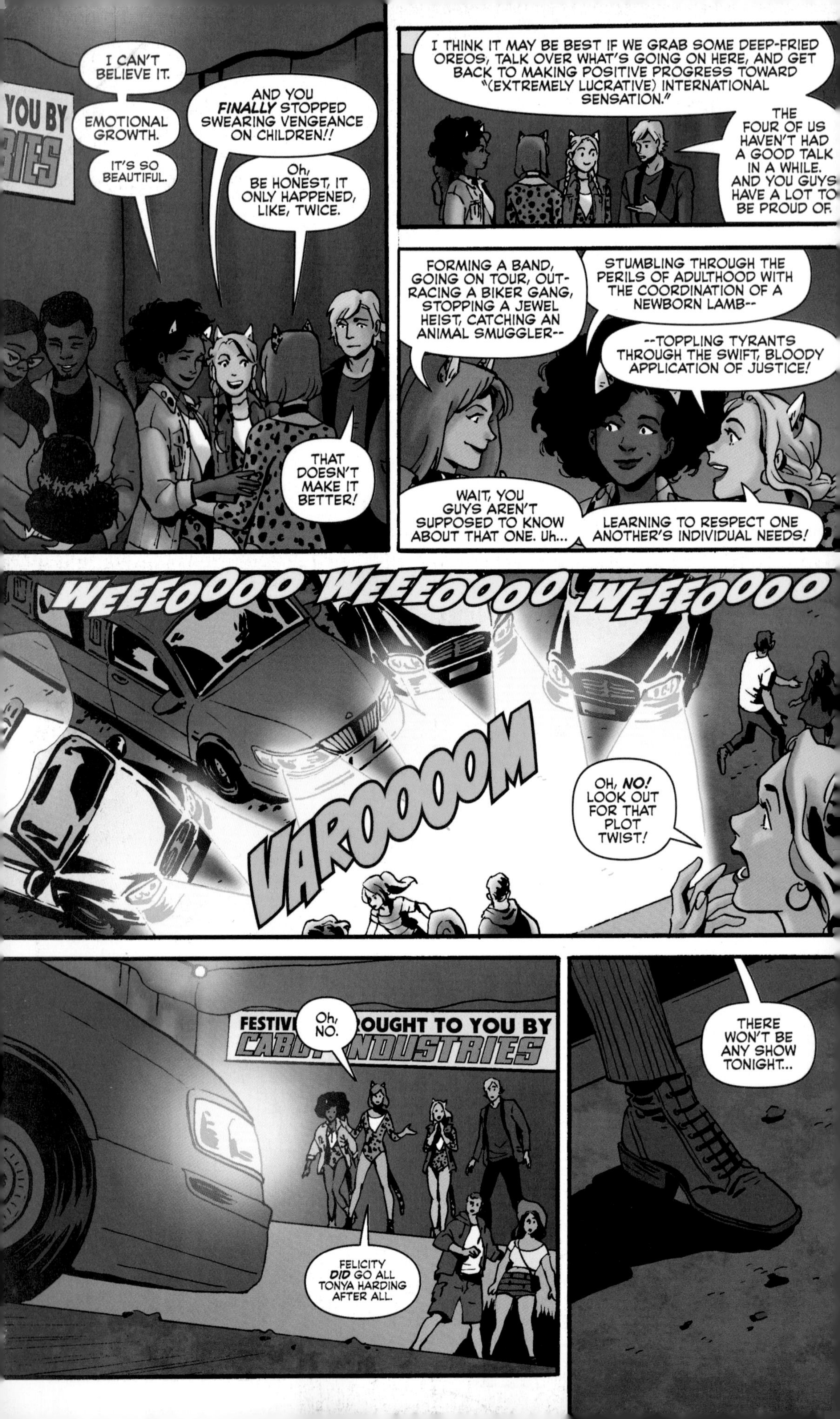
YOU BY
BIES
I CAN'T BELIEVE IT.
EMOTIONAL GROWTH.
IT'S SO BEAUTIFUL.
AND YOU *FINALLY* STOPPED SWEARING VENGEANCE ON CHILDREN!!
Oh, BE HONEST, IT ONLY HAPPENED, LIKE, TWICE.
THAT DOESN'T MAKE IT BETTER!
I THINK IT MAY BE BEST IF WE GRAB SOME DEEP-FRIED OREOS, TALK OVER WHAT'S GOING ON HERE, AND GET BACK TO MAKING POSITIVE PROGRESS TOWARD "(EXTREMELY LUCRATIVE) INTERNATIONAL SENSATION."
THE FOUR OF US HAVEN'T HAD A GOOD TALK IN A WHILE. AND YOU GUYS HAVE A LOT TO BE PROUD OF.
FORMING A BAND, GOING ON TOUR, OUT-RACING A BIKER GANG, STOPPING A JEWEL HEIST, CATCHING AN ANIMAL SMUGGLER--
STUMBLING THROUGH THE PERILS OF ADULTHOOD WITH THE COORDINATION OF A NEWBORN LAMB--
--TOPPLING TYRANTS THROUGH THE SWIFT, BLOODY APPLICATION OF JUSTICE!
WAIT, YOU GUYS AREN'T SUPPOSED TO KNOW ABOUT THAT ONE. Uh...
LEARNING TO RESPECT ONE ANOTHER'S INDIVIDUAL NEEDS!
WEEEOOOO WEEEOOOO WEEEOOOO
VAROOOOM
OH, **NO!** LOOK OUT FOR THAT PLOT TWIST!
FESTIV ROUGHT TO YOU BY
CAB NDUSTRIES
Oh, NO.
FELICITY ***DID*** GO ALL TONYA HARDING AFTER ALL.
THERE WON'T BE ANY SHOW TONIGHT...

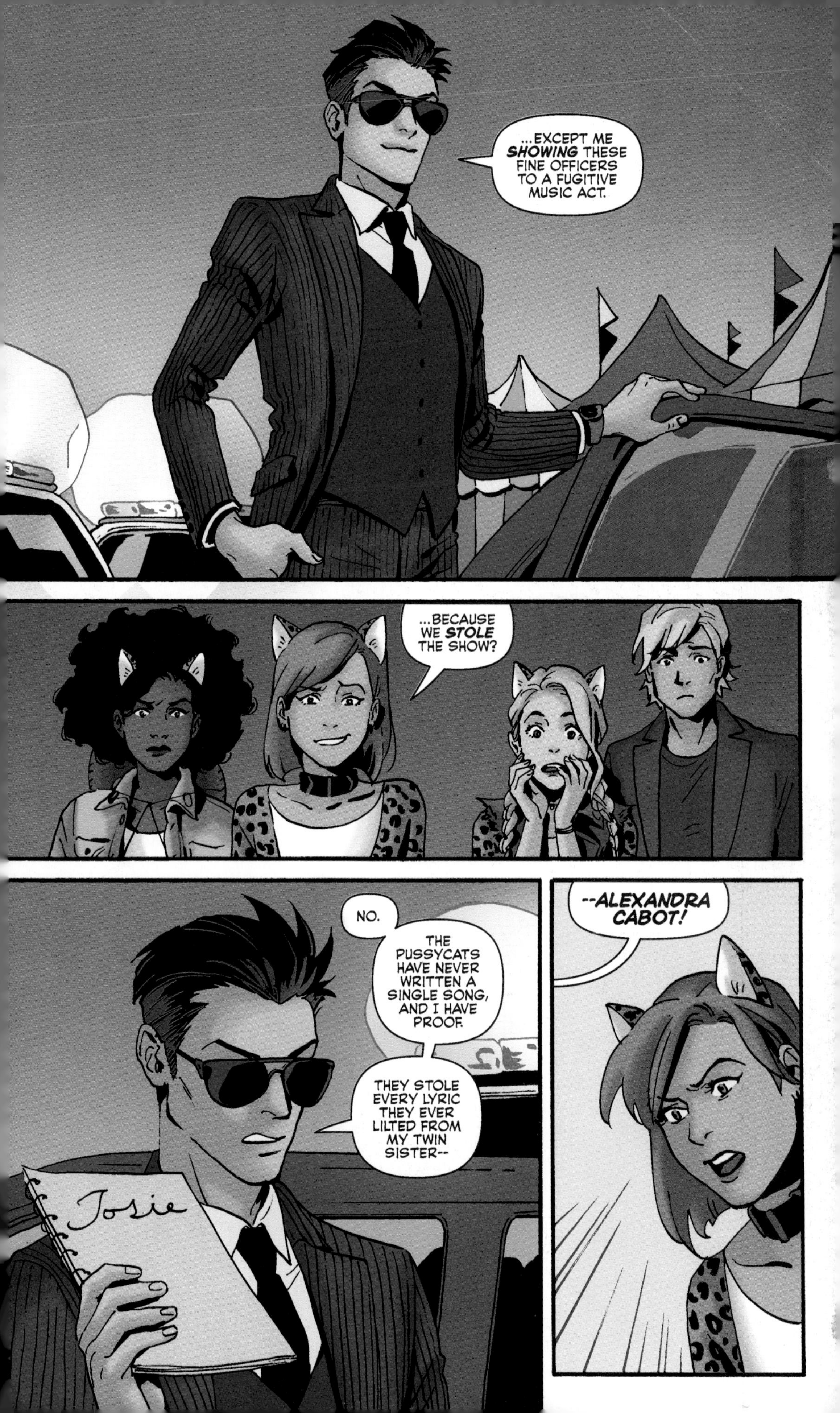
...EXCEPT ME SHOWING THESE FINE OFFICERS TO A FUGITIVE MUSIC ACT.
...BECAUSE WE STOLE THE SHOW?
NO.
THE PUSSYCATS HAVE NEVER WRITTEN A SINGLE SONG, AND I HAVE PROOF.
THEY STOLE EVERY LYRIC THEY EVER LILTED FROM MY TWIN SISTER--
Josie
--ALEXANDRA CABOT!

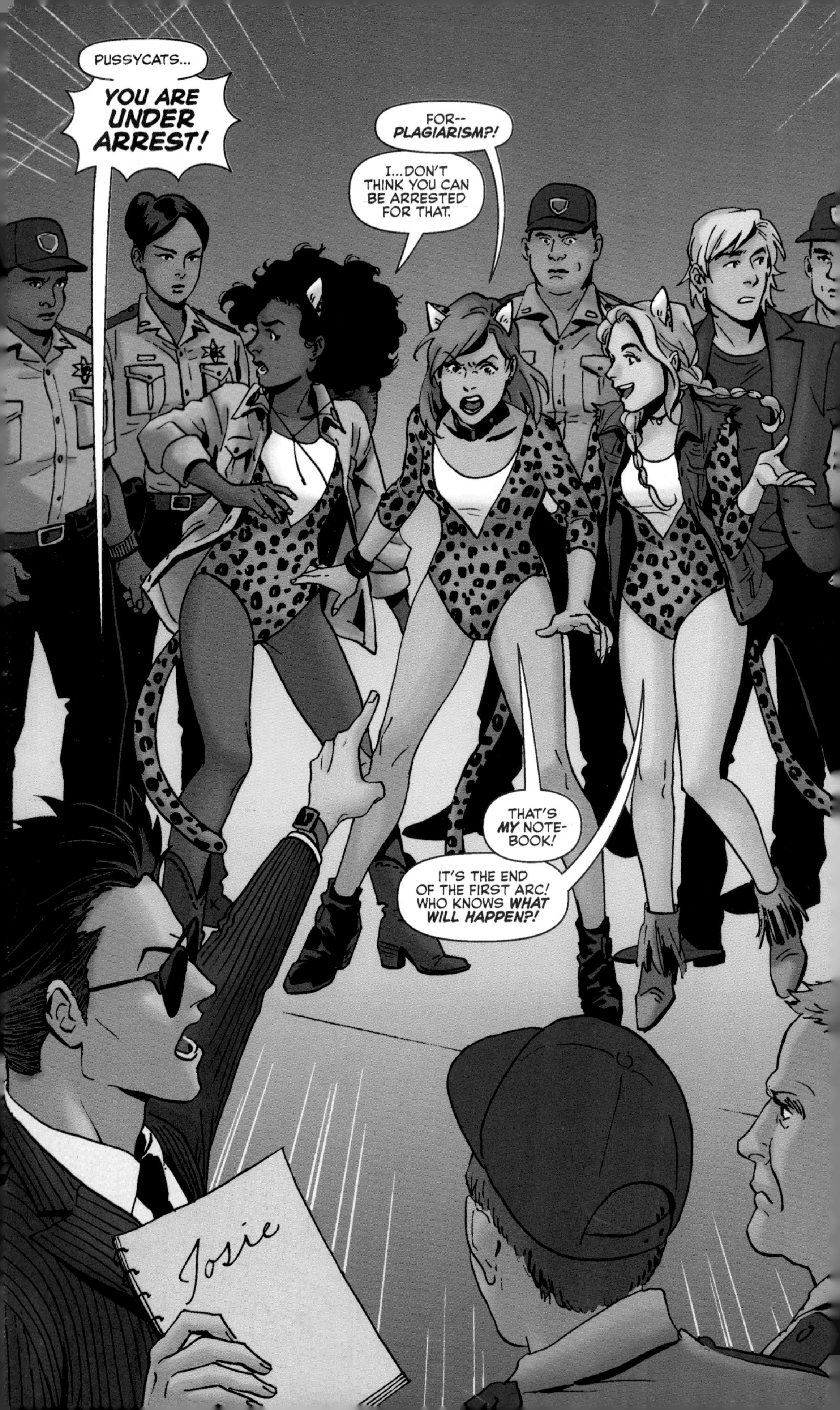
PUSSYCATS...
YOU ARE UNDER ARREST!
FOR-- PLAGIARISM?!
I...DON'T THINK YOU CAN BE ARRESTED FOR THAT.
THAT'S MY NOTE-BOOK!
IT'S THE END OF THE FIRST ARC! WHO KNOWS WHAT WILL HAPPEN?!
Josie

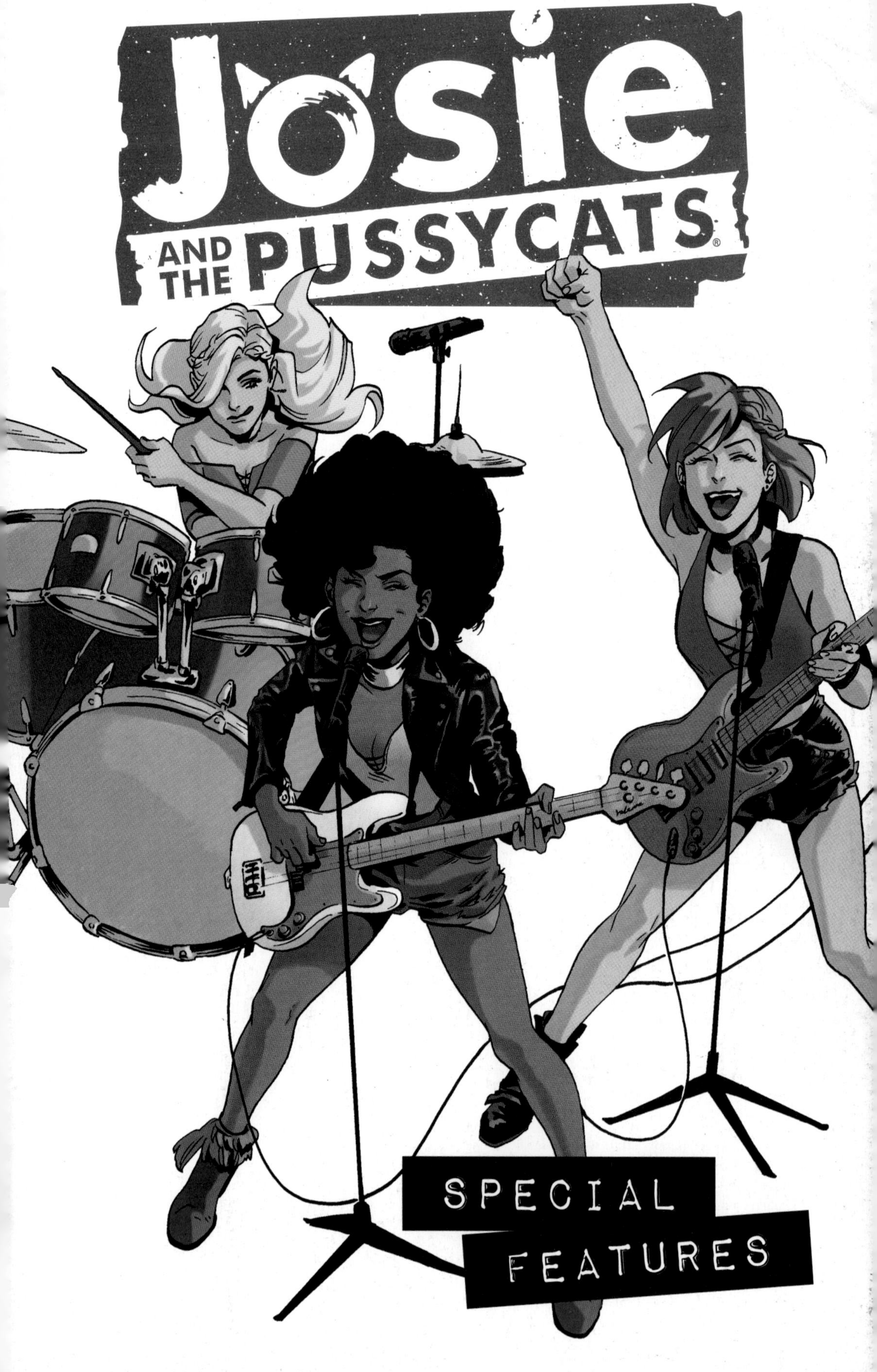
JOSIE AND THE PUSSYCATS®
SPECIAL FEATURES

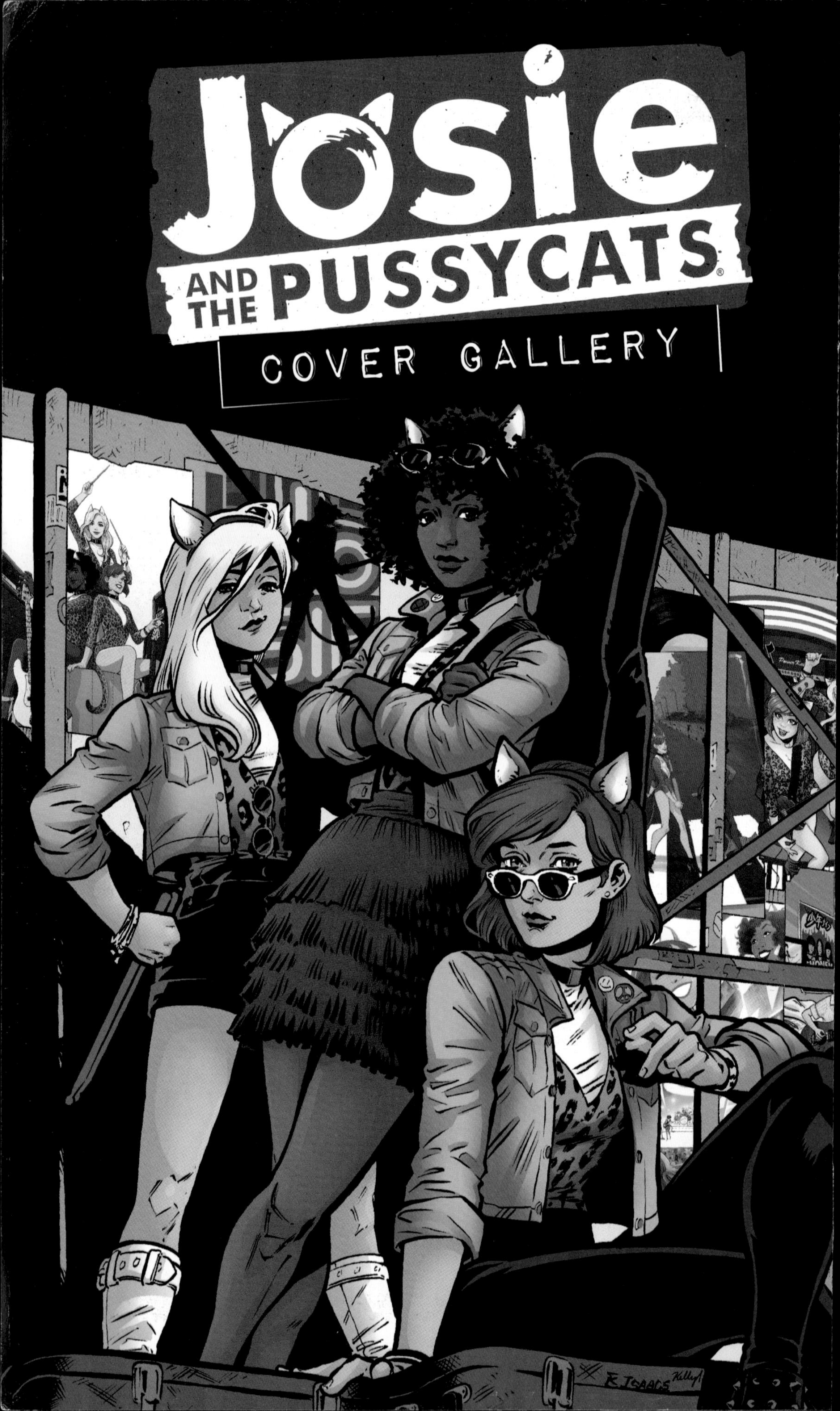

Josie
AND THE PUSSYCATS®
COVER GALLERY

ISSUE ONE

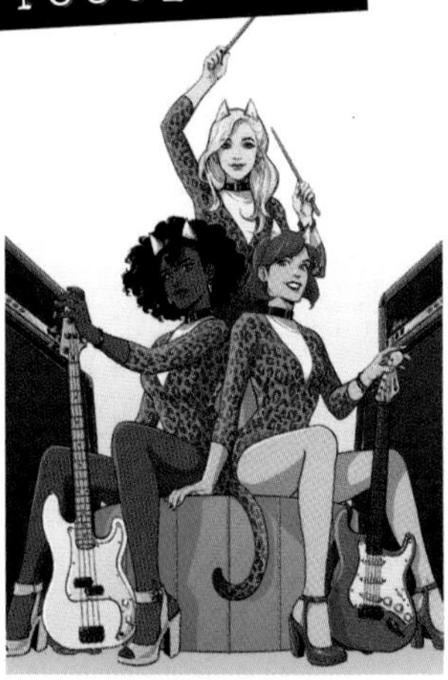

AUDREY MOK

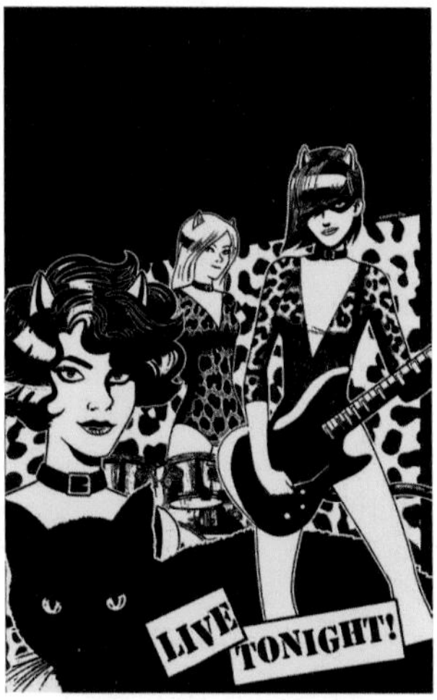
LIVE
TONIGHT!

DEREK CHARM

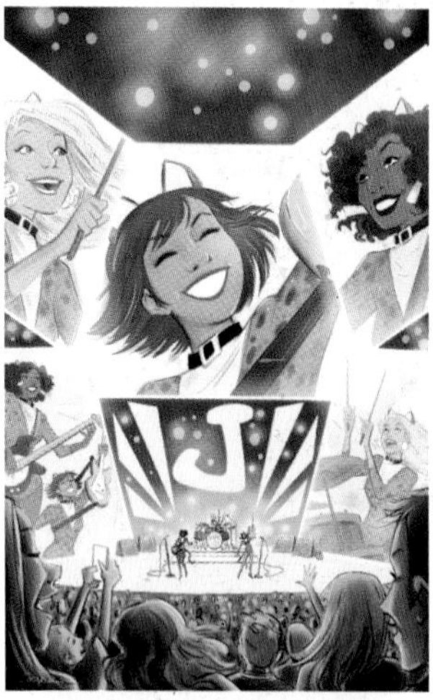

COLLEEN COOVER

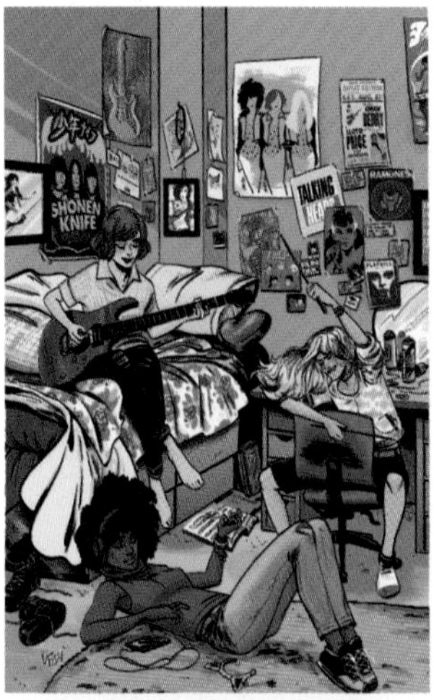
SHONEN KNIFE
TALKING

VERONICA FISH

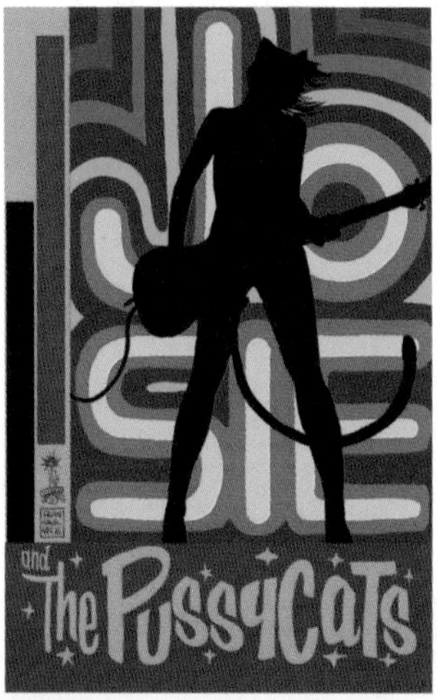
and
The PussyCats

FRANCESCO FRANCAVILLA

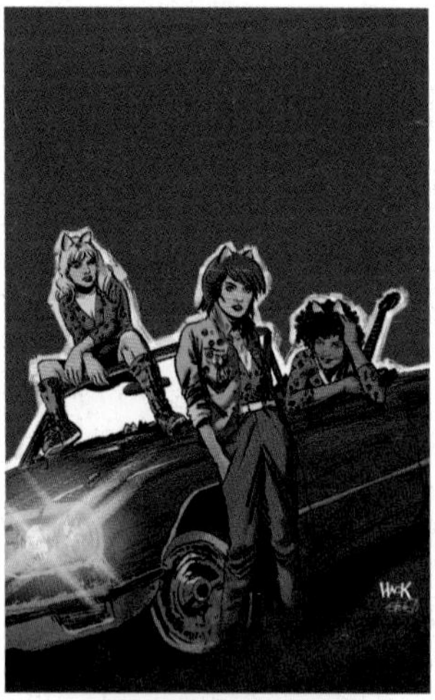
HACK

ROBERT HACK

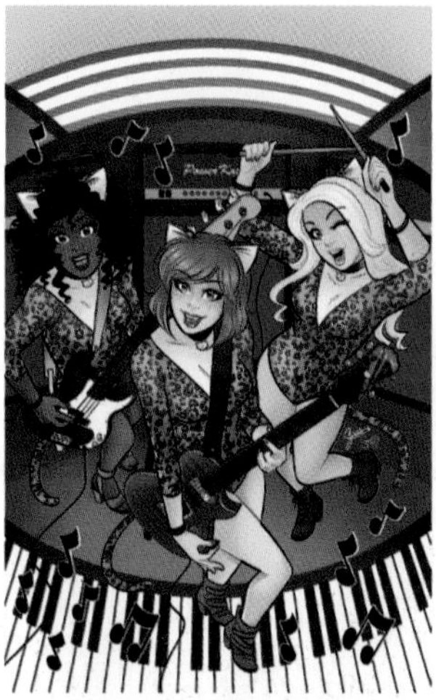

GISELE LAGACE

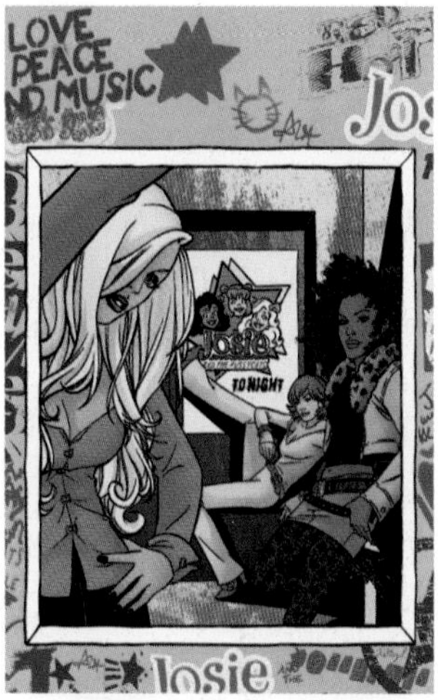
LOVE
PEACE
ND MUSIC
TONIGHT
Josie

ALITHA MARTINEZ

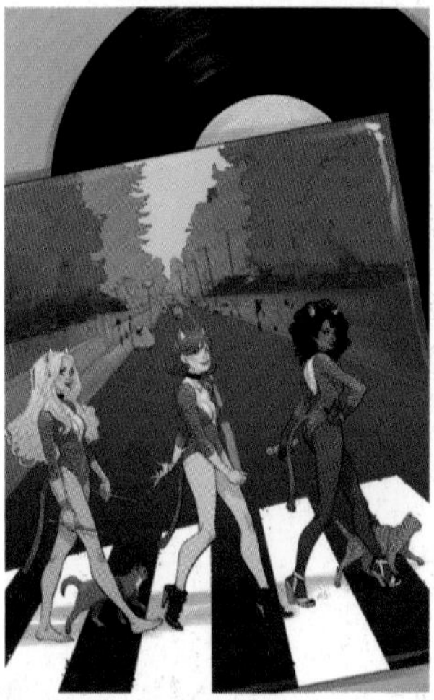

MARGUERITE SAUVAGE

ISSUE TWO

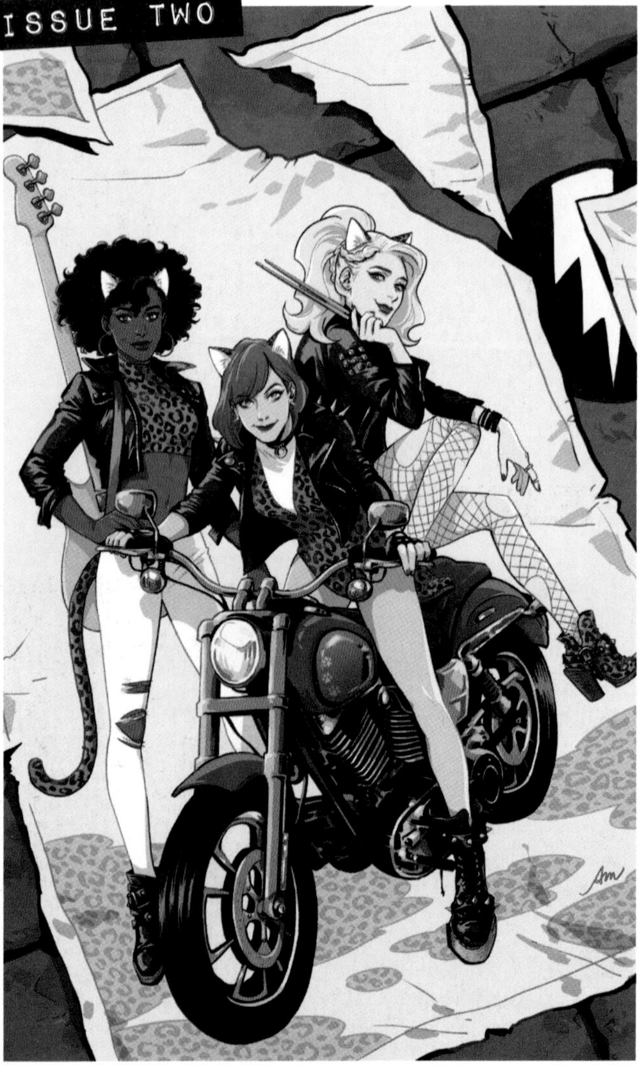

AUDREY MOK

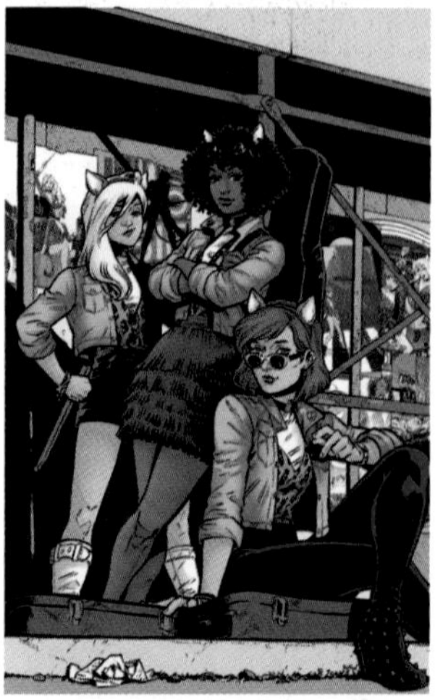

REBEKAH ISAACS

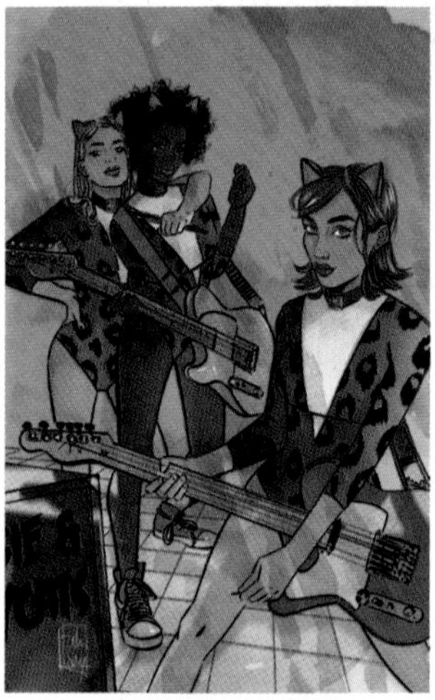

TULA TOTAY

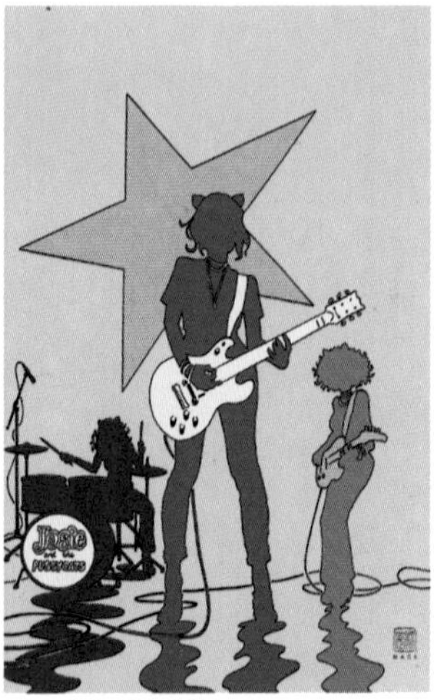

DAVID MACK

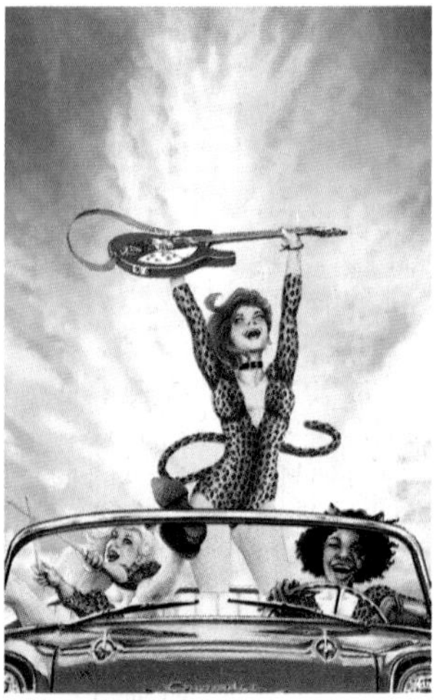

ALLISON SOHN

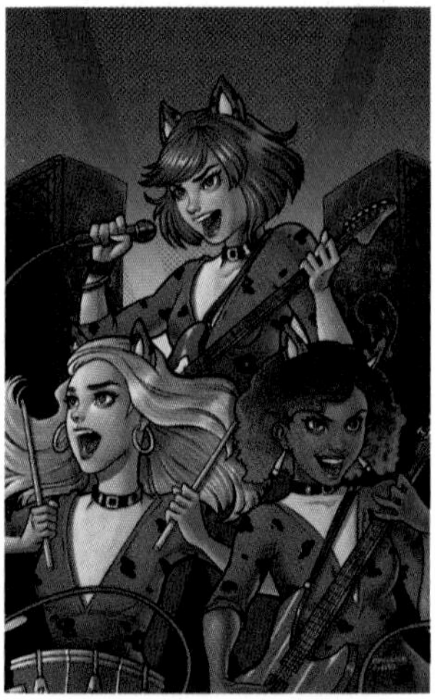

CHRISSIE ZULLO

ISSUE THREE

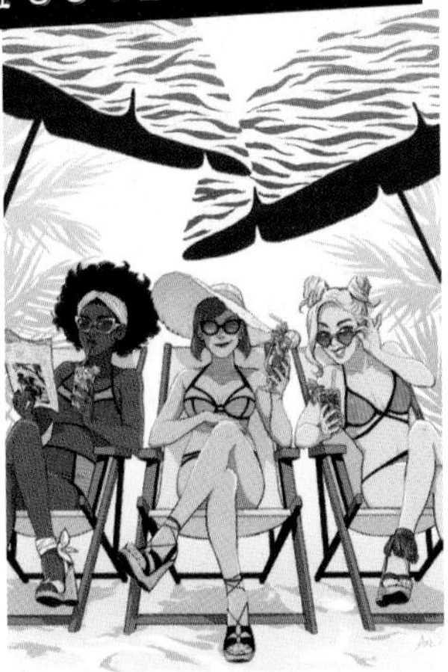

AUDREY MOK

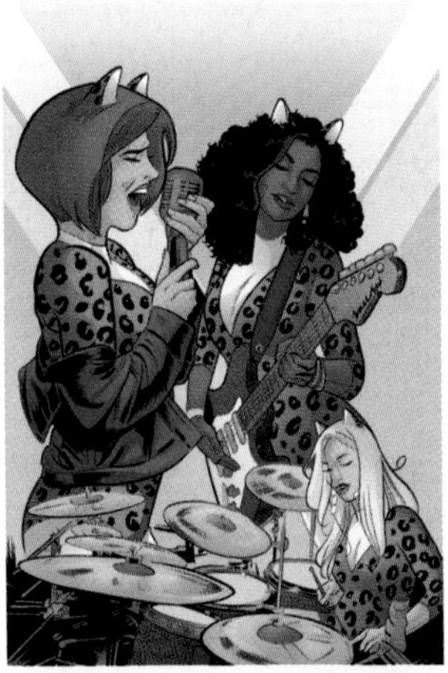

WILFREDO TORRES

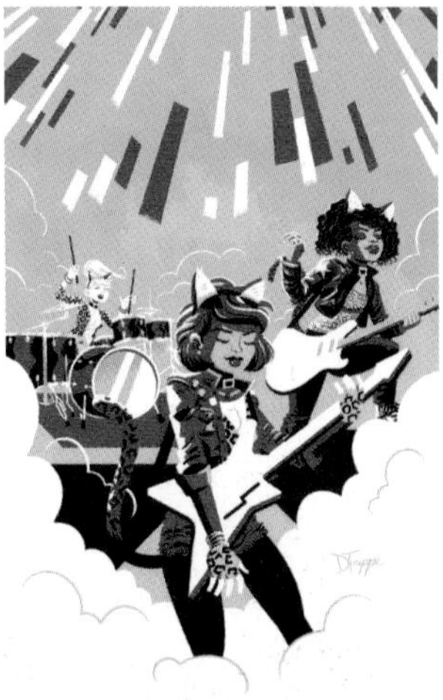

DEAN TRIPPE

ISSUE FOUR

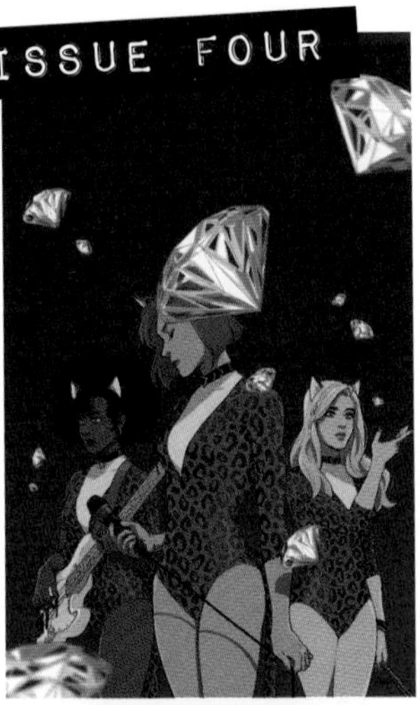

AUDREY MOK

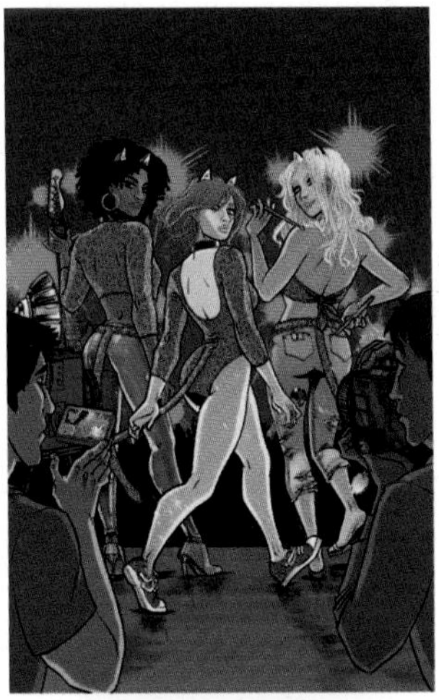

SANYA ANWAR

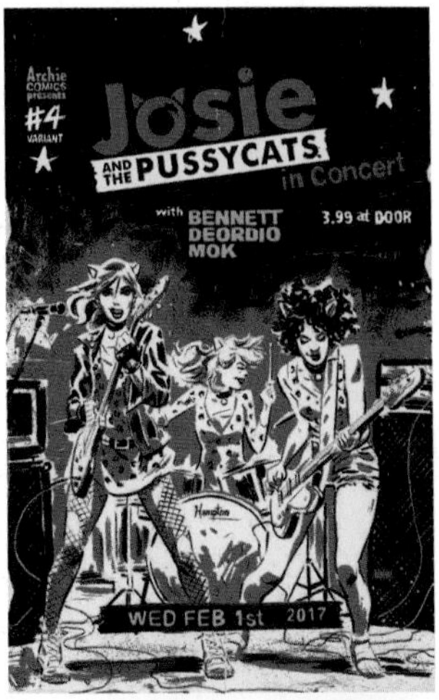
Archie COMICS presents
#4 VARIANT
Josie AND THE PUSSYCATS in Concert
with BENNETT DEORDIO MOK
3.99 at DOOR
WED FEB 1st 2017

MICHAEL WALSH

ISSUE FIVE

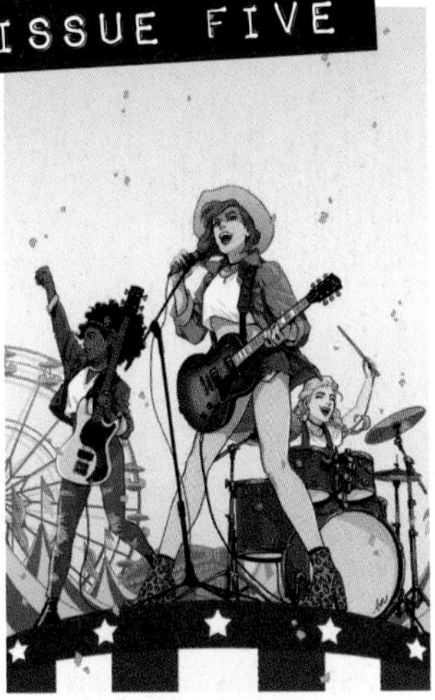

AUDREY MOK

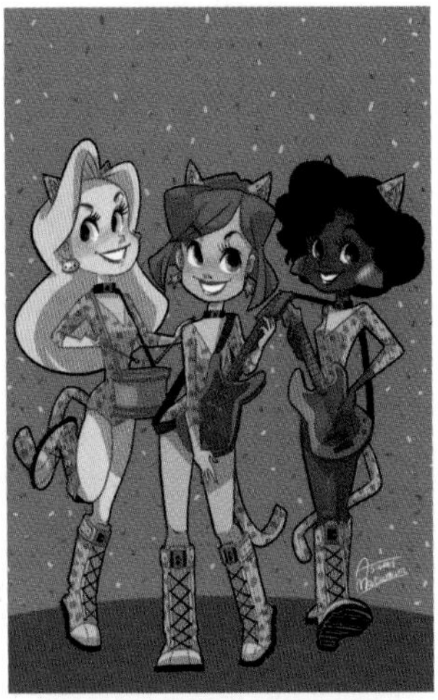

ASAMI MATSUMURA

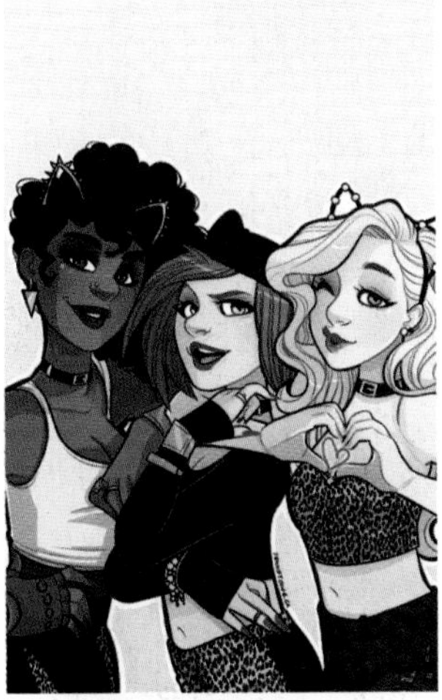

JENN ST. ONGE

JO'SIE AND THE PUSSYCATS

ORIGINAL SKETCHES

JOSIE McCOY

Lead singer and guitarist. Her style lands somewhere between country girl-next-door and mega rock star. She can easily translate to playing at local dives or amphitheaters.

VALERIE BROWN

Singer and bassist. She keeps her style casual, yet sophisticated, especially when she's spending long hours working at the animal shelter.

MELODY VALENTINE

Drummer and backup vocals. Her style is reminiscent of Baby Spice but with an edge. Cute but comfy--perfect for long tour bus rides spent listening to audiobooks!

ALAN M.

Manager of Josie and the Pussycats. Keeps his appearance sharp and classy, ideal for his world travels.

ALEXANDRA CABOT

Former friend-former rival-current friend of Josie McCoy. Her family's wealth has given her an impeccable sense of style, which she uses to showcase her individuality.

THE PUSSYCATS

The ladies donning their famous catsuits, complete with their long tails and ears for hats!

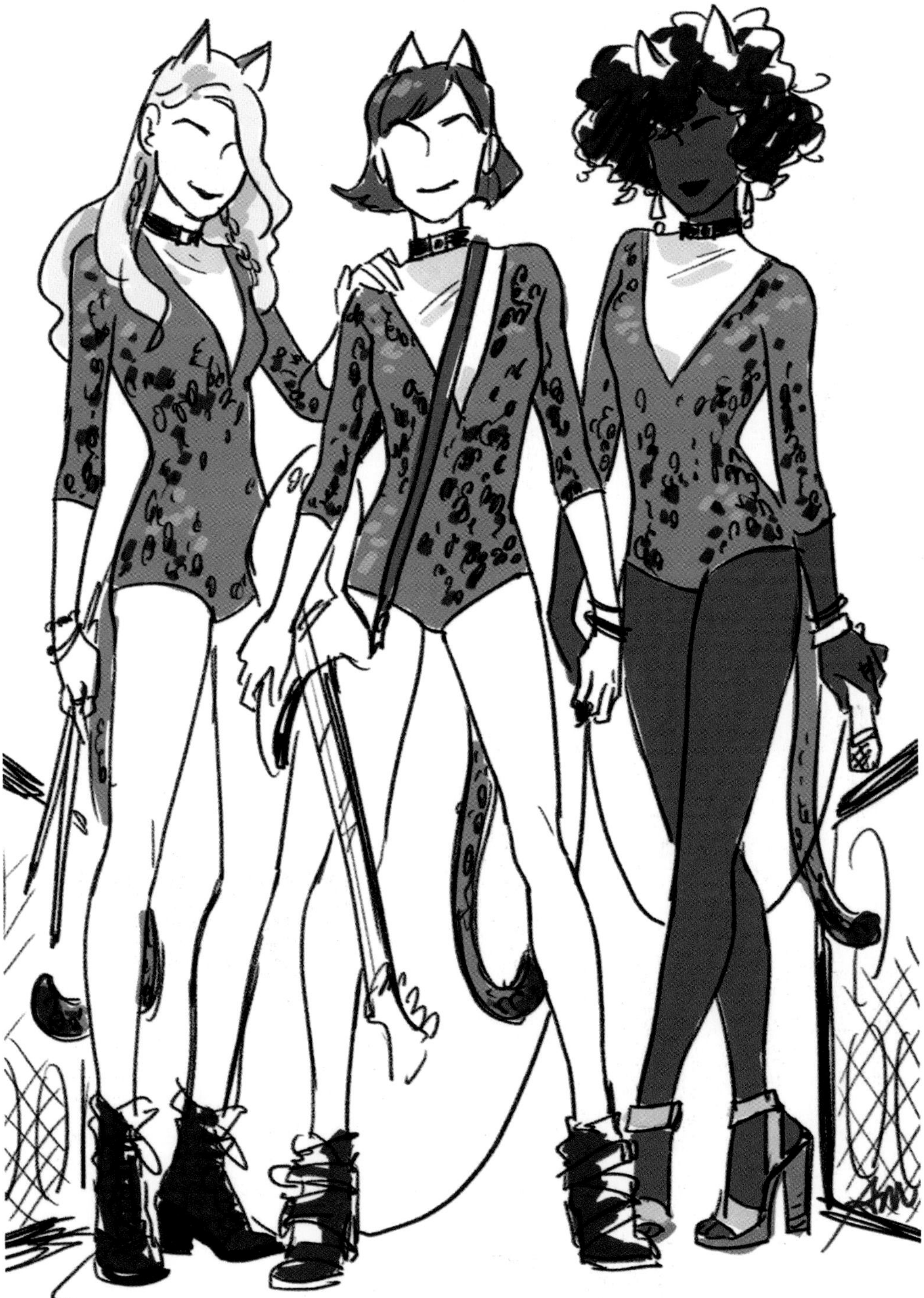

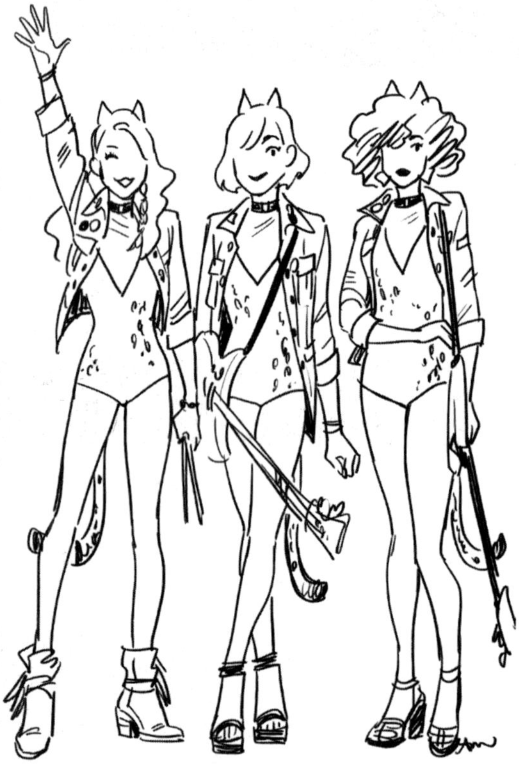

FRONT

Audrey Mok finds the best ways to make their individual styles shine through even when they're wearing matching catsuits!

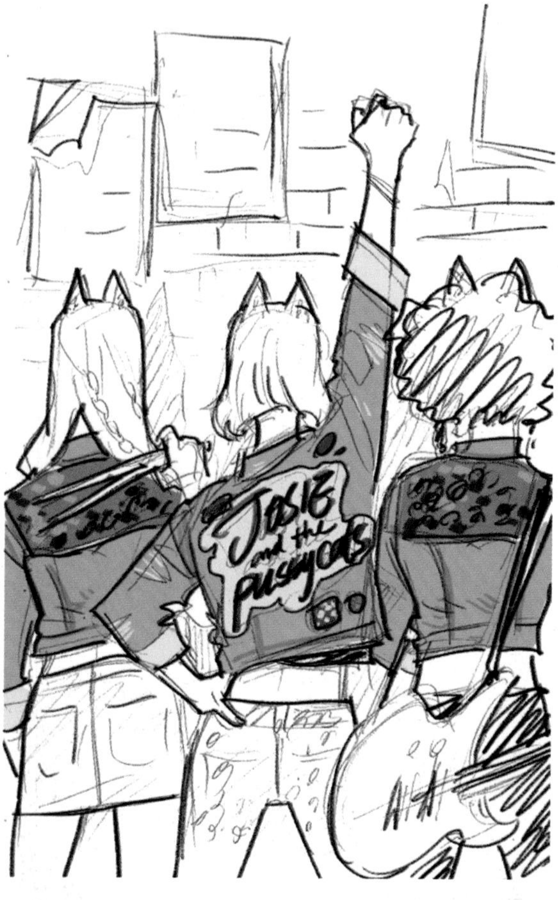

Josie and the Pussycats

BACK

The girls are ready to rock! Who wouldn't want an awesome *Josie and the Pussycats* back patch?!

SPECIAL PREVIEW

Jughead®

ISSUE NINE

Here's a special look at **JUGHEAD VOL. 2**, which sees our beloved crowned hero making a new friend: **SABRINA THE TEENAGE WITCH.** Magic and mayhem abound in this second graphic novel collection, on sale in finer bookstores and comic shops now!

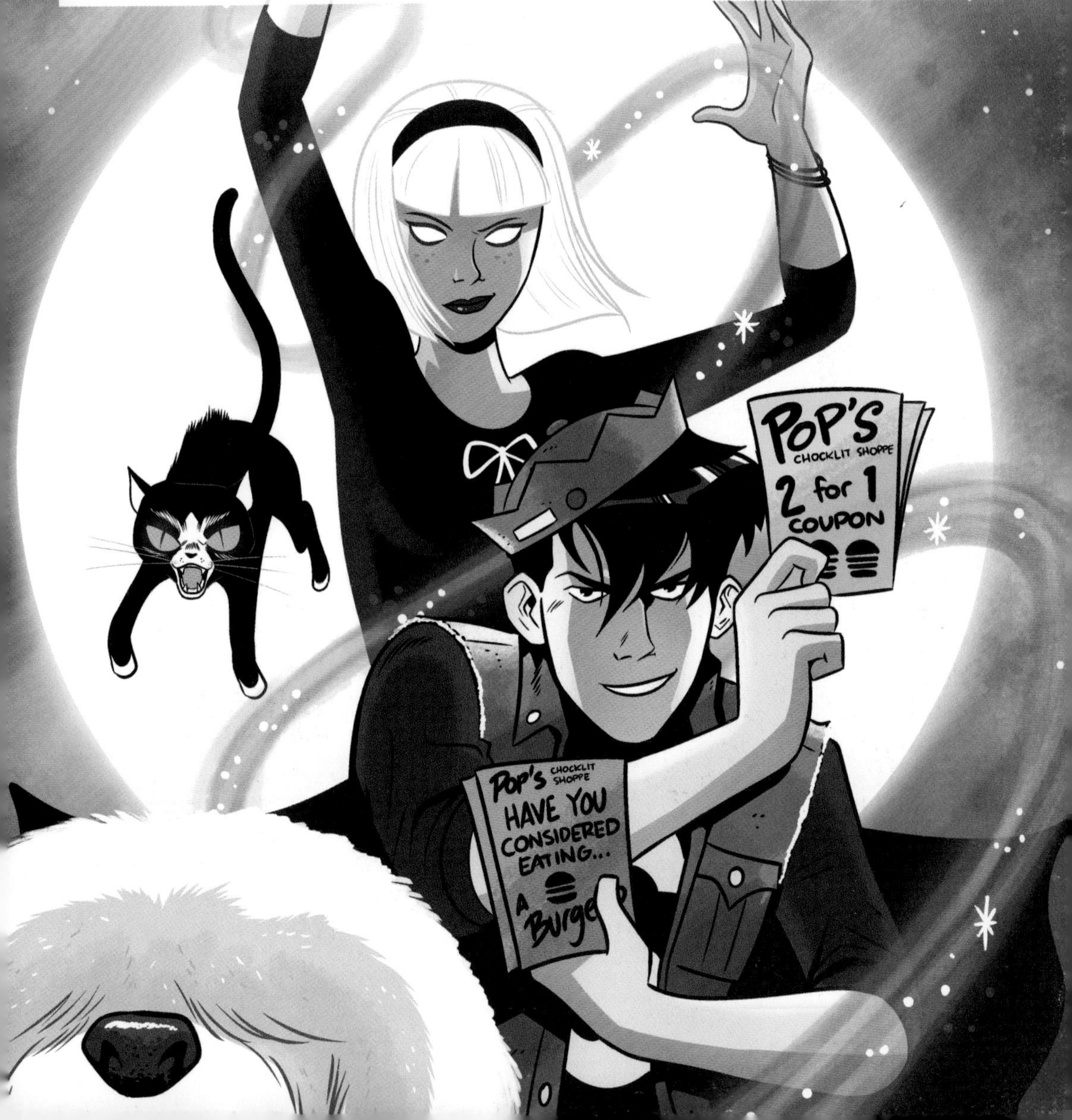
POP'S CHOCKLIT SHOPPE
2 for 1 COUPON
POP'S CHOCKLIT SHOPPE
HAVE YOU CONSIDERED EATING...
A Burge

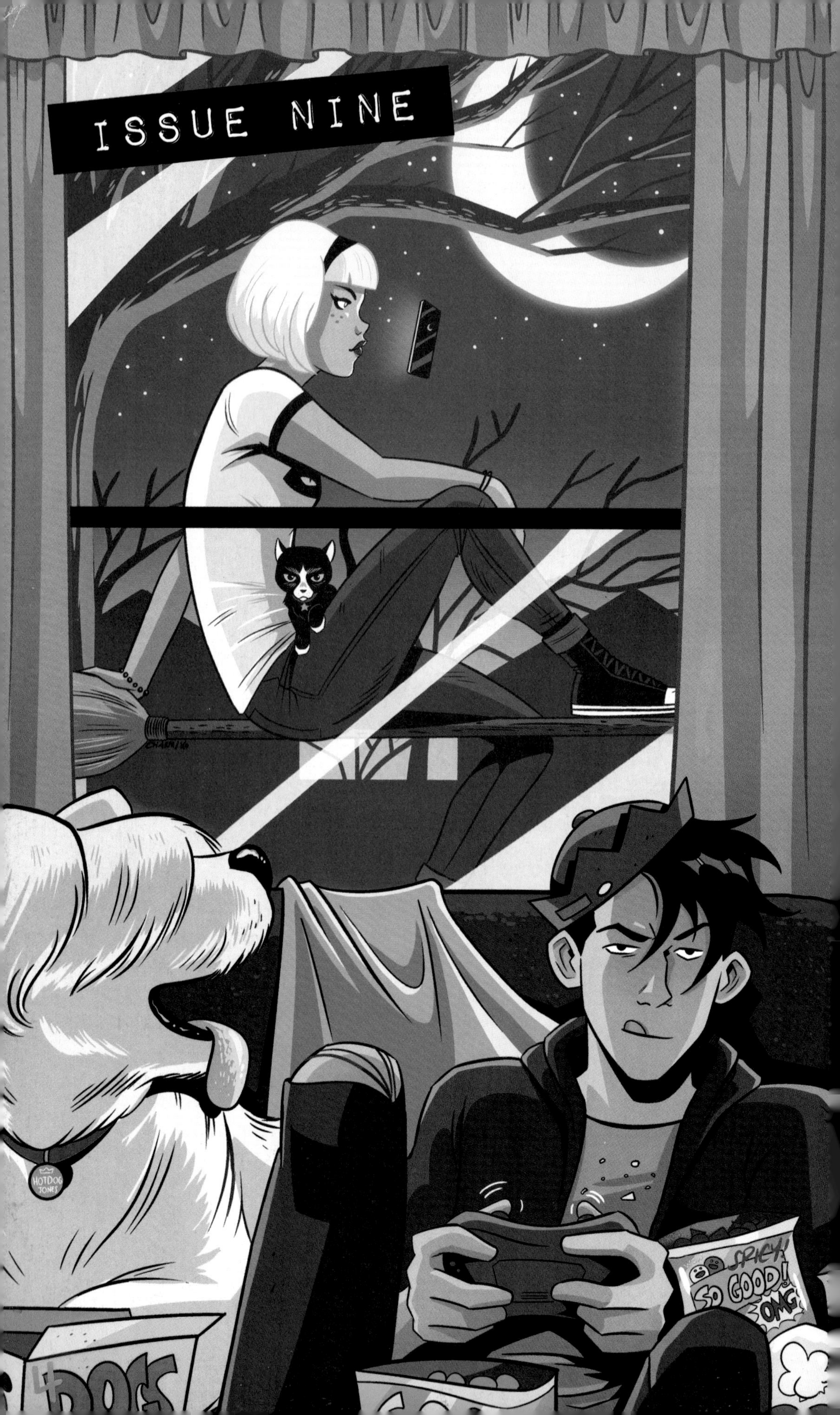
ISSUE NINE
HOTDOG JONES
SPICY!
SO GOOD!
OMG

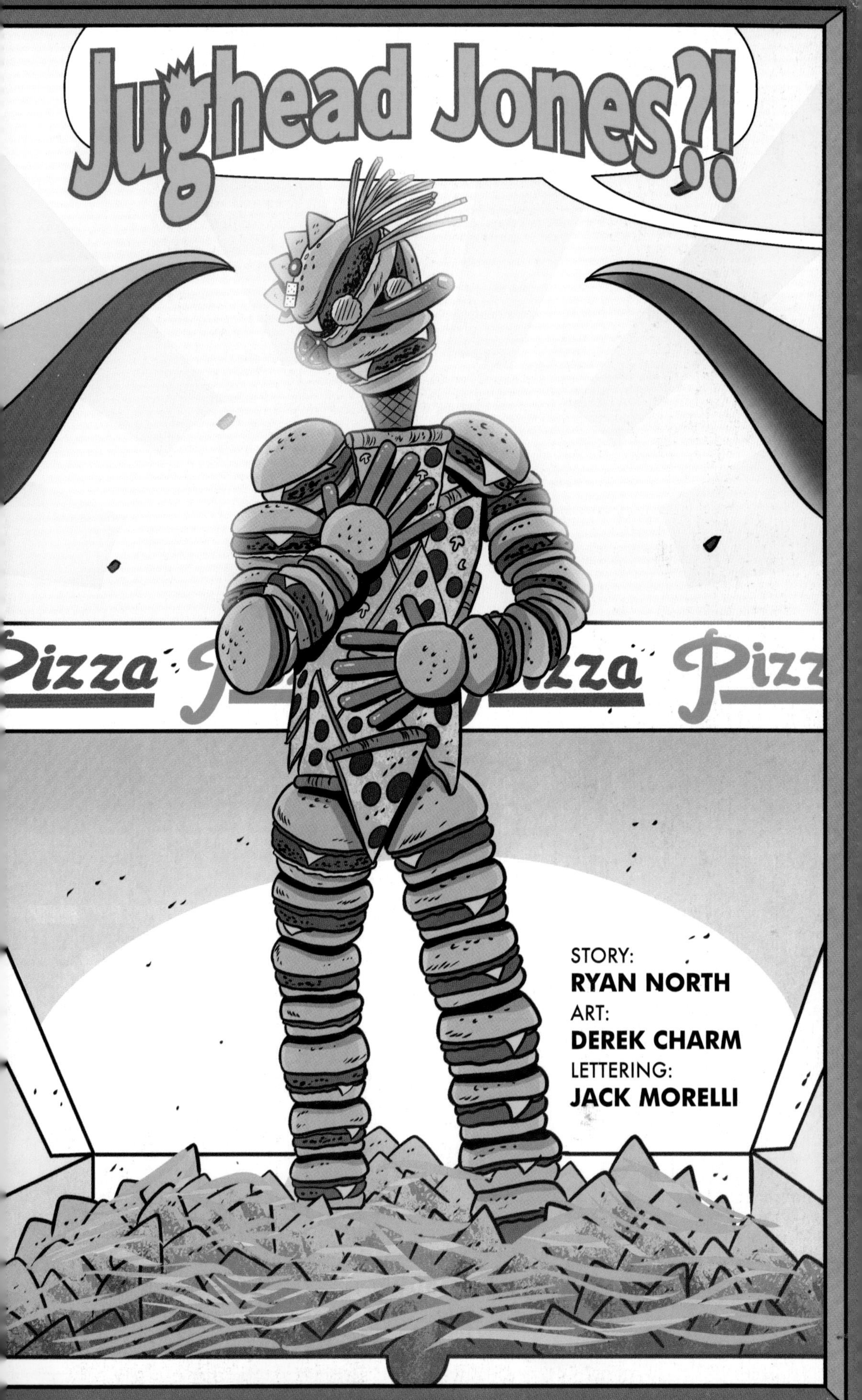
Jughead Jones?!
Pizza
Pizza
STORY:
RYAN NORTH
ART:
DEREK CHARM
LETTERING:
JACK MORELLI

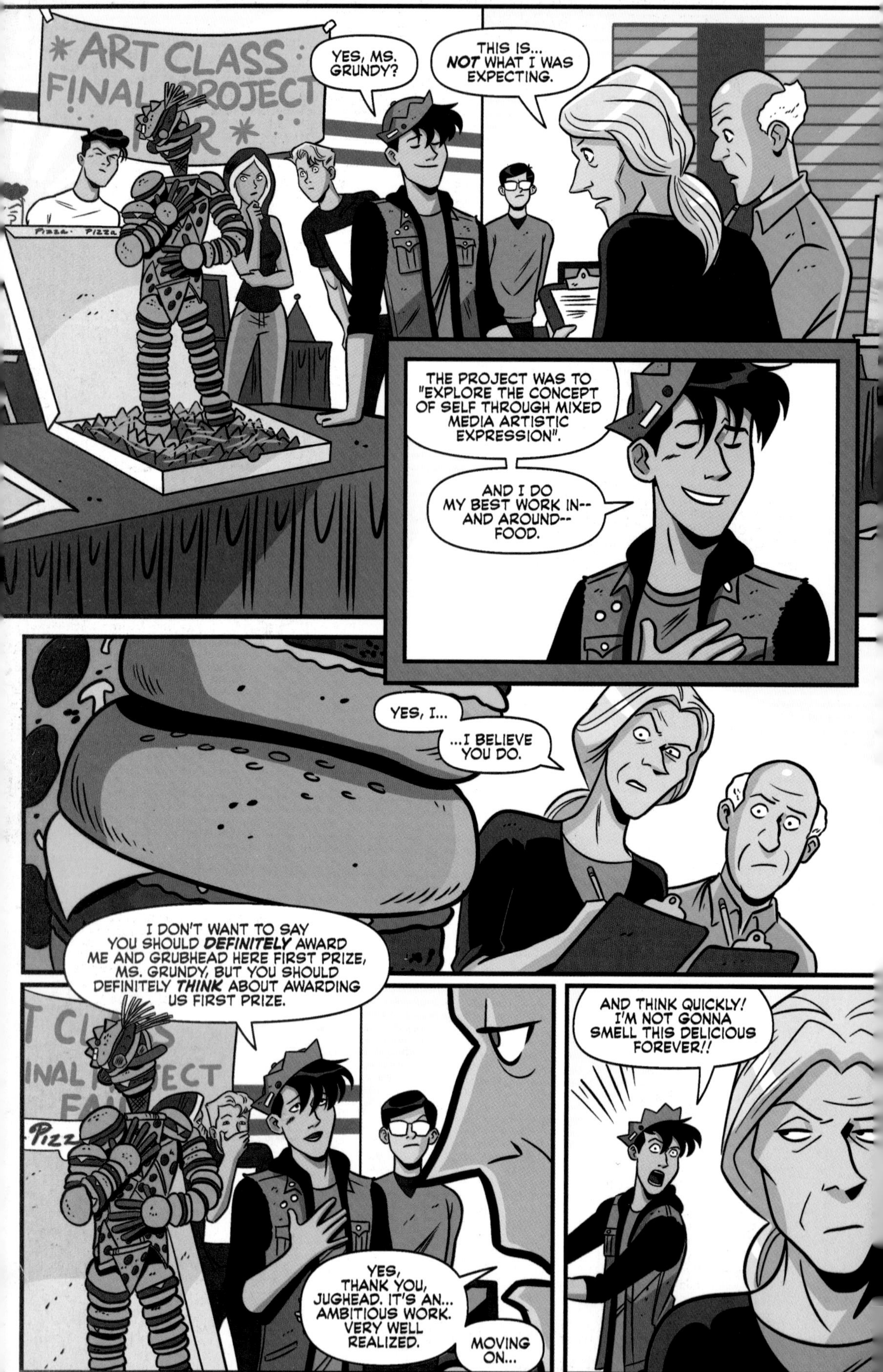
ART CLASS FINAL PROJECT
YES, MS. GRUNDY?
THIS IS... NOT WHAT I WAS EXPECTING.
PIZZA PIZZA
THE PROJECT WAS TO "EXPLORE THE CONCEPT OF SELF THROUGH MIXED MEDIA ARTISTIC EXPRESSION".
AND I DO MY BEST WORK IN-- AND AROUND-- FOOD.
YES, I...
...I BELIEVE YOU DO.
I DON'T WANT TO SAY YOU SHOULD DEFINITELY AWARD ME AND GRUBHEAD HERE FIRST PRIZE, MS. GRUNDY, BUT YOU SHOULD DEFINITELY THINK ABOUT AWARDING US FIRST PRIZE.
YES, THANK YOU, JUGHEAD. IT'S AN... AMBITIOUS WORK. VERY WELL REALIZED.
MOVING ON...
AND THINK QUICKLY! I'M NOT GONNA SMELL THIS DELICIOUS FOREVER!!

Pfft, like Jughead has ever not eaten food long enough to find out it can go bad. Also, hello, I'm Ryan and I like to put little jokes in the margins of my comics. It's ***extra jokes*** in your comic, **FOR THE SAME LOW, LOW PRICE!!** That's right: Chip was **RIPPING YOU OFF**.

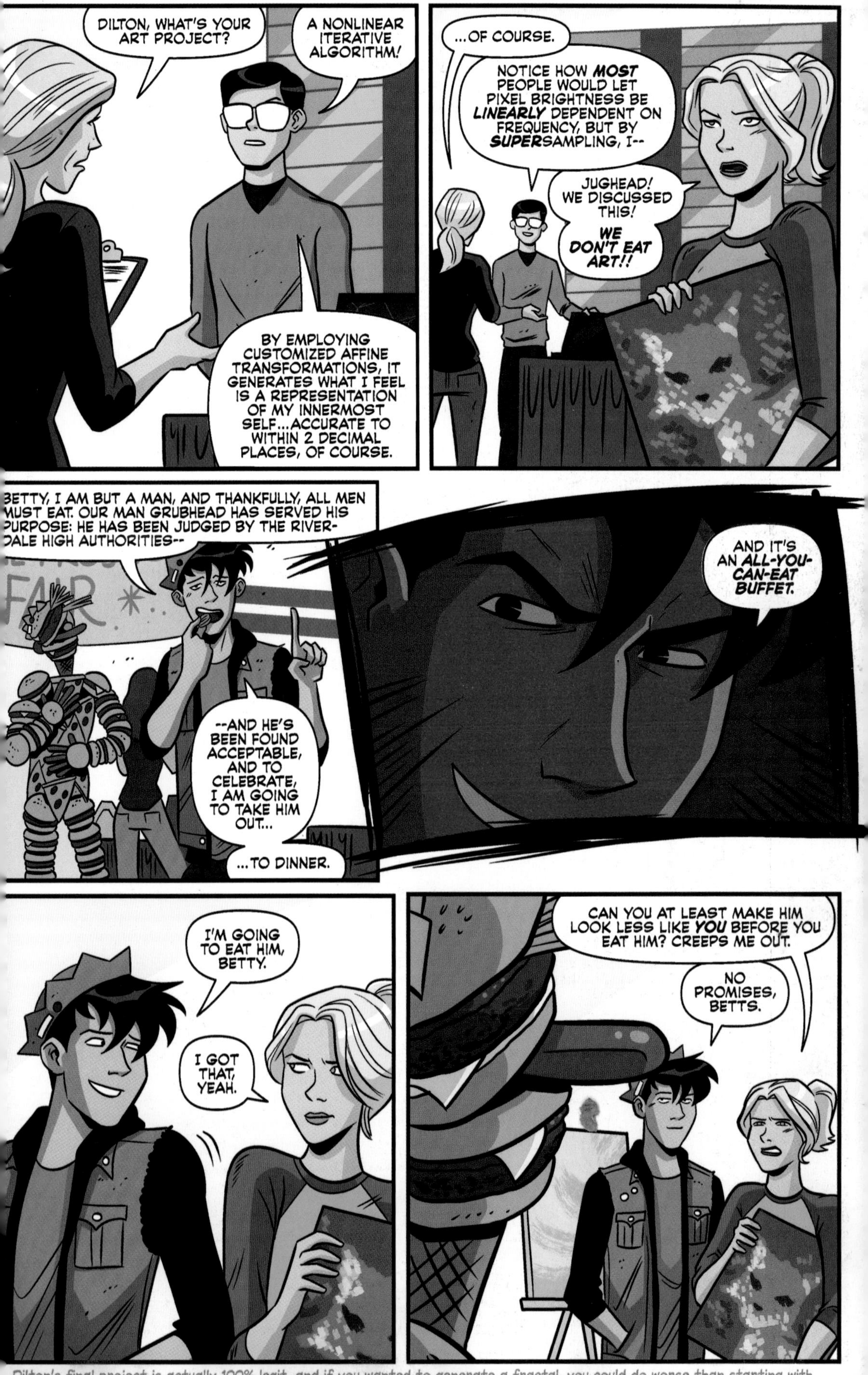
DILTON, WHAT'S YOUR ART PROJECT?
A NONLINEAR ITERATIVE ALGORITHM!
BY EMPLOYING CUSTOMIZED AFFINE TRANSFORMATIONS, IT GENERATES WHAT I FEEL IS A REPRESENTATION OF MY INNERMOST SELF...ACCURATE TO WITHIN 2 DECIMAL PLACES, OF COURSE.
...OF COURSE.
NOTICE HOW **MOST** PEOPLE WOULD LET PIXEL BRIGHTNESS BE **LINEARLY** DEPENDENT ON FREQUENCY, BUT BY **SUPER**SAMPLING, I--
JUGHEAD! WE DISCUSSED THIS! **WE DON'T EAT ART!!**
BETTY, I AM BUT A MAN, AND THANKFULLY, ALL MEN MUST EAT. OUR MAN GRUBHEAD HAS SERVED HIS PURPOSE: HE HAS BEEN JUDGED BY THE RIVER-DALE HIGH AUTHORITIES--
--AND HE'S BEEN FOUND ACCEPTABLE, AND TO CELEBRATE, I AM GOING TO TAKE HIM OUT...
...TO DINNER.
AND IT'S AN **ALL-YOU-CAN-EAT BUFFET.**
I'M GOING TO EAT HIM, BETTY.
I GOT THAT, YEAH.
CAN YOU AT LEAST MAKE HIM LOOK LESS LIKE **YOU** BEFORE YOU EAT HIM? CREEPS ME OUT.
NO PROMISES, BETTS.

Dilton's final project is actually 100% legit, and if you wanted to generate a fractal, you could do worse than starting with a nonlinear iterative algorithm with affine transformations. Those of you big into both nonlinear iterative algorithms *and* teen comedy comics are nodding your heads right now. I can tell.

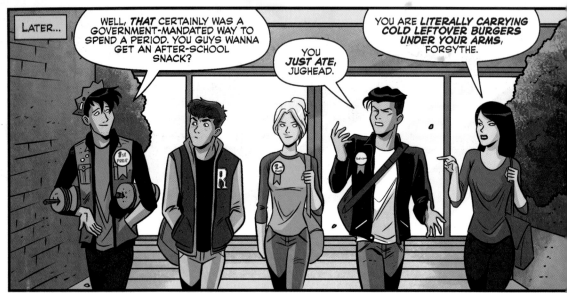

WELL, *THAT* CERTAINLY WAS A GOVERNMENT-MANDATED WAY TO SPEND A PERIOD. YOU GUYS WANNA GET AN AFTER-SCHOOL SNACK?

YOU *JUST ATE*, JUGHEAD.

YOU ARE *LITERALLY CARRYING COLD LEFTOVER BURGERS UNDER YOUR ARMS*, FORSYTHE.

WHAT, THESE? MERELY ROAD SNACKS. HEY, YOU'RE WELCOME TO SOME IF YOU WANT!

NO THANK YOU.

NO.

Participant

YEAH--I'LL TAKE ONE, ACTUALLY.

THERE'S MY BUDDY!

YOU GOT ANY VEGGIE PATTIES ON THERE?

GRUBHEAD'S ENTIRE LEFT LEG WAS VEGETARIAN!

HE WAS A COMPLICATED MAN, AND WE SHALL MISS HIM.

At this point you're probably wondering why we didn't just put Grubhead's name on the cover. Fine. I promise we'll stop talking about him right...*NOW.*

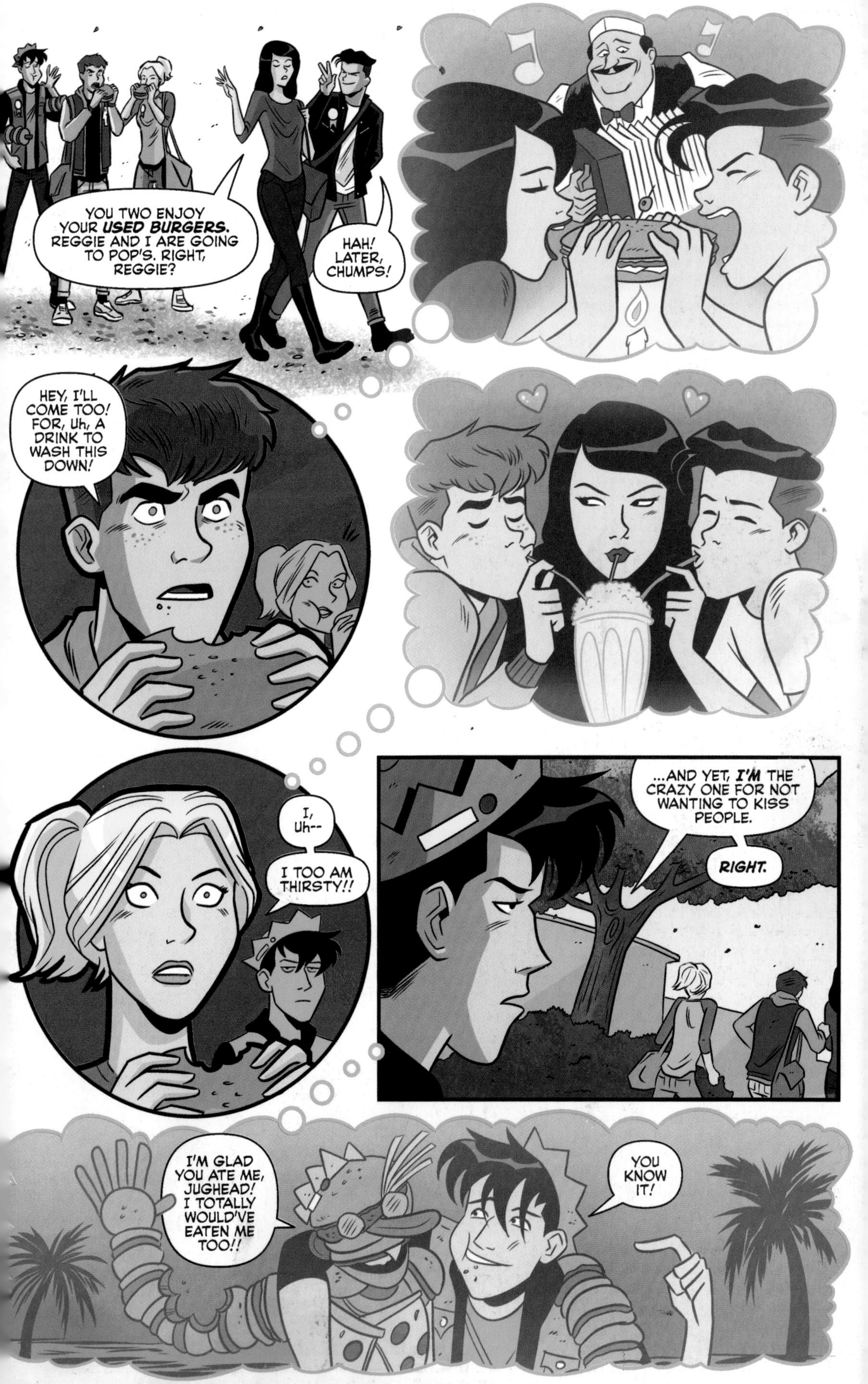

YOU TWO ENJOY YOUR USED BURGERS. REGGIE AND I ARE GOING TO POP'S. RIGHT, REGGIE?
HAH! LATER, CHUMPS!
HEY, I'LL COME TOO! FOR, Uh, A DRINK TO WASH THIS DOWN!
I, Uh--
I TOO AM THIRSTY!!
...AND YET, I'M THE CRAZY ONE FOR NOT WANTING TO KISS PEOPLE.
RIGHT.
I'M GLAD YOU ATE ME, JUGHEAD! I TOTALLY WOULD'VE EATEN ME TOO!!
YOU KNOW IT!

GRUBHEAD RETURNS, LOOKS LIKE I'M A UNRELIABLE NARRATOR!! HAH HAH HAH OH WELL

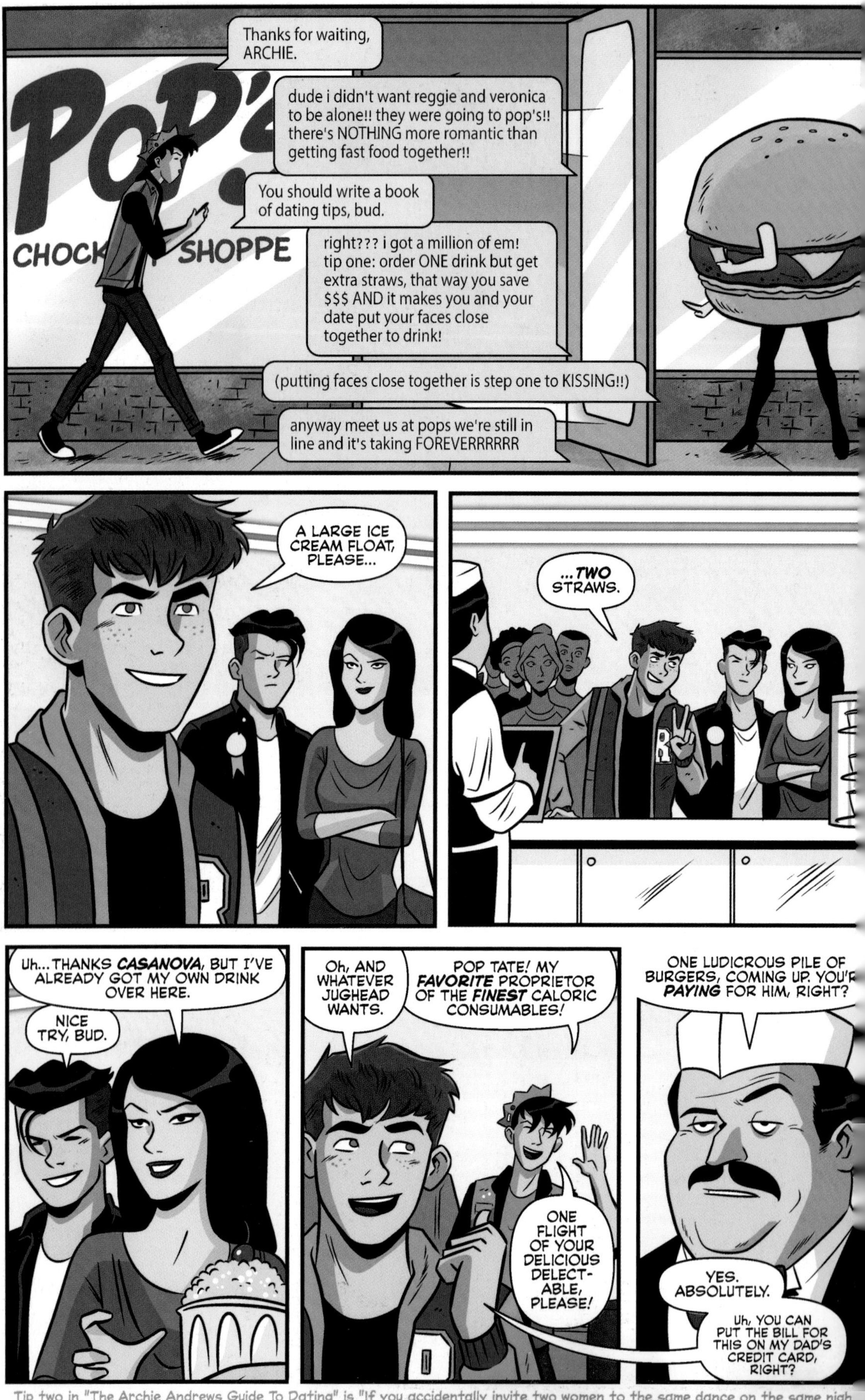
Thanks for waiting, ARCHIE.
dude i didn't want reggie and veronica to be alone!! they were going to pop's!! there's NOTHING more romantic than getting fast food together!!
You should write a book of dating tips, bud.
right??? i got a million of em! tip one: order ONE drink but get extra straws, that way you save $$$ AND it makes you and your date put your faces close together to drink!
(putting faces close together is step one to KISSING!!)
anyway meet us at pops we're still in line and it's taking FOREVERRRRRR
POP'S
CHOCK SHOPPE
A LARGE ICE CREAM FLOAT, PLEASE...
...TWO STRAWS.
Uh... THANKS CASANOVA, BUT I'VE ALREADY GOT MY OWN DRINK OVER HERE.
NICE TRY, BUD.
Oh, AND WHATEVER JUGHEAD WANTS.
POP TATE! MY FAVORITE PROPRIETOR OF THE FINEST CALORIC CONSUMABLES!
ONE FLIGHT OF YOUR DELICIOUS DELECT-ABLE, PLEASE!
ONE LUDICROUS PILE OF BURGERS, COMING UP. YOU'R PAYING FOR HIM, RIGHT?
YES. ABSOLUTELY.
Uh, YOU CAN PUT THE BILL FOR THIS ON MY DAD'S CREDIT CARD, RIGHT?

Tip two in "The Archie Andrews Guide To Dating" is "If you accidentally invite two women to the same dance on the same nigh wear a different outfit with each of them. This will prevent them from spotting you in the crowd, and is absolutely preferabl to a forthright and mature apology and explanation about your error in scheduling."

THREE MINUTES LATER...

SERIOUSLY, JUGHEAD. A) HOW DO YOU EAT SO QUICKLY, AND B) WHERE DO ALL THOSE CALORIES GO?

A) 10,000 HOURS OF PRACTICE, *THANKS GLADWELL*, AND B) STRAIGHT TO MY BRAIN. IT'S HOW COME I'M SO SMART AND STUFF.

RIGHT.

BEEPITY BLOOP

SO WHAT'D YOU THINK OF POP'S NEW MASCOT, HUH? YOU THINK IT'LL HELP DRUM UP BUSINESS?

I MEAN, POP'S GOT A CRAZY LINE NOW, SO I'D SAY IT'S WORKING.

UGH. IT'S SO *DEMEANING.*

BLOOPITY BLEEP

HUH? WHAT MASCOT?

WHAT ARE YOU TALKING ABOUT?

BLOOLOOLOO

THE BURGER LADY? AT THE ENTRANCE?

BURGER...

...LADY?

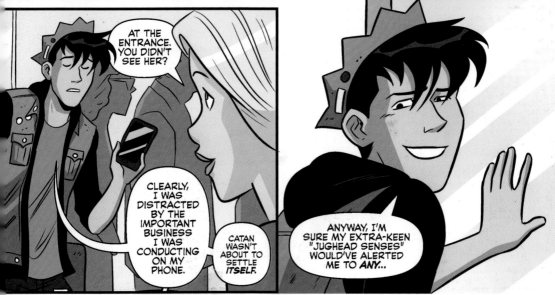

AT THE ENTRANCE. YOU DIDN'T SEE HER?

CLEARLY, I WAS DISTRACTED BY THE IMPORTANT BUSINESS I WAS CONDUCTING ON MY PHONE.

CATAN WASN'T ABOUT TO SETTLE *ITSELF.*

ANYWAY, I'M SURE MY EXTRA-KEEN "JUGHEAD SENSES" WOULD'VE ALERTED ME TO ANY...

Gladwell said that to become an expert in anything required at least 10,000 hours of practice! It's sort of crazy though because I've been writing comics for 9999.9999 hours and I've never discovered any new techniques that make me feel like an exp--*WAIT! SUDDENLY EVERYTHING IS CLEAR TO ME, NEVERMIND*

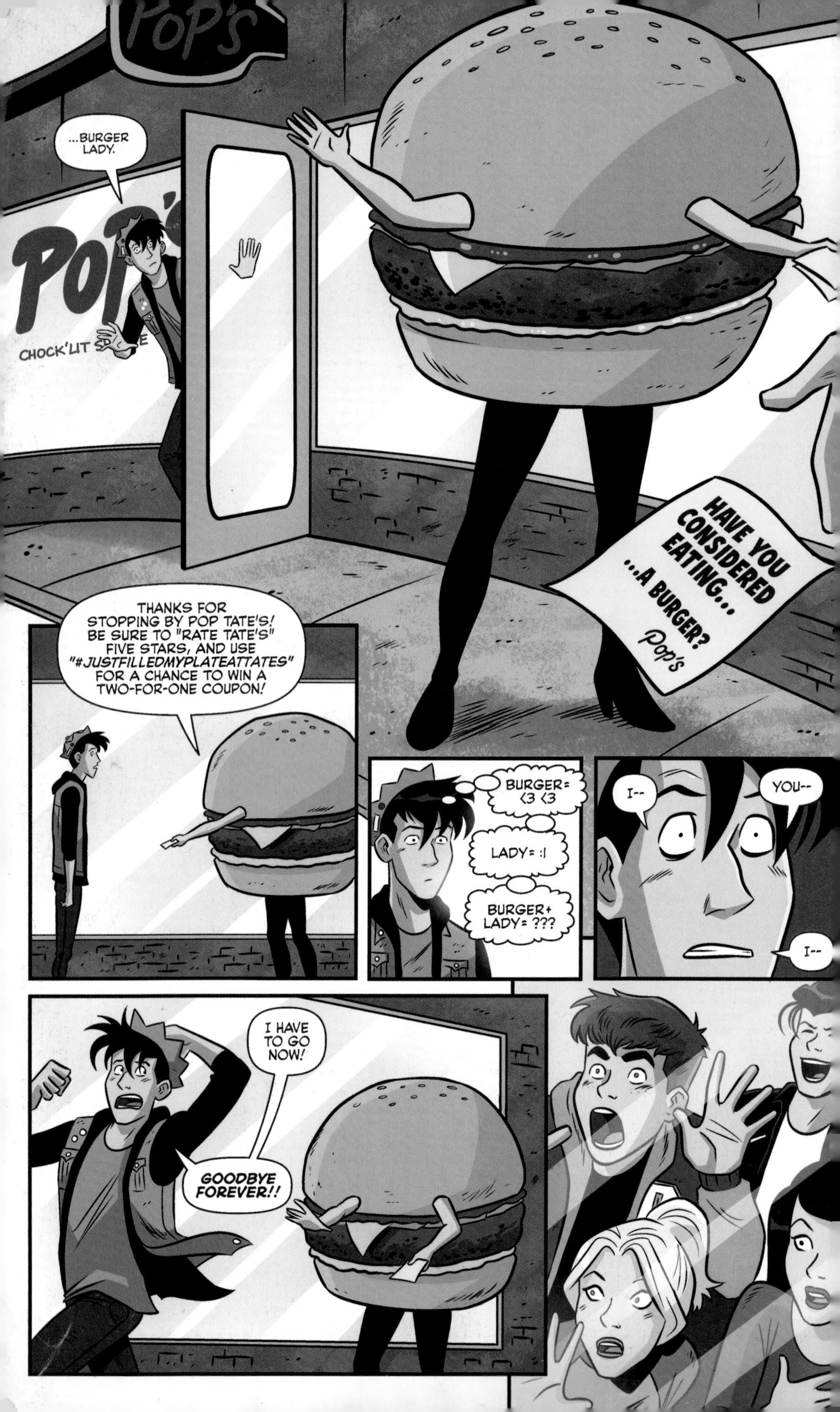

POP'S
...BURGER LADY.
POP'S
CHOCK'LIT SHOPPE
HAVE YOU CONSIDERED EATING... ...A BURGER?
Pop's
THANKS FOR STOPPING BY POP TATE'S! BE SURE TO "RATE TATE'S" FIVE STARS, AND USE "#JUSTFILLEDMYPLATEATTATES" FOR A CHANCE TO WIN A TWO-FOR-ONE COUPON!
BURGER= <3 <3
LADY= :|
BURGER+ LADY= ???
I--
YOU--
I--
I HAVE TO GO NOW!
GOODBYE FOREVER!!

JUGHEAD HAS A CRUSH!

I DON'T!!

YOU GOT NERVOUS AROUND HER! TONGUE-TIED! YOU, JUGGIE, THE GUY WITH A ZINGER FOR EVERY SITUATION!

YOU LIIIIIKE HER!

I DON'T GET CRUSHES. I JUST--FOUND HER INTERESTING! IT'S A FRIENDSHIP CRUSH, IF ANYTHING. WHAT DRIVES A WOMAN TO DRESS UP LIKE A BURGER AND ENCOURAGE OTHERS TO EAT THEM? AND WHY DID I NEVER THINK OF DOING THAT FIRST?

MOST IMPORTANTLY: HAVE I FINALLY MET SOMEONE WHOSE LOVE OF BURGERS EXCEEDS...EVEN MY OWN??

IT WAS MONEY, JUGHEAD. THAT'S WHAT MOTIVATES HER. SHE WAS BEING PAID MONEY.

I KEEP THINKING ABOUT HER, BETTS. IS THIS WHAT IT'S LIKE FOR YOU? THINKING ABOUT BOYS ALL THE TIME? WONDERING WHAT IT'D BE LIKE TO DO ACTIVITIES WITH THEM??

EH, YOU GET USED TO IT. ALSO, HELLO, I DON'T JUST THINK ABOUT BOYS. I THINK ABOUT SUSTAINABILITY, SOCIAL JUSTICE, ETHICAL--

HOW DO YOU GET THINGS DONE? HOW DO YOU LIVE LIKE THIS??

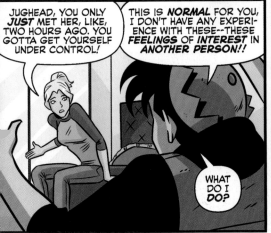

JUGHEAD, YOU ONLY JUST MET HER, LIKE, TWO HOURS AGO. YOU GOTTA GET YOURSELF UNDER CONTROL!

THIS IS NORMAL FOR YOU, I DON'T HAVE ANY EXPERIENCE WITH THESE--THESE FEELINGS OF INTEREST IN ANOTHER PERSON!!

WHAT DO I DO?

EASY, JUGGIE. YOU'RE GONNA SEE HER AGAIN.

TONIGHT.

To be fair, feelings *are* pretty boring. Real snorefest most of the time. You gotta pull up your socks, feelings. Feelings, get your head in the game.

NO. NOOOO WAY. I'LL JUST FIND SOME *OTHER* PLACE TO EAT BURGERS FROM NOW ON!

YES. *YES.* IT IS A PERFECT SOLUTION, BOTH EASIER *AND* LAZIER THAN ANY ALTER-NATIVE.

YOU AND I BOTH KNOW YOU CAN'T ABANDON POP. REMEMBER THE ONE TIME HE ALLOWED YOU TO GLADLY PAY HIM TUESDAY FOR A BURGER TODAY?

YOU'RE RIGHT, BETTY. *I CAN'T ABANDON HIM.*

HERE'S WHAT YOU'RE GONNA DO, JUGGIE: YOU'RE GONNA GO SAY HI TO BURGER LADY CASUALLY, SUCH THAT SHE CAN FOLLOW UP IF SHE'S INTERESTED, BUT ALSO--AND THIS IS CRITICAL--YOU'RE *NOT* GOING TO GO BEYOND WHAT'S NATURAL IN A BURGER-PATRON/BURGER-MASCOT RELATIONSHIP!

SHE'S A WOMAN WHO WORKS RETAIL, BELIEVE ME, SHE'S GOT *PLENTY* OF CREEPERS BOTHERING HER.

YOU'VE GOT TO PUT THE BALL ENTIRELY IN HER COURT. SHOW HER YOU'RE NOT LIKE OTHER GUYS.

OOF...NOW THAT I THINK ABOUT IT, OPENING WITH "I'M NOT LIKE OTHER GUYS" IS LIKE THE #1 PLAY IN THE PICK-UP ARTIST HANDBOOK.

...SO THAT'S PROBLEMATIC.

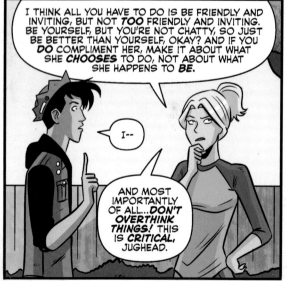

I THINK ALL YOU HAVE TO DO IS BE FRIENDLY AND INVITING, BUT NOT *TOO* FRIENDLY AND INVITING. BE YOURSELF, BUT YOU'RE NOT CHATTY, SO JUST BE BETTER THAN YOURSELF, OKAY? AND IF YOU *DO* COMPLIMENT HER, MAKE IT ABOUT WHAT SHE *CHOOSES* TO DO, NOT ABOUT WHAT SHE HAPPENS TO *BE.*

I--

AND MOST IMPORTANTLY OF ALL...*DON'T OVERTHINK THINGS!* THIS IS *CRITICAL,* JUGHEAD.

YOU DONE?

ROMANCE IS COMPLICATED!!

Betty's "compliment people on what they choose to do, not what they happen to be" is an actual, real-life, industrial-grade romance tip. Try it out! And when you're kissing on someone attractive down the road, think of me! *CONSTANTLY.*

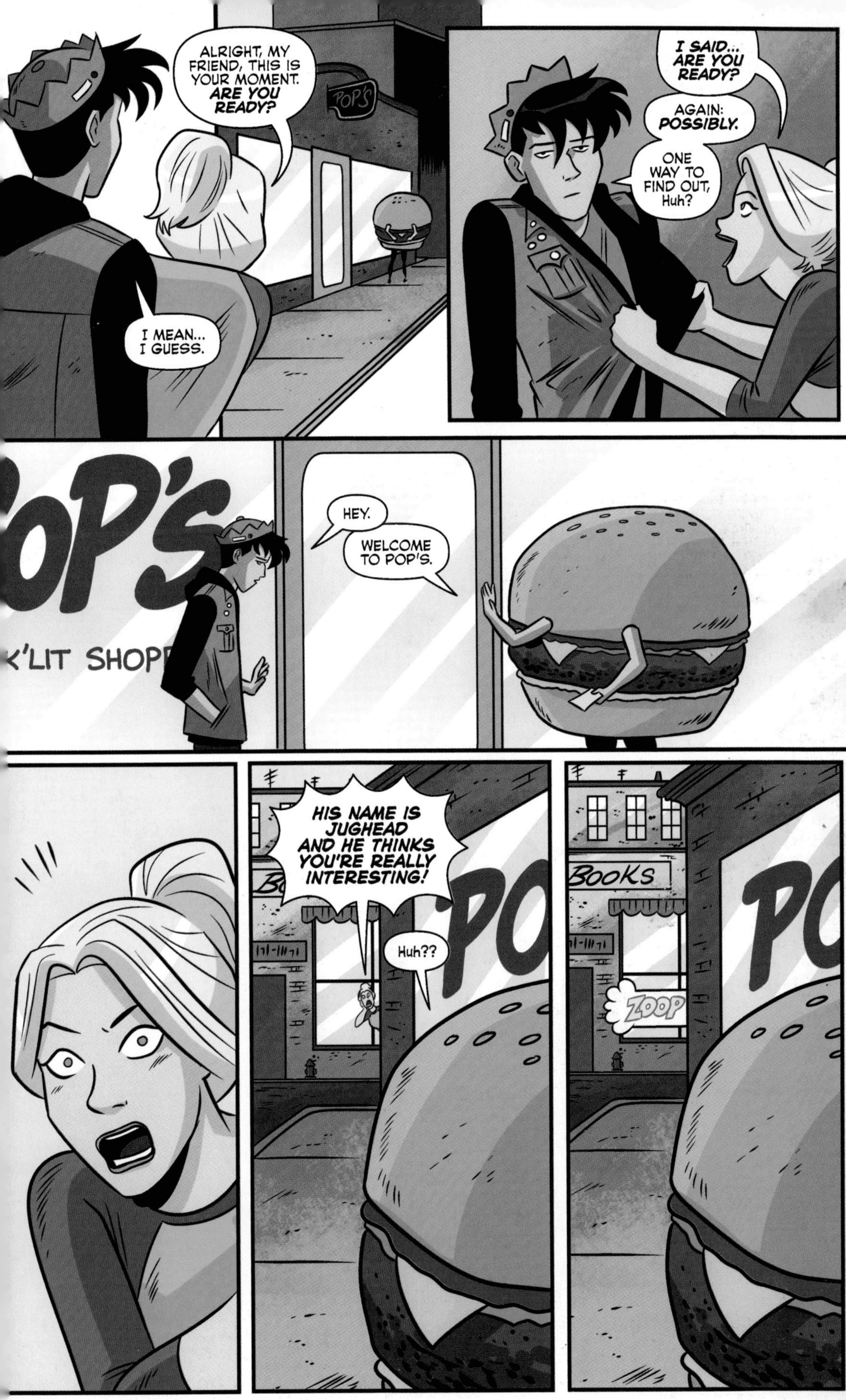
ALRIGHT, MY FRIEND, THIS IS YOUR MOMENT. ARE YOU READY?
POP'S
I MEAN... I GUESS.
I SAID... ARE YOU READY?
AGAIN: POSSIBLY.
ONE WAY TO FIND OUT, Huh?
POP'S
'LIT SHOP
HEY.
WELCOME TO POP'S.
HIS NAME IS JUGHEAD AND HE THINKS YOU'RE REALLY INTERESTING!
Huh??
BOOKS
ZOOP

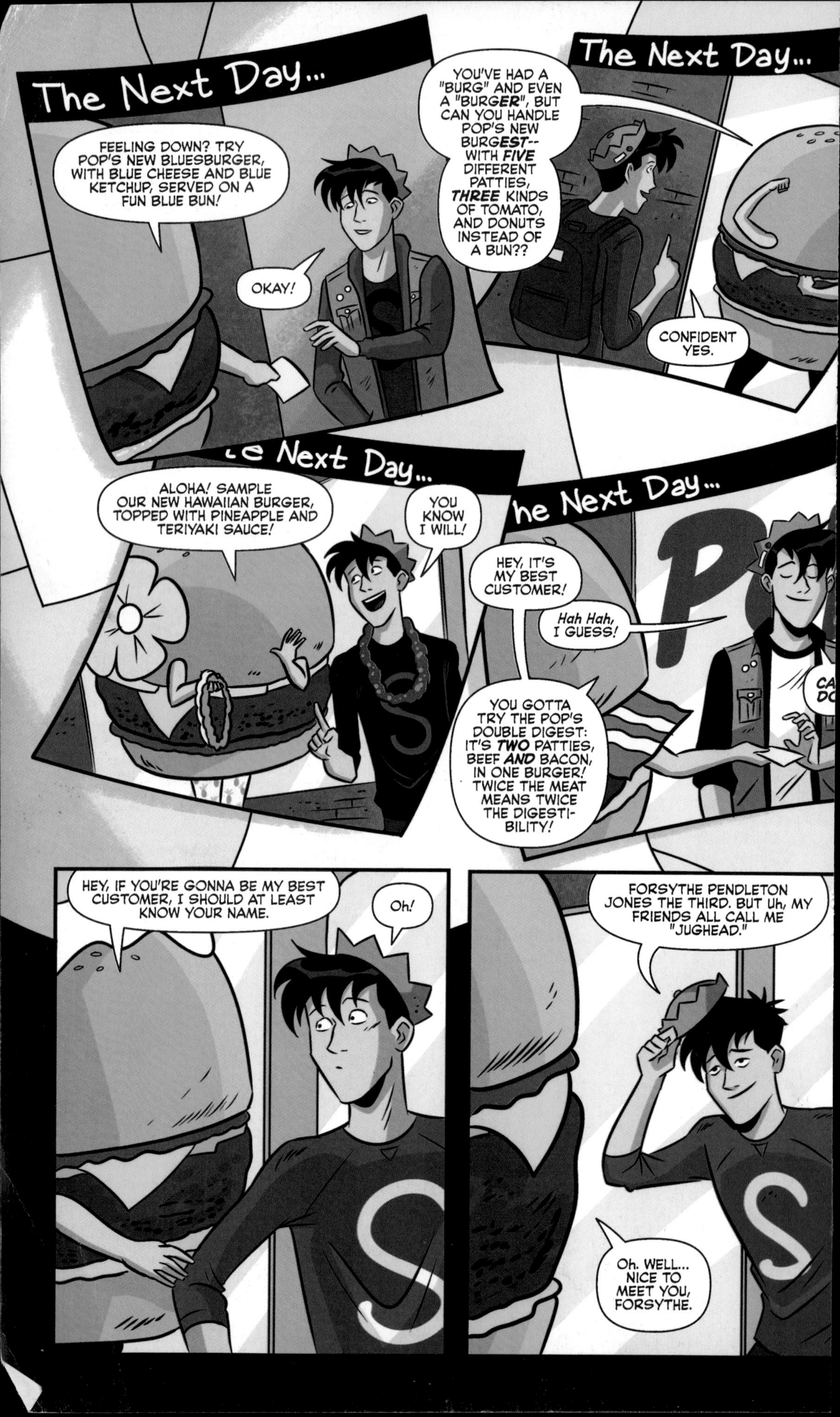

The Next Day...
FEELING DOWN? TRY POP'S NEW BLUESBURGER, WITH BLUE CHEESE AND BLUE KETCHUP, SERVED ON A FUN BLUE BUN!
OKAY!
The Next Day...
YOU'VE HAD A "BURG" AND EVEN A "BURGER", BUT CAN YOU HANDLE POP'S NEW BURGEST-- WITH FIVE DIFFERENT PATTIES, THREE KINDS OF TOMATO, AND DONUTS INSTEAD OF A BUN??
CONFIDENT YES.
e Next Day...
ALOHA! SAMPLE OUR NEW HAWAIIAN BURGER, TOPPED WITH PINEAPPLE AND TERIYAKI SAUCE!
YOU KNOW I WILL!
he Next Day...
HEY, IT'S MY BEST CUSTOMER!
Hah Hah, I GUESS!
YOU GOTTA TRY THE POP'S DOUBLE DIGEST: IT'S TWO PATTIES, BEEF AND BACON, IN ONE BURGER! TWICE THE MEAT MEANS TWICE THE DIGESTI-BILITY!
HEY, IF YOU'RE GONNA BE MY BEST CUSTOMER, I SHOULD AT LEAST KNOW YOUR NAME.
Oh!
FORSYTHE PENDLETON JONES THE THIRD. BUT Uh, MY FRIENDS ALL CALL ME "JUGHEAD."
Oh. WELL... NICE TO MEET YOU, FORSYTHE.

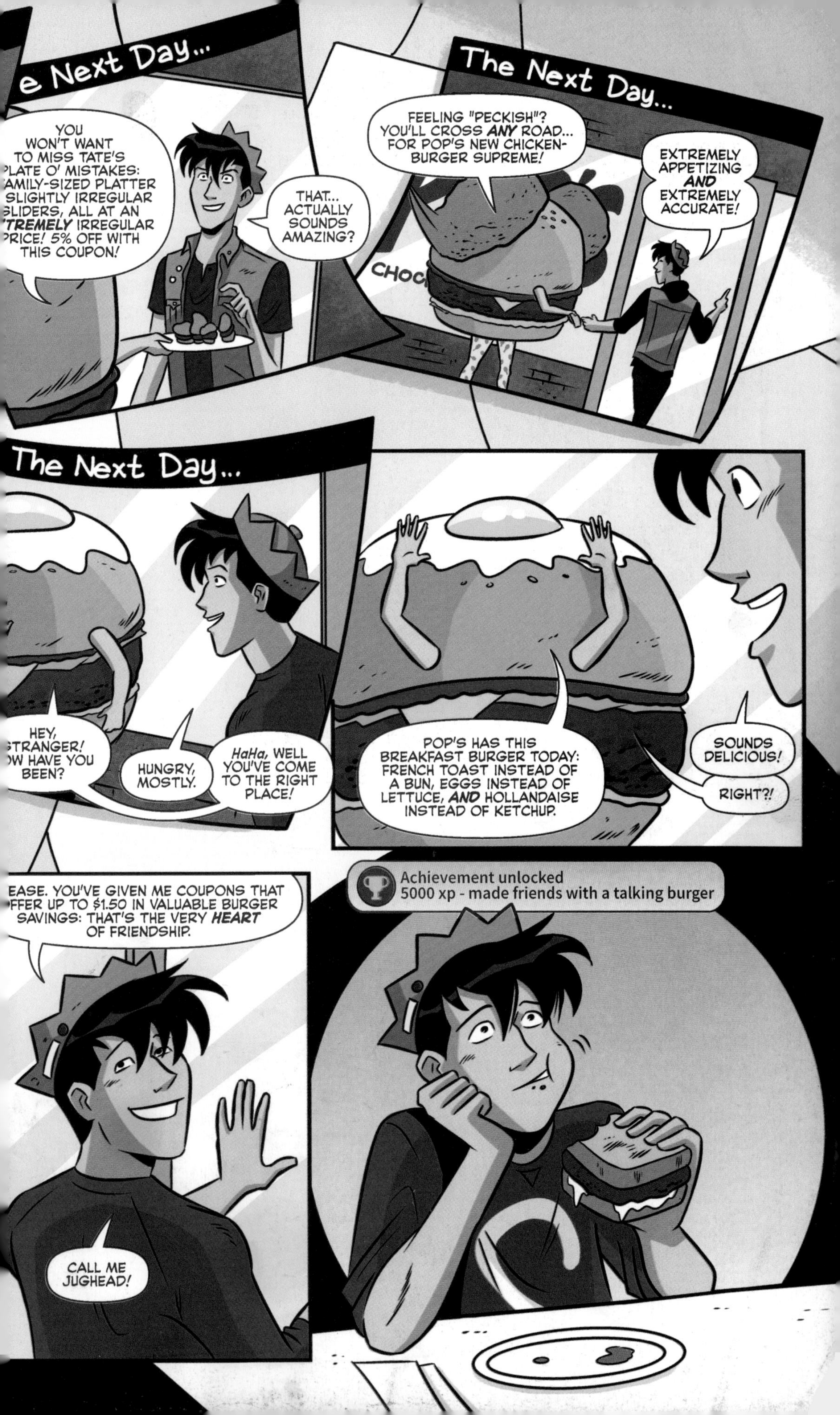
e Next Day...
YOU WON'T WANT TO MISS TATE'S PLATE O' MISTAKES: FAMILY-SIZED PLATTER SLIGHTLY IRREGULAR SLIDERS, ALL AT AN XTREMELY IRREGULAR PRICE! 5% OFF WITH THIS COUPON!
THAT... ACTUALLY SOUNDS AMAZING?
The Next Day...
FEELING "PECKISH"? YOU'LL CROSS ANY ROAD... FOR POP'S NEW CHICKEN-BURGER SUPREME!
EXTREMELY APPETIZING AND EXTREMELY ACCURATE!
CHOC
The Next Day...
HEY, STRANGER! OW HAVE YOU BEEN?
HUNGRY, MOSTLY.
HaHa, WELL YOU'VE COME TO THE RIGHT PLACE!
POP'S HAS THIS BREAKFAST BURGER TODAY: FRENCH TOAST INSTEAD OF A BUN, EGGS INSTEAD OF LETTUCE, AND HOLLANDAISE INSTEAD OF KETCHUP.
SOUNDS DELICIOUS!
RIGHT?!
EASE. YOU'VE GIVEN ME COUPONS THAT OFFER UP TO $1.50 IN VALUABLE BURGER SAVINGS: THAT'S THE VERY HEART OF FRIENDSHIP.
CALL ME JUGHEAD!
Achievement unlocked
5000 xp - made friends with a talking burger

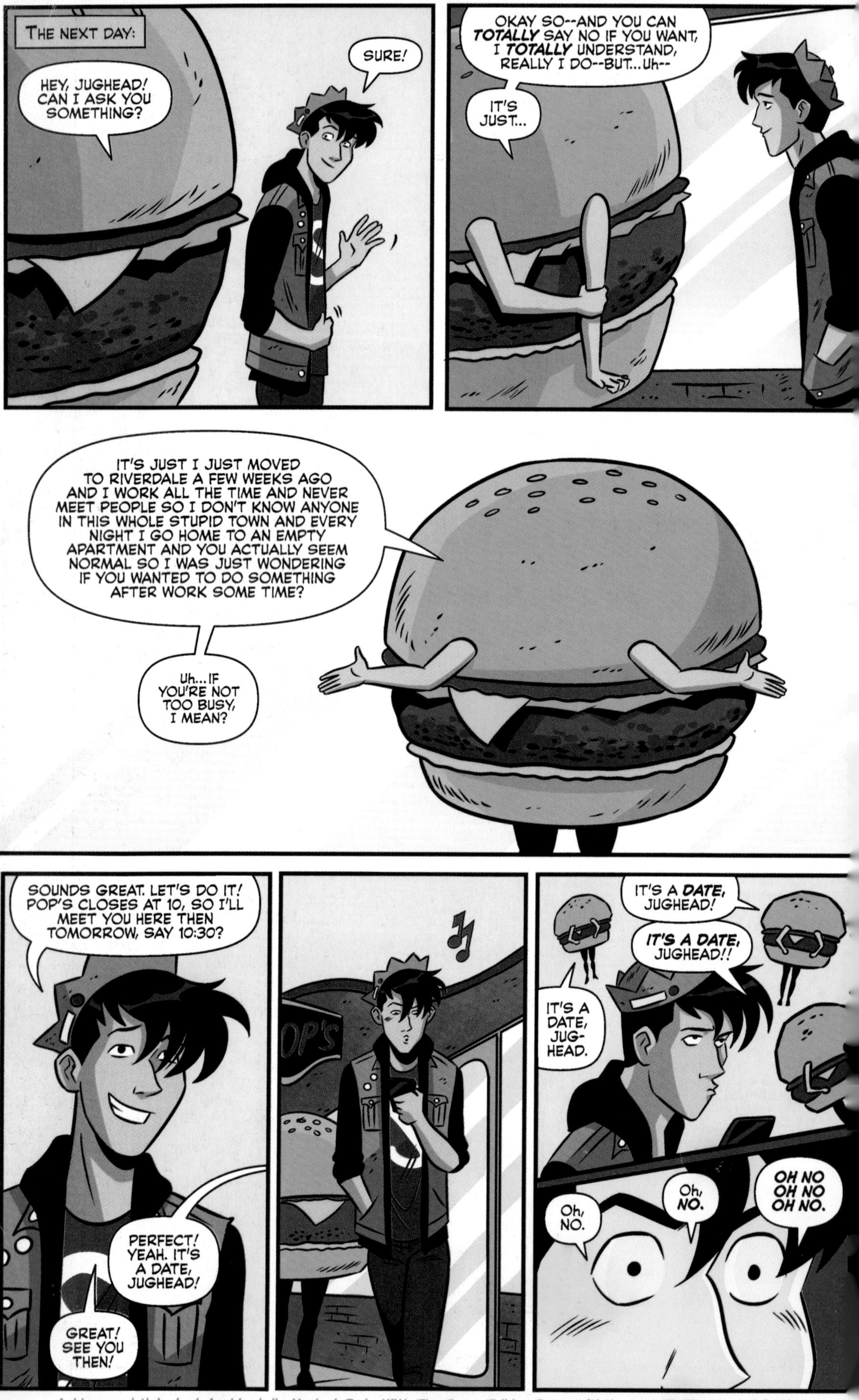
THE NEXT DAY:
HEY, JUGHEAD! CAN I ASK YOU SOMETHING?
SURE!
OKAY SO--AND YOU CAN TOTALLY SAY NO IF YOU WANT, I TOTALLY UNDERSTAND, REALLY I DO--BUT...Uh--
IT'S JUST...
IT'S JUST I JUST MOVED TO RIVERDALE A FEW WEEKS AGO AND I WORK ALL THE TIME AND NEVER MEET PEOPLE SO I DON'T KNOW ANYONE IN THIS WHOLE STUPID TOWN AND EVERY NIGHT I GO HOME TO AN EMPTY APARTMENT AND YOU ACTUALLY SEEM NORMAL SO I WAS JUST WONDERING IF YOU WANTED TO DO SOMETHING AFTER WORK SOME TIME?
Uh...IF YOU'RE NOT TOO BUSY, I MEAN?
SOUNDS GREAT. LET'S DO IT! POP'S CLOSES AT 10, SO I'LL MEET YOU HERE THEN TOMORROW, SAY 10:30?
PERFECT! YEAH. IT'S A DATE, JUGHEAD!
GREAT! SEE YOU THEN!
OP'S
IT'S A DATE, JUGHEAD!
IT'S A DATE, JUGHEAD!!
IT'S A DATE, JUG-HEAD.
Oh, NO.
Oh, NO.
OH NO OH NO OH NO.

Achievement Unlocked: Accidentally Made A Date With The Same Talking Burger (It Happens To The Best Of Us)

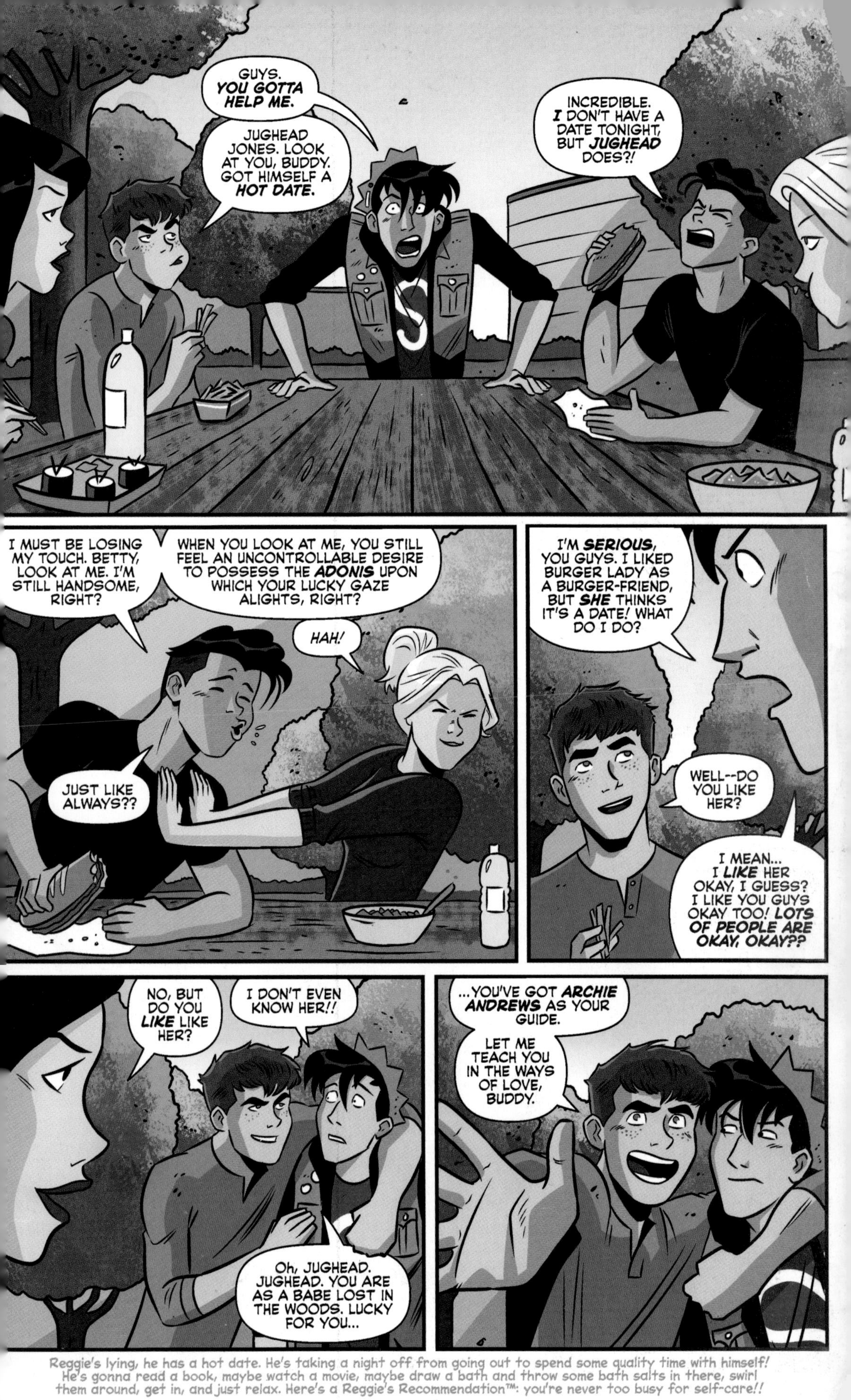
GUYS. YOU GOTTA HELP ME.
JUGHEAD JONES. LOOK AT YOU, BUDDY. GOT HIMSELF A HOT DATE.
INCREDIBLE. I DON'T HAVE A DATE TONIGHT, BUT JUGHEAD DOES?!
I MUST BE LOSING MY TOUCH. BETTY, LOOK AT ME. I'M STILL HANDSOME, RIGHT?
WHEN YOU LOOK AT ME, YOU STILL FEEL AN UNCONTROLLABLE DESIRE TO POSSESS THE ADONIS UPON WHICH YOUR LUCKY GAZE ALIGHTS, RIGHT?
HAH!
JUST LIKE ALWAYS??
I'M SERIOUS, YOU GUYS. I LIKED BURGER LADY AS A BURGER-FRIEND, BUT SHE THINKS IT'S A DATE! WHAT DO I DO?
WELL--DO YOU LIKE HER?
I MEAN... I LIKE HER OKAY, I GUESS? I LIKE YOU GUYS OKAY TOO! LOTS OF PEOPLE ARE OKAY, OKAY??
NO, BUT DO YOU LIKE LIKE HER?
I DON'T EVEN KNOW HER!!
Oh, JUGHEAD. JUGHEAD. YOU ARE AS A BABE LOST IN THE WOODS. LUCKY FOR YOU...
...YOU'VE GOT ARCHIE ANDREWS AS YOUR GUIDE.
LET ME TEACH YOU IN THE WAYS OF LOVE, BUDDY.

Reggie's lying, he has a hot date. He's taking a night off from going out to spend some quality time with himself! He's gonna read a book, maybe watch a movie, maybe draw a bath and throw some bath salts in there, swirl them around, get in, and just relax. Here's a Reggie's Recommendation™: you're never too busy for self-care!!

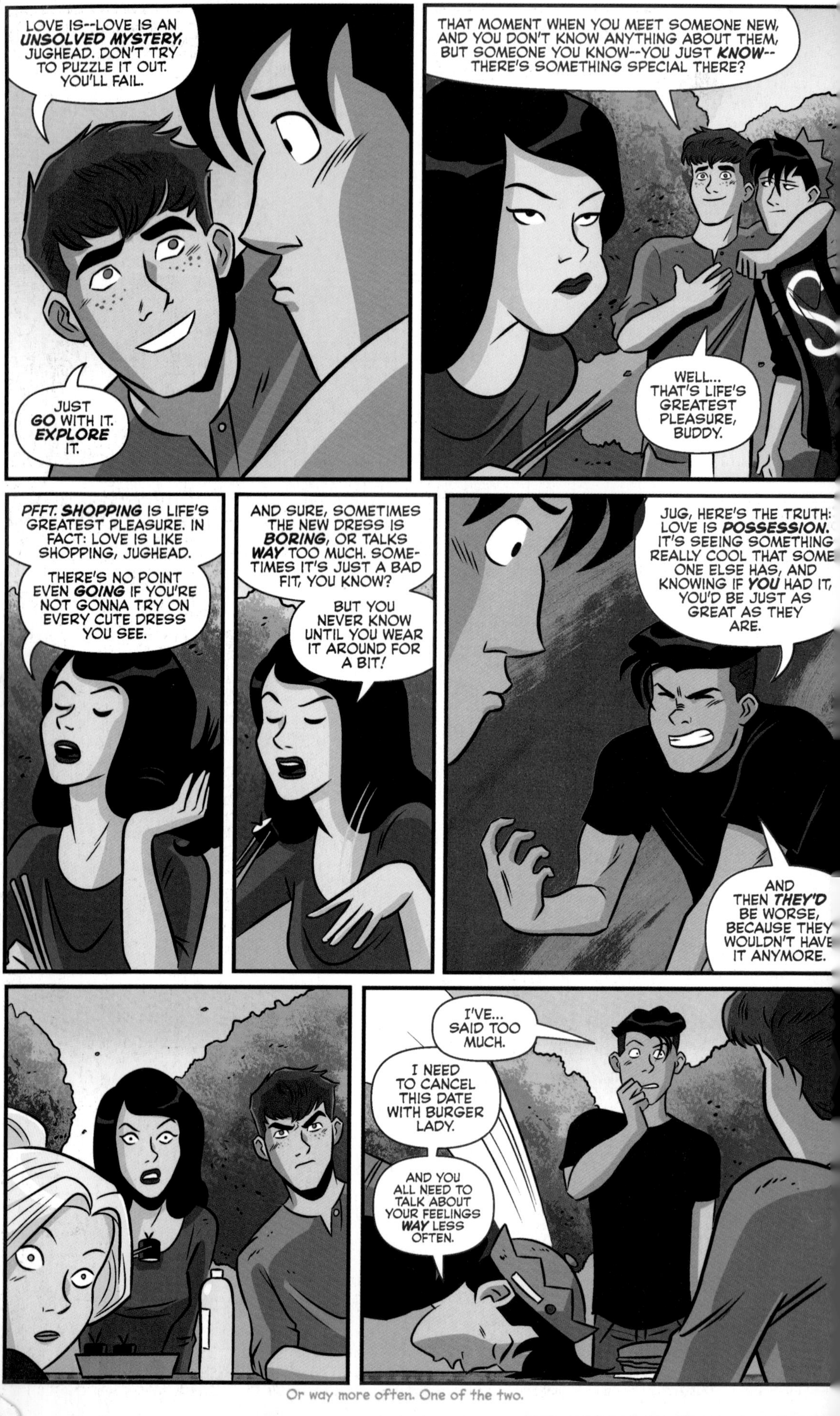

LOVE IS--LOVE IS AN ***UNSOLVED MYSTERY,*** JUGHEAD. DON'T TRY TO PUZZLE IT OUT. YOU'LL FAIL.
JUST **GO** WITH IT. ***EXPLORE*** IT.
THAT MOMENT WHEN YOU MEET SOMEONE NEW, AND YOU DON'T KNOW ANYTHING ABOUT THEM, BUT SOMEONE YOU KNOW--YOU JUST ***KNOW***-- THERE'S SOMETHING SPECIAL THERE?
WELL... THAT'S LIFE'S GREATEST PLEASURE, BUDDY.
PFFT. **SHOPPING** IS LIFE'S GREATEST PLEASURE. IN FACT: LOVE IS LIKE SHOPPING, JUGHEAD.
THERE'S NO POINT EVEN **GOING** IF YOU'RE NOT GONNA TRY ON EVERY CUTE DRESS YOU SEE.
AND SURE, SOMETIMES THE NEW DRESS IS ***BORING***, OR TALKS ***WAY*** TOO MUCH. SOME-TIMES IT'S JUST A BAD FIT, YOU KNOW?
BUT YOU NEVER KNOW UNTIL YOU WEAR IT AROUND FOR A BIT!
JUG, HERE'S THE TRUTH: LOVE IS ***POSSESSION.*** IT'S SEEING SOMETHING REALLY COOL THAT SOME ONE ELSE HAS, AND KNOWING IF ***YOU*** HAD IT, YOU'D BE JUST AS GREAT AS THEY ARE.
AND THEN ***THEY'D*** BE WORSE, BECAUSE THEY WOULDN'T HAVE IT ANYMORE.
I'VE... SAID TOO MUCH.
I NEED TO CANCEL THIS DATE WITH BURGER LADY.
AND YOU ALL NEED TO TALK ABOUT YOUR FEELINGS ***WAY*** LESS OFTEN.

Or way more often. One of the two.

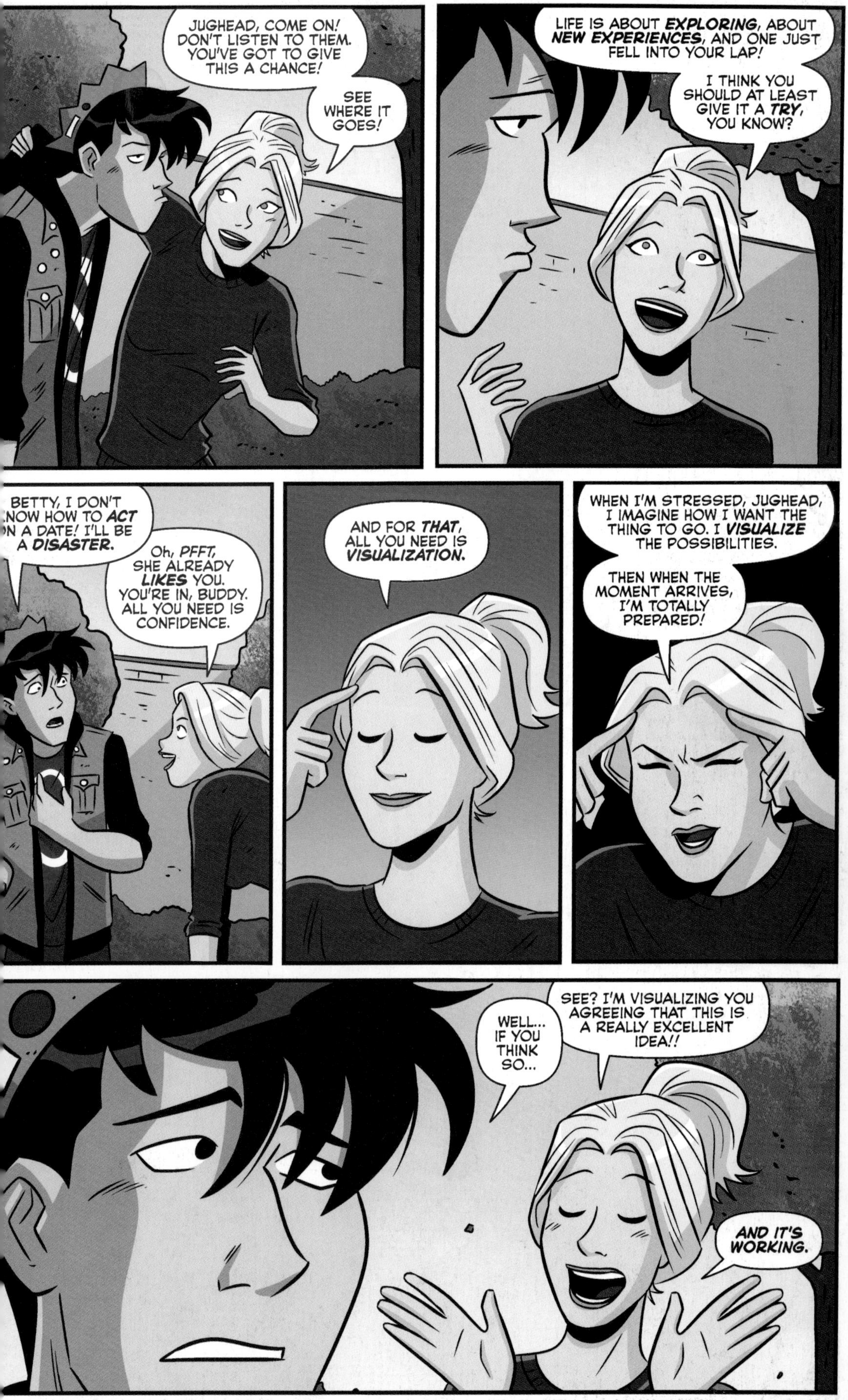
JUGHEAD, COME ON! DON'T LISTEN TO THEM. YOU'VE GOT TO GIVE THIS A CHANCE!
SEE WHERE IT GOES!
LIFE IS ABOUT EXPLORING, ABOUT NEW EXPERIENCES, AND ONE JUST FELL INTO YOUR LAP!
I THINK YOU SHOULD AT LEAST GIVE IT A TRY, YOU KNOW?
BETTY, I DON'T KNOW HOW TO ACT ON A DATE! I'LL BE A DISASTER.
Oh, PFFT, SHE ALREADY LIKES YOU. YOU'RE IN, BUDDY. ALL YOU NEED IS CONFIDENCE.
AND FOR THAT, ALL YOU NEED IS VISUALIZATION.
WHEN I'M STRESSED, JUGHEAD, I IMAGINE HOW I WANT THE THING TO GO. I VISUALIZE THE POSSIBILITIES.
THEN WHEN THE MOMENT ARRIVES, I'M TOTALLY PREPARED!
WELL... IF YOU THINK SO...
SEE? I'M VISUALIZING YOU AGREEING THAT THIS IS A REALLY EXCELLENT IDEA!!
AND IT'S WORKING.

ersonally, ***I'M*** visualizing you turning the page to see what happens next. ***DON'T TURN MY VISUALIZATIONS INTO LIES!!***

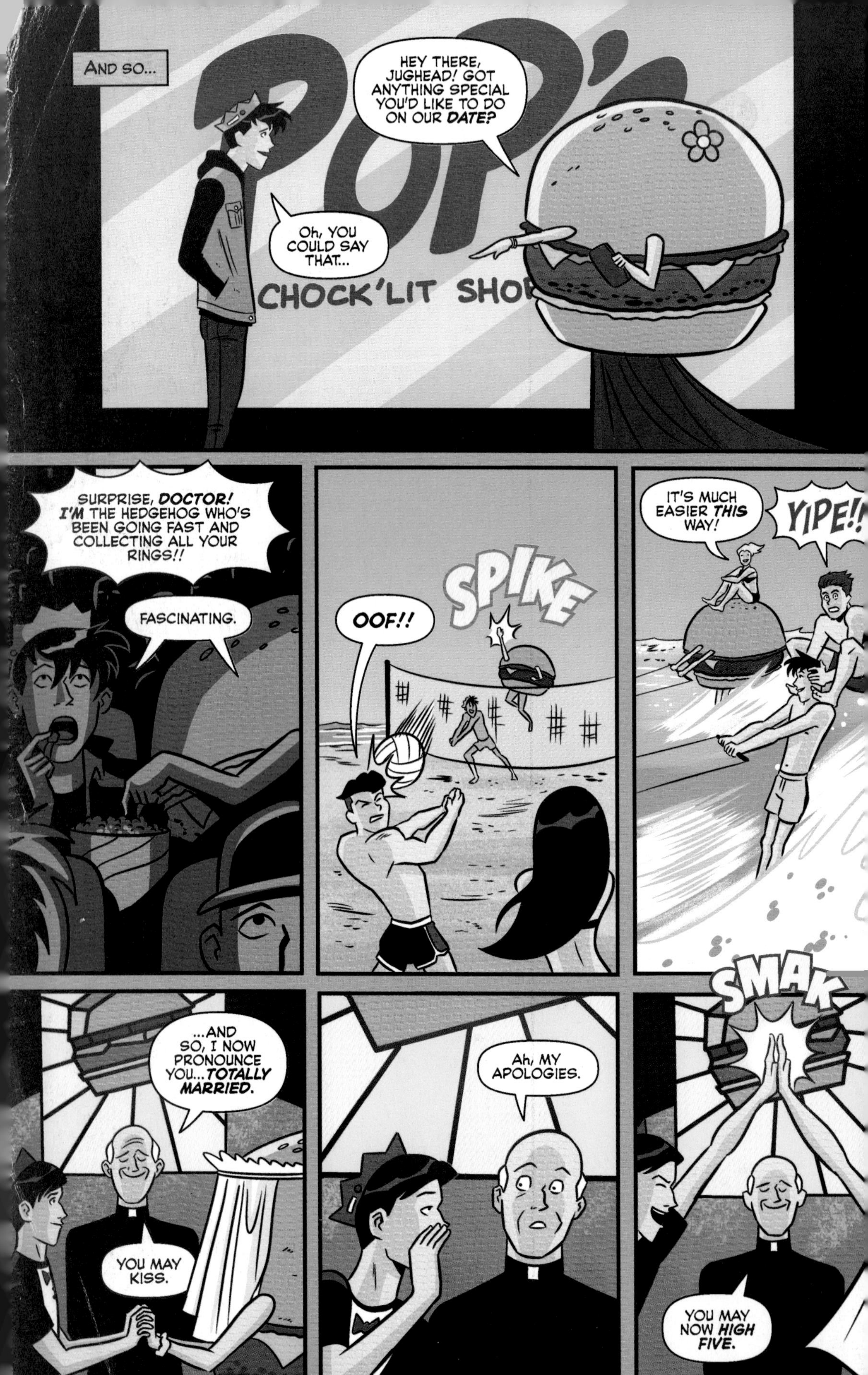
AND SO...
HEY THERE, JUGHEAD! GOT ANYTHING SPECIAL YOU'D LIKE TO DO ON OUR DATE?
Oh, YOU COULD SAY THAT...
POP'S
CHOCK'LIT SHOP
SURPRISE, DOCTOR! I'M THE HEDGEHOG WHO'S BEEN GOING FAST AND COLLECTING ALL YOUR RINGS!!
FASCINATING.
SPIKE
OOF!!
IT'S MUCH EASIER THIS WAY!
YIPE!!
...AND SO, I NOW PRONOUNCE YOU...TOTALLY MARRIED.
YOU MAY KISS.
Ah, MY APOLOGIES.
SMAK
YOU MAY NOW HIGH FIVE.

You may now wink and make finger guns at each other, and then do that thing where you mush perfectly good cake into each other's faces.

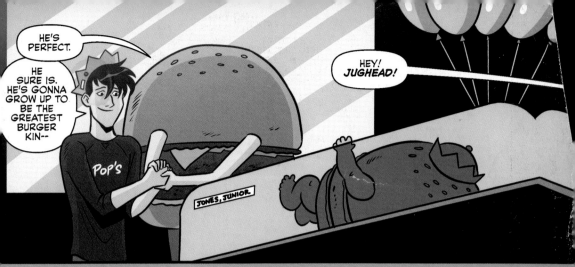

HE'S PERFECT.

HE SURE IS. HE'S GONNA GROW UP TO BE THE GREATEST BURGER KIN--

HEY! *JUGHEAD!*

JONES, JUNIOR

YOU WERE MILES AWAY, BUDDY.

YEAH, I WAS JUST, UH-- VISUALIZ- ING? I GUESS?

Oh, COOL!

I'M SORRY, DO I KNOW YOU?

Hah! WHAT, DID YOU THINK I WAS GONNA WEAR MY *COSTUME* ON OUR DATE?

Uh...

IT'S ME, DUDE. *BURGER LADY.* THIS IS ME WITHOUT TEN POUNDS OF FOAM BURGER ON MY HEAD.

MOST BOYS WOULD SAY IT'S A MARKED IMPROVEMENT.

AND I REALIZED WE NEVER INTRODUCED OURSELVES TO EACH OTHER PROPERLY, SO LET ME GIVE YOU MY NAME.

IT'S VERY NICE TO MEET YOU, JUGHEAD JONES...

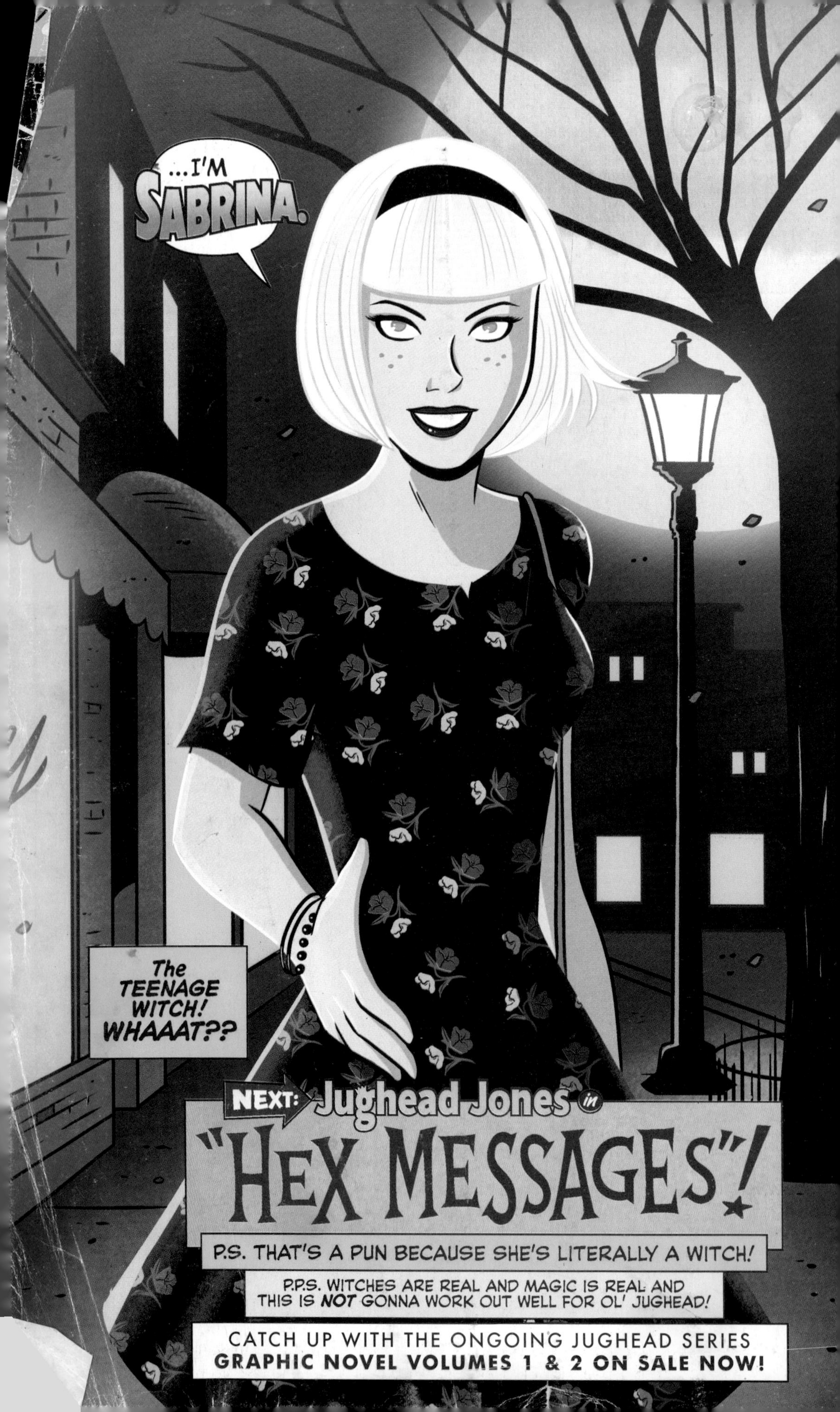
...I'M SABRINA.
The TEENAGE WITCH! WHAAAT??
NEXT: Jughead Jones in
"HEX MESSAGES"!
P.S. THAT'S A PUN BECAUSE SHE'S LITERALLY A WITCH!
P.P.S. WITCHES ARE REAL AND MAGIC IS REAL AND THIS IS NOT GONNA WORK OUT WELL FOR OL' JUGHEAD!
CATCH UP WITH THE ONGOING JUGHEAD SERIES GRAPHIC NOVEL VOLUMES 1 & 2 ON SALE NOW!